LEGITIMATING INTERNATIONAL ORGANIZATIONS

Legitimating International Organizations

Edited by
DOMINIK ZAUM

OXFORD
UNIVERSITY PRESS

OXFORD
UNIVERSITY PRESS

Great Clarendon Street, Oxford, OX2 6DP,
United Kingdom

Oxford University Press is a department of the University of Oxford.
It furthers the University's objective of excellence in research, scholarship, and education by publishing worldwide. Oxford is a registered trade mark of Oxford University Press in the UK and in certain other countries

First Edition published in 2013

Impression: 1

Published in the United States of America by Oxford University Press
198 Madison Avenue, New York, NY 10016, United States of America

British Library Cataloguing in Publication Data
Data available

Library of Congress Control Number: 2013937732

ISBN 978–0–19–967209–7

Printed and bound in Great Britain by
CPI Group (UK) Ltd, Croydon, CR0 4YY

Acknowledgements

This book has been a rather long time in the making, and I am deeply indebted to the authors for their patience. The project started with a small exploratory workshop in January 2008 on some case studies of legitimation by international and regional organizations, hosted by the Centre for Political Theory and the Department of Politics and International Relations at the University of Reading. The Department has offered me a very supportive research environment over the last seven years. I am grateful to the Centre and Professor Alan Cromartie for their support launching the project, and the workshop participants for identifying some of the key themes and conceptual issues addressed by this book. A further two-day workshop was held at Reading in January 2009, which included many of the authors, and some additional chapters were commissioned after that.

My greatest debt is to the contributors to the volume, for the knowledge and insight reflected in their contributions, and for the thoughtful and careful revisions of their chapters. A range of people have also commented on the book as a whole and on individual chapters. In addition to the excellent and very constructive comments by three anonymous reviewers for Oxford University Press, these have included Ademola Abass, Andreas Behnke, Mats Berdal, Chris Bickerton, Alan Cromartie, Carolyn Haggis, Beatrice Heuser, Chris Hilson, Hiro Katsumata, Kundai Sithole, Alex Warleigh-Lack, and Peter Woodward.

The British Academy (Award No SG-47719) provided generous support without which the project would not have been possible. It supported both the authors' workshop and several weeks of fieldwork in New York for the chapter on the UN Security Council. As most of the interviews were confidential, I cannot name those diplomats and UN officials who generously made time available and shared their insights, but their help was essential to writing the chapter. I am also grateful to Dominic Byatt and his editorial team at Oxford University Press for their patience and support for this project.

DZ, Reading, January 2013

Contents

List of Acronyms

AEC	African Economic Community
AMIB	African Union Mission to Burundi
AMIS	African Union Mission in Sudan
AMISOM	African Union Mission in Somalia
APC	Asia Pacific Community
APEC	Asia Pacific Economic Cooperation Forum
APF	Africa Peace Facility
APSA	African Peace and Security Architecture
ARF	ASEAN Regional Forum
ASEAN	Association of Southeast Asian Nations
ASF	African Standby Force
AU	African Union
AUC	African Union Commission
AUV	African Union Volunteers
CAR	Central African Republic
CEWS	Continental Early Warning System
CFE	Conventional Forces in Europe Treaty
CIS	Commonwealth of Independent States
CNC	Council of National Coordinators
CNPC	China National Petroleum Corporation
CPC	Conflict Prevention Center
CSBM	Confidence and Security-building Measures
CSCE	Conference on Security and Cooperation in Europe
CSO	Civil Society Organization
CSSDCA	Conference on Security, Stability, Development and Cooperation in Africa
DPKO	Department for Peacekeeping Operations
DRC	Democratic Republic of the Congo
ECCAS	Economic Community of Central African States
ECOMICI	ECOWAS Mission in Côte d'Ivoire
ECOMIL	ECOWAS Mission in Liberia
ECOMOG	ECOWAS Ceasefire and Monitoring Group
ECOWAS	Economic Community of West African States
EST	European Security Treaty
EU	European Union
EUFOR RD	European Union Force in the Congo
GCC	Gulf Cooperation Council
HCNM	High Commissioner on National Minorities

IMF	International Monetary Fund
MAES	African Union Electoral and Security Assistance Mission to the Comoros
MBFR	Mutually Balanced Forces Reduction
MSC	Mediation and Security Council
MSC	Military Staff Committee
NATO	North Atlantic Treaty Organization
NGO	Non-Governmental Organization
NTC	National Transitional Council
OAS	Organization of American States
OAU	Organization for African Unity
ODIHR	Office for Democratic Institutions and Human Rights
ONUB	*Operation des Nations Unies au Burundi*
OSCE	Organization for Security and Cooperation in Europe
PCRD	Post-Conflict Reconstruction and Development
PSC	Peace and Security Council
PSOD	Peace Support Operations Division
RATS	Regional Anti-Terrorism Structure
RCI LRA	Regional Cooperation Initiative against the Lord's Resistance Army
REC	Regional Economic Community
RM	Regional Mechanism
SAARC	South Asian Association for Regional Cooperation
SADC	South African Development Community
SCO	Shanghai Cooperation Organization
SMC	Standing Mediation Committee
TAC	Treaty of Amity and Cooperation
UN	United Nations
UNAMID	United Nations/African Union Mission in Darfur
UNDP	United Nations Development Programme
UNOMIL	United Nations Observer Mission in Liberia
UNOMSIL	United Nations Observer Mission in Sierra Leone
UNSC	United Nations Security Council
UNV	United Nations Volunteers
WACSOF	West African Civil Society Forum
WANEP	West Africa Network for Peace-Building
WTO	World Trade Organization

List of Contributors

Alice D. Ba is Associate Professor of Political Science & International Relations at the University of Delaware. Her research focuses on the politics and processes of regionalism in East Asia and the Asia Pacific, especially the Association of Southeast Asian Nations (ASEAN); questions of institutional change and regional integration; and Southeast Asia's relations with China and the United States. She is the author of *(Re)Negotiating East and Southeast Asia: Region, Regionalism, and the Association of Southeast Asian Nations* (Stanford 2009) and co-editor of *Contending Perspectives on Global Governance* (Routledge 2005). She also serves as Director of Asian Studies at the University of Delaware.

Alhaji Sarjoh Bah is Head of the African Union Liaison Office to the Southern African Development Community (SADC). He was the Lead Facilitator of an Executive Post-Graduate Program at the Institute for Peace and Security Studies at Addis Ababa University, and Senior Fellow at New York University's Center on International Cooperation where he served as Lead Scholar and editor of the Annual Review of Global Peace Operations. He worked as a Senior Researcher at the Institute for Security Studies, and is on the editorial board of the *African Security Review*. He has published widely on issues of peace and security and is the co-editor of *A Tortuous Road to Peace—The Dynamics of Regional, UN and International Humanitarian Interventions in Liberia* (Institute for Security Studies 2005). Dr. Bah has been a consultant to several international organizations and research institutes.

Mervyn Frost, BA (Stellenbosch), MA (Stellenbosch), BPhil (Oxford), DPhil (Stellenbosch) is Professor and Head of the Department of War Studies at King's College, London. He has held lectureships at the University of Cape Town and at Rhodes University. He was appointed to the Chair of Politics at the University of Natal in Durban in 1986. In 1996 he was appointed Professor of International Relations at the University of Kent in Canterbury. Publications include: *Towards a Normative Theory of International Relations* (CUP, 1986), *Ethics in International Relations* (CUP, 1996), *Constituting Human Rights: Global Civil Society and the Society of Democratic States* (Routledge, 2002) and *Global Ethics: Anarchy, Freedom and International Relations* (Routledge, 2009).

Christopher Lord is Professor at ARENA, The Centre for European Studies at the University of Oslo. He is an author of several books and articles on

Legitimacy, Democracy and the European Union, as well as the European Parliament. He is currently working on a (further) Democratic Audit of the European Union and on a study of the Legitimacy of Monetary Union.

Walter Lotze works in the Peace Support Operations Division of the African Union Commission. Prior to joining the AU he worked as a visiting researcher at the Norwegian Institute of International Affairs (NUPI), before which he headed the peacebuilding division of the African Centre for the Constructive Resolution of Disputes (ACCORD). Walter holds a PhD in International Relations from the University of St Andrews in Scotland.

Ingo Peters is Associate Professor of Political Science, Freie Universität Berlin, and Executive Director of the Center for Transnational Relations, Foreign and Security Policy at the Otto-Suhr-Institut of Political Science. His major research interests are European security policy, German foreign policy and transatlantic relations. His recent publications include *Transatlantic Tug-of-War: Prospects for US-European Cooperation* (Lit Verlag, 2006) and *20 Years since the Fall of the Berlin Wall. Transitions, State Break-Up and Democratic Politics in Central Europe and Germany*, co-edited with Elizabeth Bakke (Berliner Wissenschafts-Verlag/Intersentia, 2011).

Jochen Prantl is Associate Professor in International Relations, College of Asia and the Pacific, Australian National University. His research focuses on global governance, international security, institutional diversity, and collective action. Prior to this, he held positions in the Department of Politics and International Relations, and Nuffield College, University of Oxford, and the Lee Kuan Yew School of Public Policy, National University of Singapore. He also served as Acting Director of Oxford's Centre for International Studies. Dr Prantl is Senior Research Associate at the Centre for International Studies and at the Global Economic Governance Programme, University of Oxford. He holds degrees in Political Science (M) from the University of Bonn and International Relations (DPhil) from the University of Oxford.

Jennifer Welsh is Professor in International Relations at the University of Oxford, and co-director of the Oxford Institute for Ethics, Law and Armed Conflict. She is the author and editor of a series of books and articles related to humanitarian intervention, 'the responsibility to protect', and the UN Security Council, including *Humanitarian Intervention and International Relations* (Oxford 2004), *The United Nations Security Council and War: The Evolution of Thought and Practice Since 1945* (Oxford 2008) and *Just and Unjust Interventions* (Cambridge 2013). She currently directs a research project funded by the Australian Government on the prevention of mass atrocity crimes. She is a former adviser to the Canadian government on international policy, and a frequent commentator in the Canadian and UK media on international affairs.

Paul D. Williams is Associate Professor in the Elliott School of International Affairs at the George Washington University and a Non-Resident Senior Adviser at the International Peace Institute in New York. His books include *War and Conflict in Africa* (Polity, 2011), *Understanding Peacekeeping* (Polity, second edition, 2010), and *Providing Peacekeepers: The Politics, Challenges and Future of United Nations Peacekeeping Contributions* (Oxford University Press, 2013).

Dominik Zaum is Professor in Governance, Conflict, and Security at the University of Reading, and a Senior Research Fellow in Conflict and Fragility at the UK's Department for International Development (DFID). His research focuses on the politics of international organizations, especially the UN, and on the political economy of international peace- and state-building efforts. His publications include *The Sovereignty Paradox: The Norms and Politics of International Statebuilding* (Oxford 2007), *The United Nations Security Council and War: The Evolution of Thought and Practice Since 1945* (Oxford 2008), and *Political Economy of Statebuilding: Power after Peace* (Routledge 2012).

Part I

Conceptual Questions

1

International Organizations, Legitimacy, and Legitimation

Dominik Zaum

This book examines and evaluates the legitimation practices of international and regional organizations and their member states.[1] It is not an effort to assess the legitimacy—or lack thereof—of different international organizations. Rather than examining legitimacy as the property of institutions, and in judging their legitimacy claims, it is interested in understanding the practices of legitimacy: the practices employed by international organizations to communicate and to justify their legitimacy claims.[2] It examines both the similarities and differences between the legitimation efforts of international organizations, and the factors that can help to explain these.

Why do the legitimation practices of international organizations merit such examination? Over the last two decades, the growing scope of international organizations' efforts to regulate the actions of states (and increasingly individuals), and the intrusiveness of some organizations into areas considered by many states to be within their sovereign domain has resulted in a greater interest in the legitimacy of international organizations and their actions.[3] On the one hand, the debate this has spurred has focused both on the structures and on the decision-making processes of international organizations. Proponents of UN Security Council reform, for example, have focused very much on the lack of representativeness of the fifteen-member Council dominated by the victors of the Second World War, and argue that this has fuelled a legitimacy deficit that threatens the credibility and authority of the institution. They note

[1] For simplicity, the chapter refers to international organizations to describe both international and regional organizations, unless it is made explicit in the text.

[2] Ian Clark, *Legitimacy in International Society* (Oxford: Oxford University Press, 2005).

[3] Jean-Marc Coicaud and Veijo Heiskanen (eds.), *The Legitimacy of International Organizations* (Tokyo: United Nations University Press, 2001); Bruce Cronin and Ian Hurd, *The UN Security Council and the Politics of International Authority* (Abingdon: Routledge, 2008); see also the contributions in the special issue of *International Politics* (2007), Vol. 44, nos. 2–3, on 'Resolving Crises of Legitimacy', edited by Ian Clark and Christian Reus-Smit.

the absence of any African and Latin American permanent members, and the need to accommodate the changes in international order since the end of the cold war, in particular the emergence of a number of non-Western rising powers such as India and Brazil. Similarly, an extensive literature has emerged on the challenge that the European Union's 'democratic deficit' poses to the organization's legitimacy.[4] On the other hand, it has also led to the examination of the actions of international organizations through the lens of legitimacy, in particular of diplomatic and military interventions by international organizations into the domestic affairs of their member states, for example by the Economic Community of West African States (ECOWAS), the Organization for Security and Cooperation in Europe (OSCE), NATO, and the UN Security Council.

These debates about the roles of international organizations have also raised questions about the character of legitimacy in international society more generally,[5] and the roles that international organizations play as 'collective legitimizers' of state actions, to use Inis Claude's famous phrase.[6] These debates have largely focused on the role of international organizations with regard to the authorization of the use of force,[7] and the legitimacy of the use of force without the authorization by international organizations, especially the UN, in particular in the context of the wars in Kosovo and Iraq in 1999 and 2003 respectively.[8]

From the perspective of mainstream International Relations (IR) theory, the prominence of legitimacy talk in recent IR debates might seem surprising. Legitimacy is normally associated with relationships of authority, with hierarchical relationships between rulers and ruled.[9] Most IR theories, on the

[4] Thomas Pogge, 'Creating Supra-National Institutions Democratically: Reflections on the European Union's "Democratic Deficit"', *Journal of Political Philosophy*, Vol. 5/2 (1997), 163–82; Vivien Schmidt, 'The European Union: Democratic Legitimacy in a Regional State?', *Journal of Common Market Studies*, Vol. 42/5 (2004), 975–97.

[5] Clark, *Legitimacy in International Society;* Thomas Franck, *The Power of Legitimacy Among Nations* (Oxford: Oxford University Press, 1990).

[6] Inis L. Claude, 'Collective Legitimization as a Political Function of the United Nations', *International Organization*, Vol. 20/3 (1966), 367–79.

[7] Alex Bellamy and Paul Williams, 'Who's Keeping the Peace? Regionalization and Contemporary Peace Operations', *International Security*, Vol. 29/4 (2005), 157–95; Katharina Coleman, *International Organisations and Peace Enforcement: The Politics of International Legitimacy* (Cambridge: Cambridge University Press, 2007); Andrew Hurrell, 'Legitimacy and the Use of Force: Can the Circle be Squared?', *Review of International Studies*, Vol. 31, special issue on Force and Legitimacy in World Politics (2005), 15–32.

[8] Independent International Commission on Kosovo, *The Kosovo Report: Conflict, International Response, Lessons Learned* (Oxford: Oxford University Press, 2000); Justin Morris and Nicholas J. Wheeler, 'The Security Council's Crisis of Legitimacy and the Use of Force', *International Politics*, Vol. 44, nos. 2/3 (2007), 214–31; Adam Roberts, 'Law and the Use of Force after Iraq', *Survival*, Vol. 45/2 (2003), 31–56.

[9] Hannah Arendt, 'What is Authority', in Hanna Arendt, *Between Past and Future: Eight Exercises in Political Thought* (New York: Viking Press, 1954), 91–141; See also Chapter 2 by Mervyn Frost in this volume.

other hand, have identified anarchy as one of the overriding characteristics of international politics,[10] even if anarchy is socially constructed,[11] or governed and sustained by international institutions such as diplomacy, international law, and great powers.[12] Until the 1990s, legitimacy questions were therefore rarely asked of international institutions,[13] restricting theorizing about legitimacy mostly to sociologists, political theorists, and psychologists interested in questions of institutional legitimacy at the level of the state and below, where the existence of hierarchy and authority is not contested.[14] To the extent that legitimacy was discussed at the level beyond the state, it was mainly explored in studies of the European Communities/Union, where the relative autonomy of the European Commission and the European Court of Justice, and the primacy of European Union over national legislation have created hierarchical relationships.[15]

The growing interest in questions of legitimacy at the international level over the last two decades, especially the legitimacy of international organizations, has been fuelled by three factors in particular. First, there has been a growing recognition that within the broadly anarchic international environment, there have always been pockets of hierarchy in international society.[16] Such hierarchies can take two different forms: formal and informal. Formal hierarchies describe the establishment of formal authority structures above the state, where international organizations have the power to take binding decisions with an expectation of compliance from states. Prominent examples include the UN Security Council's power to take decisions binding on all member states, under Chapter VII of the

[10] Robert O. Keohane, *After Hegemony: Cooperation and Discord in the World Political Economy* (Princeton: Princeton University Press, 1984); Kenneth Waltz, *Theory of International Politics* (New York: Addison-Welsey, 1979).

[11] Alexander Wendt, 'Anarchy Is What States Make of It: The Social Construction of Power Politics', *International Organization*, Vol. 46/2 (1992), 391–425.

[12] Hedley Bull, *The Anarchical Society: A Study of Order in World Politics*, 2nd edition (Basingstoke: Macmillan, 1995).

[13] For important exceptions, see Inis L. Claude, 'Collective Legitimization as a Political Function of the United Nations', *International Organization*, Vol. 20/3 (1966), 367–79; and Jerome Slater, 'The Limits of Legitimization in International Organizations: The Organization of American States and the Dominican Crisis', *International Organization*, Vol. 23/1 (1964), 48–72.

[14] For an overview of this literature, see Morris Zelditch, 'Theories of Legitimacy', in John T. Jost and Brenda Major (eds.) *The Psychology of Legitimacy: Emerging Perspectives on Ideology, Justice, and Intergroup Relations* (Cambridge: Cambridge University Press, 2001), 33–53.

[15] David Beetham and Christopher Lord, *Legitimacy and the EU* (London: Longman, 1998); Fritz Scharpf, *Governing in Europe: Democratic and Effective?* (Oxford: Oxford University Press, 1999).

[16] Ian Clark, *The hierarchy of states: Reform and resistance in the international order* (Cambridge: Cambridge University Press, 1998); Edward Keene, 'A Case Study of Construction of International Hierarchy: British Treaty-Making Against the Slave Trade in the Early Nineteenth Century', *International Organization*, Vol. 61/2 (2007), 311–39; David A. Lake, 'Escape from the State of Nature: Authority and Hierarchy in World Politics', *International Security*, Vol. 32/1 (2007), 47–79.

UN Charter;[17] and the EU, where Union law takes precedence over national law, and can be enforced through the European Court of Justice.[18] Similarly, unequal regimes such as the Nuclear Non-proliferation Treaty (NPT), which aims to limit the possession of nuclear weapons to certain states (who now also happen to be the permanent members of the UN Security Council) establish and reinforce formal hierarchies in international society.

Informal hierarchies, on the other hand, describe hierarchies between states whose relationship is otherwise characterized by sovereign equality, where states accept that certain powerful states, the great powers, can legitimately exercise control over certain policy areas of subordinate states.[19] Historians examining the nineteenth-century great power concert and balance of power politics have long argued that great power status is not just a question of military and economic resources, as neo-realists suggest, but a social status involving certain rights and responsibilities on behalf of the putative great power,[20] which define the character of the informal hierarchy.[21] During the cold war, both the Soviet Union's and the US's role in Europe could be described as informal hierarchies or informal empires;[22] and since the end of the cold war, informal hierarchies have been reflected in particular in the identification of some states as 'rogue' or 'outlaw' states,[23] who are not accorded the unconditional right of sovereign non-interference because of their unwillingness or inability to protect the human rights of their citizens.[24]

[17] The expectation of compliance with Security Council decisions is reflected in Article 25 of the UN charter: 'The Members of the United Nations agree to accept and carry out the decisions of the Security Council in accordance with the present Charter.'

[18] Karen Alter, *Establishing the Supremacy of European Law: The Making of an International Rule of Law in Europe* (Oxford: Oxford University Press: 2001).

[19] Lake, 'Escape from the State of Nature'.

[20] Paul Schroeder, 'The nineteenth century system: balance of power or political equilibrium?' *Review of International Studies*, Vol. 15 (1989), 135–53.

[21] This social dimension of great power status is also highlighted by Hedley Bull, who argued that 'great powers are powers recognised by others to have, and conceived by their own leaders and peoples to have, certain special rights and duties... States which... are military powers of the front rank, but are not regarded by their own leaders or others as having these rights and responsibilities, are not properly speaking great powers' (Bull, *Anarchical Society*, 196).

[22] Geir Lundestad, 'Empire by Invitation? The United States and Western Europe, 1945–1952', *Journal of Peace Research*, Vol. 23/2 (1986), 263–77; Alexander Wendt and Daniel Friedheim, 'Hierarchy under anarchy: informal empire and the East German state', in Thomas Biersteker and Cynthia Weber (eds.), *State sovereignty as social construct* (Cambridge: Cambridge University Press, 1996), 240–77.

[23] Gerry Simpson, *Great Powers and Outlaw States: Unequal Sovereigns in the International Legal Order* (Cambridge: Cambridge University Press, 2004).

[24] International Commission on Intervention and State Sovereignty, *The Responsibility to Protect* (Ottawa: International Development Research Centre, 2001); Robert O. Keohane, 'Political authority after Intervention: gradations in sovereignty' in J. L. Holzgrefe and Robert O. Keohane (eds.) *Humanitarian Intervention: Ethical, Legal, and Political Dilemmas* (Cambridge: Cambridge University Press, 2003), 275–98; Stephen Krasner, 'Sharing Sovereignty: New Institutions for Collapsed and Failing States', *International Security*, Vol. 29/2 (2004), 85–120.

Second, as noted earlier, international organizations have increasingly involved themselves in the domestic affairs of states. This involvement has taken several forms, three of which stand out. First, international and regional economic organizations like the WTO and the EU have taken on regulatory functions, in particular to promote market liberalization, which have limited the sovereign autonomy of their members. Second, international organizations have increasingly resorted to diplomatic and economic sanctions to promote and protect human rights, and attached human rights conditionalities to development aid or preferred marked access.[25] Third, in the last two decades a range of international organizations, including the UN, the AU, NATO, the EU, and ECOWAS have intervened militarily in member states (and non-member states) to end civil conflicts or humanitarian emergencies.[26]

Finally, the rapid social and political change since the end of the cold war has fuelled perceptions of legitimacy gaps—or even crises—which have shaped the debate about the legitimacy of international organizations. An institution is deemed legitimate if its exercise of power is justified by moral and other socially embedded beliefs.[27] If an international organization fails to reflect these shared beliefs in its practices and objectives, either because of normative change or because it imposes rules in contexts where supporting beliefs are lacking, it develops a legitimacy deficit, which in the worst case can turn into a legitimacy crisis, when the 'decline in legitimacy, or its failure to cultivate sufficient legitimacy, has reached a critical turning point'.[28] The rapid international political and social change of the last decades has challenged many of the underlying beliefs on which the legitimacy of international organizations rested. As Veijo Heiskanen has argued,

> Over the past fifty years, fundamental changes have taken place in the operating environment of these international organisations... As a result of these changes, many international organizations... have been struggling to maintain or re-establish the role that they once were perceived, or expected to have in international relations.[29]

[25] Emilie Hafner-Burton, 'Trading Human Rights: how Preferential Trade Agreements Influence Government Repression', *International Organization*, Vol. 59/3 (2005), 593–629.

[26] See the Chapter 3 by Williams in this volume. See also Mats Berdal and Spyros Economides (eds.), *United Nations Interventionism: 1991–2004* (Cambridge: Cambridge University Press, 2007); Coleman, *International Organisations and Peace*; Vaughan Lowe, Adam Roberts, Jennifer Welsh, and Dominik Zaum (eds.), *The United Nations Security Council and War: The Evolution of Thought and Practice since 1945* (Oxford: Oxford University Press, 2008).

[27] David Beetham, *The Legitimation of Power* (Basingstoke: Palgrave Macmillan, 1991), 15–25.

[28] Christian Reus-Smit, 'International Crises of Legitimacy', *International Politics*, Vol. 44 (2007), 166–67.

[29] Veijo Heiskanen, 'Introduction', in Jean-Marc Coicaud and Vaijo Heiskanen (eds.) *The Legitimacy of International Organizations* (Tokyo: United Nations University Press, 2001), 1–2.

To address such legitimacy gaps, international organizations need to engage in legitimation, to justify their roles and practices and ground them in their wider social context.[30] As Inis Claude astutely observed of states, 'lovers of naked power are far less typical than those who aspire to clothe themselves in the mantle of legitimate authority; emperors may be nude, but they do not like to be so, and think of themselves so, or to be so regarded'.[31] This insight into the preferences and behaviour of states certainly also holds for international organizations which lack the coercive capacities that characterize (most) states, and that therefore do not have the privilege of resorting to naked power. They therefore rely strongly on legitimacy to achieve compliance with their rules and decisions.[32]

The contributions to this book examine in greater detail the legitimation practices of different international organizations, and the distinct and changing normative environments within which these efforts take place. The concept of legitimacy is complex and diffuse, not least because of the variety of sources and objects associated with it,[33] and different chapters emphasize different aspects of legitimacy and legitimation. To provide a framework for these contributions, this introductory chapter examines some of the key aspects of legitimacy and legitimation that inform the enquiries in the different chapters. It is divided into three sections. The first examines the concepts of legitimacy and legitimation as they pertain to international organizations. The second discusses three conceptual challenges to understanding the legitimacy challenges and legitimation efforts of international organizations: first, their Janus-faced character as both actors and frameworks for action; second, the need of international organizations to address different and diverse audiences; and third, the multifaceted relationship between power and legitimation. The chapter concludes with a brief overview of the remaining chapters.

[30] Rodney Barker, *Legitimating Identities: The Self-Representation of Rulers and Subjects* (Cambridge: Cambridge University Press, 2001); Herbert Kelman, 'Reflections on Social and Psychological Processes of Legitimization and Delegitimization', in John T. Jost and Brenda Major (eds.), *The Psychology of Legitimacy: Emerging Perspectives on Ideology, Justice, and Intergroup Relations* (Cambridge: Cambridge University Press, 2001), 54–73; Talcott Parsons, 'Authority, Legitimation, and Political Action' in Carl Friedrich (ed.), *Authority* (Cambridge, Mass: Harvard University Press, 1958), 197–221.

[31] Claude, 'Collective Legitimization', 386.

[32] Franck, *The Power of Legitimacy Among Nations.*

[33] Zelditch, 'Theories of Legitimacy'.

LEGITIMACY AND LEGITIMATION

An institution is legitimate if its power is justified in terms of moral and other socially embedded beliefs, and if those subject to its rule recognize that it should be obeyed.[34] We can broadly distinguish between three different kinds of beliefs that give rise to different forms of legitimacy. First, they can be beliefs about the ends towards which power should be exercised and about the effectiveness of an institution in promoting these shared goals.[35] If institutions fail to achieve the desired outcomes, be they welfare gains arising from cooperation, the promotion of particular human rights, or placing effective limitations on the use of force, their legitimacy will be challenged and decline. These are beliefs about what Fritz Scharpf has called output legitimacy.[36] Second, they can be beliefs about the ways in which power is exercised, the processes by which rulers are selected and by which decisions are made, and the processes that ensure that power is exercised in a procedurally fair manner.[37] In contrast to the former, which emphasizes the effectiveness of promoting shared goals, the latter emphasizes procedural fairness, which in the case of international organizations might involve even-handedness vis-á-vis those subject to its authority, a perception that all member states have appropriate opportunity to participate in decision-making, and the equal application of its rules to all member states. As will be discussed further below, in an international order without centralized coercive power and characterized by unequal power, procedural fairness and legitimacy are very difficult to achieve. A third set of legitimating beliefs are beliefs about the identity and particular qualities of an institution, contributing to what Mark Sutchman has called 'structural legitimacy'.[38] In Sutchman's words, '[t]he structurally legitimate organization becomes a repository of public confidence because it is "the right organization for the job." '[39] An international organization's structural legitimacy might arise from shared beliefs about its epistemic capacities, its perceived ability to muster particular resources and expertise, or from certain qualities of its membership. In particular the latter has featured prominently in the debates about the legitimacy of international organizations, amidst (controversial) suggestions

[34] Beetham, *Legitimation of Power*, 15–35.

[35] Lake, 'Escape from the Scape of Nature'.

[36] Scharpf, *Governing Europe*.

[37] Thomas M. Franck, *Fairness in International Law and Institutions* (Oxford: Clarendon Press, 1995); Tom R. Tyler, 'A Psychological Perspective on the Legitimacy of Institutions and Authorities', in John T. Jost and Brenda Major (eds.), *The Psychology of Legitimacy: Emerging Perspectives on Ideology, Justice, and Intergroup Relations* (Cambridge: Cambridge University Press, 2001), 416–36.

[38] Mark Sutchman, 'Managing Legitimacy: Strategic and Institutional Approaches', *Academy of Management Review*, Vol. 20/3 (1995), 571–610.

[39] Ibid., 582.

that institutions made up of democratic states enjoy greater legitimacy because of the representative institutions and the constitutional constraints that characterize democratic states.[40]

Approaching the concept of legitimacy from this perspective highlights that it is problematic to neatly distinguish between what Robert Keohane and Allen Buchanan call the normative dimension of legitimacy (the right to rule) and the sociological dimension of legitimacy (a widely held belief in the right to rule).[41] Normative legitimacy is usually ascribed to an institution if its structure, processes, and actions fulfil particular criteria, such as being based on some expression of consent, institutional integrity, or the promotion of justice. However, one cannot just assert universal criteria against which legitimacy claims can be judged, as these criteria are dependent on the particular audience making a normative judgement on an institution's legitimacy. They are the consequence of social processes of argumentation, persuasion, and socialization, and subject—as discussed above—to social change. Similarly, judgements on an institution's sociological legitimacy, ascribed as the result of the congruence of the institution's objectives and practices with the beliefs, values, and expectations that provide a justification for its power, are made on the basis of certain normative suppositions. Thus, in practice both the normative and sociological dimensions of legitimacy are closely interlinked.

While legitimacy can be seen as an attribute of an institution, it also encompasses the social practice of legitimation: it needs to be claimed, sustained, and recognized.[42] As a social practice, it involves both the rulers and the ruled. It is these practices of legitimation by international and regional organizations and their member states, the ways in which they communicate and justify their claims to authority, and in which these claims are recognized and validated, that are at the heart of this book.

Legitimation can be practised both by rulers from above, and by the ruled from below.[43] Legitimation from below, by those subject to an institution's authority, recognizes and validates this institution's legitimacy claims. Thus, voting is a prominent example of such 'bottom-up' legitimation in the domestic context, democratically validating the authority claims of office holders. In international society, legitimation can occur through a range of social practices. One of the most important forms of legitimation emphasized by

[40] G. John Ikenberry and Anne-Marie Slaughter, Final Report of the Princeton Project on National Security, *Forging a World of Liberty Under Law: US National Security in the 21st Century* (Princeton, NJ: Woodrow Wilson School of Public and International Affairs, 2006); Stephen Schlesinger, 'Why a League of Democracies Will Not Work', *Ethics and International Affairs*, Vol. 23/1 (2009), 13–18.

[41] Allen Buchanan and Robert Keohane 'The Legitimacy of Global Governance Institutions', *Ethics and International Affairs*, Vol. 20/4 (2006), 405–37.

[42] Barker, *Legitimating Identities;* Clark, *Legitimacy in International Society.*

[43] Barker *Legitimating Identities*, 22–5.

international lawyers and international relations theorists has been the practice of consent by states to an institution or rule.[44] International organizations are legitimized from below through the consent that states express by joining an institution, and accepting its rules and regulations. In addition, they are legitimized by the day-to-day practices of their member states confirming their recognition of an institution's authority. Thus, practices such as demanding Security Council authorization of the use of force and criticism of military action without the Council's imprimatur confer legitimacy onto the Council (see Chapter 4 by Welsh and Zaum) as do statements from OSCE member states like the US or Germany defending its election monitoring practices (see Chapter 10 by Peters), to highlight just two examples.

The second form of legitimation is from above, by the actors claiming legitimacy. From this perspective, legitimation is 'an action or series of actions—speech, writing, ritual, display—whereby people justify to themselves or others the actions they are taking and the identities they are expressing or claiming'.[45] In other words, it is a process of self-legitimation, where institutions communicate their claims sideways to other institutions that might make competing claims, or downwards towards their membership and the wider international community, to justify particular activities. Drawing on Weber's famous definition of the state, Rodney Barker suggests that this form of legitimation—of *claiming* legitimacy—is a defining component of government.[46]

A third form of legitimation, which, to stay in the spatial metaphor used above one could call 'horizontal' or 'sideways', is legitimation by actors who are outside the hierarchical relationship governed by legitimacy. Here, legitimacy claims are recognized by outsiders who are not directly affected by the claim, or might be able to make rival claims. In international society, the most prominent example of this form of legitimation is the practice of state recognition, constituting a political community as a member of the society of states with the concomitant rights and responsibilities, and legitimating its participation in the practices of international society. With regards to international relations, such legitimation can be practiced by a least three kinds of actors: by other international organizations recognizing and affirming the activities of a particular organization; by non-members of an organization, especially great and regional powers that are politically, economically, or strategically important

[44] Terry Nardin, 'Legal Positivism as a Theory of International Society', in David Maple and Terry Nardin (eds.), *International Society: Diverse Ethical Perspectives* (Princeton, NJ: Princeton University Press, 1998), 17–35; Bruno Simma, 'From Bilateralism to Community Interest in International Law: Bilateralism and Community Interest Confronted', *Recueil des Cours*, Vol. 250 (1994), 229–55; Dominik Zaum, 'The Authority of International Administrations in International Society', *Review of International Studies*, Vol. 32/3 (2006), 458–61.

[45] Rodney Barker, 'Legitimacy, Legitimation, and the European Union: What Crisis?', in P. Craig and R. Rawlings (eds.), *Law and Administration in Europe: Essays in Honour of Carol Harlow* (Oxford: Oxford University Press, 2003), 163–4.

[46] Barker, *Legitimating Identities*, 24.

for many member states of an organization; and by prominent NGOs that can galvanize international public opinion.

Depending on the context, such legitimation efforts address three distinct challenges. First, they confirm the desirability of the status quo, affirming existing authority structures and defending them against rival authority claims. Thus, many states who regularly emphasize the central role of the Security Council with regard to the lawful authorization of force do so in response to claims that force used unilaterally or by other multilateral organizations such as NATO and justified in humanitarian terms could undermine the Council's Charter-based monopoly on authorizing military force other than in self-defence.[47] Second, legitimization efforts can re-categorize or extend authority relationships.[48] As Clark argues, legitimation describes the processes by which the distinct normative beliefs of actors are reconciled and applied to a particular case.[49] These processes of negotiating both applicable norms and the role that a particular international organization should play in their promotion or protection both lead to normative change and to changed understandings of the legitimate objectives and practices of international organizations. A very good example of such a legitimation process is the shift by the AU and ECOWAS from a 'principle of non-intervention' to a 'principle of non-indifference', which Sarjoh Bah and Walter Lotze examine in their respective chapters in this volume. Third, legitimation efforts can confirm legitimacy claims in the light of social change, maintaining an international organization's legitimacy when the original grounds for legitimacy and obedience no longer exist because of social change. A good example of such efforts legitimating the role of an international organization in a changed environment is NATO's change from a cold war alliance to a security organization addressing a much broader range of security challenges outside its previous regional focus, most notably in Afghanistan or Libya.

CONCEPTUAL CHALLENGES

The complex characters of both legitimacy and of international organizations, and the environment within which they operate, impose a range of challenges to conceptualizing and understanding the legitimation practices of international organizations, and the legitimacy challenges that they face. Three problems stand out: the Janus-faced character of many intergovernmental

[47] Martha Finnemore, 'Fights about rules: the role of efficacy and power in changing multilateralism', *Review of International Studies*, Vol. 31/S1 (2005), 187–206.

[48] Kelman, 'Reflection on Processes of Legitimization and Delegitimization'.

[49] Clark, *Legitimacy in International Society*, 20.

organizations as corporate entities and actors on the one hand and frameworks for cooperation between states on the other; the challenge that international organizations often address a range of different audiences with their legitimation efforts, with different values, interests, and expectations; and the huge power inequalities between different member states of international organizations, and the hegemonic role that some states come to play in their decision-making.

The Janus-faced Character of International Organizations

The international organizations examined in this book are all predominantly intergovernmental organizations. They are deeply political institutions, and one of their central roles is to act as a focal point facilitating the cooperation between states to address collective action problems in a complex, globalized world. However, in their communications, international organizations often strive to give the impression of being a single, relatively homogenous corporate entity, implying that the organization as a whole 'endorses', 'authorizes', 'regrets' or 'criticizes' particular actions or state of affairs. In addition, many international organizations have supranational, at times relatively autonomous bureaucracies or secretariats that further foster this impression, most notably the European Commission, or the UN Secretariat. Most of these international organizations are therefore best understood as having a Janus-faced character, defying easy characterization as either a coherent, autonomous supranational body or an institutional framework for intergovernmental cooperation. This ambiguity is captured best in Inis Claude's notion of the 'two United Nations'—the supranational UN of the Secretariat and its specialized agencies on the one hand, and the UN of the member states in the Security Council and the General Assembly on the other.[50]

However, the perception of international organizations as relatively autonomous, corporate entities pervades much of the literature on the legitimacy of international organizations.[51] On the basis of this perception, a range of scholars, for example Jens Steffek,[52] and Michael Barnett and Martha Finnemore,[53]

[50] Inis L. Claude, 'Peace and Security: Prospective Roles for the Two United Nations', *Global Governance*, Vol. 2 (1996), 289–98.

[51] Michael N. Barnett and Martha Finnemore, 'The Politics, Power, and Pathologies of International Organizations', *International Organization*, Vol. 53/4 (1999), 699–732; Corneliu Bjola, 'Legitimating the Use of Force in International Politics: A Communicative Action Perspective', *European Journal of International Relations*, Vol. 11/2 (2005), 266–303; Michael Matheson, *Council Unbound: The Growth of UN Decision Making on Conflict and Post-Conflict Issues after the Cold War* (Washington D.C.: USIP Press, 2006); Jens Steffek, 'The Legitimation of International Governance: A Discourse Approach', *European Journal of International Relations*, Vol. 9/2 (2003), 249–75.

[52] Steffek, 'Legitimation of International Governance'.

[53] Barnett and Finnemore, *Politics, Power, and Pathologies*'.

have suggested that Weber's study of bureaucracies provides an insight into the character of international organizations, and the way in which their legitimacy can be understood. They argue that like bureaucracies, international organizations have issue-specific authority (rather than the discretionary and plenipotentiary authority of a government), and their decision-making is subject to closely prescribed and codified processes, which are well understood by the relevant audiences—they embody what Weber has termed rational-legal authority.[54] Consequently, the legitimacy of decisions can be rationally debated on the basis of these decision-making rules.

Such an understanding of international organizations undoubtedly captures a range of very important aspects of their roles, their power, their legitimacy, and their legitimation practices. However, for two reasons in particular such an understanding is at best partial. First, as the following chapters show, while the scope of different organizations' authority might on paper be issue specific, relating to international or regional peace and security or to economic cooperation, in reality their activities have often reached beyond these, and some of them have exercised significant discretion in the interpretation of their mandates. Thus, as Sarjoh Bah discusses in Chapter 5, ECOWAS with its mandate to promote economic cooperation and integration in West Africa decided to intervene with military force into two member states—Liberia and Sierra Leone—in the early 1990s. Similarly, the UN Security Council has substantially broadened its understanding of what constitutes a threat to peace and security.[55] This highlights that these organizations are best seen as deeply political, rather than bureaucratic, institutions, challenging the view of some scholars of multilateral institutions, who suggest that legitimacy is fostered by the ability of such organizations to appear depoliticized.[56] Second, decision-making is often not based on clear, well-understood decision-making rules against which the legitimacy of an action can be judged. Instead, decision-making is frequently characterized by political bargaining between members, and often dominated by a few powerful states. These bargaining processes by which decisions are reached are more likely to be opaque and secretive, rather than subject to closely prescribed and codified processes.

Any analysis of the legitimacy and legitimation practices of international organizations needs to take into account their Janus-faced character, and the tensions and the constraints this imposes on their legimation efforts. It also needs to take account of the deeply political nature of these organizations. While they provide focal points that enable states to cooperate through their structures and processes, as neoliberal institutionalist theories have powerfully argued,[57] the case studies in this book also show that they also act as

54 Max Weber, *Economy and Society* (New York: Bedminster Press. 1968).
55 See Zaum and Welsh in this volume, and Lowe et al., *The UN Security Council and War.*
56 Barnett and Finnemore, 'Politics, Power, and Pathologies'.
57 Keohane, *After Hegemony.*

frameworks through which states pursue the legitimation—and de-legitimation—of different conceptions of international order, and the role of respective international organizations within that order. Legitimation is therefore not only pursued collectively by an international organization as a whole, but also by different members individually, through the structures and processes of the organizations, and with reference to their mandates. We therefore must not only look at international organizations as relatively coherent, corporate entities, but also unpack the political dynamics occurring within their different organs, and the ways in which these dynamics affect strategies of legitimation.

From these two distinct aspects of the character of international organizations arise two broad categories of legitimation, which one could term *collective* and *pluralist*. Collective legitimation practices describe the efforts of international organizations and their members as coherent actors to improve the normative properties of an institution to defend or sustain authority claims against both internal and external challenges. A good example of such a collective legitimation effort is ASEAN's admission of Myanmar in 1997, in spite of strong external pressure especially from the US and the European Union to deny it membership, to assert ASEAN's institutional integrity and its autonomy from outside interference;[58] and the promotion of a norm of non-indifference in Africa by the AU and ECOWAS. Pluralist legimation efforts, on the other hand, are conducted by individual states and groups of states using the structures and processes of particular international organizations instrumentally to protect or promote their particular vision of international or regional order. The debates between Russia and CIS states on the one hand, and the US and Western European states on the other, about the degree of OSCE involvement in the domestic affairs of its member states through its monitoring missions of human rights and democratization practices in particular, are a clear case of pluralist legitimation, where different groups of states use the OSCE and its processes to promote their conflicting conceptions of international order.[59] States have used the UN and the Security Council in particular to promote similar conflicting conceptions of international order, reflected for example in debates about the responsibility to protect and the Security Council's role in this regard.[60]

Why are international organizations useful frameworks within which to contest competing norms? Two reasons stand out. First, the structured character of interaction in the context of international organizations can constrain the exercise of coercion and power politics,[61] creating a more permissive environment for norm-based discourses. This offers a platform for states who would

[58] See Chapter 7 by Alice Ba in this volume.

[59] See Chapter 10 by Ingo Peters in this volume.

[60] Alex Bellamy, 'The Responsibility to Protect—Five Years On', *Ethics and International Affairs*, Vol. 24/2 (2010), 143–69.

[61] Finnemore, 'Fights about Rules'.

otherwise find it more difficult to have their voices heard, and to advance their visions of order. Second, international organizations are frequently characterized by a 'repertoire of collective understandings',[62] that structure the debate between states, and mean that arguments that reflect these shared normative frameworks are more likely to resonate with an organization's membership than those that do not reflect them, that such arguments are 'better' and more persuasive than others.[63] International organizations are therefore particularly conducive environments for norms-based discourses, and offer a structured yet permissive framework for states to contest competing norms.

The Problem of Different Audiences

In modern international society, characterized by value pluralism and a diverse range of actors (both states and non-state actors), international organizations seeking legitimacy have to address a range of distinct audiences with different interests, expectations, and normative reference points, and face the difficulty of reconciling these competing demands.[64] The extensive debate about the EU's 'democratic deficit' is a prime example of such a tension, where the EU and its institutions might be successfully legitimated vis-à-vis European elites, but have failed to do so successfully with regard to the wider population of the EU's member states, as highlighted by the fate of the constitutional convention and treaty.[65] Similarly, the literature on international peace operations has increasingly focused on the tensions between international and local legitimacy.[66]

These audience problems pose three specific challenges to international organizations and their collective and pluralist legitimation practices. First, as noted earlier, processes of social and political change can result in legitimacy gaps as the objectives and practices of an organization no longer match the normative beliefs and expectations of its members. Such change, however,

[62] Thomas Risse, 'Let's Argue! Communicative Action in World Politics', *International Organization*, Vol. 54/1 (2000), 11.

[63] Ian Johnstone, 'Security Council Deliberations: The Power of the Better Argument', *European Journal of International Law*, Vol. 14/3 (2003), 437–80.

[64] Andrew Hurrell, 'Legitimacy and the Use of Force: Can the Circle be Squared?', *Review of International Studies*, Vol. 31 (2005), special issue on Force and Legitimacy in World Politics, 15–32.

[65] See Chapter 9 by Chris Lord in this volume. See also Thomas Risse and Mareike Kleine, 'Assessing the Legitimacy of the EU's Treaty Revision Methods', *Journal of Common Market Studies*, Vol. 45/1 (2007), 69–80.

[66] Noah Feldman, *What We Owe Iraq: War and the Ethcis of Nationbuilding* (Princeton: Princeton University Press, 2004); Jeni Whalan, 'The power of friends: The Regional Assistance Mission to Solomon Islands' *Journal of Peace Research*, 47/5 (2010), 627–37; Dominik Zaum, *The Sovereignty Paradox: The Norms and Politics of International Statebuilding* (Oxford: Oxford University Press, 2007).

is likely to affect different states in different ways, depending on their internal characteristics, their economic or military capacity, or their geopolitical position. Thus, rather than simply depriving international organizations of their normative underpinnings, political and normative change opens them up for contestation again, as the expectations of member states towards the organization diverge, or because previously existing differences come into the open. As Chris Lord highlights in his Chapter 9, the governments of European Union member states have used very different (and conflicting) understandings of the kind of Union the ill-fated Constitutional Treaty would have created to legitimize it vis-à-vis their respective populations. The cases of the UN Security Council and the OSCE highlight how fissures about the nature of the international order that both organizations should uphold have emerged over the last decade: whether they should promote a liberal 'solidarist' vision that rests on a commitment to individual human rights, or the more restrictive 'pluralist' order that emphasizes sovereign equality and non-intervention. For those states concerned to protect and enhance sovereignty, the Security Council's 'coercive solidarism',[67] involving the Council ever deeper into the domestic affairs of its member states on the basis of a broadened understanding of what constitutes a threat to international peace and security, and the OSCE's intrusive monitoring of elections, democracy promotion, and assistance to civil society, are eroding the legitimacy of these organizations. For those states supporting a more liberal interpretation of these organizations' mandates, it is the failure to do more to challenge the sovereign prerogatives of states that threatens to undermine the legitimacy of the UNSC and OSCE. The normative divisions within the membership of international organizations, and the existence of multiple internal audiences for legitimacy claims on behalf of international organizations, highlight the importance of considering international organizations not only as actors legitimating other actors and practices, or as institutions in need of legitimation, but also as frameworks for contesting and legitimating different international orders.

Second, most discussions of legitimacy are concerned with the hierarchical relationship between a power-holder and those subject to this power, often because their analytical concern is the issue of compliance. Thus, in the case of international organizations, the focus has been on member states and their publics as the relevant audiences of legitimacy claims. However, as Alice Ba highlights with regard to ASEAN in Chapter 7, international organizations without a near-universal membership, in particular regional and sub-regional organizations in the developing world whose members are not amongst the economic and military great powers, are equally concerned about their legitimacy in the eyes of this external audience of non-member states. Such regional

[67] Andrew Hurrell, *On Global Order: Power, Values, and the Constitution of International Society* (Oxford: Oxford University Press, 2007), 63.

organizations are embedded into a wider global order that reflects the values, interests, and expectations of the major powers, and they have to negotiate the requirements and expectations of this global order. The external recognition of an organization's legitimacy can strengthen its legitimacy amongst its members, however, as internal and external values and expectations might conflict it can also detract from it and limit the political space available to an organization and its members, within which they can successfully pursue their legitimation efforts. Furthermore, powerful global actors often fulfil important economic and security functions in a region, and might even financially support some of the core activities of regional organizations in the developing world. Thus, most of the conflict resolution and peacekeeping activities of the African Union (AU) have been financially supported by external actors, in particular the European Union.[68] The AU therefore relies heavily on external support to be able to legitimize itself internally vis-à-vis its members and their publics (see also Chapter 6 by Lotze in this volume). If the practices of regional organizations and their member states fail to fulfil or actively disappoint the expectations of such powerful actors, states in the region are likely to suffer material consequences as external actors withdraw support to the organization and member states, or attempt to de-legitimize an organization.

Third, the audience of legitimacy claims not only includes states and their publics, but also NGOs and civil society, who do not easily fall into the categories of internal and external audiences discussed earlier. Scholars have highlighted the role that NGOs can play in the diffusion of norms,[69] and in shaping and influencing international organizations' policymaking.[70] However, NGOs and civil society also constitute an important audience for international organizations' legitimation practices, because through their advocacy and lobbying efforts, their ability to mobilize networks of activists, and their promotion of particular norms they can legitimisze international organizations vis-à-vis governments and their publics, complementing the efforts of international organizations and their members. Unlike other audiences discussed here, legitimation towards NGOs and civil society is not important to achieve compliance or to counter rival authority claims, but to co-opt NGOs and civil society into an international organization's legitimation efforts. Thus, NGOs, for example through the International Coalition for the Responsibility

[68] Between 2000 and 2007, the EU supported peace support operations by African regional and sub-regional organizations (in particular the AU) with almost €350 million, and has allocated another €300 million allocated to support the Security activities of the AU and sub-regional organizations in Africa from 2008–10. Nicoletta Pirozzi, *EU Support to African Security Architecture: funding and training components*, Occasional Paper 76 (Paris: European Union Institute for Security Studies, 2009).

[69] Margaret Keck and Kathryn Sikkink, *Activists beyond Borders: Advocacy Networks in International Politics* (Ithaca: Cornell University Press, 1998).

[70] Thomas G. Weiss, Tatiana Carayannis, and Richard Jolly, 'The "Third" United Nations', *Global Governance*, 15/1 (2009), 123–42.

to Protect, have contributed to anchoring the responsibility to protect in the language used to discuss humanitarian crises and conflicts,[71] thus re-affirming (and legitimating) the role of the UN as the guardian of R2P. The nature and depth of the relationship that international and regional organizations have with civil society, however, varies widely. While some organizations such as the OSCE have strong, almost organic links with civil society (going back to the OSCE's predecessor, the CSCE, and the mutually supportive relationship between the CSCE and civil rights organizations in Eastern Europe),[72] others, especially security organizations and regional organizations in the developing world, have for a long time been very reluctant to actively engage with NGOs and civil society.[73]

The existence of different and distinct audiences for legitimacy claims therefore creates a challenge both for the legitimation efforts of international organizations, and for analysing them. With regard to legitimation practices, it means that expectations towards an organization by different audiences are likely to conflict, limiting the political space within which different legitimation strategies can be successfully reconciled. Analytically, it highlights the need to look beyond the internal, hierarchical relationship when examining legitimation practices, to critically explore the tensions and relationships between the expectations of different legitimacy audiences, and to closely examine which audiences matter for the legitimacy of particular international organizations.

The Problem of Power

Legitimacy, and legitimation practices, cannot be understood without regard for the complex and ambiguous relationship between legitimacy and power. Legitimacy is often invoked to imply a particular quality of the exercise of power, morally justifying its use,[74] and associating it with authority.[75] On the one hand, legitimacy is seen as a source of power as it exercises a 'compliance pull' without a need for coercion or the threat of coercion, most famously expressed in Joseph Nye's notion of 'soft power'.[76] As Michael Barnett and

[71] Bellamy, 'The Responsibility to Protect—Five Years On'.

[72] Daniel Charles Thomas, *The Helsinki Effect: International Norms, Human Rights, and the Demise of Communism* (Princeton: Princeton University Press, 2001).

[73] Margaret Karns and Karen Mingst, *International Organizations: The Politics and Process of Global Governance* (Boulder, Co.: Lynne Rienner, 2010), 244–5. See also the Chapters 5, 7, and 8, by Ba, Bah, and Prantl respectively, in this volume.

[74] Allen Buchahnan, 'Political Legitimacy and Democracy', *Ethics*, Vol. 122 (2002), 689–719; William E. Connolly, *The Terms of Political Discourse*, 2nd ed. (Oxford: Martin Robertson, 1983).

[75] Ian Hurd, 'Theories and tests of international authority', in Bruce Cronin and Ian Hurd (eds.) *The UN Security Council and the Politics of International Authority* (Abingdon: Routledge, 2008), 24–6.

[76] Joseph Nye, *Soft Power: The Means to Success in World Politics* (Jackson: PublicAffairs, 2004).

Raymond Duvall highlight, power has a range of different dimensions in the context of global governance, and legitimacy arguably pertains to several of them.[77] Legitimacy matters with regard to what they call compulsory power, where it is key to understanding the role of normative and symbolic resources as sources of power.[78] Legitimacy is also a source of institutional power, and is central to understanding compliance with institutional rules and procedures that constrain actors' behaviour. On the other hand, legitimacy constrains the unchecked exercise of power. The legitimation of power requires powerful states to exercise self-restraint,[79] for if powerful states want to maintain the legitimacy of institutions that reflect their conceptions of order and long-term interests, and ensure continued compliance with them, they have to accept being bound by their rules just as weaker states are.[80] Given the focus of this book on practices of legitimation, it is worth highlighting two particular facets of the relationship between legitimacy and power.

First, power is central to the reproduction of its own legitimacy. As Beetham observes, 'the important point to stress about the maintenance and reproduction of legitimacy—the maintenance of rules, the reproduction of beliefs, the continued expression of consent—is that these do not take place independently of the structures of power that they legitimate'.[81] Beetham identifies two accounts of how power contributes to its own legitimacy. First, powerful actors have superior resources they can deploy to influence the beliefs that legitimate both institutions and power relationships. In the context of international organizations, powerful states cannot control these beliefs and the practices by which they are communicated (as ultimately they need to be judged by the relevant audiences that include those subject to power, rather than exercising it), however, recent scholarship on international organizations (and institutions more generally) highlights the dominant voice that powerful states have within them.[82] Second, power relationships can be constitutive of actors' identities,

[77] Michael N. Barnett and Raymond Duvall (eds.) *Power in Global Governance* (Cambridge: Cambridge University Press, 2005).

[78] Ian Hurd, *After Anarchy: Legitimacy and Power at the UN Security Council* (Princeton: Princeton University Press, 2007).

[79] G. John Ikenberry, *After Victory: Institutions, Strategic Restraint, and the Rebuilding of Order after Major Wars* (Princeton: Princeton University Press, 2001).

[80] Nico Krisch, 'The Security Council and the Great Powers'. In Vaughan Lowe et al. (eds.), *The United Nations Security Council and War: The Evolution of Thought and Practice since 1945* (Oxford: Oxford University Press, 2008), 133–53.

[81] Beetham, *Legitimation of Power*, 104.

[82] Jane Boulden, 'Double Standards, Distance, and Disengagement: Collective Legitimization in the Post-Cold War Security Council', *Security Dialogue*, Vol. 37/3 (2006), 409–23; Andrew Hurrell, 'Power, Institutions, and the Production of Inequality', in Michael Barnett and Raymond Duval (eds.) *Power in Global Governance* (Cambridge: Cambridge University Press, 2005), 33–58; Ngaire Woods, 'The United States and the International Financial Institutions: Power and Influence within the World Bank and the IMF' in Rosemary Foot, Neil MacFarlane, and Michael Mastanduno (eds.) *US Hegemony and International Organizations* (Oxford: Oxford University Press, 2003), 92–114.

shaping the interests and expectations of those governed by relationships of power (see also Chapter 2 by Frost in this volume). Beetham points in particular to claims that the exercise of power by dominant groups serves the general interest, including those of subordinate groups.[83] One example of this are claims about the benefits of the liberalization of developing economies and their integration into global markets, even if the benefits of such policies have been rather unevenly distributed between the developed and the developing world. The need for market liberalization has been invoked to justify the intrusive regulatory powers assumed by the international financial institutions, as only they are said to provide a way out of the collective action problems that the maintenance of free global markets pose.

The second facet of the power-legitimacy relationship concerns the importance of power for procedural legitimacy. As Tom Tyler highlights, perceptions of fairness are central to procedural legitimacy, hence the emphasis on transparency, inclusiveness, and rule-based decision-making that feature prominently in efforts to improve the procedural legitimacy of institutions.[84] One way to ensure fairness and general compliance with the rules of international organizations would be to endow them with the coercive capacity to ensure compliance. If non-compliance has no consequences, other actors have no incentive for compliance either, and cannot reasonably be expected to comply.[85] However, international and regional organizations normally do not have such coercive power, and even if they formally do, as the EU has with regard to the stability pact in the Eurozone, they have normally been unable to enforce rules against powerful states. Thus, Germany and France faced no sanctions when they breached the stability pact by running budget deficits exceeding the agreed limits in the early years of the 21st century, and Spain and Italy have faced more lenient treatment than Greece during the Euro crisis.

In an international society that lacks strong formal hierarchies with the power to ensure procedurally fair treatment of all states, substantial power differences between states threaten to undermine procedural legitimacy, as it enables powerful states to manipulate or break the rules designed to enable and sustain cooperation. As Andrew Hurrell has argued, 'The problem of unbalanced power is not that unchecked power will lead inevitably to tanks rolling across borders. It is rather that radically unbalanced power will…undermine the procedural rules on which stable and sustained cooperation must inevitably depend.'[86] Substantial power imbalances thus threaten to undermine the procedural legitimacy of international organizations, and raises questions about the viability of legitimation on the basis of reforming

[83] Beetham, *Legitimation of Power*, 106–7.

[84] Tyler, 'A Psychological Perspective on the Legitimacy of Institutions'.

[85] Joseph Raz, 'Introduction', in Joseph Raz (ed.), *Authority* (New York: New York University Press, 1990), 15–16.

[86] Hurrell, *On Global Order*, 281.

and opening up decision-making processes. This is particularly important as such reforms have been central to the legitimation efforts of a range of international and regional organizations, ranging from efforts to reform Security Council decision-making structures and processes, to debates about greater civil society involvement at ECOWAS and ASEAN, and to reforms about EU decision-making. Few, if any, of these seem to offer any answer as to how to deal with the problem of power imbalances amongst the membership of different organizations.

PLAN OF THE BOOK

To examine these issues, this book is divided into two parts. Part I (Chapters 1–3), which includes this introduction, examines a range of conceptual problems that arise from the study of the legitimation practices of international and regional organizations. In Chapter 2, Mervyn Frost examines the changing international ethical context within which international organizations pursue their legitimation practices. Frost argues that legitimacy questions arise for international organizations for even though many of them were established by states as functional mechanisms to instrumentally address cooperation problems (thus constituting 'enterprise associations', in Michael Oakeshott's words), many have evolved into something more complex that elicits compliance from states not only for instrumental, but also for ethical reasons. Membership in international organizations can also contribute to the constitution of state identities—UN membership, for example, has become a constitutive element of statehood,[87] while membership in the EU constitutes a state as a liberal democracy in line with the EU's Copenhagen criteria. For these reasons, legitimacy questions have become a pertinent issue for many international organizations, arising in particular, Frost argues, when the ethical reasons for accepting an institution's authority have become contentious, for example in times of rapid social change.

In his analysis in Chapter 3 of the different legitimation claims made by regional organizations and the UN with regard to their activities to maintain international peace and security, Paul Williams highlights that the authority and legitimation relationships between the UN Security Council and regional organizations are more complex than the clear normative and institutional hierarchy outlined in the UN Charter suggests. He highlights the absence of a hierarchy of legitimacy, with some regional organizations (such as the EU) relying on UN Security Council mandates for their legitimation claims,

[87] James Crawford, *The Creation of States in International Law*, 2nd ed. (Oxford: Oxford University Press, 2006), 544–5.

while in other cases the Council has sought the support of regional organizations before authorizing a peace operation or the use of force—for example in Libya in spring 2011, where Arab League support was crucial to the Council's approval of the no-fly zone.[88] Williams's analysis also highlights how the legitimation dynamics between the UN and regional organizations are shaped by the audiences who need to recognize different legitimation claims, with some more responsive to justifications for the use of force based on regional normative frameworks, in particular norms of democratic government and the protection of civilians.

Part II (Chapters 4–10) contains seven case studies examining the legitimation practices of particular international and regional organizations. They analyse the different factors that shape these practices, discuss the challenges that specific legitimation efforts face, and evaluate the legitimacy of the specific organization in the eyes of different relevant audiences for their legitimacy claims.

In Chapter 4, Jennifer Welsh and Dominik Zaum examine the UN Security Council's legitimation efforts. Through the lens of three different legitimation practices they highlight how the tensions between these different practices inherently limit their effectiveness in strengthening Council legitimacy, and how different practices are shaped by the particular normative and political environment within which the Council operates. They also show how the legitimation efforts of member states are not only focused on legitimizing the organization, but also on using the structures and processes of the Security Council to advance and legitimize competing visions of international order (including competing visions for the role of the UN Security Council in this order).

This role of international organizations as a framework within which the character and rules of international and regional orders are contested is also reflected in other case studies, such as Ingo Peters' analysis of the OSCE (Chapter 10), and Sarjoh Bah's analysis of ECOWAS (Chapter 5). Bah's chapter highlights how a need for legitimation arises from rapid social change. The military interventions by ECOWAS into the domestic affairs of some of its member states in the 1990s to address problems posed by civil wars in Liberia and Sierra Leone strongly challenged the legitimacy of the organization in the eyes of a number of its member states and states in the wider region not only because they lacked a mandate from the UN Security Council, but also because they were at odds with the traditional principle of non-intervention. As Bah shows, the contestations over ECOWAS' legitimacy claims in the wake of these interventions resulted in the development of strong new regional 'intervention norm', emphasizing 'non-indifference', over the traditional 'non-interference'. This normative change informed the development of ECOWAS'

[88] SC Res. 1973 of 17 March 2011.

security architecture to further legitimize ECOWAS' new role by strengthening its ability to enforce a principle of 'non-indifference', an architecture that has remained, however, strongly dependent on the willingness of the regional hegemon, Nigeria, to provide the necessary human and financial resources.

In his chapter on the African Union (AU), Walter Lotze examines how the change from the Organization of African Unity (OAU) to the AU was strongly shaped by legitimacy concerns and the expectations of both African states and publics, and external audiences, especially Western states. The chapter charts the evolution of a complex institutional architecture to support the AU's legitimation claims, but also highlights how the lack of substantive consensus on the scope of AU authority among member states, and the continued reliance on external funding to support legitimation claims through actions and not only rhetoric have undermined the AU's legitimation efforts.

While ECOWAS and the AU have modified (at least formally) their traditional stance on non-interference, this principle has remained at the heart of the normative framework underlying the legitimation claims of Asian regional organizations such as ASEAN and the Shanghai Cooperation Organization (SCO), discussed in Chapters 7 and 8 respectively. As Alice Ba contends in her chapter on ASEAN, the non-intervention norm, the support for a state-centric regional order, and a consensus-based process of decision-making have been central to ASEAN's internal legitimation efforts, vis-à-vis its member states. However, since the end of the cold war, and under the influence of greater interaction, both economically and politically, with actors outside ASEAN, the organization has made increasing efforts to legitimate itself vis-à-vis external actors, in particular powerful states like the US, for example through institutional reforms such as the new ASEAN charter. As Ba's analysis shows, internal and external legitimacy are often interdependent, as ASEAN's external legitimacy affects the organization's ability to protect the interests of its members and hence its internal legitimacy. However, despite this interdependence, the conflicting demands of distinct internal and external audiences of legitimacy claims has led to tensions that have required ASEAN members to make difficult choices and prioritize one dimension of legitimacy over another. This has been evident in particular over decisions such as Myanmar's ASEAN membership, which undermined its external legitimacy but became central to assert the institution's autonomy and integrity in the light of external pressure not to admit Myanmar, and thus to its internal legitimacy.

Jochen Prantl's analysis of the Shanghai Cooperation Organization (SCO) in Chapter 10 shows that despite its very weak institutions and close resemblance to 'enterprise association', legitimation offers an important perspective for understanding the roles the SCO plays for its member states. On the one hand it legitimates itself with regards to its members by addressing regional functional cooperation problems; for example with regard to dealing with separatism and counter-terrorism; by providing an institutionalized framework for managing relations between the region's hegemonic powers, China and Russia; and by occupying political space in the region that could otherwise be entered by more liberal organizations and states. On the other hand, the SCO also legitimizes non-liberal norms in these areas (and exceptions to otherwise applicable international norms) that are advanced by its members, especially China and Russia, and provides states that want to escape the scrutiny of Western-dominated international organizations (such as Iran) with an institutional alternative and an attractive alternative model.

In Chapter 9, Chris Lord focuses on the role of member states in the legitimation of the EU, comparing the justifications put by the French and British governments to their own populations for the organization's powers and for their own participation in the Union. Taking on arguments in the literature that the legitimation of the EU has been predominantly affected by its rules and decisions (i.e. through direct elections, as to the European Parliament), Lord shows that both Britain and France relied on a hybrid of direct and indirect legitimacy claims when defending the ultimately ill-fated Constitutional Treaty to their respective publics. Furthermore, he shows how both the study and practice of legitimation of the EU has given rise to a hybrid form of indirect legitimacy that emphasizes the strengthening of democratic mechanisms at the domestic level to establish greater control and accountability over supranational EU institutions.

In Chapter 10, Ingo Peters examines the contestation of the OSCE's legitimacy by Russia on the one hand, and the US and Germany on the other. His analysis highlights that international organizations are not only institutions whose authority needs to be constantly legitimated both towards internal and external audiences, but are also institutional frameworks through which states advance and contest competing conceptions of international order. The competing conceptions of order are examined through debates on the forms and functions of the OSCE, in particular the issue of its legal personality, the unequal involvement of the OSCE into the domestic affairs of its member states, and the autonomy from member-state control of OSCE institutions such as the Office for Democratic Institutions and Human Rights (ODIHR). His analysis also highlights the limits that value pluralism, exemplified in the OSCE by the split between Russia and CIS states on the one hand, and North American and Western European states on the other, undermines the efficacy of efforts to legitimate any international organization.

The concluding chapter discusses the key findings that emerge from a parallel reading of all the cases.

2

Legitimacy and International Organizations: *The Changing Ethical Context*

Mervyn Frost

Before turning to consider the legitimation of international organizations in the contemporary context and to the changing political and normative context in which this takes place, let me make a few points about the notion of legitimacy in general. 'Legitimacy' is one of the more slippery concepts in political studies.[1]

Questions of legitimacy normally only arise when there is a perceived problem in some social arrangement or institutional practice (I use these terms interchangeably). When an institution is working well both from the point of view of the participants and from those outside of it, questions about legitimacy are seldom asked. This is true of all institutions, including international organizations.

If the above is true then we must ask, what kinds of problem give rise to questions about legitimacy? Consider some simple examples of cases where questions about legitimacy have arisen. During the Second World War many French citizens queried the legitimacy of the Vichy regime.[2] In South Africa during the *apartheid* period many people queried the legitimacy of the, so called, 'bantustans' and queried the legitimacy of the governmental systems that operated in them.[3] Many people both within and outside South Ossetia at present question the legitimacy of the political arrangements in place there. The legitimacy query, in each of these cases, points to a problem in the relationship between the government and the governed—to a problem between

[1] 'The concept of legitimacy has attracted considerable interest for generations, yet it has so far led to little true systematic analysis.' Jean Blondel, *Comparative Government: An Introduction* (New York: Philip Allan, 1990), 62 fn 1.

[2] In a famous speech made via the BBC, Gen Charles de Gaulle, on 18 June 1940, challenged the legitimacy of the government set up by the military leaders in France after their defeat by German forces. See the text of his speech at http://www.guardian.co.uk/theguardian/2007/apr/29/greatspeeches1 (accessed 19 October 2010).

[3] See the graphic accounts of those who had withdrawn support for the state of South Africa during the struggle against *apartheid* provided in Shaun Johnson, *Strange Days Indeed* (London: Bantam Press, 1993), passim.

those who have authority (or claim it) and those who are subject to it.[4] The legitimacy question within a given state may be posed by those not actually living there, for example, as happens when members of the Palestinian diaspora challenge the legitimacy of the governing arrangements in Israel. It is clear that where this relationship becomes severely problematic, the stability of the whole social practice might be under threat. The threat could lead to gross instability or it could lead to the institution simply failing to function at all, as happens in failed states. Where the legitimacy question is posed from outside a given state it might point to a lack of international support for the state itself or the arrangements within it.

Let us look at this problem between the governed and those who govern more closely. When we say that a given institution lacks legitimacy we are not simply saying that it *lacks support* from the people involved in it. For it is perfectly possible for people to support an institution while at the same time regarding it as illegitimate. This happens for example when people uphold a corrupt organization such as the Mafia.[5] When we are enquiring about legitimacy, the inquiry is not just about the fact of support, but, seeks to uncover the ethical reasons people have for giving that support. When we ask: 'Do you regard the constitutional arrangements in your state as legitimate?' a positive answer would indicate not just support, but that the support was given for ethical reasons. When people ask questions about legitimacy, underlying the questioning are ethical concerns such as: 'Are these arrangements just? Are they democratic? Do they protect human rights?' and so on.

I wish to argue in this chapter that whenever the legitimacy question is posed it is always:

- posed about people within some social institution;
- posed about the relationship between government and governed (about authority) in that institution;
- posed about the ethical reasons people have for accepting or rejecting the authority of an institution and its rules.

The legitimacy question is usually posed when the ethical reasons for accepting the specified authority relationships in an institution have become contentious for the participants. Where the arrangements are stable (consider the constitutional arrangements in any of the Nordic states) it is not likely that the legitimacy question would be posed. There would seem to be little point or

[4] For Max Weber this problem arises when there is a lack of 'subjective belief in the validity of an order' by the people within that order. See Max Weber, *Economy and Society* (New York: Bedminster Press, 1968).

[5] For a description of the contested status of the Mafia see Diego Gambetta, *The Sicilian Mafia: The Business of Private Protection* (Cambridge, Ma: Harvard University Press, 1996).

purpose in doing so. It is usually change (or the threat of change) of one kind or another which brings the legitimacy question to the fore.

Social institutions are not static, but change in the face of changing circumstances. The factors that move institutions towards change include changing historical circumstances; the emergence of new political forces; scientific discoveries that pose challenges to traditional ways of doing things; and both natural and man-made disasters that force institutions to reconsider their institutional arrangements with a view to transformation. So for example, as India emerges as a great power, this poses challenges to the legitimacy of the structure of the Security Council of the United Nations, and, similarly, as the consequences of climate change become apparent, this will provoke challenges to the legitimacy of national and international institutions which may be seen as inadequate to cope with the emerging problems.

Social institutions consist of a set of people who interact with one another in terms of a set of commonly recognized social rules in order to realize certain values that are of importance to them. This is true of micro institutions such as the family and of macro institutions such as the state. The changes mentioned in the previous paragraph often pose problems that lead participants to question the fit between the commonly recognized rules of the institution and the values that these are considered to serve. For example, the invention of collateralized debt obligations (CDOs) and the consequences that followed from the selling of these instruments, has lead governments and citizens everywhere to reconsider the regulatory framework within which these transactions took place. A key part of this whole process has been a bringing to light of the core values served by the existing framework in order to evaluate how the operation of the CDOs either advanced or threatened these core values. To what extent did they strengthen or undermine the core commitments of the global free market (human rights, property rights, freedom of association, freedom of contract, and so on) and to what extent did they advance or undermine the ethical commitments that are at the core of the society of democratic states; undermine, that is, the core values of democratic citizenship?

In the face of pressure for change, participants in social institutions have to consider what changes to their arrangements would be legitimate given the ethical underpinnings of the institution in question. Often, there are divergent opinions about what changes ought to be accepted as legitimate. In such cases participants within such institutions come to argue about the legitimacy of the proposed changes. Such arguments reveal the deep ethical disputes and fault lines within the institutions in question. The ongoing stability of such institutions depends on a resolution being found to the legitimacy question.

Two easy examples of this process in action spring to mind, both taken from within the sphere of religion. Participants within the Anglican Church have recently faced pressure from the homosexual community within the church for change to some of its fundamental rules. For example, they have demanded a change to the rule that specifies that only hetero-sexual priests are qualified to be considered for the office of bishop. Would such a change be legitimate in terms of the underlying value commitments of the Anglican Church seen as a whole? The argument still rages. A similar argument goes on within the Roman Catholic Church about the legitimacy of a rule change that would allow the appointment of women as priests. Such disputes require of the participants that they look at the whole institution in the round, that they consider at a profound level what the values are on which the institutions in question are founded. If the participants cannot, through argument, reach an agreed conclusion then, there is a real sense in which the institution cannot continue to exist. At this point, one solution might be that the institution divide itself into two separate institutions—each one with its own legitimating ethical background theory. The religious examples that I have used above are fundamental for the churches in question. If the legitimacy problem is not resolved it could have drastic consequences for each of the institutions concerned. But in normal everyday life within the many institutions we engage with, there are less dramatic, but ongoing disputes about the legitimacy of proposed changes within them. Even in vibrant, successful and functioning institutions the legitimacy question is regularly posed. This is true of clubs, learned societies, universities, sports clubs, families, companies, states, and, of course, international corporations and international organizations.

It is therefore worth repeating the central point: institutions regularly face a range of pressures for change. The proposed changes often call forth the legitimacy question: is what is proposed legitimate? This question is not a synonym for the question, do you support the proposed change? It is more profound than that. It asks whether the proposed changes accord with the deep values embedded in the institution. The arguments that ensue about the nature of these values are themselves expressive of a deep value commitment. Arguments about legitimacy are part of the stuff of life within social institutions.[6]

When discussing the legitimacy of a particular social institution we are not concerned with a single act of a particular institutional actor. The legitimacy question arises with regard to the whole structure of authority within an institution, that is, the legitimacy question usually refers to the constitution of an institution. For example, with regard to *apartheid* South Africa the opponents of that form of government (both in South Africa and abroad) challenged the legitimacy of the constitution and this challenge was directly linked to challenges to the legitimacy of the government and the individual decision-makers within the government itself.

[6] For a discussion of how leaders in most institutions produce arguments making the case for their legitimacy see Rodney Barker, *Political Legitimacy and the State* (Oxford: Clarendon Press, 1990).

INTERNATIONAL ORGANIZATIONS

Let me now turn to the legitimacy question as applied to international organizations. Can we and do we ask the legitimacy question outlined above about international organizations? We clearly can and do. For example, the question often arises in connection with the UN and also with regard to the EU, and it could arise about any international organization. Yet, *prima facie*, this seems odd for there are several features of international organizations that seem to suggest that asking questions about their legitimacy would be inappropriate.

First, international organizations do not establish structures of authority akin to those established within states. Organizations such as the UN, EU, AU, ASEAN, OAS, and others do not establish government over their member states or over the people in them. While they clearly have some kind of authority, their authority is over states rather than over individuals. Even with regard to states, these international organizations certainly do not have a general sovereign authority.

Second, the members of these organizations are states, not individual men and women. This raises the question whether states, like individual men and women, have ethical reasons for accepting the authority of these organizations within which they are participants. While it is clear that they might have functional reasons for belonging, it is, on the face of it, not certain that they have ethical reasons for doing so. Many would argue that these organizations are simply what Oakeshott called enterprise associations (sometimes referred to as 'purposive practices') put in place by states for specific instrumental reasons (*inter alia*, to promote international peace and security, regional goals, trade, and so on).[7] We know that individual men and women have ethical reasons for recognizing key institutions such as churches or states as legitimate, but do states do this too? This question is linked to the question whether states are ethical subjects or not. We often talk about states and other collective actors in ways that suggest that these entities themselves may be considered subjects of moral responsibility. We discuss them as having duties, making promises, being generous (or not) and so on.[8]

A third problem arises from the fact that the member states of these organizations consider themselves to be *sovereign* states, that is, they are subject to no higher authority. This would seem to exclude there being any legitimacy problem about such international organizations. If member states are sovereign and if the international organizations are not sovereign bodies, then there cannot (by definition) be a legitimacy question, because, as defined

[7] For a discussion of Oakeshott's idea about enterprise association see Terry Nardin, *Law Morality and Relations of States* (Princeton, NJ.: Princeton University Press, 1983), Introduction.

[8] For an excellent discussion of this see Toni Erskine (ed.), *Can Institutions Have Responsibilities?* (Basingstoke: Palgrave MacMillan, 2003), Introduction.

above, this question always has to do with an authority relationship that has become problematic. If there is no authority relationship (of a sovereign international organization over its member states) then there cannot be a problem of legitimacy.

The fourth and final problem is this: international organizations are voluntary organizations. If the member states have not walked away from the association (have not resigned), then it must follow that member states must, in some broad sense, accept or support the organization—that is, they must see it as legitimate. The mere fact of membership might be seen as proof of their having granted legitimacy to the organization. This last point does indeed seem to be a plausible one when considering international organizations such as the International Postal Union or the Southern African Customs Union. In such purposive and instrumental associations it seems perfectly reasonable to assume that if the members have not resigned from the organization, then it must be the case that they see it as legitimate.[9] For such narrowly defined associations created for a specific purpose, it would seem that 'is legitimate' amounts to 'is fit for purpose'.

In spite of all these *prima facie* reasons for thinking that it is implausible to suppose that the legitimacy question might arise *re* international organizations such as the UN, it seems to me that the legitimacy of international organizations is often an important question and it often arises for the actors who participate in international organizations.

First, many actors such as the UN and other international organizations, such as the EU, are not completely understood if judged only in terms of their fitness for purpose. The UN and the EU (and others) are not properly understood as simply instrumental organizations. Although at the outset it might seem that they were set up as purposive organizations (what Oakeshott calls 'enterprise associations') with the mission of securing 'international peace and security', or 'promoting intra-European trade' and so on, they can no longer be fully understood in this way. They have evolved into something altogether more complex. For the sake of brevity here, let me focus on the UN. The UN has become something much more like a 'civil association' as defined by Michael Oakeshott.[10] My interpretation of such associations (sometimes called 'authoritative practices') is that they do not merely serve as instruments for the achievement of specific ends, but they are social arrangements within which,

[9] The argument here is similar to the 'tacit consent' argument in social contract theory. According to these it can be argued that if citizens do not leave the state within which they are living, then they may be said to have tacitly consented to the state's rule over them. There are many well known arguments against this argument from tacit consent. See in this regard David Hume's argument. Paul Kelly, 'Hume', in David Boucher and Paul Kelly (eds.), *Political Thinkers: From Socrates to the Present* (Oxford: Oxford University Press, 2003), 211.

[10] David Boucher, 'Oakeshott', in David Boucher and Paul Kelly (eds.), *Political Thinkers: From Socrates to the Present* (Oxford: Oxford University Press, 2003), 470.

through processes of mutual recognition, people come to recognize one another in ways that are of value to them.[11] In other words, in such authoritative practices, the participants come to constitute one another as valued beings of one kind or another. There is nowadays a lot more to the UN and the EU than was originally envisaged in the initial instrumental phase. The significant features of the UN that support my contention are that it includes almost all states in the world and that resignations from the UN do not occur and, as far as I can tell, resignation from the UN is not even contemplated. Nowadays, membership of the UN is a constitutive feature of statehood. Indeed, it is the case that the UN is the organization which grants or withholds international recognition from entities that aspire to be autonomous states. The UN is not merely a 'peace and security' operation, but is also active in dozens of different ways in the promotion of human rights, the promotion of international law, and the promotion of democracy. It is recognized by the member states as a norm creator. It has done this with regard to the rights of women, the rights of the child, the rights of peoples, and so on.[12] The UN is recognized as having the right to specify when some or other action has become a threat to peace and security. It gives the authoritative determination on this matter. It has the authority to grant status to peacekeeping operations. I could produce a long list of the normative roles played by the organization. What all this reveals to me is that this organization and its members form an authoritative community. To be a participant in this community is to be a participant in *the* authoritative global norm-creating institution. It is difficult to imagine a state leaving the UN voluntarily (as yet no state has done this) and rejecting all the values embedded in it. My suggestion is that, were a state to do this, then the other states would deem it to have lost moral standing in the community of states.[13] Such a loss of standing would not occur to a state leaving an enterprise association like a postal union. Leaving such a union does not earn the leaver any moral opprobrium from the remaining member states. The argument I have presented with regard to the UN could also be made with regard to the EU. It too is no longer merely an enterprise association.

At the heart of my argument about international organizations such as the UN and the EU is that they are social institutions that do not simply serve purposes external to the organizations, but create for their participants certain valued standings within these organizations. In other words, they are not unlike those other organizations that I briefly discussed earlier (churches and

[11] For an outline of constitutive theory see Mervyn Frost, *Ethics in International Relations: A Constitutive Theory* (Cambridge: Cambridge University Press, 1996).

[12] See United Nations, *Human Rights: A Compilation of International Instruments* (New York: United Nations, 1988).

[13] More than a hint of this was to be found in the community of states' attitude to the USA during the administration of George W. Bush when the US attempted to distance itself from the UN.

states). If this is correct, it follows that the UN and the EU are precisely the sort of organizations within which we would expect the legitimacy question to be posed. In such organizations there are important authority relationships. Let us consider the UN. Given that it is a worldwide organization incorporating most people in the world and most states in the world, it is reasonable to assume that it will face regular and ongoing pressures to change in order to adapt to evolving circumstances.[14] Where the issue of change comes to the fore it will raise the issue of its legitimacy which will only be solvable by delving into the embedded ethics which underpin the organization as a whole. Answering the legitimacy question with regard to the UN will not simply require finding out whether the participants support it or not—it is not simply about getting participants to tick (or not) a box which says 'I support the United Nations Organization'. Instead, an inquiry into the legitimacy of the organization will have to delve into questions about the underlying ethical philosophy of the UN. For it is this philosophy that will guide what participants do when it comes to changing the rules of the basic structure. As the pace of change in world politics increases (across a wide range of different dimensions), the question is likely to be posed with increasing frequency.[15]

At this point it is important to specify the changes in the world that might prompt us to think there is a need for the United Nations to adapt and change its basic structure. I shall just mention a few of the major ones. First, there is the rise of new great powers in the East (India and China). Second, there is the increase in the number of states that has taken place since the inception of the organization. Third, there is the collapse of the bipolar world. Fourth, there is the emergence of something that is often referred to as 'global terror'. Fifth, there is the emergence of a global set of environmental problems. Sixth, there is the rise of a global communications network, including the internet. Seventh, there is the growth of a highly sophisticated network of international criminals. Eighth, there is the problem of what has come to be called the global 'credit crunch'. Ninth, there is the emergence of so called 'new wars'. I'm sure there are many other important things that should be on this list. The point is that these developments, singly and as a group, pose challenges to the UN, and in particular to the legitimacy of the UN as seen from the point of view of the participants. Each one of the developments listed above may pose a challenge to its legitimacy. Let us consider two of them.

Consider the rise of new great powers. These powers and their allies are making strong claims that the existing arrangement of the Security Council is illegitimate and that it ought to be reformed to include some of them as

[14] An instance of the UN itself acknowledging this pressure is to be found in United Nations, *A More Secure World—Our Shared Responsibility: Report of the Secretary General's High Level Panel on Threats, Challenges and Changes*, UN doc. A/59/565 of 2 December 2004.

[15] Similar points can be made about the EU.

permanent members. These demands directly challenge the legitimacy of the existing arrangements. South Africa and Nigeria argue that they ought to be permanent members of the SC as do India, Brazil, Germany, and Japan. Consider too, the rise of 'new wars'. The inability of the UN effectively to deal with these has weakened the legitimacy of the UN and has precipitated a call for new mechanisms within the UN to deal with them.

All of these developments give rise to calls for change. The proposed changes then have to be submitted to the members to see whether they pass the legitimacy test. Once the legitimacy question is posed, the answer has to be sought in arguments that refer to the underlying values of the UN institution understood in the round. What are the ethics embedded in this international organization? What are the key arguments about the organization's legitimacy that take place between the participants?

Before turning to these, let me reiterate a point made earlier. Although there may be arguments about the background theory which justifies the UN, the organization itself is very strong. Were it a weak organization one would expect defections and widespread absenteeism and a general apathy towards organization. None of these are widespread. Newly recognized states always want to join the organization immediately after having achieved recognition as sovereign states. The existing member states regularly attend the sessions of the component parts of the UN. When they encounter global crises, member states turn to the UN with alacrity. Even the most hostile critic of the UN, the USA under President Bush, did not reject the organization outright. He criticized it, but still sought its approval at various key points in his foreign policy ventures. From this I conclude that the debates that do take place about the legitimacy of the organization are conducted by members who may be taken to be strongly committed to the organization.

I have argued that the UN is an authoritative practice that in the face of a fast changing world, regularly encounters changing circumstances which allow critics to challenge the legitimacy of its existing institutional arrangements. Furthermore, I have argued that when this happens the participants are called upon to evaluate the existing arrangements in terms of the ethical commitments on which the organization is built. In the light of such evaluations, the participants can modify the institutional structures where appropriate. I now need to turn to the process of ethical evaluation that follows whenever the legitimacy question is posed. What are the ethical underpinnings of the UN that the participants call on when confronted with questions of legitimacy? What values do its members have in common?

The UN is a universal organization in that the vast majority of states belong to it. Within this multiplicity of states there are any number of different national communities, religious communities, tribes, clans, and other social groups. The people in them are committed to a large set of different ethical codes. At first glance it might seem as if there is no universal ethic common to all the peoples participating, through their states, in the UN system. This supposition would be wrong, because in spite of this multiplicity of ethical commitments, there are communal values on which the participants in the UN can call to answer questions of legitimacy as and when they arise. The arguments about the legitimacy of the UN draw on the ethical commitments of the two major global practices of our time. Participants in these two practices include everyone, everywhere. It is out of these two global practices that the UN has grown and it is clear that in seeking to legitimate the UN, people will call on the values embedded in them. There are no others to draw on.

OUR GLOBAL PRACTICES

All international organizations are embedded in the two major global practices of our time. These are global civil society (GCS) and the society of sovereign states (SOSS). It is within these that we are constituted as the rights holders and citizens that we understand ourselves to be. Our sense of ourselves as rights holders depends on the recognition we receive from others in the practice of global civil society. Our sense of ourselves as citizens derives from the recognition we receive from other citizens in the society of sovereign states.[16] In the contemporary world it often appears to be the case that there is a contradiction between these two practices such that full involvement in the practice of rights seems to pull us in a different ethical direction to full involvement in the society of states. But there are ways in which this tension can be overcome as we shall see later in this chapter. For the time being what we need to notice is that no international organization will be legitimate that does not cohere with the underlying values embedded in both of these practices. International organizations have to show that they are coherent with the values embedded in GCS and the SOSS.

Global Civil Society

The first practice with global reach is global civil society. This is the society of people who claim first-generation rights for themselves and recognize them in others. Rights holders in the society consider they have their rights no matter where they are. Their fundamental rights are not territorially bound. In some places in the world, rights holders have adequate machinery to protect their rights (in

[16] For further elucidation of these forms of reciprocal recognition see Mervyn Frost, *Ethics in International Relations: A Constitutive Theory* (Cambridge: Cambridge University Press, 1996), last two chapters.

well-established democratic states, for example) whereas in other places their rights are less well protected (for example, in weak and failed states). A key feature of this practice that we need to notice is that claiming rights is not dependent on being a member of this or that sovereign state. At least in concept the idea of a rights-respecting society does not require the idea of a sovereign state. Quite the contrary, the society of rights holder provides us with a vantage point from which we can criticize those states that fail to respect and protect the individual human rights of their citizens. A prominent portion of global civil society is what has come to be known as the global free market. Within this market, rights holders exercise their rights to freedom of movement, speech, property, contract, association, and so on, in order to advance their individual interests. There is no shortage of evidence that most people in the world envisage themselves as members of this global civil society. The primary piece of evidence supporting this contention is the fact that they participate in the global market, even if only in a minimal fashion by simply selling their labour.

Also, in many parts of the world the impoverished and downtrodden sections of the population appeal to the international community to uphold their human rights. A good recent example of this is to be found in the Israeli/Palestinian conflict in Gaza. The people of Gaza and sympathizers elsewhere often appeal to the international community to help protect the human rights of the people of Gaza. A good example of this kind of work is to be found in the reports of *Human Rights Watch*.[17] Further evidence is provided by the fact that most states are signed up to the United Nations Charter which endorses human rights in many different ways through a range of different institutional structures.[18] Most states are also signed up to one or more of the major human rights conventions. Many states have now incorporated human rights components into their constitutions. What is more, international law is shot through with human rights considerations. Also, in contemporary wars the parties involved frequently make claims about human rights infringements by the other side.[19] Taken together all these things indicate wide spread participation by people everywhere in global civil society.[20]

Given that global civil society exists, we must then ask: 'What values are held and promoted by this society of rights holders? The primary values are freedom and diversity.[21] This judgement tallies with what the participants in

[17] See the *Human Rights Watch* website at www.hrw.org.

[18] For a full discussion of the diverse range of international instruments that protect human rights in the international domain see United Nations, *Human Rights*.

[19] For a good discussion of how these are intertwined see Matthew Evangelista, *Law, Ethics and the War on Terror* (Cambridge: Polity Press, 2008).

[20] As a general point here it is worth noting that one determines the existence of a social practice by noting what people say about their interactions with others. Where they refer to common laws, rules, norms, and values, and where they criticize one another in cases where these are flouted, this indicates the existence of a social practice.

[21] For a more detailed exposition of this argument see Mervyn Frost, *Global Ethics: Anarchy, Freedom and International Relations* (London: Routledge, 2009).

global civil society say. The ethical reasons that rights holders give for participating in global civil society are that it allows every participant the freedom to pursue his or her interests subject only to the constraint that others are granted the same freedom. Doing this allows for a huge diversity of people with very different interests and life plans to live together in relative harmony. It seems reasonable to assume that the participants are committed to this diversity as a value. There is no feature of the practice which suggests that participants are seeking to eradicate this diversity.

The Society of Sovereign States

The second global practice is the society of sovereign states. This, as is well known, is an anarchical society of free states.[22] The reference to anarchy does not indicate a lack of order, but simply points to the fact that in this society there is no central government. Just as global civil society is one in which, through a process of mutual recognition, individuals create one another as free actors, so, in the society of sovereign states, the states, through reciprocal recognition, create one another as free actors in an anarchical order. They confer on one another the status of free-states. There is no world government. The states within the society are each free to pursue their own vision of their national interest subject only to the constraint that they allow a similar freedom to the other states.

Here again, it is easy to establish that such a society exists. It is self-evident that everyone in the world is a member of a sovereign state and that they indicate their participation in the system through the language they use. Even those groups who are seeking secession for their nations, make use of the language of the system of sovereign states. They rest their case on the right of a people to self determination. It is significant that none of them seeks anything other than full statehood for their group. Few seek alternative forms of political arrangement such as regional or cultural autonomy within an existing state. The language of self determination allows them to claim sovereignty for their nation, to claim high ethical significance for their borders, the ethical importance of their national interests, their ethical right to protect national security, and their right to internal autonomy. We know that the system of states is widely regarded as legitimate because all new political entities aspire to become members of the system of sovereign states. In all such cases they indicate that on gaining independence they wish to join the society of sovereign states. They do not propose the establishment of an alternative

[22] Hedley Bull, *The Anarchical Society: A Study of Order in World Politics*, 2nd edition (Basingstoke: Macmillan, 1985).

international practice. Both in the seeking of membership and in acquiring it the participants indicate that they understand the society of sovereign states as a legitimate society.

What are the values that are promoted (embedded) in the society of sovereign states? Here, once again, the key values are freedom and diversity, however, in this case the actors for whom freedom is secured are states, and the diversity to be promoted is one that allows diverse policies between states. In this society of sovereign states, a social practice has been established within which the participants (states) are free to pursue their own conceptions of the national interest provided they reciprocate and allow other states to do the same. Each state is free within this anarchical order. Overall, this practice makes possible the coexistence of a great diversity of ways of life for individual states. It seems fair to assume that the participants in this practice value the diversity that it makes possible. If they did not, one would expect to encounter repeated calls for conformity. Only a few such calls are made and these are from a fringe of religious fundamentalists of one kind or another.

When international organizations such as the UN, the EU, the AU, and others, seek legitimacy it has to be sought from the total population of our world, all of whom are participants in the two practices we have outlined: global civil society, the practice of individual human rights; and the society of sovereign states, the practice of states' rights. Many of the problems encountered in the search for legitimacy arise because of an apparent tension between the two practices, a tension, that is, between individual human rights and individuals states' rights. A single example of this must suffice here. The African Union often appears to stand before a stark choice: respect, protect and promote the rights of states to sovereign independence or respect, protect and promote the rights of individual men and women. Nelson Mandela encountered this tension within the Commonwealth when he became involved in the Ken Sara Wewa case. Here it seemed he could either demand that the Commonwealth strive to have the rights of Sara Wewa (and his co-accused) protected or he could respect the right of Nigeria as a sovereign state to deal with the 'rebels' as it saw fit. The tension between the state's rights and individual rights in this case appeared to be unresolvable. The tension in that case and many others appears to make the achievement of legitimacy for the international organizations involved impossible.

GLOBAL SHOCKS

The global social practices that I have considered have recently suffered major shocks which might well have been expected to call forth challenges to their overall legitimacy. Yet, both of them have survived remarkably well and have come through with their legitimacy intact.

The first shock was that posed to the society of sovereign states by the rise of global terror. On the face of it, this appeared to pose a threat to the system of states as a whole. In the aftermath of 9/11 most states of the world recognized that the attack was not confined, in its implications, to the USA. It could be interpreted, they realized, as part of a much wider campaign against the system of sovereign states as a whole. In the event, what we have seen since then, is a strong commitment by all states to the maintenance of their sovereignty and the stability of the practice of states as a whole. There has been widespread reassertion of the values core to this practice. Huge amounts of money have been poured into preserving national security and beefing up national and international intelligence operations. States have started cooperating on an unprecedented scale in their efforts to secure these goals. The populations of sovereign states, while quibbling about the means used, have supported the notion that the security of the states' system is important. There is little demand for a completely new set of international arrangements. The legitimacy question has not been raised.

The rise of global terrorism has also presented a major shock to GCS. The attacks of 9/11, 7/7, and others seemed to signal an all out attack on human rights by terrorist groups. This in turn prompted a response by states, in particular the USA and the UK, which itself seemed to threaten the rights of individual men and women. Such threats were made manifest in Abu Graib, Guantanamo prison, the practice of water-boarding, and the practice of special renditions. In spite of these very real threats, GCS has proved to be resilient. There has been wide spread critical reaction to the practices mentioned above. The vast majority of civil society actors have been highly critical of the rights-threatening measures taken in response to the shocks posed by global terrorism.

The second shock was that presented to global civil society by the so-called 'credit crunch' which threatened the global financial market. This might have been expected to raise questions about the legitimacy of the global market as a whole. Instead, what we have found is that there has been little or no fundamental questioning of the market and global civil society itself. The legitimacy of this social institution has been taken for granted and a great effort is being directed towards regulating the market better. This is true around the world. What hasn't emerged is any significant group seeking to undermine the whole structure of global civil society. As a whole its legitimacy has been reasserted.

THE LEGITIMACY OF INTERNATIONAL ORGANIZATIONS

All international organizations exist within the two practices outlined in this chapter. Thus the participants in these organizations are all also simultaneously participants in these global practices and are, therefore, constrained to make sure that the international organizations are legitimate in terms of the values embedded in these two practices.

The international organization most closely associated with the society of sovereign states is, of course, the United Nations, although there are many other international organizations such as the African Union, the European Union, the Association of American States, ASEAN, and many others, that are designed to promote and protect sovereign states. The organizations most closely focused on the health of global civil society are the International Monetary Fund, the World Bank, and the informal associations the G8 and the G20. These are focused on the global market component of GCS. Other organizations protect other aspects of GCS. Here mention must be made of organizations directed towards protecting press freedom, the rights of women, the rights of political prisoners (Amnesty International), individual human rights (Human Rights Watch), and the rights of children, amongst others.

As these international organizations struggle to cope with the aftermath of these two global shocks and further unforeseen developments in the future, in order to preserve their legitimacy, they will have to demonstrate that they are upholding the values of freedom and diversity which, as we have seen, are core to both global practices. If they fail in this, then, their standing in the international order will become suspect and their legitimacy will wane.

The key point to note here is that these international organizations will have to demonstrate to the participants in them, that they are upholding freedom and diversity in both global civil society and the society of sovereign states. Their legitimacy will suffer if they are seen to be favouring states' rights at the expense of the rights of individual men and women. Similarly, their legitimacy will weaken if they do the converse, which is to favour the rights of individual men and women at the expense of states' rights. The tension between states' rights and individual rights has become particularly difficult to solve in recent times, especially in connection with the following issue areas: armed intervention in the domestic affairs of sovereign states; the rights of refugees and asylum seekers; the regulation of the international financial system; the conduct of asymmetrical 'new wars'; the treatment of combatants before and after such wars; the sharing of intelligence between states in the so called 'war on terror'; and the protection of the international environment. There is insufficient space to go into the details of the ethical arguments to be had in connection with each of these issue areas, but there is no doubt that when the legitimacy question is posed within international organizations in the coming years, the major arguments will be about achieving the appropriate balance between states' rights and individual rights. The United Nations can already be seen to be active in this regard upholding its commitment to sovereign statehood, but at the same time seeking to advance the value of human rights. In the coming decades it will have to devote a significant amount of attention to harmonizing these value commitments.

3

Regional and Global Legitimacy Dynamics: *The United Nations and Regional Arrangements*

Paul D. Williams

Legitimacy is about why actors feel a sense of obligation to behave in certain ways or try and live up to particular norms *in the absence of coercion.* After a period in the doldrums, the concept of legitimacy is back in vogue in academic International Relations with the last decade witnessing a variety of important studies within the broad constructivist tradition which have attempted to demonstrate how and why legitimacy matters for a range of international issues. They include analyses which show how international organizations are important sites of legitimacy claims in world politics;[1] how historically, legitimacy crises have acted as important motors for change within international society;[2] how understanding legitimacy dynamics raises fundamental challenges to orthodox (political realist) conceptions of international anarchy;[3] how the concept sheds important light on the use of military force in contemporary world politics;[4] as well as more specific issues relating to multinational peace enforcement and peace operations more generally.[5]

[1] Michael Barnett and Martha Finnemore, *Rules for the World: International Organizations in Global Politics* (Ithaca, NY: Cornell University Press, 2004).

[2] Ian Clark, *Legitimacy in International Society* (Oxford: Oxford University Press, 2005); Ian Clark and Christian Reus-Smit (eds.), Legitimacy Crises in World Politics special issue of *International Politics*, Vol. 47/1 (2007).

[3] Ian Hurd, *After Anarchy: Legitimacy and power in the United Nations Security Council* (Princeton, NJ: Princeton University Press, 2007). Specifically, Hurd argues that since authority is 'the relationship that exists between a legitimised rule or institution and its audience', where this exists in the international realm, there cannot be anarchy (p. 65). See also Emmanuel Adler and Michael N. Barnett (eds.), *Security Communities* (Cambridge: Cambridge University Press, 1998).

[4] Nicholas J. Wheeler, *Saving Strangers: Humanitarian Intervention in International Society* (Oxford: Oxford University Press, 2000); *Force and Legitimacy in World Politics*, special issue of *Review of International Studies*, Vol. 31 (2005).

[5] Katharina P. Coleman, *International Organisations and Peace Enforcement* (Cambridge: Cambridge University Press, 2007); Sharon Wiharta, 'The legitimacy of peace operations', *SIPRI Yearbook 2009* (Oxford: Oxford University Press, 2009), 95–116.

This chapter contributes to this debate by analysing the different dimensions of legitimacy claims made by the United Nations (UN) Security Council and regional arrangements with reference to what the UN Charter calls the maintenance of international peace and security. This is an important area for analysis because international organizations are simultaneously significant sites of legitimacy claims and important audiences for judging legitimacy claims made by other actors. Within this broad issue area I focus on legitimacy claims made about the authorization, conduct and effectiveness of peace operations and how international organizations generate compliance with their relevant objectives.[6] Here, issues of peace enforcement—operations mandated to use military force beyond situations of self-defence—and humanitarian military intervention—using military force for human protection purposes without host government consent—are particularly noteworthy because they highlight the sometimes conflicting moral, legal and political imperatives evident within and between different international organizations.

In order to address these issues the chapter begins with a short discussion of the meaning of legitimacy in world politics. It then uses Andrew Hurrell's framework for thinking about five important dimensions of international legitimacy, namely, procedure, shared values, expertise, effectiveness, and persuasion, in order to explore the various claims related to peace operations made by the UN Security Council and some regional arrangements. The overall argument is that when it comes to peace operations there is not a uniform relationship between the UN and regional arrangements. In part, this stems from the huge variation across the world's regional arrangements, many of which have little experience with peace operations and hence have not formed part of this debate. UN–regional relationships, and hence legitimacy dynamics, thus vary considerably depending on the regional organization in question and the 'threat' to international peace and security under consideration. But the relationship also varies because the same legitimacy claims made by an international organization and/or peace operation can generate a variety of often conflicting verdicts from different audiences. Hence an actor or institution which may be perceived as legitimate by one audience may be reviled by another. Overall, the UN Security Council remains the single

[6] Peace operations involve the expeditionary use of uniformed personnel (police and/or military) with a mandate from an international institution or at the invitation of all parties to a peace agreement to: (1) assist in the prevention of armed conflict by supporting a peace process; (2) serve as an instrument to observe or assist in the implementation of ceasefires or peace agreements; or (3) enforce ceasefires, peace agreements or the will of the UN Security Council in order to build stable peace. See Paul D. Williams, 'Peace Operations' in Robert A. Denemark (ed.), *The International Studies Encyclopedia: Volume IX* (Malden, MA: Wiley-Blackwell, 2010), 5551–78.

most authoritative institution on issues of international peace and security across the globe. But its primacy has been subject to challenges and it has often relied upon so-called 'partnerships' with regional arrangements in an attempt to solidify its own legitimacy credentials. Moreover, since the end of the Cold War the flow of international norms has not all been one-way traffic from the UN down to regional arrangements. Instead, some regions have played an important role in shaping international legitimacy dynamics. For example, Western policies related to human rights, liberal democracy, and military doctrine have influenced the shape of UN peace operations although they have generated pushback in some parts of the world. On other occasions, as in Darfur and Somalia, the mantra of 'African solutions for African problems' influenced the UN's approach to peacekeeping and international legitimacy dynamics, although in both these cases the results were far from successful.

LEGITIMACY: NECESSARY BUT SLIPPERY

Legitimacy dynamics influence the authorization, conduct and effectiveness of peace operations in several ways. First, as Ian Hurd has shown, the interactions between states and between international organizations do not occur in a truly anarchic realm but instead one where various forms of authority exist above the state, most notably the UN Security Council but also regional arrangements involved in developing peace and security policies. It is in this context of overlapping and multiple sources of supranational authority that the legitimacy claims made by different states and organizations compete.[7] Second, as Katarina Coleman has demonstrated with reference to peace enforcement operations, legitimacy dynamics provide the best explanation for why states usually choose to launch such missions through international organizations.[8] In addition, legitimacy is also an important part of understanding why particular peace operations succeed or fail.[9]

Yet legitimacy remains 'an extremely slippery concept' for several reasons.[10] First, legitimacy is slippery because it is historically contingent and dynamic: it

[7] Hurd, *After Anarchy*.

[8] Coleman, *International Organisations*.

[9] On which, see Béatrice Pouligny, *Peace Operations Seen from Below: UN Missions and Local People* (London: Hurst, 2006); Wiharta, 'The legitimacy of peace operations'; Jeni Whalan, 'The power of friends: The Regional Assistance Mission to Solomon Islands', *Journal of Peace Research*, Vol. 47/5 (2010), 627–37.

[10] Andrew Hurrell, 'Legitimacy and the use of force: can the circle be squared?', *Review of International Studies*, Vol. 31: Special Issue (2005), 17.

literally makes no sense to talk about the meaning of legitimacy outside of a particular set of historical structures and conventions. Indeed, some analysts have suggested that not only does legitimacy vary historically but systemic historical change is often the hallmark of changing conceptions of political legitimacy.[11] As a consequence, notions of legitimacy as well as definitions of what constitute legitimate practices will alter as normative and political contexts change.

It is also slippery because ideas of legitimacy bring together and straddle a social terrain populated by sometimes conflicting legal, moral, and political claims. As Ian Clark put it, since 'legitimacy possesses no independent normative content of its own [... it] is always mediated through a composite of other norms' (legal, moral, political/constitutional). This means that at any given time, our understanding of legitimacy is 'a composite of, and an accommodation between, a number of other norms, both procedural and substantive, and does not possess its own independent standard against which actions can be measured'.[12]

A third reason for legitimacy's slipperiness is its inherent inter-subjectivity. Consequently, meanings of legitimacy are the property of groups/societies which cannot be controlled unilaterally, even by superpowers. Put simply, legitimacy is for collectivities to judge not for 'us' to control. In particular, it is centrally concerned with those elements that explain why certain actors and/or activities can generate normative compliance—that is, compliance pull without coercion—amongst relevant audiences.[13] Importantly, this inherent intersubjectivity does not completely rule out the possibility of strategic action and resistance to shape the substance of legitimacy; in fact, it calls for it.[14]

Finally, legitimacy is slippery because it 'cannot be divorced from power'.[15] Legitimacy is not only an important dimension of power—now commonly discussed with reference to Joseph Nye's idea of 'soft power'—but it is also a political force in its own right that can constrain powerful actors.[16] At the same time, power shapes the type of procedures and values that may be perceived as legitimate in a particular social context. Legitimacy, as Ian Clark observed, is thus both 'poacher and gamekeeper'.[17]

In addition to these issues, a further layer of complexity is added when legitimacy dynamics are assessed in the context of international organizations which are, by definition, unique institutional amalgamations of their member

[11] Clark, *Legitimacy*, 13.

[12] Clark, *Legitimacy*, 207.

[13] See Thomas M. Franck, *The Power of Legitimacy Among Nations* (Oxford: Oxford University Press, 1990), 16.

[14] Hurd, *After Anarchy*, 66.

[15] Clark, *Legitimacy*, 20. See also Hurrell, 'Legitimacy', 16.

[16] For a discussion see Christian Reus-Smit, *American Power and World Order* (Cambridge: Polity, 2004).

[17] Clark, *Legitimacy*, 21.

states and transnational bureaucracies. There are four major complications raised by focusing on international organizations. First, international organizations are simultaneously social environments from which legitimacy claims emerge and audiences which judge legitimacy claims made by other actors.[18] Second, as amalgamations of state governments and transnational bureaucracies they have many moving parts which do not always interact in a uniform or particularly transparent manner. Thus understanding the inner workings of many international organizations is difficult for outside observers without privileged access. Third, because major schools of IR theory disagree so vehemently about the nature and political consequences of international organizations it is hardly surprising that these disagreements carry over into debates about legitimacy.[19] Discussions of legitimacy thus tend to reflect the analyst's deeper theoretical assumptions about the nature of world politics and their preferences with regard to IR theory (I favour the constructivist side of the spectrum[20]). Fourth, the UN Charter provides no definition of what it refers to as 'regional arrangements'. The problem is that the entities that fall under this broad category vary considerably in terms of their structure, intent, resources, and conflict management capabilities.[21] As such it is unwise to generalize about 'regional arrangements'. This chapter's focus is limited to those organizations that have conducted two or more peace operations in the post-Cold War period.[22] Such organizations are principally found in Europe and Africa and include the European Union (EU), the North Atlantic Treaty Organization (NATO), the Commonwealth of Independent States (CIS), the Organization of African Unity/African Union (OAU/AU), and the Economic Community of West African States (ECOWAS). There are large parts of the world where the most relevant regional organizations have chosen not to conduct peace operations at all, such as south Asia (SAARC), the Middle East (GCC), and southeast Asia (ASEAN). In these regions, unlike Europe and Africa, the UN has rarely faced competing legitimacy claims about its peacekeeping role, in part because large, multidimensional UN missions have been relatively uncommon with regional states wary of breaching traditional principles of non-interference.[23]

[18] See Alastair Iain Johnston, 'Treating International Institutions as Social Environments', *International Studies Quarterly*, Vol. 45 (2001), 487–515.

[19] For a good overview see John S. Duffield, 'International Security Institutions' in R.A.W. Rhodes et al. (eds.), *The Oxford Handbook of Political Institutions* (Oxford: Oxford University Press, 2006).

[20] Paul D. Williams, 'From Non-Intervention to Non-Indifference: The Origins and Development of the African Union's Security Culture', *African Affairs*, Vol. 106, no. 423 (2007), 253–79.

[21] See Chester Crocker et al. (eds.), *Rewiring Regional Security in a Fragmented World* (Washington DC: US Institute of Peace Press, 2011); Rodrigo Tavares, *Regional Security: The capacity of international organizations* (Abingdon: Routledge, 2009).

[22] For an overview of how different regions have adopted different approaches to peace operations see Donald C.F. Daniel et al. (eds.), *Peace Operations: Trends, Progress and Prospects* (Washington DC: Georgetown University Press, 2008).

[23] See Michael Gilligan and Stephen John Stedman, 'Where do the peacekeepers go?', *International Studies Review*, Vol. 5/4 (2003), 37–54.

With these points in mind, this chapter proceeds on the basis that legitimacy refers to some notion of perceived obligation akin to what Ian Clark has described as 'a belief in being bound' and Thomas Franck has labelled 'normative compliance' i.e. compliance without coercion.[24] Crucially, this sense of obligation is held by actors even if such a situation might generate outcomes which go against their 'specific interests at specific times.'[25]

Such obligations are often described as being owed to an institution (such as international society or the Security Council) or a norm (such as non-intervention or racial equality). Ian Hurd, for example, describes legitimacy as 'the normative belief by an actor that a rule or institution ought to be obeyed'.[26] This is true as far as it goes but legitimacy does not only attach to institutions and norms; it can also inhere within specific activities and actors such as peace operations and peacekeepers. As a result, Katharina Coleman's definition provides a more useful point of departure because it conceives of legitimacy as 'a social status that can adhere to an actor or an action' and which is 'recognised as good, proper, or commendable by a group of others'.[27]

Coleman's definition is useful, in part, because it raises the question of how particular actions and actors gain or lose legitimacy. In general terms, the answer seems to lie in the extent to which relevant audiences judge that some combination of fairness and the following of appropriate correct procedures has occurred.[28] In substantive terms, the central issue is how the UN Security Council and regional arrangements have generated legitimacy for their organization's peace and security activities. But Coleman's definition is also useful because her focus on recognition highlights the importance of specific audiences in judging legitimacy claims.[29] From this flows the need to inquire which audiences are the most significant judges of legitimacy, why, and who benefits and loses out as a result.

FIVE DIMENSIONS OF LEGITIMACY

In a recent discussion of legitimacy, Andrew Hurrell has identified five dimensions of the concept which have had a significant bearing on debates about the use of force in world politics.[30] I refer to these dimensions as a way of

[24] Clark, *Legitimacy*, 23; Franck, *The Power*.

[25] Hurrell, 'Legitimacy', 16.

[26] Ian Hurd, 'Legitimacy and Authority in International Politics', *International Organization*, Vol. 53/2 (1999), 381.

[27] Coleman, *International Organisations*, 20.

[28] See the persuasive discussion in Hurd, *After Anarchy*, 67–72.

[29] See also Clark and Reus-Smit (eds.), *Legitimacy Crises*.

[30] Hurrell, 'Legitimacy', 18–25.

organizing my discussion of the legitimacy claims concerning peace operations made by the UN Security Council and the various regional organizations listed above.

Process and Procedure

Hurrell's first dimension suggests that the behaviour or objectives of actors are legitimate to the extent that they conform to generally accepted procedures. Arguably the three most significant sources of procedural legitimacy in contemporary world politics have revolved around international law and democratic or consensual notions of taking decisions. In this sense, the activities of international organizations could be judged legitimate to the extent that they conformed to the relevant international law or obtained broad consensus among the relevant parties. This is not to suggest that international legality or consensual decisions automatically guarantee legitimacy. It is merely to note that as procedures they are often taken to be significant markers in debates over legitimacy. For example, decision-making processes might be considered legitimate even though they are not democratic (e.g. UN Security Council resolutions), consensus might be criticized on substantive grounds (e.g. the Southern African Development Community's decision not to censure Robert Mugabe's regime in Zimbabwe for its breaches of the rule of law and electoral manipulation), and action in conformity with international law might be considered illegitimate when judged according to other standards (e.g. withdrawing peacekeepers during Rwanda's 1994 genocide rather than conducting a military intervention to rescue its victims).

Historically, international legal standards have been popular with weaker governments and international organizations because their inherent inter-subjectivity made it impossible for single states, even superpowers, to control the interpretation or development of international law. This trend was apparent in various criticisms of NATO's Operation Allied Force in Serbia/Kosovo (1999), notably from members of the Non-Aligned Movement.[31] Such criticisms were based on the claim that in bombing Serbia, NATO violated international law because it was neither an act of self-defence nor conducted with the explicit authorization of the UN Security Council. In contrast, when ECOWAS had engaged in peace enforcement activities in Liberia in the early 1990s without Security Council authorization—and in contravention of ECOWAS' own internal rules of procedure—many African states argued that this was a legitimate response to a crisis in the face of UN neglect (see also Chapter 5 by Sarjoh Bah in this volume). Moreover, the UN Security Council eventually

[31] See Albrecht Schnabel and Ramesh Thakur (eds.), *Kosovo and the Challenge of Humanitarian Intervention* (Tokyo: UN University Press, 2000).

endorsed the ECOWAS operation as a useful contribution to the maintenance of international peace and security despite the fact that arguably it breached Article 53 of the UN Charter.

Alternatively, it might be argued that legitimacy adheres to actions and institutions to the extent that they conform to fair and consensual decision-making procedures. The UN Security Council, for example, is the classic case where its decisions are considered legitimate and lawful despite the fact that they are clearly not democratic. Thus while the Council is widely regarded as the most authoritative institution to pronounce on threats to international peace and security (in large part because its decisions conform with international law and take place with a degree of consensus between the permanent five members) its decision-making procedures are based on the distinctly undemocratic principle that five veto-wielding permanent members hold the key to the institution's pronouncements and activities. In sum, a hierarchy based on privileges flowing to the permanent five members continues to define the procedural basis for some of the most legitimate decisions on international peace and security in the twenty-first century.

Regional organizations in Africa have also adopted a distinctly ambiguous position with regard to democratic norms of decision-making, although none of them have adopted the model of permanent, veto-wielding members evident at the UN Security Council. The AU and ECOWAS, for example, both delegate crucial decisions about peace and security issues to small subsets of their membership (through the Peace and Security Council and the Mediation and Security Council respectively).[32]

Regardless of their institutional specifics, all international organizations defend the legitimacy of their decision-making procedures in some manner, often by making the claim that they involve a serious attempt to forge consensus among competing interests and positions. In the UN Security Council there is a clear hierarchy inasmuch as the consensus that really counts is between the permanent five members. But passing a substantive resolution also requires nine affirmative votes (i.e. involving the support of at least four of the ten elected members). Similarly, the ECOWAS Mediation and Security Council can establish a peace operation with a two-thirds majority of a quorum (i.e. technically, this could occur with the affirmation of only four of the organization's fifteen members). In the case of the AU Peace and Security Council, so far, all of its decisions have been taken on the basis of a consensus reached by all of its 15 members but this is still less than one-third of the AU's total membership. (The caveat to this consensus principle is that a member of the Peace and Security Council which is considered a party to the conflict

[32] The AU Peace and Security Council is comprised of 15 of the organization's 54 members while the ECOWAS Mediation and Security Council comprises 9 of the organization's 15 members.

under discussion is not supposed to participate in the substantive portion of the deliberations.) NATO also has mechanisms to ensure that consensus does not always mean the same as complete unanimity among all its members.[33] Indeed, it appears that the EU is unique in requiring unanimity from all its members to define common positions for its foreign and security policies.

To summarize, processes and procedures are clearly a significant part of the legitimacy claims related to peace operations made by all these international organizations. But not only is there considerable variation in the type of procedures that are considered appropriate for addressing peace and security issues, a focus on them alone leaves much of the legitimacy story untold.

Shared Substantive Values and Goals

Hurrell's second dimension suggests that for an institution or action to be legitimate 'its core principles need to be justifiable on the basis of shared goals and values'.[34] With regard to peace operations, some substantive values clearly generate widespread consensus across both the UN and regional arrangements while others are much more divisive. At the most consensual end of the spectrum, there is a very strong consensus that peace operations conducted by the UN and regional organizations should respect the laws of war and international humanitarian law.[35] Indeed, contemporary peace operations occur in a context where the substantive parameters of legitimacy have been framed by the just war tradition and its concepts of *jus ad bellum*, *jus in bello*, and, to a lesser extent, *jus post-bellum*.[36] It is precisely because the AU's mission in Somalia has been regularly accused of killing local civilians in Mogadishu by acting disproportionately and indiscriminately in retaliation to *al-Shabaab* attacks that it has lost considerable legitimacy in the eyes of the local population and to a lesser extent within international society as well.[37]

At the other end of the spectrum, however, questions over the extent to which peace operations should protect human rights and promote liberal democracy have generated considerable disagreement. While some organizations (notably the EU and NATO) have made an explicit commitment to uphold democratic norms of domestic governance, others (including the ECOWAS, AU, CIS, and UN) have preferred to base their legitimacy claims on other criteria.

[33] On NATO's caveats see Paul Gallis, *NATO Decision-making Procedures* (Washington, DC: Congressional Research Service Report RS-21510, 5 May 2003).

[34] Hurrell, 'Legitimacy', 20.

[35] See, for example, Siobhán Wills, *Protecting Civilians: The Obligations of Peacekeepers* (Oxford: Oxford University Press, 2009).

[36] For an overview see Alex J. Bellamy, *Just Wars* (Cambridge: Polity, 2006).

[37] See, for example, Sarah Childress, 'Civilian casualties dog troops in Somalia', *Wall Street Journal*, 29 July 2010.

This issue has prompted some prominent politicians in Western states, such as US Senator John McCain, to call for the formation of an international 'league of democracies' on the grounds that there is a clear relationship between democratic forms of domestic governance and international legitimacy.[38] A similar argument was made by US Secretary of State Madeleine Albright when trying to justify NATO's military intervention in Kosovo/Serbia (1999). She argued that the Alliance did not need UN Security Council authorization because the North Atlantic Council, which at that time comprised 15 liberal democracies, was a more legitimate voice on the use of force than the Security Council, which included many non-democracies. According to Albright, repressive regimes such as Russia and China should not be given the opportunity to veto action intended to prevent a humanitarian catastrophe by a coalition of liberal democracies.[39]

Since the end of the Cold War, many of the UN's new peace operations involved mandates which explicitly sought to turn war-torn states into market democracies.[40] This occurred to such a degree that the UN's standard approach was often dubbed 'liberal peacebuilding' and generated a large critical literature on the dangers of such policies.[41] While it was not surprising that NATO and the EU also regularly supported democratization initiatives, especially but not solely in their Balkans operations, other organizations clearly did not prioritize this agenda. In their peace operations during the 1990s, for example, the CIS (in Tajikistan, Moldova and Georgia) and ECOWAS (in Liberia and Guinea-Bissau) did not make any significant effort to build liberal democratic governance structures.[42] More recently, the AU's peace operations have varied on this issue. While the Union explicitly sought to facilitate democratic processes in its operations in Burundi (2003–4) and the Comoros (2006–8) its peace operations in Sudan and Somalia were not mandated to produce democratic structures.[43]

[38] For a sensible critique of the idea see Charles A. Kupchan, 'Minor League, Major Problems', *Foreign Affairs*, Vol. 87/6 (2008), 96–109.

[39] Alex J. Bellamy, *Kosovo and International Society* (Basingstoke: Palgrave-Macmillan, 2002), 87.

[40] See Roland Paris, *At War's End* (Cambridge: Cambridge University Press, 2004); Alex J. Bellamy and Paul D. Williams, *Understanding Peacekeeping* (Cambridge: Polity, 2nd edition, 2010).

[41] On this debate see, for example, Michael N. Barnett, 'Building a Republican Peace: Stabilizing States after War', *International Security*, Vol. 30/4 (2006), 87–112; Edward Newman, Roland Paris and Oliver Richmond (eds.), *New Perspectives on Liberal Peacebuilding* (Tokyo: UN University Press, 2010); and Roland Paris, 'Saving Liberal Peacebuilding', *Review of International Studies*, Vol. 36 (2010), 337–65.

[42] ECOWAS forces in Sierra Leone, however, were involved in democracy promotion inasmuch as they were used to help reinstall the elected President Ahmed Kabbah, who had been deposed in a coup d'etat in May 1997.

[43] See Paul D. Williams, 'The African Union's Peace Operations: A Comparative Analysis', *African Security*, Vol. 2/2–3 (2009), 97–118.

The other major bone of contention between the UN and some regional organizations has been the extent to which peace operations should play a role in protecting civilians facing imminent threats of physical violence. In one sense there has been a gradual convergence around the idea that once they have deployed on the ground peace operations will lose legitimacy if they do not protect civilians in danger.[44] During the 1990s, there were also several operations conducted with the explicit aim of saving foreign civilians, perhaps most notably the US-led United Task Force in Somalia (1992), the NATO-UN Operation Deliberate Force in Bosnia (1995), NATO's Operational Allied Force in Kosovo/Serbia (1999), and the UN-authorized Intervention Force in East Timor (1999). Only Operation Allied Force generated a large degree of international controversy because it occurred against the wishes of the host government. Since September 1999, the majority of the UN's new peacekeeping missions have included explicit civilian protection components in their mandates.[45] Similarly, civilian protection played an important role in ECOWAS operations in Liberia (2003) and Côte d'Ivoire (2003–4), the EU's operations in the Democratic Republic of Congo (DRC) (Operation Artemis, 2003 and EUFOR RD, 2006), and the AU's mission in Sudan (2004–7).

On the other hand, the issue of when it is legitimate to conduct a humanitarian military intervention has been the source of significant controversy between the UN and various regional arrangements. While most international lawyers regard the practice as illegal without UN Security Council authorization, proponents have put forward a variety of moral, political, and legal arguments in support of its legitimacy.[46] In this context, the AU is a particularly interesting case. Despite the fact that many African states were quick to condemn NATO's military intervention in Kosovo in 1999 precisely because it was conducted without Security Council authorization, shortly thereafter the newly established AU Constitutive Act (2000) contained a clause (Article 4h) which institutionalized the Union's right to conduct humanitarian military intervention in one of its member states in what it called 'grave circumstances', namely war crimes, genocide, and crimes against humanity. Although the AU has yet to invoke Article 4h to override the will of a sovereign government, its members were initially keen to emphasize the point that it would be legitimate

[44] The key codification of this norm came in the *Report of the Panel on United Nations Peace Operations* (UN doc. A/55/305-S/2000/809, 2000), commonly referred to as the Brahimi report after its chairman, former Algerian Foreign Minister Lakhdar Brahimi.

[45] For a detailed overview see Victoria Holt and Glyn Taylor with Max Kelly, *Protecting Civilians in the Context of UN Peacekeeping Operations* (New York: UN DPKO/OCHA, November 2009).

[46] See Adam Roberts, 'The so-called "right" of humanitarian intervention', *Yearbook of International Humanitarian Law*, Vol. 3 (Summer 2001), 3–51; Wheeler, *Saving Strangers*; Simon Caney, *Justice Beyond Borders* (Oxford: Oxford University Press, 2005), chapters 6–7.

for the AU to conduct a humanitarian military intervention under Article 4h *without* UN Security Council authorization. As the legal adviser to the AU recounted, during the Union's internal debates:

> When questions were raised as to whether the Union could possibly have an inherent right to intervene other than through the Security Council, they were dismissed out of hand. This decision reflected a sense of frustration with the slow pace of reform of the international order, and with instances in which the international community tended to focus attention on other parts of the world at the expense of more pressing problems in Africa. Furthermore, the process of drawing up the Constitutive Act took place not long after the OAU Assembly of Heads of State and Government had adopted the Ouagadougou decision defying the sanctions imposed by the UN Security Council on Libya in connection with the Lockerbie crisis... [African] leaders have shown themselves willing to push the frontiers of collective stability and security to the limit without any regard for legal niceties such as the authorisation of the Security Council.[47]

In early March 2005 the AU was still claiming that it did not need to abide by the letter of Article 53 of the UN Charter but could instead secure UN Security Council approval 'after the fact' in circumstances requiring urgent action.[48] Just a few weeks later, however, the *Roadmap for the Operationalization of the African Standby Force* explicitly stated that 'the AU will seek UN Security Council authorisation of its enforcements actions. Similarly, the RECs [regional economic communities] will seek AU authorisation of their interventions'.[49]

In sum, while substantive consensus exists around the legal rules governing peace operations the legitimacy of democratization is much more open to question. Similarly, while it is clear that most UN and regional peacekeepers are expected to protect civilians in imminent danger of physical violence in their areas of deployment, there is no consensus over when and how to authorize a humanitarian military intervention where a government is either unwilling or unable to stop the slaughter. It is therefore fair to conclude that the lack of shared goals and values remain partly responsible for competing legitimacy claims related to peace operations evident among the UN and some regional organizations.

[47] Ben Kioko, 'The Right of Intervention under the African Union's Constitutive Act', *International Review of the Red Cross*, Vol. 85, no. 852 (2003), 821. See also Jeremy L. Levitt, 'The Peace and Security Council of the African Union: The Known Unknowns', *Transnational Law and Contemporary Problems*, Vol. 13 (Spring 2003), 125–6.

[48] *The Common African Position on the Proposed Reform of the United Nations: 'The Ezulwini Consensus'* (AU doc. Ext/EX.CL/2(vii), 7–8 March 2005), 6.

[49] *Roadmap for the Operationalization of the African Standby Force* (AU doc. EXP/AU-RECs/ASF/4(I), Addis Ababa, 22–23 March 2005), 5.

Specialized Knowledge and Expertise

Hurrell's third dimension suggests that institutions and actors are legitimate to the extent that they possess relevant expertise. For example, he argues that the legitimacy of claims made to justify preventive and/or pre-emptive war rest upon the privileged knowledge available to those actors about an enemy's capabilities and intentions. In relation to peace operations, one route to gain expertise is through experience of conducting numerous operations over time. Hence an organization like the UN which has conducted over 60 peacekeeping operations involving over 1.3 million uniformed personnel over the course of six decades can claim a degree of legitimacy on the basis of its accrued knowledge. In comparison, and with the exception of the EU and the AU, most regional organizations have yet to conduct more than half a dozen peace operations.[50]

In addition to judging the expertise of an international organization on the basis of its prior experience, another method is to examine whether the organizations have bureaucracies with sufficient resources, including competent and qualified staff, to carry out their tasks. As Michael Barnett and Martha Finnemore have argued, the size and scope of bureaucracies within international organizations reveal at least two important points. First, the level of resources devoted to the bureaucracies and/or secretariats of international organizations provides a good indicator of how seriously they are viewed by their member states. Bureaucracies kept famished by the member states suggest the organization has been designed to fail or is useful primarily for cosmetic/symbolic purposes. Second, and of most relevance here, the size and effectiveness of the bureaucracy will also significantly influence the potential of these organizations to develop what Barnett and Finnemore refer to as 'autonomous power', that is, the capacity of international organizations to develop a degree of autonomy from the states that created them. Such autonomous power derives from the legitimacy of the rational-legal authority embodied by the organization in question, their control over technical expertise and information, and overseeing administrative processes and procedures. Put conceptually, autonomous power thus derives from the ability of organizations to '(1) classify the world, creating categories of problems, actors and action; (2) fix meanings in the social world; and (3) articulate and diffuse new norms and rules'.[51] It is through these processes that certain organizations and their officials gain legitimacy as experts in the relevant field.

[50] As of April 2013, the EU had conducted nine (military) peace operations in Bosnia, Macedonia, DRC, Chad/Central African Republic, Mali, Somalia, and Sudan; while the AU had conducted eight in Burundi, the Comoros, Mali, Somalia, and Sudan.

[51] Barnett and Finnemore, *Rules for the World*, 31. See also Peter M. Haas, 'Introduction: Epistemic Communities and International Policy Coordination', *International Organization*, Vol. 46/1 (1992), 1–35.

With this in mind, it is notable that regional arrangements around the world display huge variation in the size and effectiveness of their bureaucracies engaged in peace and security issues.[52] At one end of the spectrum, organizations such as the EU and NATO have relatively well-resourced and numerous bureaucrats, whereas at the other end of the scale, officials of organizations such as ECOWAS, CIS, and the AU are relatively few and chronically under-resourced. At the UN, the fact that the Department of Peacekeeping Operations (DPKO) was only established in 1992 reflects the organization's long struggle to generate and retain an institutional home for expertise on peace operations. However, since then the growth of the DPKO and its ability to construct an institutional memory on these issues has been significant and the UN can now claim a reasonably high degree of competence and professionalism in the way it conducts and manages peace operations.[53] Although it is widely acknowledged that the UN's lack of standing armed forces means it struggles with tasks at the higher end of the military spectrum the same could be said for every international organization with the exception of NATO. Indeed, during the 1990s the UN peacekeeping brand became so significant that on several occasions CIS soldiers engaged in operations tried to pretend they were UN peacekeepers by painting their helmets blue (in Moldova) and their trucks white (in Tajikistan). As Ian Hurd noted, the CIS actions in these cases demonstrated the extent to which UN peacekeeping had become a trademark imbued with 'discursive power'.[54] The AU's attempt to create a similar trademark with its peacekeepers wearing green helmets suggests the UN does not retain a monopoly on such discursive power.

This bureaucratic dimension affects the prospects for competing legitimacy claims between the UN and regional organizations in several ways. All other things being equal, international organizations with better resourced bureaucracies are more likely to be able to generate autonomous power as well as collect, interpret, and disseminate information relevant to conducting effective peace operations. Of course, expert bureaucracies are not always listened to by the member states. In mid-November 2008, for example, in response to Somalia's ongoing conflict the UN Secretary-General recommended an International Stabilisation Force of 'approximately two brigades' to support the implementation of the Djibouti peace agreement. However, after explicitly approaching more than 50 UN member states the Secretary-General secured

[52] See Amitav Acharya and Alastair Iain Johnston (eds.), *Crafting Cooperation* (Cambridge: Cambridge University Press, 2007); Daniel et al. (eds.), *Peace Operations*; Tavares, *Regional Security*.

[53] It could be argued that the UN Security Council has undergone a broader trend towards the bureaucratization of its functions as reflected in the management of its sanctions regimes (many of which occur in similar areas to its peace operations) which now involve extensive committee structures and panels of experts.

[54] Hurd, *After Anarchy*, 125–8.

only two offers of funding, no offers of troop contributions and the idea of a multinational force quickly died.

In the field of peacekeeping, it is interesting to note how organizational doctrine and guidelines have often been developed either in interaction with other organizations or passed directly from one organization to another. For example, it is notable how military doctrine within NATO states on peace support operations appears to have been reflected in the UN's attempts to formulate guidelines and principles for its own operations in the twenty-first century.[55] Officials from several African regional organizations including the AU and ECOWAS have been provided with substantive training, advice, and assistance on peace and security issues from secretariats and officials from the UN, the EU, and NATO as well as a wide range of bilateral initiatives from Western states.[56] This includes the writing of operational guidelines for the African Standby Force, the proposed centrepiece of the AU's peacekeeping architecture. Similarly, although there are five institutions in Africa that claim to be centres of excellence for peacekeeping training, almost all of them rely on foreign sponsorship, and all of them have serious practical limitations.[57]

In this sense, while recognized expertise is clearly an important dimension of international legitimacy, it appears that in the realm of peace operations such expertise and evolving 'best practices' are generally flowing from North to South. That said, the precise impact of security experts from EU and NATO states on the development of UN guidelines and principles is harder to determine.

Effectiveness

Hurrell's fourth dimension suggests that the legitimacy of processes, actors and institutions can also be judged on their ability to deliver 'effective solutions to shared problems'.[58] Put crudely, approaches or instruments that consistently prove their effectiveness stand a higher chance of acquiring legitimacy than those which persistently fail to deliver positive outcomes. In relation to the UN Security Council, Hurrell observes that one of the most common arguments used to fend off calls for the Council to democratize (by increasing its membership and perhaps changing its voting rules) is that such a move would render the institution less effective. In short, this perspective argues that democracy at the UN looks like the General Assembly, arguably one of the most dysfunctional

[55] See *UN Peacekeeping Operations: Principles and Guidelines* (UN DPKO: 2008).

[56] Interestingly, although China has provided considerable sums of financial support to the AU it has not provided much comparable support in the peacekeeping realm.

[57] Mark Malan, 'Africa: Building Institutions on the Run', in Daniel et al. (eds.), *Peace Operations*, 104–7.

[58] Hurrell, 'Legitimacy', 22.

organizations on the planet.[59] A similar logic underlies the decision-making structures of several African organizations. As noted above, both the AU and ECOWAS have delegated their core decision-making powers on peace and security issues to subsets of their membership because they consider their full complement of members too unwieldy to take effective decisions quickly.

Of course, legitimacy cannot simply be reduced to effectiveness alone. For example, although an imperial police force might make a better job of defeating an insurgency than a multilateral organization, in the contemporary era global norms dictate that colonialism is usually something to be avoided.[60] Nevertheless, effectiveness does matter. The problem is that there remains no consensus on how to measure the effectiveness of peace operations.[61]

On the issue of effectiveness, the UN is in a stronger position than it is often given credit for. Despite suffering a wide variety of criticisms—some quite reasonable, some badly misplaced—UN peace operations have a reasonably good record in several respects. As Virginia Page Fortna's extensive work concludes, 'The answer to the question of whether peacekeeping works is a clear and resounding yes.'[62] UN peacekeeping does not do everything well, however. For instance, there is no evidence that the presence of peacekeeping operations facilitates peace agreements.[63] On the other hand, UN peace operations *do* significantly reduce the likelihood of wars reigniting after such agreements have been concluded.[64] Specifically, where peacekeepers have deployed, the likelihood of war reigniting fell by at least 75–85% compared to those cases where no peacekeepers were deployed.[65] In the post-Cold War era, traditional peacekeeping operations deployed with the consent of the belligerents reduced the likelihood of war reigniting by as much as 86%. For large and complex multidimensional operations—often deployed in regions with unstable consent and lingering violence—the figure remained above 50%.[66]

[59] There is, of course, the important caveat that the Assembly is democratic only in the sense that each member state gets one vote i.e. the governments of the People's Republic of China and Tuvalu get the same number of votes despite the vastly different number of people they represent.

[60] For a relevant discussion see Roland Paris, 'Peacekeeping and the Constraints of Global Culture', *European Journal of International Relations*, Vol. 9/3 (2003), 441–73.

[61] The usual candidates are saving lives, war termination, state-building, and democratisation. For two good discussions see Charles T. Call, 'Knowing peace when you see it: Setting standards for peacebuilding success', *Civil Wars*, Vol. 10/2 (2008), 173–94; Paul F. Diehl and Daniel Druckman, *Evaluating Peace Operations* (Boulder, CO: Lynne Rienner, 2010).

[62] Virginia Page Fortna, *Does Peacekeeping Work? Shaping Belligerents' Choices after Civil War* (Princeton, NJ: Princeton University Press, 2008), 173.

[63] J. Michael Greig, and Paul F. Diehl 'The Peacekeeping–Peacemaking Dilemma', *International Studies Quarterly*, Vol. 49/4 (2005), 621–45.

[64] Virginia Page Fortna, 'Inside and Out: Peacekeeping and the Duration of Peace after Civil and Interstate Wars', *International Studies Review*, Vol. 5/4 (2003), 97–114; 'Does Peacekeeping Keep Peace? International Intervention and the Duration of Peace after Civil War', *International Studies Quarterly*, Vol. 48/2 (2004), 269–92; and *Does Peacekeeping Work?*

[65] Fortna, *Does Peacekeeping Work?*, 171.

[66] Fortna, 'Does Peacekeeping Keep Peace?', 283.

In comparison, on most criteria the record of regional peace operations is not obviously better. Indeed, in the case of peace operations conducted by Africa's regional organizations it has usually been considerably worse, not least because of their lack of funds, human resources, and management mechanisms as well as appropriate military capabilities.[67] In Darfur, for example, there was a widespread push from late 2004 to deploy UN peacekeepers because of the obvious inability of the AU force to protect civilians. This practical failure significantly detracted from the legitimacy of the AU's mantra that Darfur was an 'African problem' requiring an 'African solution'.[68] The EU and NATO operations in the Balkans fared reasonably well if the measure of success is preventing loss of life from direct violence. But they have been less effective if judged on their ability to resolve the underlying conflicts.[69] Similarly, while both these organizations have the world's best high level military power projection capabilities, the EU has only been willing to deploy its troops in small numbers for very short periods of time while NATO has spent almost all its energies on operations in the Balkans and (since 2003) Afghanistan, suggesting there is little evidence that it would take part in the kind of operations the UN is asked to undertake on a regular basis.

This huge difference in capabilities and the global division of labour apparent in post-Cold War peace operations raises the question of whether the relationship between UN and regional peace operations should be seen as complementary or competitive. The aspiration at the UN is that the Security Council 'and regional organisations should play complimentary roles in facing the challenges to peace and security'.[70] In this sense, the legitimacy of these organizations is intertwined and dependent in large part on their effectiveness at maintaining international peace and security. Yet there is good reason to see the relationship as simultaneously complementary and competitive, which opens up the space for competing legitimacy claims between the UN and regional organizations. In terms of the numbers of peacekeepers deployed by the UN and various regional arrangements—primarily the EU, the NATO, and the AU—the relationship has been complimentary inasmuch as the post-Cold War period has seen a significant increase in the number of peacekeepers deployed by both the UN and these regional organizations. As Birger Heldt put it, the relevant data about the numbers of peacekeepers deployed between

[67] See Herbert M. Howe, *Ambiguous Order: Military Forces in African States* (Boulder, CO: Lynne Rienner, 2001), chapter 4; Adekeye Adebajo, *Building Peace in West Africa* (Boulder, CO: Lynne Rienner, 2002); Coleman, *International Organisations*, chapters 3–5; Williams, 'The African Union's Peace Operations'.

[68] Paul D. Williams, 'Keeping the peace in Africa: Why "African solutions" are not enough', *Ethics and International Affairs*, Vol. 22/3 (2008), 309–29.

[69] See, for example, William J. Durch (ed.), *Twenty-first Century Peace Operations* (Washington DC: US Institute of Peace Press, 2006), chapters 2 and 5.

[70] Report of the UN Secretary-General, *In Larger Freedom: Towards Security, Development and Human Rights for All* (UN A/59/2005, 21 March 2005), paragraph 213.

1948 and 2005 do 'not offer support for concerns that non-UN operations may undermine the UN's future global role'.[71] Similarly, at a strategic level, the fact that the UN often works in partnership with regional organizations suggests that invoking the support of multiple organizations is thought to enhance the legitimacy of a particular operation, such as in UN collaboration with the Organization of American States (OAS) in Haiti during the 1990s, or the UN and the AU in Darfur, Sudan after 2006, or in Somalia after 2009. Yet if the focus switches from a concern with the number of peacekeepers and the strategic relationship between these international organizations to the quality and capabilities of the peacekeeping operations themselves, then the UN–regional relationship can be seen in a more competitive light. In particular, the recent trend of Western states to reduce their military contributions to UN peacekeeping and invest their capabilities in regional or coalition missions has undermined the UN's ability to carry out robust peace operations—missions capable of effectively using military force in situations beyond self-defence[72]—especially in parts of the world which are not considered of major strategic interest to Western powers.[73]

Overall, therefore, the UN's peacekeeping record stands in a favourable light compared to most of the relevant regional organizations. This has helped it to retain a considerable degree of international legitimacy. As discussed earlier, this record of relative effectiveness is reinforced by the increasing professionalism evident at the DPKO and the newly created Department of Field Support. Although the EU and NATO are clearly capable of conducting effective peace operations, the former has been badly limited in terms of its ambition and the scope of its missions while the latter's ongoing identity crisis means it is highly unlikely to play a significant peacekeeping role in theatres beyond its current commitments in the Balkans and Afghanistan.[74] The African organizations have faced the opposite problem: an overdose of ambition and expectations and a huge deficit of funds and material capabilities.[75]

[71] Birger Heldt, 'Trends from 1948 to 2005: How to view the relation between the United Nations and non-UN entities' in Daniel et al. (eds.), *Peace Operations*, 25.

[72] See *Robust Peacekeeping: The Politics of Force* (New York University: Center on International Cooperation, 2009), at www.cic.nyu.edu/peace_ssr/docs/robustpeace.pdf.

[73] Alex J. Bellamy and Paul D. Williams, 'The West and Contemporary Peace Operations', *Journal of Peace Research*, Vol. 46/1 (2009), 39–57.

[74] See Anand Menon, 'Empowering Paradise? The ESDP at Ten', *International Affairs*, Vol. 85/2 (2009): 227–46.

[75] See *Report of the African Union-United Nations panel on modalities for support to African Union peacekeeping operations* (UN doc. A/63/666-S/2008/813, 31 December 2008).

Persuading Audiences

Hurrell's final dimension suggests that actors and institutions are more likely to enhance their legitimacy if they give reasons and make arguments which persuade important audiences of the merits of their behaviour. Unlike Hurrell's four previous dimensions which represented grounds on which legitimacy claims are made, this one reflects the process through which legitimacy claims become accepted (or rejected) by powerful audiences. Audiences are crucial for understanding legitimacy dynamics for several reasons. First, it is ultimately audiences, not the actors authorizing and conducting peace operations, which get to deliver the most important verdicts on a mission's legitimacy. Second, the existence of multiple audiences raises the thorny topic of whose judgements about the legitimacy of a particular operation are most important and whether it is ever possible to deliver a final verdict. Indeed, the ability to adjudicate between different verdicts presupposes that some shared framework of understanding or mode of communication exists across the various organizations and audiences in question. This might not always hold true. Third, different audiences may have competing and conflicting expectations about what a peace operation is for or use different criteria to assess its legitimacy.

In policy terms, the existence of multiple audiences means that in order to be effective legitimacy claims need to address the concerns of distinct audiences. Thus policymakers need to know who the distinct audiences are and which ones are the most important in the situation at hand. At a generic level, Katharina Coleman's work on peace enforcement operations has identified four recurring audiences: domestic opinion in the state(s) conducting the enforcement action, public opinion within the recipient state, countries bordering the recipient state, and the wider global community of states.[76] Actors seeking to enhance their legitimacy must make their claims persuasive to these different audiences even though each may have different expectations and objectives which are not easily reconciled. The task is complicated even further by the fact that different audiences might become more or less important at different times during an operation. For instance, the crucial audience(s) during the initial decision to create and deploy a peace operation might be different from the crucial audience(s) when attempting to assess its ongoing performance in the field, or when trying to develop an appropriate exit strategy.

A final issue is whether different organizations are better at persuading particular audiences. For example, are regional organizations better at persuading the neighbourhood that their approach is legitimate? Regional organizations have often argued that regional problems should have regional solutions, they make better conflict managers in their neighbourhood because of local

[76] Coleman, *International Organisations*, 24–6.

knowledge and proximity, and they are sometimes forced to fill the vacuum when the UN has failed to act effectively to maintain international peace and security. Similarly, is the UN better at addressing wider international society, thereby generating resources which might otherwise be lacking within a particular region? If so, this division of labour might help explain the growing number of cases of 'partnership peacekeeping' whereby multiple organizations are engaged in peace operations in the same theatre, either sequentially or simultaneously.[77] The problem is that definitive answers to such questions can only be developed in light of detailed empirical analysis of the case/context in question—much of which remains to be done.

Nevertheless, based on her study of peace enforcement operations, Coleman argued that these generic audiences existed in a global legitimacy pyramid where endorsement from the UN Security Council represented the pinnacle of international legitimacy but authorization from a regional organization was the next best thing.[78] The problem with this formulation is that the Security Council's actions (or inactions) are not always perceived as more legitimate than all other actors by all the relevant audiences. In this sense at least the analogy of a fixed pyramid with the UN Security Council at the top does not work equally well for all audiences in all contexts. Nor does it reflect the fact that in certain circumstances, the UN's legitimacy relies upon the support of the relevant regional arrangement(s).[79] Moreover, even when the UN is at the top of the pile, in absolute terms it remains far from perfect: 'a deeply flawed and heavily politicised body in which arguments can be presented and policies defended because other, better, forums simply don't exist'.[80] And in relative terms it may well be the case that, as discussed above, the states in the neighbourhood in question view actions by the regional organization as more legitimate than the UN.

CONCLUSIONS

The preceding analysis suggests that there is no single general relationship between the UN Security Council and even the small subset of regional organizations which have conducted multiple peace operations in the post-Cold War

[77] The phrase 'partnership peacekeeping' is taken from Norrie MacQueen's, *Peacekeeping and the International System* (Abingdon: Routledge, 2006). For an overview of different types of partnerships see Bellamy and Williams, 'The West'; Bruce Jones with F. Cherif, *Evolving Models of Peacekeeping* (UN: Peacekeeping Best Practices Unit External Study, 2004).

[78] Coleman, *International Organisations*, 57–8.

[79] See Linnea Bergholm, *The African Union-United Nations Relationship and Civilian Protection in Darfur, 2004-2007* (Unpublished PhD thesis, Aberystwyth University, Department of International Politics, 2009).

[80] Hurrell, 'Legitimacy', 24.

era. Legitimacy dynamics depend on the regional organization as well as the type of peace operation in question. To the extent that the UN Security Council does lead the way it is important to note that UN peace operations doctrine appears to have been more heavily influenced by powerful members within the EU and NATO than states in other regions. It is also notable that the EU and NATO are the only regional arrangements which have sought to legitimize the conduct of peace operations beyond their own borders. While the EU has always sought prior Security Council authorization for such activities, in Operation Allied Force NATO acted without such permission. African organizations appear to have received most external assistance in their peace and security activities, including from the UN Security Council, and EU and NATO states.

Nor is it entirely accurate to suggest that a fixed hierarchy of legitimacy exists between the UN and regional organizations because legitimacy dynamics fluctuate depending on the audience in question. The existence of multiple relevant audiences also makes it very difficult to come to a definitive verdict on the legitimacy of a particular peace operation. On the pertinent policy question of whether particular organizations are especially good at generating compliance for their activities among specific audiences, more detailed empirical research of recent operations is required to come to any definitive answers.

In terms of the different grounds for basing legitimacy claims suggested by Hurrell's framework, decision-making processes and procedures play a significant part in the legitimacy claims of all international organizations but there is considerable variation in the institutional design and type of procedures that are considered appropriate for addressing peace and security issues.

As for shared substantive values as a basis for legitimacy claims, a strong international consensus exists that peace operations should uphold the laws of war and international humanitarian law. In contrast, whether peace operations should promote democratization and how and when they should protect civilians remains the source of considerable debate among and within a variety of international organizations. The continued lack of shared goals and values remains partly responsible for the competing legitimacy claims made by the UN and some regional organizations on issues related to peace operations.

Perceptions of expertise and specialized knowledge are also clearly important ingredients in legitimacy claims for both the UN and regional arrangements. Here, there was considerable variation in the size, capabilities and competence of the bureaucracies across the organizations in question. However, even where bureaucracies were relatively well respected, expert opinions have often been overruled by member states. Expert officials have also played important roles in terms of the production of peacekeeping doctrine and codes of 'best practice'. To date, the flow of expertise has tended to be primarily from the North to the South. Within the UN itself, it is harder to determine the precise impact of Western peacekeeping experts on the formulation of UN guidelines and principles.

Effectiveness also affects legitimacy although there is little consensus over the best criteria to measure success. Nevertheless, on most counts the UN's peacekeeping record is better than most regional organizations and this has helped the Council to retain its strong legitimacy credentials despite some very public failures and setbacks. The EU and NATO are clearly capable of conducting robust peace operations and projecting their power over great distances. Yet their ambition and scope has been severely limited in areas beyond their immediate strategic interests, principally the Balkans, Iraq, and Afghanistan. African organizations have faced the opposite problem: their peacekeepers have been deployed in pursuit of hugely ambitious mandates thereby raising many international, and crucially, local, expectations, but they have lacked adequate funds and material capabilities to succeed.

Overall, we remain at the early stages of figuring out the complicated legitimacy dynamics that exist between the UN and regional arrangements on matters concerning peace operations. More detailed studies of particular operations and the relationships between particular organizations are needed to help fill this considerable knowledge gap.

Part II

Case Studies

4

Legitimation and the UN Security Council

Jennifer Welsh and Dominik Zaum

In the aftermath of the wars in Kosovo (1999) and Iraq (2003), member states and observers of the UN increasingly openly questioned the effectiveness of the institution, and its legitimacy with regard to authorizing (and withholding authorization) of the use of force. Some Western commentators, in particular the US, suggested that the non-democratic character of certain Security Council (UNSC) members compromised the institution's legitimacy and effectiveness, leaving the Council paralyzed because of divisions between democratic and autocratic states, for example over Kosovo, Iran, or Syria.[1] Members of the non-aligned movement, on the other hand, have regularly highlighted the underrepresentation of large parts of the world in the Council, and the concomitant 'democratic deficit' of an institution dominated by the threat and exercise of the veto reserved for five privileged permanent members.[2] As global opinion polls have shown, this perception of an unrepresentative Council dominated by a few great powers chimes with public opinion in countries across the world.[3] Such challenges to the Council seem to be supported by common scholarly accounts of institutional legitimacy, focussing on the character of its decision-making procedures,[4] its effectiveness,[5]

[1] See for example Alex J. Bellamy, *Kosovo and International Society* (London: Palgrave, 2002), 87; Robert Kagan, 'The world divides... and democracy is at bay', *Sunday Times*, 2 September 2007; Rosemary Righter, 'Let's join the new democracy gang', *The Times*, 29 May 2008.

[2] See for example Address by Dr Manhoman Singh, Prime Minister of India, at the High-Level plenary Meeting of the 60th Session of the United Nations General Assembly, New York, 15 September 2005, 3.

[3] See *Views of the UN in Majority-Muslim Nations*, 3 December 2008, available at http://www.worldpublicopinion.org; and BBC, *23-Country Poll Finds Strong Support for Dramatic Changes at UN, and for Increased UN Power*, 21 March 2005, available at http://www.worldpublicopinion.org. Interestingly, amongst the P5 support for enlargement was smallest in China and Russia. The latter was the only country without a majority supporting enlargement.

[4] Thomas Franck, *The Power of Legitimacy Among Nations* (Oxford: Oxford University Press, 1990); Tom R. Tyler, 'A Psychological Perspective on the Legitimacy of Institutions and Authorities', in John T. Jost and Brenda Major (eds.), *The Psychology of Legitimacy: Emerging Perspectives on Ideology, Justice, and Intergroup Relations* (Cambridge: Cambridge University Press, 2001).

[5] Fritz Scharpf, *Governing Europe: Effective and Democratic?* (Oxford: Oxford University Press, 1999).

or the degree to which it reflects and promotes shared values.[6] However, the record of the UNSC is sketchy at best with regard to all of those. Critics highlight its secretive decision-making procedures that favour the five permanent members; point to its inability to prevent the unauthorized use of force by powerful states as in Iraq (2003) or Georgia (2008); to its failure to decide on strong action in response to the genocides in Rwanda and Srebrenica; and to the deep normative split among member states over issues such as the substance of the international 'Responsibility to Protect'.

However, despite these criticisms and shortcomings, the UNSC continues to be widely regarded as a keystone of the international security architecture. Scholars and policymakers alike continue to assert its central role in legitimating actions to address threats to international peace and security.[7] Regional organizations may have increasingly complemented the UNSC's role as a 'collective legitimizer' of the use of force since the end of the Cold War (see Chapter 3 by Williams in this volume), but they have not challenged or replaced it.[8] Without having the 'hard' power envisaged by the original drafters of the Charter at its disposal,[9] its impact is seen to flow from its status as a repository of collective political judgement on the 'rightness' of particular uses of military force by states or groups of states. In some cases the Council's endorsement can make a direct material difference, by enabling those leading a military action to obtain troops and financial support from other members of international society. More commonly, however, the UN stamp of approval has a more intangible benefit, by enhancing both the lawfulness and the political acceptability of the proposed actions. As a result, states have invested significant diplomatic capital in garnering Security Council authorization for their actions.

While references to the Council's legitimating function are frequent, it is harder to find compelling explanations for *how* the UNSC obtains legitimacy

[6] Allen Buchanan and Robert Keohane, 'The Legitimacy of Global Governance Institutions', *Ethics and International Affairs*, Vol. 20, no. 4 (2006), 405–37.

[7] One of the earliest articulations of this notion is found in Inis Claude, 'Collective Legitimization as a Political Function of the United Nations', *International Organization*, Vol. 20, no. 3 (Summer 1966), 367–79. For more recent discussions, see for example Ian Hurd, *After Anarchy: Legitimacy and Power in the United Nations Security Council* (Princeton: Princeton University Press, 2007).

[8] Alex Bellamy and Paul Williams, 'Who's Keeping the Peace? Regionalization and Contemporary Peace Operations', *International Security*, Vol. 29/4 (Spring 2005), 157–95; Katharina Coleman, *International Organisations and Peace Enforcement: The Politics of International Legitimacy* (Cambridge: Cambridge University Press, 2007); Alexander Thompson, *Channels of Power: The UN Security Council and U.S. Statecraft in Iraq* (Ithaca: Cornell University Press, 2009).

[9] Articles 43–5 of the UN Charter call for armed forces to be made available to the Security Council (including national air-force contingents). Articles 46 and 47 outline the make-up and role of the Military Staff Committee (drawn from representatives of the Permanent Five), which was to be responsible 'for the strategic direction of any armed forces placed at the disposal of the Security Council'. These provisions of the Charter have never been implemented.

in international society. This leaves us with a puzzle: there is broad agreement by scholars (on the basis of empirical evidence) that the Council acts as a collective legitimizer, but the sources of its own legitimacy, and the practices that sustain it, have remained largely unexplored. This chapter addresses this gap, examining the practices of the UNSC to explain how it is attempting to legitimate itself in contemporary international society, and to assess how successful these efforts have been. To that end, we begin by identifying some of the inherent constraints the Council faces in its legitimation efforts. The chapter then examines three key legitimation practices pursued to strengthen and sustain the Council's legitimacy. It concludes with an assessment of these efforts, and of their impact on the Council's role in international order.

THE CHARACTER OF THE COUNCIL AND CONSTRAINTS FOR LEGITIMATION

The introductory chapter to this volume identifies several challenges to examining the legitimacy of international organizations, which are also of relevance to the study of the UNSC. These include the Janus-faced character of many international organizations; and the need of such organizations to address diverse audiences with their legitimation claims.

The UNSC's Janus-faced character, defying easy characterization as a coherent, supranational body or as a framework for intergovernmental cooperation complicates the question of who claims legitimacy. While the former feature of the Council suggests that legitimation claims are made by 'the UNSC', the latter role highlights the agency of member states rather than the Council as a whole. These states make claims about the legitimacy of the UNSC, or use the Council's legitimating role instrumentally, to advance their interests and conceptions of international order. Much of the recent literature on the legitimacy of international organizations more generally, and the Council in particular, has employed the former vision of an autonomous corporate entity,[10] however,

[10] Michael N. Barnett and Martha Finnemore, 'The Politics, Power, and Pathologies of International Organizations'. *International Organization*, Vol. 53, no. 4 (1999), 699–732; Corneliu Bjola, 'Legitimating the Use of Force in International Politics: A Communicative Action Perspective', *European Journal of International Relations*, Vol. 11, no. 2 (2005), 266–303; Paul Kennedy, *The Parliament of Man: The Past, Present, and Future of the United Nations* (New York: Random House, 2006); Michael Matheson, *Council Unbound: The Growth of UN Decision Making on Conflict and Post-Conflict Issues after the Cold War* (Washington DC: USIP Press, 2006); and Jens Steffek, 'The Legitimation of International Governance: A Discourse Approach', *European Journal of International* Relations, Vol. 9, no. 2 (2003), 249–75. Toni Erskine goes further, arguing that the UNSC meets the criteria of an institutional moral agent, and can therefore be said to bear collective responsibility for acts and omissions. See Toni Erskine, '"Blood on the UN's Hands?" Assigning Duties and Apportioning Blame to an Intergovernmental Organisation', *Global Society*, Vol. 18, no. 1 (2004), 21–42.

there are clear limits on the degree to which the Council can be attributed agency, and the powers and responsibilities which flow from it. While the UNSC has an identity greater than the sum of its parts, its decision-making structures and processes, along with its capacity to implement those decisions, are more ad hoc than its characterization as a coherent body suggests. UNSC decision-making is frequently dominated by a few powerful states, and is opaque and secretive rather than based on the application of well-understood rules.[11] Furthermore, unlike formal bureaucracies, the UNSC's authority is not issue-specific, as the Council has exercised significant discretion when determining what constitutes a threat to international peace and security. This also underlines the UNSC's deeply political character, challenging the view that international organizations' legitimacy is fostered by their ability to appear depoliticized.[12]

To establish who is claiming legitimacy, we therefore conceive of the Council as a collective enterprise, rather than as a coherent institutional agent. In so doing, we distinguish between those cases in which Council members are consciously deliberating and acting collectively (e.g. in retreats or summit meetings which seek to take stock of the Council's performance or to discuss specific aspects of reform), and those instances in which particular member states are taking the lead. In what follows, we refer to these as 'collective' and 'pluralist' legitimation practices respectively. The latter cases necessitate close examination of the political dynamics occurring within the Council chamber—particularly those arising from the privileged position of the P5—and the ways in which these shape legitimation practices.

The Council's legitimation efforts are further constrained by the need to address distinct audiences with different interests, expectations, and normative reference points.[13] Across member states, one confronts deep divisions on a range of important issues, including the grounds for intervention, the relationship between security and development, and the severity of new so-called security threats. In particular, there is a notable divide between the US and its allies on the one hand, and many developing countries on the other, about how to conceive of security in a twenty-first century world. Powerful developed states continue to fear that the UN will not act decisively on the threats that preoccupy them (terrorism, weapons of mass destruction, and transnational crime) and developing countries continue to insist that the greatest threats to their security reside elsewhere—in poverty, infectious disease, and collapsing state structures.

[11] See, for example, Chinmaya Gharekan, *The Horseshoe Table: An Inside View of the UN Security Council* (Delhi: Dorling Kindersley, 2006), 13–44.

[12] Barnett and Finnemore, 'Politics, Power, and Pathologies'.

[13] Andrew Hurrell, 'Legitimacy and the Use of Force: Can the Circle be Squared?', *Review of International Studies*, Vol. 31 (2005), special issue on Force and Legitimacy in World Politics, 24.

Another, arguably more profound, fissure within international society concerns the very character of the international order that the Council should seek to pursue: are its values congruent with the liberal 'solidarist' vision that rests on the UN's commitment to individual human rights, or the more restrictive 'pluralist' order that emphasizes sovereign equality and non-intervention?[14] For those states that see the UN as a body to protect and enhance sovereignty, the Council's 'coercive solidarism',[15] adopting a wide interpretation of what constitutes a threat to international peace and security and involving the Council ever deeper into the domestic affairs of member states, has exceeded its authority and is eroding its legitimacy. For those states promoting a liberal interpretation of the Council's mandate, its legitimacy is under threat because it is doing *too little*, leading some states to investigate alternative mechanisms for responding to contemporary threats to peace and security—whether these be existing regional organizations such as NATO or a new, selective grouping of states (based on liberal democratic credentials) that can act as a forum for legitimizing the use of force.[16] This fissure has prominently divided the five permanent members on a range of occasions, such as the NATO intervention in Kosovo and the broader agenda of the 'responsibility to protect', the question of peacekeeping in Darfur, the imposition of sanctions on Iran because of its alleged clandestine nuclear programme, and the issue of climate change.[17]

The Council's audience for legitimacy claims includes not only states and international organizations, but also NGOs and civil society. They constitute a particularly important audience for the UNSC's legitimation practices, because through their advocacy and lobbying efforts, their ability to mobilize networks of activists, and their promotion of particular norms they can legitimize the Council vis-à-vis sceptical member states, complementing the efforts of particular Council members. Thus, for example through the International Coalition for the Responsibility to Protect, NGOs have contributed to anchoring the principle of the 'Responsibility to Protect' in the language used to discuss humanitarian crises and conflicts,[18] legitimating the role of the UNSC as the guardian of this principle within the United Nations system.

[14] On solidarism and pluralism, see Hedley Bull 'The Grotian Conception of International Society', in Herbert Butterfield and Martin Wight (eds.), *Diplomatic Investigations: Essays in the Theory of International Politics*, (London: Allen and Unwin, 1966), 51–73.

[15] Andrew Hurrell, *On Global Order: Power, Values, and the Constitution of International Society* (Oxford: Oxford University Press, 2007), 63.

[16] L. Feinstein and Anne-Marie Slaughter, 'The Duty to Prevent', *Foreign Affairs*, Vol. 83, no. 1 (2004), 136–50.

[17] For a detailed discussion of these fissures in the Security Council, in particular with regard to humanitarian intervention, see Jennifer Welsh, 'The Security Council and Humanitarian Intervention', in Lowe et al. (eds.), *The United Nations Security Council and War*, 535–62.

[18] Alex Bellamy, 'The Responsibility to Protect—Five Years On', *Ethics and International Affairs*, Vol. 24, no. 2 (2010), 143–69.

The Importance of SC Legitimacy for Member States

Finally, while member states share an interest in a legitimate Council that would not be marginalized by other actors in matters relating to international peace and security, they have different reasons that inform that interest, and consequently view legitimacy, and the practices that sustain it, differently. For the wider UN membership, in particular for smaller and weaker states, a legitimate Security Council imposes constraints on the ability of great powers to act unilaterally, and strengthens the institutionalization of the restraint to use military force.[19] A legitimate Council makes obtaining non-permanent membership an attractive perk for most states, and is seen as enhancing their status amongst their peers. While non-permanent membership in the UNSC does not substantially increase the decision-making power of states, it confers, as Ian Hurd has pointed out, 'status and recognition on a state and allows the state to appropriate some of the authority derived from the legitimacy of the Council'.[20] Consequently, states continue to commit substantial resources to obtain a non-permanent seat.[21]

For the permanent members, the benefits of a legitimate SC are more substantial. For those whose relative military and economic power has declined since 1945 or 1989, such as Britain, France, and Russia, permanent membership in the UNSC and the associated veto power increases their influence and confers prestige on them.[22] The veto gives those permanent members inclined to challenge US hegemony—China, France, and Russia—an instrument to extract concessions from the US, either in form of adjustments to its policy, or in form of support on other issues.[23]

However, even for a hegemonic power like the US, which in light of its unique military, economic and political power is arguably most constrained by acting through the Security Council, a legitimate Council offers substantial practical benefits. It has, for example, simplified international lawmaking with regard to key US security interests such as counterterrorism, where Chapter VII resolutions have imposed binding obligations on member states that would otherwise have required extensive bilateral or multilateral bargaining.[24] Furthermore, not only does it enable the US to share the financial and manpower burden of addressing threats to international peace and security, in

[19] Nico Krisch, 'The Security Council and the Great Powers', 147–9.

[20] Ian Hurd, 'Legitimacy, Power, and the Symbolic Life of the UN Security Council', *Global Governance* Vol. 8 (2002), 43.

[21] David M. Malone, 'Eyes on the Price: The Quest for Nonpermanent Seats in the UN Security Council', *Global Governance*, Vol. 6 (2000), 3–23.

[22] Mats Berdal, 'The UN Security Council: Ineffective but Indispensable', *Survival*, Vol. 45/2 (2003), 11–14.

[23] Mats Berdal, '*The UN Security Council: Ineffective but Indispensable*', 9–10.

[24] Krisch, 'Great Powers', 143–5. On the Security Council's role as a 'lawmaker', see also José E. Alvarez, *International Organizations as Law-Makers* (Oxford: Oxford University Press, 2005).

particular through peacekeeping operations financed by UN assessed contributions, but can also limit the political costs, both domestically and internationally, of using force, through signalling acceptance of such actions by other states.[25]

LEGITIMATING THE SECURITY COUNCIL

The Council's legitimation efforts are therefore shaped by its dual character, its need to appeal to different audiences, and the differing priorities of its key member states. These constraints limit the kind of justifications that the Council and its members can advance in support of legitimacy claims. They also create methodological challenges for observing and analysing what we call a 'legitimation practice'. For the purposes of our analysis, we define a legitimation practice as a conscious attempt by states—either collectively or individually—to enhance an aspect of the Council's legitimacy. This focus on intention has three implications. First, while legitimation must be the goal of action, the practices employed will not always succeed in enhancing legitimacy. Second, while an action must be aimed at increasing or improving legitimacy in order to be called a 'legitimation practice', we accept that there may be a variety of motives behind such an action. These multiple reasons for action do not compromise the label 'legitimation', as long as a key purpose of the action is to enhance legitimacy. Third, while we recognize that legitimacy can also arise unintentionally—for example, as a product of informal practices that build up over time[26]—we maintain that a *practice* of legitimation requires some evidence of a conscious desire to enhance a procedural or substantive aspect of an institution's activity.

Council members are not only aware of the legitimacy problems facing the UNSC, but at times also make conscious efforts to address these challenges. During the rare moments when the Council collectively reflects on its role, for example at its annual retreat for newly elected members,[27] or its occasional summit meetings, member states regularly identify what they view as the key areas where the Council can strengthen its legitimacy. These issues also emerge from the priorities articulated by elected members to the Council, in particular when they take over the rotating presidency. From these documents, as well as from interviews with diplomats in a range of member state missions

25 See for example Voeten, 'Political Origins'; Thompson, *Channels of Power*.

26 We are grateful to Duncan Snidal for pointing out the distinction between intentional and non-intentional legitimacy.

27 While these annual meetings are held under Chatham House Rules, the Finnish Mission to the UN, which has organized the retreats, has in recent years published a report on the discussions which identifies the key issues and positions taken.

to the UN,[28] we have identified three key legitimation practices. Two are pursued by the Council collectively: improving the Council's decision-making processes; and enhancing its capacity to collect and manage information. A third is engaged in by individual UN member states (either on their own or in smaller coalitions) and we call it 'pluralist': asserting the relevance of the Council to key contemporary security issues. Although all three of these legitimation practices seek to sustain and enhance the Council's role as the preeminent institution addressing threats to peace and security, the pluralist practice is frequently accompanied by mixed motives, most notably the desire to use the Council to protect or promote a particular vision of international order.

Collective Legitimation: Improving UNSC Decision-Making

Ever since the Security Council moved from the relative margins of international relations that it occupied during much of the Cold War to the centre of attempts to address international political and military crises in the early 1990s, its decision-making mechanisms have come under increasing scrutiny, and have elicited regular calls for reform. These calls have been driven by three factors. First, the six decades since the creation of the UN have seen fundamental changes in the composition of international society and the realities of power, in particular a large increase in the membership of developing countries and the rise of new powers such as Japan, India, and Brazil. Many argue that the Council needs to reflect these changed realities. Second, the workload of the Security Council has grown dramatically. Council members meet several times a week for formal sessions and consultations, and participate in the growing number of subsidiary bodies, such as sanctions committees. This imposes a huge workload in particular on smaller countries without large missions in New York. Third, the scope of the UNSC's activities has expanded. Not only has it increasingly involved itself in the domestic affairs of member states, but through its subsidiary organs has taken on a more operational role, such as the management and monitoring of sanctions regimes. Together, these changes have led to calls for structural reforms, enlarging the Council and achieving wider representation and participation in Council business, greater effectiveness, and greater transparency and accountability.

Structural Reform

Demands for Council enlargement and reform of the veto culminated in Secretary-General Kofi Annan's proposals in 2005 to expand the Council to 24

[28] Interviews were conducted during two weeks fieldwork in July 2008, and one week in September 2008, with a range of follow-up interviews in late 2011.

members, following the recommendations of the High-level Panel Report.[29] Ultimately, these recommendations made little headway, as political consensus on who should join this enlarged Council as a permanent member remained elusive.[30] Moreover, it is questionable whether these reforms would have strengthened the legitimacy of the UN in the current global political context.

The underlying assumption of the proposals, that the Council's weaknesses are the consequence of its composition rather than the complexity of the problems it faces, and of the inherent limitations member states face when tackling them, is not supported by the Council's record.[31] Moreover, it is not clear that a reconfigured and expanded permanent membership will necessarily result in more agreement. In 2011, for example, the Council's membership was uniquely configured to include most of those states that have been touted for permanent status: India, Germany, Brazil, and South Africa. Nevertheless, the body remained divided on contentious issues such as the crises in Iran and Syria, where it was unable to agree on a robust, unified response. Even where Resolutions have been passed, they have been accompanied by deep-seated concerns on the part of so-called aspirants about the proper role of the Council in crises occurring inside member states of the UN. For example, when the UNSC passed Resolution 1975 with respect to the crisis in Côte d'Ivoire, which UN peacekeepers and French troops interpreted as permitting the use of attack helicopters against military camps and weaponry belonging to former Ivorian president Laurent Gbagbo, the South African President, Thabo Mbeki, argued that the UN had overstepped its authority and abandoned its operating principle of impartiality.[32] Similarly, while the Council was able to pass a resolution authorizing the 'use of all necessary means' to protect civilians in Libya in 2011, most of the aspirant members abstained on the resolution, citing concerns about the lack of a clear 'end game', and subsequently criticized Western members of the Council for exceeding the mandate given in

[29] For details of the two reform proposals, see Kofi Annan, *In Larger Freedom: Towards Security, Development and Human Rights for All—Report of the Secretary General*, UN Doc. A/59/2005 of 21 March 2005, paras. 165–83.

[30] The enlargement debate moved to intergovernmental negotiations in September 2008. Three models for UNSC reform have been at the heart of the negotiations: first, a proposal by the G4 (Brazil, Germany, India, Japan) to enlarge the UNSC to 25 members (six new permanent members without a veto [subject to review after 15 years] and four new non-permanent members); second, an African Union proposal to enlarge the UNSC to 26 members (six permanent and five non-permanent), with a veto for new permanent members; and the Uniting for Consensus group proposal to enlarge the UNSC by ten new non-permanent members. Divisions over the veto and over the categories of new members have so far prevented any agreement.

[31] For a further discussion, see Edward C. Luck, 'The UN Security Council: Reform or Enlarge?', in Paul Heinbecker and Patricia Goff (eds.), *Irrelevant or Indispensable? The United Nations in the 21st Century* (Waterloo, On: Wilfred Laurier University Press, 2005), 143–52.

[32] Thabo Mbeki, 'What the world got wrong in Cote D'Ivoire', *Foreign Policy*. 29 April 2011, http://www.foreignpolicy.com/articles/2011/04/29/What_the_world_got_wrong_in_cote_d_ivoire, accessed 26 November 2012.

Resolution 1973 and failing to provide on-going updates to the UNSC on the progress of the NATO-led mission.[33] These kinds of deep divisions demonstrate that efforts to improve the UNSC's structural legitimacy, through expansion of Council membership, will not necessarily enhance its output legitimacy.

Working Methods Reform

Nonetheless, calls for structural changes to the UNSC have continued. Partly to compensate for their absence, Council members have collectively pursued a range of smaller procedural reforms, in order to address perceived legitimacy gaps that have arisen from the secretive character of UNSC decision-making, and the growing 'collusion' among the P5 in informal meetings (which exclude the Council's elected members) that decide upon the content of key resolutions. More specifically, in response to criticism and pressure from non-permanent members and the General Assembly, the UNSC has agreed not only to formalize and publicize its working methods, but also to endorse a series of changes to such methods that have been under discussion since the early 1990s.[34] These efforts to enhance the Council's input legitimacy have included the quicker publication of Council documents; increased involvement of troop contributing countries (TCCs) in debates on peace-keeping mandates;[35] increased use of open debates on important issues, where non-Council members—particularly from regions directly affected by the topic under discussion—can present their views; regular informal meetings with non-state actors, often under the so-called Arria formula;[36] and regular briefings and publication of information about work of sanctions committees and other subsidiary bodies. However, the impact of these measures and their success in addressing perceived legitimacy gaps is to date relatively limited. TCC's continue to complain about limited meaningful involvement into the drafting of mandates, and UNSC decision-making continues to be dominated by a small group of states and informal meetings—to the dissatisfaction of many member states. Similarly, the Council's working methods in the realm of counter-terrorism have been

[33] See 'R2P and RwP after Libya and Syria', Speech by the Hon. Gareth Evans to the Global Centre for the Responsibility to Protect, New York, 23 August 2012. Available at http://www.responsibilitytoprotect.org/index.php/component/content/article/1-default/4324-gareth-evans-speech-the-rtop-after-libya-and-syria

[34] These reforms are encapsulated in a Presidential Note and Annex issued by the Security Council. See *Note by the President of the Security Council*, UN doc. S/2010/507 of 26 July 2010. For detailed discussions of efforts at working methods reform, see Security Council Report, *Security Council Working Methods—A Work in Progress?* New York, 30 March 2010.

[35] SC Res. 1353 of 13 June 2001.

[36] Arria meetings are confidential private meetings of all Council members, where no official record is kept. See Sydney Bailey and Sam Daws, *The Procedure of the UN Security Council*, 3rd Edition (Oxford: Oxford University Press, 1998), 73–4.

criticized by the wider UN membership, and challenged in the courts—most notably by the European Court of Justice in 2008, which annulled the EU regulation implementing the Council's counter-terrorism sanctions as it infringed basic human rights and was in violation of EU law.[37]

Furthermore, increased transparency and openness in Council sessions can make it more difficult for states to make the compromises necessary to reach diplomatic agreement, and to be frank and outspoken in their exchanges. As some Council members have suggested, the lack of confidentiality in Council sessions has effectively shifted decision-making into bilateral negotiations or informal fora such as groups of friends or contact groups, which often include important non-Council members with a special stake or interest in a particular conflict. These groups allow for greater flexibility and privacy, and can help to mobilize extra diplomatic and other resources for conflict resolution, strengthening the output legitimacy of the Council by producing substantial outcomes.[38] Critics, however, suggest that the use of informal groups undermines the function of the UNSC as a collective legitimizer, as they avoid the hard diplomatic work required to achieve a real consensus within the Council itself.[39] The possible gains in output legitimacy achieved through informal groups thus come at the cost of the perception amongst a substantial number of states that the Council might not reflect the shared values of the whole membership, but is promoting the normative agenda of a small group of powerful states.[40]

The debate over transparency came to a head in May 2012, when a draft General Assembly resolution on Security Council working methods from the co-called S5 (Costa Rica, Jordan, Liechtenstein, Singapore, and Switzerland) was withdrawn. While the proposals detailed in the resolution were designed primarily to ensure that the Council lived up to its own pledges concerning transparency, the S5 initiative was nonetheless viewed by the P5 as undue 'interference' by non-Council members in its working methods.[41] The episode illustrates the limitations of working methods reform as a legitimation

[37] Joined Cases C-402/05 P and C-415/05 P *Yassin Abdullah Kadi and Al Barakaat International Foundation* v *Council and Commission*.

[38] Jochen Prantl, 'Informal Groups of States and the Security Council', *International Organization*, Vol. 59, no. 3 (2005), 584.

[39] Confidential Interview with UN diplomat, New York, 9 July 2008.

[40] Gharekan *Round the Horseshoe Table*.

[41] Failure to put the draft resolution to a vote was also due to the fact that the proposals included two recommendations concerning the use of the veto by permanent members. Opposing states argued that these recommendations constituted fundamental reform of the Council, rather than merely working methods reform, and would therefore require Charter revision. Since a 2/3 majority of the General Assembly is required for Charter revision, and this was unlikely to be achieved, the S5 withdrew the resolution. Confidential interview with Permanent Representative to the UN, 14 September 2012.

practice, and the degree to which permanent members believe that output legitimacy is compromised by greater transparency.

Collective Legitimation: Improving the Council's Knowledge and Expertise

An organization's claim to specialist knowledge can be an important source of legitimacy, and a means of warding off challenges to its authority.[42] Central to justifying such claims are the organization's epistemic capacities: how it processes information and generates knowledge that is viewed as credible for its core audiences. Though the Council has been consistently constrained by its lack of an independent intelligence capability,[43] it has nonetheless attempted to strengthen its ability to gather and manage more information to inform its decision-making about matters related to international peace and security. These efforts to improve the Council's epistemic capacities have taken three main forms: the dispatch of missions; the increased use of expert witnesses; and the expansion of the committee structure to manage complex sanctions regimes.

Security Council Missions

Since the mid-1960s, the Council has occasionally dispatched fact-finding missions,[44] but it has significantly expanded this practice since the end of the Cold War. Between 1992 and December 2012, it sent 44 missions to different conflict areas, most of them (28) to Africa. While these are primarily fact-finding missions, aimed at helping Council members to better understand the dynamics of a conflict and the issues at stake, they have also been used to demonstrate Council engagement in resolving a conflict, to push conflict parties towards a settlement, or to convey the disapproval of the international community with regard to particular actions by the parties.

Some missions have enabled Council members (especially elected members) to develop a more nuanced appreciation of the complexities of a conflict, and have played a key role in shaping the Council's response, as in East Timor in 1999.[45] In the view of the former British permanent representative to the

[42] Barnett and Finnemore, 'Politics, Power, and Pathologies'.

[43] Simon Chesterman, 'Does the UN have Intelligence?' *Survival*, Vol. 48, no. 3 (2006), 149–64.

[44] The first mission was sent to Cambodia and Vietnam in 1964. Between 1964 and 1992, the Security Council formed 10 missions, deployed for fact-finding purposes. See also Alexandra Novosseloff 'Les 'missions spéciales' du Conseil de Sécurité des Nations Unies', *Annuaire français de droit international*, Vol. 49 (2003), 165–75.

[45] Stewart Eldon, 'East Timor', in David Malone (ed.), *The UN Security Council: From the Cold War to the 21st Century*, ed. David Malone (Boulder: Lynne Rienner, 2004), 551–66.

UN, Sir Jeremy Greenstock, these missions have been 'a good move, helping to sharpen the understanding by Council members of the particular issue and to dilute the impression of UN remoteness from the field of action'.[46] Despite some reservations about the effectiveness of the missions as a fact-finding tool (not least because of the political nature of decisions as to whether or not to establish a mission), this is an assessment shared by most of the UN diplomats interviewed for this study.

However, the effectiveness of the missions is inherently limited by the deeply political nature of the Council and the fact that it is not a unitary or coherent agent. As a result, the specific terms of reference for particular missions often reflect the divisions within the Council over the issue at hand.[47] For example, the explicit limitation of the mission to Kosovo in May 2007 to fact finding, and the unwillingness to broaden the mandate to support efforts to resolve the territory's status, reflected fundamental disagreement on Kosovo's future between Russia and Western states.[48] In addition, controversies over the nature of a conflict can make decisions about who to consult during a mission a divisive issue, lest consultation might be seen as endorsement of one side's narrative of the conflict.[49] While the Council is under pressure to talk to all sides in a conflict, these controversies, and the limited time available to the missions, make wide consultation very difficult to achieve. Finally, the publicity associated with the missions can, in the words of one diplomat, turn them into a 'court of appeal' for all the conflict parties to voice their grievances, giving those parties 'shouting loudest' undue influence over the mission's perception of a situation.[50] The growing prominence of the missions, and their inherently political nature, has also affected their composition and size: while until the late 1990s missions normally had between four and seven members, they now include representatives of all 15 members—hardly the most effective way for the Council to gather information.

[46] Jeremy Greenstock, 'The Security Council in the Post-Cold War World', in Lowe et al., *The United Nations Security Council and War* (Oxford: Oxford University Press, 2008), p. 255.

[47] While the terms of reference are now negotiated in advance of the missions, in the past it was often left to the mission itself to decide on its terms of reference—as with the mission to Bosnia and Herzegovina in 1993 at the height of the conflict. See UN doc. S/25700* of 30 April 1993.

[48] Interview with UN diplomat, New York, 30 June 2008. See also Marc Weller, 'Kosovo's Final Status', *International Affairs*, Vol. 84, no. 6 (2008), 1223–43.

[49] This is clearly reflected in the reports of UNSC missions. While earlier reports, e.g. from the UNSC's mission to Bosnia and Herzegovina in 1993 (UN doc. S/25700*) used very blunt language identifying the Bosnian Serbs as the aggressors, the 2007 mission's report on Kosovo (UN doc. S/2007/256 of 4 May 2007) carefully emphasized the 'balanced programme' of the visit and avoided taking sides in the conflict.

[50] Confidential Interview with UN diplomat, 17 September 2008. A further issue noted in several interviews was that SC missions can affect the local dynamics of a conflict because of their high profile. Thus, Greenstock suggests that the Security Council Mission to Eritrea and Ethiopia in 2000, while failing to negotiate an end to the conflict, made it easier to subsequently deploy a peacekeeping operation. Greenstock, 'The Security Council in the Post-Cold War World', 256.

Expert Witnesses at Council Meetings

Security Council members have increasingly relied on outside experts, in particular from NGOs and the wider UN system, to provide them with information about particular issues and conflicts.[51] With the Council's growing workload, NGOs—often with a presence on the ground in conflict areas—are an invaluable source of information, especially for smaller elected Council members.[52] The UNSC for the first time sought systematic input from NGOs during the Rwandan genocide in April 1994, when the Council's President asked NGOs with a presence on the ground in Rwanda to brief him on the situation in the country to complement the sketchy information provided by the UN Secretariat.[53] As the UN's own report into its failure to address the Rwandan genocide states: 'For a number of the non-permanent members at the time, a key to realizing the genocidal perspective to the killings in Rwanda was information provided to them by the NGO community.'[54] However, any consultation with non-state actors who can only participate on invitation of the Council is necessarily selective; it therefore makes the issue of who is allowed to speak crucial and often contested.

To avoid these problems, the Council has regularly held meetings with NGOs and other non-state actors under the Arria formula. Such meetings make the problem of selectivity in consultations politically less salient, and allow for wider consultations than is possible in formal sessions. The epistemic consequences of selectivity, however, are only partially addressed by Arria meetings, since, as UN diplomats have cautioned, such meetings are sometimes used by the convenor to support particular claims about an issue or conflict.

Expansion of the Council's Committee Structure

The increasing complexity of the sanctions regimes authorized by the UNSC has led to the development of a bureaucratic structure of committees and supporting offices to assist with the implementation of these regimes and monitor their impact. To support the committees, which consist of diplomats from UNSC members, the Council has established expert panels to investigate both compliance and impact. The first of these was the United Nations International Commission of Inquiry (UNICOI), established in 1995 to investigate the effect

[51] Weiss et al., 'The 'Third' United Nations'.

[52] James Paul, 'Working with Non-Governmental Organizations', in Malone, *The United Nations Security Council* (Boulder, Co.: Lynne Rienner, 2004), 374.

[53] Michael Barnett, *Eyewitness to Genocide: The United Nations and Rwanda* (Ithaca: Cornell University Press, 2002); Colin Keating, 'Rwanda: An Insider's Account', in Malone, *The UN Security Council*, 500–11.

[54] Report of the Independent Inquiry into the Actions of the United Nations during the 1994 Genocide in Rwanda, 15 December 1999.

of the arms embargo against Rwandan Hutu rebels in the Eastern Congo after the 1994 genocide.[55]

In the aftermath of the 9/11 attacks, the Council established the Counter Terrorism Committee (CTC),[56] which has been at the core of the UN's counterterrorism efforts. In addition to monitoring the progress of states in passing and implementing counter terrorism legislation required under Resolution 1373, the CTC also has the task of facilitating assistance and capacity building—a mandate that goes far beyond those of the classic sanctions committees.[57] Since 2004, it has been supported by a Counter Terrorism Executive Directorate (CTED), based in the UN Secretariat.[58] With around 40 permanent staff, it is significantly bigger than the expert groups of other sanctions regimes, and highlights the increasingly operational role of the Council in the sanctions domain.

This structure of committees and expert groups—described by a Council member as the 'de facto executive branch of the Council'[59]—has been indispensable for managing the vast quantity of information related to the sanctions and counter terrorism regimes, and has made an important contribution to the Council's legitimation efforts. However, Council members have expressed concerns about the expansion of the committee structure, as it stretches the resources of the elected members who chair the vast majority of committees. In addition, the overall effect of this legitimation practice is ambiguous, given that discussion of issues in the normally closed sessions of committees removes issues from public discussion, raising further concerns about the Council's transparency.[60]

Overall, strengthening the epistemic capacities of the Council does reinforce its position as the preeminent institution for managing international peace and security. This legitimation practice succeeds for two reasons: it helps to improve Council members' understanding of the dynamics of particular conflicts and the impact of the UNSC's own policies on these conflicts; and it allows the Council to more effectively manage the large amounts of information that some of its activities require. However, while better knowledge can help the Council to defend controversial actions and decisions, there are two inherent limitations to the degree to which stronger epistemic capacities can 'solve' the UNSC's legitimacy challenges.

The first stems from the increased demands on the Council to act preventively, before conflicts or humanitarian crises spiral out of control. However,

[55] SC Res. 1013 of 7 September 1995.

[56] SC Res. 1373 of 28 September 2001.

[57] For a more detailed discussion, see Jane Boulden, 'The Security Council and Terrorism', in Lowe et al., *The United Nations Security Council and War*, 614–17.

[58] SC Res. 1535 of 26 March 2004.

[59] UN doc. S/2006/483, 6.

[60] Confidential Interview with UN diplomat, New York, 7 July 2008.

the 'facts' established by fact-finding missions, commissions of inquiry, or expert witnesses may not be delivered in a timely or definitive way that would enable the Council to act decisively. In the case of Syria, for example, the initial report of the Independent International Commission of Inquiry could not categorically pronounce on the responsibility for the May 2012 massacre at Houla, in which over 100 people (half of them children) were killed.[61] Two months later, in its final report, the Commission concluded that the killings had indeed been committed by militia backed by Syrian government officials at the highest levels, and that the actions met the requirements of the war crime of murder.[62] But by this point, a key moment for decisive action had passed, and the Council was hopelessly deadlocked over how to respond to the escalating crisis.

Furthermore, like other collective legitimation practices which focus on procedural legitimacy, it assumes a particular understanding of the Council's character, and of the environment within which it operates. It implies that the weakness in UNSC decision-making is a consequence of incomplete information rather than the different interests, political goals, and values of its members. This view offers at best a partial understanding of how the Council operates and the legitimacy challenges it faces. Ultimately, collective legitimation practices cannot address many of the legitimacy concerns of member states, which derive from more fundamental questions about the Council's authority: its role and purpose in managing threat to international peace and security. This limitation underlines the importance of investigating alternative, pluralist approaches to legitimating the Council.

Pluralist Legitimation: Asserting the Relevance of the Security Council to Key Policy Issues

The changing character of war and the decline in the number of inter-state wars over the past two decades has made the question of what kind of threats to international peace and security the UNSC should address more pertinent. Member states—acting either on their own, or in smaller coalitions—have responded to this change by encouraging the Council to consider within its agenda not only different kinds of war, but also new species of threat, such as humanitarian crises, refugee flows, climate change, or the development of weapons of mass destruction, in order to maintain the body's relevance in

[61] Oral Update of the Independent International Commission of Inquiry on the Syrian Arab Republic. See UN doc. A/HRC/20/CRP.1, 26 June 2012. The Commission was not able to visit the site of the killings before issuing this update, and therefore relied on interviews with witnesses, information provided by governmental and non-governmental sources, and satellite imagery.

[62] Report of the Independent International Commission of Inquiry on the Syrian Arab Republic, UN doc. A/HRC/21/50, 15 August 2012.

contemporary international society. As stated by the permanent representative of one prominent developing country: 'The greatest threat to the Council's legitimacy today is that it will become irrelevant—that the P5 will circumvent it in order to address the issues that concern them. We need to make sure that the Council remains the place where consensus is reached on the key threats of today.'[63]

For those employing this third legitimation practice, the challenge facing the Council is less about addressing legitimacy gaps that arise from its procedures, and more about its capacity to respond to new kinds of security threats. In other words, the goal of legitimation is to reinforce and expand both the nature and extent of the Council's authority, both vertically (to UN member states) and horizontally (to other organizations involved in the management of international security). But the efforts to assert the relevance of the Council to new policy issues are also targeted, in some cases, at another audience: the domestic publics of key member states. Viewed from this perspective, the expanded agenda of the Council is the product of governments' efforts to prove to their populations that diplomatic activity at the UN is consequential to their day-to-day security.

There is ample empirical evidence for the Council's expanded definition of what constitutes a threat to international peace and security: all one need do is consult the content of its numerous resolutions since the end of the Cold War. What is less clear, however, is whether this redefinition has enhanced the body's legitimacy, by extending its authority to new actors and issues. George Andreopolus, for example, has argued that the Council's embrace of new security threats (particularly those related to human rights and humanitarian crises) has led to 'normative overstretch', given that some of the responses designed to address these threats involve either actions that encroach upon the domestic jurisdiction of states or a style of decision-making which resembles that of a legislator rather than an intergovernmental body.[64] This greater activism has led to significant controversy both among Council members and between the Council and the wider UN membership. Three areas in particular highlight the challenges associated with this legitimation practice.

First, over the past decade the Council has been very active in addressing the issue of terrorism, by providing a working definition of terrorism,[65] issuing binding resolutions with respect to terrorist financing,[66] and monitoring these efforts through the CTC. While these unprecedented actions have responded

[63] Confidential Interview with UN diplomat, New York, 17 September 2008.

[64] George Andreopoulos, 'The challenges and perils of normative overstretch', in Cronin and Hurd, *The UN Security Council*, 105–28.

[65] SC Res. 1566 of 8 October 2004.

[66] SC Res. 1373 of 28 September 2001. See also Ian Johnstone, 'The Security Council as Legislature', in Cronin and Hurd, The UN Security Council and the Politics of International Authority), 80–104.

to the demands of the US and its allies to address their primary security concern, they have created unease among many member states for three main reasons: first, unlike other Council resolutions they are not related to a particular crisis or limited in time; second, they seek to impose general obligations on all UN members; and third, the measures contained in the resolutions have in some cases had the effect of enabling states to adopt counter-terrorism measures that potentially contravene human rights obligations and basic criminal law principles.[67]

Second, by using the tool of 'thematic resolutions', states such as the United Kingdom have pushed the Council to include on its agenda the issue of climate change.[68] This move was opposed in particular by the G77 countries, who argue that the 'ever-increasing encroachment by the Security Council on the roles and responsibilities of other principal organs of the UN represents a distortion of the principles and purposes of the UN Charter, also infringes on their authority and compromises the rights of the general membership of the United Nations'.[69] China in particular has expressed concern that the Council lacks the necessary expertise to address climate change and is not a sufficiently inclusive body to generate proposals that would be widely acceptable.[70]

Finally, in response to the atrocities against civilians in the conflicts in the early 1990s, Council members have argued that large scale violations of human rights and humanitarian law constitute a threat to international peace and security, and in a range of thematic resolutions explicitly underlined the Council's commitment to the protection of civilians in times of war—a commitment further strengthened with the establishment of a working group on Children and Armed Conflict in 2005.[71] While this has not led to a new doctrine of 'humanitarian intervention', it has raised the possibility that on a case-by-case basis, the UNSC will consider the commission of massive human rights violations to override the sovereignty and non-intervention

[67] See for example Jessica Almqvist, 'A Human Rights Critique of European Judicial Review: Counter Terrorism Sanctions', *Comparative Law Quarterly*, Vol. 57, no. 2 (2008), 303–31; Alison Brysk and Gershon Shafir (eds.), *National Insecurity and Human Rights: Democracies Debate Counterterrorism* (Berkeley: University of California Press 2007); Rosemary Foot, 'Collateral damage: human rights consequences of counterterrorist action in the Asia-Pacific', *International Affairs*, Vol. 81, no. 2 (2005), 411–25.

[68] UN doc. S/PV.5663 of 17 April 2007, 2.

[69] Statement on behalf of Group of 77 China by Mr. Farukh Amil, Deputy Permanent Representative of Islamic Republic of Pakistan to the United Nations, in the Security Council Open Debate on Energy, Security and Climate, New York, 17 April 2007. Available at www.G77.org.

[70] UN doc. S/PV.5663, 13.

[71] SC Res. 1265 of 17 September1999; SC Res. 1296 of 19 April 2000; SC Res. 1674 of 28 April 2006; and SC Res. 1738 of 23 December 2006. In addition, the Council has passed thematic resolutions on related issues, such as children and armed conflict (SC Res.1612 of 26 July 2005 SC Res. 1998 of 12 July 2011, and SC Res. 2068 of 19 September 2012) and on women, peace and security (SC Res. 1820 of 19 June 2008, and SC Res. 1960 of 16 December 2010).

claims of member states.[72] The 2011 air campaign over Libya, authorized by the Council in Resolution 1973, is a prime example of this ad hoc approach to protecting civilians. Nonetheless, as suggested by the abstentions on the Libya Resolution,[73] and the Russian and Chinese veto of a draft resolution threatening sanctions against the Syrian government,[74] there remains serious opposition on the part of some states to any moves which would expand the exceptions to the prohibition on the use of force contained in the UN Charter, and suspicion that the broadened definition of what constitutes a threat to international peace and security has simply 'provided those most capable and willing to project force with more opportunities for doing so'.[75] As a result, it is still highly unusual for the Council to authorize forceful measures to protect civilians without the consent of the state in which those civilians are under threat.[76]

The Council's activity in all of these issue areas has generated two main legitimacy concerns on the part of member states. First, those countries who adopt a 'purist' conception of the Council's role insist that its legitimacy depends upon its effective execution of its core mandate as specified in the Charter: preventing armed conflict among the members of the UN. 'Human rights are an important subject for discussion by the Human Rights Council', argues one permanent representative from a developing country, 'but not by the Security Council. Its job is to focus on questions of peace and security'.[77]

According to the purists, involvement with a more expansive set of threats is viewed at best as an unhelpful distraction and at worst as undermining the Council's stature in international society as the place where 'high' politics and 'real' security issues are discussed. As another former permanent representative

[72] At the 2005 World Summit, heads of government gave clear support for a United Nations' 'Responsibility to Protect' civilians from four crimes in particular: genocide, crimes against humanity, ethnic cleansing, and war crimes. UN, *World Summit Outcome Document*, paras.138–9.

[73] China, Russia, India, Brazil, and Germany abstained on Resolution 1973. The former two states expressed particular concern about abandoning peaceful means of resolving disputes and the lack of clarity over the extent of the mission, while the latter two emphasized the dangers and unintended consequences of using military force. See UN doc. SC/10200, 17 March 2011.

[74] See UN Doc. S/PV.6810 of 19 July 2012. In addition to the Russian and Chinese veto, South Africa and Pakistan abstained.

[75] Andreopoulos, 'The challenges and perils of normative ovestretch', 123–4; Jennifer Welsh, 'The Responsibility to Protect: Securing the Individual in International Society', in Benjamin Goold and Liora Lazarus (eds.), *Security and Human Rights* (Oxford: Hart, 2007), 363–83.

[76] Resolution 1973, which authorized the bombing campaign to protect civilians in Libya, represented the first time the Council has mandated the use of force for explicitly humanitarian purposes against the wishes of a functioning state. In previous cases such as Haiti, Bosnia, the Congo, Sudan, and Cote d'Ivoire, there were pre-existing peacekeeping operations on the ground in the country operating with the consent of the target state. In the case of Somalia, in 1992, member states on the Council explicitly referred to the absence of a working government. See Welsh, 'The Security Council and Humanitarian Intervention'.

[77] Confidential Interview with UN diplomat, New York, 14 September 2012.

has put it: 'Traditional, inter-state conflicts still provide the Council with more than enough work to fully occupy its members. Why expand the agenda?'[78] For these sceptical states, the most pressing threat to the UNSC's legitimacy is its inability to deal with prominent and protracted conflicts such as those between North and South Korea and between Israel and the occupied territories. Of particular concern are the attempts to pass thematic resolutions on new security threats, which are seen by some as simply a way for the state which holds the Council presidency to securitize a 'pet project' that has resonance with that state's population. Too often, it is argued, there is insufficient follow-up on such resolutions, for it is difficult to identify what precise action the Council can mandate in a new issue area. As a result, there is a danger that the Council's legitimacy will suffer.

A second concern expressed by states wary of the expanded security agenda is that the Council is encroaching on the mandate and authority of other bodies—particularly the General Assembly—and disrupting the delicate balance of institutions within the UN system. While many of the new threats which have come to the Council table have a logical home in other parts of the UN system, there is an assumption that because the UNSC has the authority to pass binding resolutions, it is also more likely to instigate swift and decisive action. For states opposed to the practice of thematic resolutions, this assumption needs closer scrutiny. In the words of one Council diplomat: 'There are a host of Security Council resolutions which are not being complied with. So why should we believe that the Council will be more likely to spur action on, say, the Responsibility to Protect, than the General Assembly?'[79] On the other hand, defenders of the Council's foray into new issue areas insist that other parts of the UN often need a push to initiate action. As one diplomatic representative from a P5 state has remarked: 'During the Asian Tsunami, ECOSOC proved incapable of calling an emergency meeting. In this case, should the Council stand on ceremony and defer to other bodies? At the end of the day, it is only the Security Council which can produce a good, "meaty" resolution which can be acted upon.'[80]

In sum, the attempts to extend the Council's authority and assert its relevance to non-traditional security threats have had contradictory effects in terms of legitimation. On the one hand, these efforts have helped to convince powerful states such as the US to continue to work through the Council to address the issues which are of most concern to them. Yet, on the other hand, the encroaching on the domestic jurisdiction of member states as well as the authority of other organs of the UN system has been met with resistance from

[78] Confidential Interview with UN diplomat, New York, 17 September 2008.
[79] Confidential Interview with UN diplomat, New York, 17 September 2008.
[80] Confidential Interview with UN diplomat, New York, 18 September 2008.

many countries. In areas such as counter-terrorism or climate change, for example, the benefits of increased activism have not always outweighed the costs in terms of legitimacy.

Different member state perspectives on whether and how the Council should extend the reach of its authority therefore demonstrates that the political space over which legitimation takes place is inherently contested. In cases involving civil conflict or organized violence against civilians, the Council's attempts to extend the reach of its authority has encountered less resistance; through both the accumulation of practice over the past two decades, and the 2005 Summit Outcome Document endorsement of the principle of the 'Responsibility to Protect', there is now widespread acceptance of the legitimacy of Council-led efforts to respond to the threat or commission of mass atrocities occurring inside the jurisdiction of UN member states. Even here, however, the Council's legitimacy rests on a knife edge: while its resolutions designed to protect populations from atrocity crimes may be viewed as legitimate, there is not necessarily a consensus among the various audiences for the UNSC's legitimacy claims that military force is always the right means for responding to threats against innocent populations. Moreover, the Council's moves away from impartiality—for example, to pronounce on the outcome of the Ivorian elections, or to constrain the movements of forces loyal to former Libyan leader Qaddafi—are seen by some states and NGOs as stepping beyond the legitimate role of the UNSC in managing threats to international peace and security.[81]

This latter concern is particularly acute given that the Council is not an operational agent, but rather relies on member states to interpret and implement the actions which it authorizes. In the two recent cases of Libya and Cote d'Ivoire, it was not so much the precise text of the Council resolutions (1973 and 1975 respectively) which threatened the Council's legitimacy, but rather the interpretation of the mandates specified in the text by Western states (France in the Ivorian case, and France, the UK, and the US in the case of Libya).[82] Partly in response to the alleged 'mission creep' of the NATO-led action in Libya, the Brazilian government has launched an initiative,

[81] For a more detailed discussion of these two cases, see Alex J. Bellamy and Paul D. Williams, 'The new politics of protection? Cote d'Ivoire, Libya, and the Responsibility to Protect', *International Affairs*, Vol. 87, no. 4 (2011), 825–50.

[82] The concerns among member states regarding the case of Cote d'Ivoire and Libya were reflected in the Council's May 2011 debate on the Protection of Civilians in Armed Conflict. See UN doc. S/PV.6531, 10 May 2011. The views of the broader UN membership, and key NGOs, were voiced at the General Assembly's Interactive Dialogue on the Responsibility to Protect, New York, 5 September 2012. For an overview of the dialogue, see http://www.responsibilitytoprotect.org/index.php/component/content/article/35-r2pcs-topics/4331-un-general-assembly-dialogue-on-the-report-of-the-secretary-general-on-the-responsibility-to-protect-timely-and-decisive-response. Accessed on 11 December 2012.

'Responsibility While Protecting', designed to preserve the Council's legitimacy and to foreclose its association with coercive regime change. The proposals seek to enhance the UN's non-military options for protecting civilians, limit the Council's recourse to military force to instances where diplomatic and other means have been exhausted, and strengthen the accountability of those who act on behalf of the UNSC.[83] In so doing, countries such as Brazil—which is also an aspirant to UNSC permanent membership—hope to avoid expansion of the Council's role and purposes that threaten to go beyond what is specified in the UN Charter.

CONCLUSION

Discussions of the legitimacy of international organizations in general, and of the Security Council in particular, have become a common feature of the IR literature. While many examinations of the Council's legitimacy have focused on its role as a collective legitimizer, or on the challenges to its legitimacy, few have examined how the Council legitimates itself. This chapter addresses this gap.

The issue of UNSC legitimacy is important because the Council lacks the coercive power to enforce compliance with its resolutions if necessary. Instead, it relies on states to enforce resolutions on its behalf, and for this, its decisions need to be seen as legitimate. As this chapter has shown, the Council and UN member states more generally have been acutely aware of the need for Council legitimacy, and of the challenges to it, and they have consciously engaged in efforts to sustain and enhance its legitimacy. Our analysis highlights that these practices have had some successes, but also points to several issues that have inherently limited their effectiveness.

The mixed record of the Council's legitimation practices reveals that there is often a tension between different approaches: attempts to make the Council more transparent or more knowledgeable can also undermine rapid consensus-building, or lead to further politicization. Our analysis also suggests that a much greater substantive consensus amongst UN member states is required in order to address the UNSC's legitimacy gaps. The rapid social and political change that has occurred globally over the last two decades—both materially, with respect to the balance of power, and normatively, with respect to the growing influence of human rights and the increased importance of NGOs in advancing and sustaining such normative change—is unlikely to be easily

[83] See the letter and annex sent by the Permanent Representative of Brazil to the UN Secretary General, 'Responsibility while protecting: elements for the development and promotion of a concept', UN doc. A/66/551-S/2011/701, 11 November 2011.

accommodated by an institution whose formal structures are as difficult to change as the Council's. In addition, states are affected by and respond to material and normative shifts in different ways, opening up political space for contesting both emerging international norms and the broader architecture of international order—including the role of key institutions like the UNSC. This reality of differential impact and contestation underlines the difficulty in attaching the label 'legitimate' to any particular practice or institution.

These social and political changes also mean that the UNSC's legitimation practices will need to evolve. In the two decades after the end of the Cold War, the Council pursued its legitimation efforts in a challenging international environment characterized by value pluralism on the one hand, and the concentration of economic and military power in the hands of very few—arguably a single—state on the other. Today, the growing political and economic prominence of states such as Brazil and India will make their calls for substantive structural change in the UNSC harder to ignore. Similarly, the rise of China raises important questions about the legitimating effect of emphasizing 'new' security issues, particularly those related to human rights. At the same time, an increasingly active global civil society has strongly pushed the UN in general, and the UNSC in particular, to extend its activities to address humanitarian emergencies and involve itself ever deeper into the domestic affairs of its member states. The demands of this constituency frequently support the efforts of the US and key European states to use the UNSC as a platform to promote their vision of a more solidarist international order.

An increasingly diverse range of audiences means that the UNSC's legitimation claims, along with the scope of its activities, will remain contested and challenged. Given that the Council remains a collective, intergovernmental enterprise, it can only reflect the wider political environment within which it works—it cannot transcend it.

5

ECOWAS and the Legitimacy Question: *A Normative and Institutional Approach*

Alhaji Sarjoh Bah

ECOWAS, like most multi-lateral institutions, is faced with the challenge of establishing its legitimacy, especially when it comes to dealing with domestic issues in its member states. During the first one and a half decades after its establishment in 1975 the issue of ECOWAS' legitimacy was hardly contested, primarily because of the Cold War and the limitations it imposed on the organization's role. It was viewed by both its members and other states as focused on economic integration, and lacked the mandate to interfere in the internal affairs of its members. Hence, inter-state relations within ECOWAS were governed by the twin principles of sovereignty and non-intervention. Additionally, the Cold War subsumed ECOWAS' ambitions by introducing a security overlay.[1] It was not until the end of the Cold War and the disengagement by the superpowers that ECOWAS ventured into dealing with security issues in a meaningful way. While it had adopted two protocols on security during the Cold War—on Non-Aggression in 1979 and Mutual Defence in 1981—neither was operationalized during this period.

The emergence of violent domestic conflicts in the early 1990s had lasting repercussions not only for the role of ECOWAS in dealing with such conflicts, but also for its approach to and understanding of security. More critically, the legitimacy question was brought to the fore for the first time primarily due to the unprecedented military intervention in one of its member states, Liberia. Questions were raised about the legitimacy of the intervention not least because it was mounted by a sub-regional organization without the authorization of the United Nations Security Council (UNSC), the only body formally

[1] On the concept of overlay, see Barry Buzan, *People, States and Fear: An Agenda for International Security Studies in the Post-Cold War Era*, 2nd ed. (Boulder: Lynne Rienner, 1991).

empowered to authorize such interventions. The intervention in Liberia was the turning point as it triggered political and legal debates on ECOWAS's role in the security sphere. The controversies generated by this single act have resulted in the development of a strong 'interventionist norm'. Building on the humanitarian arguments for its intervention in Liberia in 1990, ECOWAS has developed intrusive norms that are not inhibited by the principle of non-interference, but instead have emphasized the principle of non-indifference. The emergence of these norms raised important questions about the limits of what was initially an organization dedicated to economic integration, but whose mandate has extended to the political and security spheres. Thus, while ECOWAS member states profess to subscribe to the new norms, eliciting compliance with them has been fraught with difficulties. Questions of legitimacy are at the heart of the compliance challenge.

This chapter looks at ECOWAS' efforts at legitimation from three different perspectives: normative, institutional, and with regard to compliance. Legitimacy for the purposes of this paper is defined as '...the fact that individuals or organizations are following rules, commands or decisions because they regard them as binding'.[2] According to Jens Steffek, '...in the creation of international regimes all contracting parties need to agree explicitly to the values, goals, and procedures for the regime. This moment of consensus in the regime...also provides consensual reference points for the regime's discursive justification and thus legitimacy'. He added that 'what creates legitimacy is less the fact of having consented, but rather having consented to a certain normative reasoning, linking shared values and principles to practice type norms'.[3] As will be demonstrated in the subsequent analysis, ECOWAS has developed a set of norms that are based on shared values and principles, and that have elicited a consensus that requires compliance by its members. In some instances, where compliance has failed, it has resorted to the use of force often without the authorization of the UNSC. The legitimacy of such actions has been the source of intense debates among scholars and practitioners.

The chapter examines the legitimacy challenges and legitimation practices of ECOWAS in broadly chronological order, and is divided into five sections: background (ECOWAS during the Cold War); First Generation Interventions—focusing on contested legitimacy rooted in normative disagreements and fears of Nigerian hegemony; ECOWAS's new security architecture, mechanisms, mandates, and institutional structures; Second Generation Interventions and the challenge of eliciting compliance; and how ECOWAS has sought legitimacy beyond its member states by increasing its engagement with civil society and cooperation with other international organizations. The

[2] Jens Steffek, 'The Legitimation of International Governance: A Discourse Approach', *European Journal of International Relations*, Vol. 9/2 (2003), 255.

[3] Steffek, 'The Legitimation of International Governance: A Discourse Approach', 263–4.

chapter concludes by arguing that even under its limited economic integration agenda, ECOWAS always attempted to legitimate its actions by a direct appeal and commitment to improving the welfare of its citizens. Unsurprisingly, the argument for upholding the welfare of citizens in the region is at the centre of the new norms and security architecture.

BACKGROUND

The inauguration of ECOWAS[4] in Lagos, Nigeria, on 28 May 1975 was hailed as a critical breakthrough in efforts to institute a framework for economic co-operation and integration that embraced the entire sub-region. The debate about the African development question in the 1970s and 1980s was sustained by Professor Adebayo Adedeji (often referred to as the father of ECOWAS). A key aspect of Adedeji's development strategy has been the concept of regional co-operation and integration. Adedeji considered a regional approach, linked to the principle of collective self-reliance, as a *sine qua non* for the achievement of national socio-economic goals.[5] Despite the high-profile nature of its engagement in the security realm in the post-Cold War era, regional economic integration remains at the centre of its long-term vision. It is worth noting that among other things, ECOWAS has taken concrete steps to ensure the free movement of persons across the region by removing visa requirements for citizens of its members with the introduction of the ECOWAS Brown Card, the equivalent of a sub-regional passport. Despite these measures, free and unimpeded movement across the sub-region is undermined by corrupt immigration and customs officials who continue to harass and extort monies from travellers in contravention of the Protocol on the Free Movement of Persons, Goods and Services. At another level, efforts are underway to introduce a common currency for its members, a move that is aimed at increasing the level and volume of intra-regional trade and commerce. ECOWAS has also embarked on infrastructural and other projects such as the trans-ECOWAS highway, the West African Power Pool, and the ECOWAS youth volunteer scheme that was launched in March 2010.[6]

[4] The fifteen signatories of the Treaty of Lagos were: Côte d'Ivoire, Dahomey (now Benin), Gambia, Ghana, Guinea, Guinea-Bissau, Liberia, Mali, Mauritania, Niger, Nigeria, Senegal, Sierra Leone, Togo, and Upper Volta (now Burkina Faso). The island of Cape Verde joined the Community in 1997. Mauritania withdrew from ECOWAS in 2000, though there is speculation that authorities in that country are planning a come back.

[5] S.K.B. Asante, *African Development: Adebayo Adedeji's Alternative Strategies* (Ibadan, Nigeria: Spectrum, 1991), 10.

[6] 'West Africa volunteers scheme launched', *BCC Africa News*, 26 March 2010.

In addition to its economic focus, ECOWAS also attempted to establish a security framework through the adoption of the Protocol on Non-Aggression in 1978 and of the Protocol Relating to Mutual Assistance on Defence in 1981.[7] These protocols further codified the principle of sovereignty as a defining characteristic of inter-state relations in the sub-region. The ECOWAS security framework prohibited interference in the internal affairs of member states. This position largely held until the outbreak of violent conflicts in Liberia and Sierra Leone in the early 1990s.

One of the most important developments during the early post-Cold War period was an emerging consensus in both the developing and some parts of the developed worlds that the concept of security needed to be redefined to include non-military security issues—*human security*. The publication of the United Nations Development Programme's (UNDP) Annual Human Development Report in 1994, which broadened the definition of security, was the turning point in the debate.[8] Prior to the publication of the report, efforts were already under way in Africa to shift the focus towards the security of people. At the continental level, the most significant initiative was what became known as the Kampala Document, which called for the establishment of a Conference on Security, Stability, Development and Cooperation in Africa (CSSDCA) in 1991. The CSSDCA points to the fact that peace, security and stability are the pillars for development and cooperation in Africa.[9] It emphasized that the

> security, stability and development of every African country are inseparably linked to that of other African countries. Instability in one country affects the stability of neighbouring countries and has serious implications for continental unity, peace and security.[10]

At the sub-regional level, ECOWAS' adoption of its revised treaty and the Protocol on Conflict Resolution in 1993 and 1999 respectively were significant milestones in norm development in the sub-region. The Protocol on Conflict Resolution incorporated some of the principles espoused by the CSSDCA. The normative shift at the sub-regional, regional, and international levels coupled with ECOWAS' new security regime in the form of its revised treaty and

[7] See ECOWAS Protocol on Non-Aggression, 1979, and ECOWAS Protocol Relating to Mutual Assistance on Defence, May 1981.

[8] For details see UNDP, *Human Development Report 1994: New Dimensions of Human Security* (New York: Oxford University Press, 1994).

[9] Ayodele Aderinwale, 'The Conference on Security, Stability, Development and Cooperation in Africa—Framework and the Role of Regional Institutions', in Moufids Goucha and Jakkie Cilliers (eds.), *Peace, Human Security and Conflict Prevention in Africa* (Paris/Pretoria: ISS/UNESCO, 2000), 59–66. Available at http://www.iss.org.za/uploads/CSSDCA.PDF.

[10] Aderinwale, 'The Conference on Security, Stability, Development and Cooperation in Africa—Framework and the Role of Regional Institutions', 64.

protocols provided it with the tools and instruments to deal with the legitimacy crisis that dogged its first military intervention in Liberia in August 1990.

FIRST GENERATION INTERVENTIONS: CONTESTED LEGITIMACY

In the immediate post-Cold War era, the West African security landscape was characterized by two main issues: first the violent internal conflicts in Liberia, Sierra Leone, Guinea-Bissau, and Côte d'Ivoire, and second, the unprecedented ECOWAS military interventions in two of these conflicts. The ECOWAS interventions had the effect of partly focusing attention on the unprecedented nature of the venture, and the temporal reawakening of regional rivalries along French–English linguistic lines. These conflicts, and ECOWAS's response to them, raised two challenges to the organization's legitimacy. First, some member states argued that it exceeded ECOWAS' mandate, and violated regional and global norms of non-intervention. These arguments were anchored on two points: first, whether the ECOWAS Ceasefire and Monitoring Group (ECOMOG) troop-contributing states violated the ECOWAS Charter—in other words, whether the intervention violated the principle of state sovereignty and non-interference; second, why should an organization set up for economic integration become involved in political/security issues? In other words, did ECOWAS have the mandate or legitimacy for the regional policing role that it undertook? Moreover, some of the opposition to the intervention was directed at Nigeria's dominance of ECOMOG, reawakening concerns over Nigerian hegemony in West Africa.[11]

Legitimating Intervention: the Invocation of Humanitarian Norms

Countries opposed to the intervention pointed to the fact that the intervention took place without the authorization of the UNSC, and that ECOWAS, with

[11] See Jimmi Adisa, 'Nigeria in ECOMOG: Political Undercurrents and the burden of Community Spirit', *Small Wars and Insurgencies*, Vol. 5/1 (1994), 83–110; Celestine Bassey, 'Nigeria in ECOMOG: Dilemma of Preventive Diplomacy?' in J. Owoeye (ed.), *Nigeria in International Institutions*, (Ibadan: College Press Ltd, 1993), 159–70; David Wippman, 'Enforcing the Peace: ECOWAS and the Liberian War', in L. F. Damrosch (ed), *Enforcing Restraint: Collective Intervention in Internal Conflicts* (New York: Council on Foreign Relations Press, 1993); Karsten Nowrot and Emily W Schabacker The Use of Force to Restore Democracy: International Legal Implications of the ECOWAS Military Intervention in Sierra Leone', *International Law Review*, Vol. 14 (1998), 312–412.

its mandate to advance economic integration, lacked the legal basis to interfere politically or militarily in domestic conflicts. The intervening countries were not deterred as they projected the intervention as purely humanitarian. They argued that the massive slaughter of civilians, coupled with the flooding of neighbouring countries with tens of thousands of refugees, posed a serious challenge to the peace and security of the sub-region. Furthermore, they cited the 1979 and 1981 ECOWAS Protocols as the legal basis for the intervention.

The humanitarian argument was summed up by the preamble to the decision setting up the Standing Mediation Committee (SMC):

> the wanton destruction of human life and property and the displacement of persons...the massive damage in various forms being caused by the armed conflict to the stability and survival of the entire Liberian nation; and concern...about the plight of foreign nationals, particularly citizens of the Community who are seriously affected by the conflict; and considering that law and order in Liberia had broken down...[12]

The SMC consisting of seven ECOWAS member states was charged with the responsibility of resolving the conflict.[13] But the SMC itself soon became the subject of controversy as two of its Francophone members—Mali and Togo—withdrew from it, setting the stage for open rifts between English and French speaking members of ECOWAS.

If ECOWAS' invocation of humanitarianism was meant to appease its critics, it failed because its peacekeeping force was hobbled by regional squabbles which played into the hands of the different warring factions, strengthening their resolve to pursue the military option. Nonetheless, the intervening states mounted an internationalist campaign, which had a receptive audience in the post-Cold War period, especially among some of its members. However, ECOWAS's humanitarian argument was also aimed at connecting with civil society in the sub-region and other international actors such as the United Nations. This was a clever move since it broadened ECOWAS' constituency from its members to include civil society, a development that resonated with calls for a more people-centred approach to security. The humanitarian argument strengthened its hand against those members that opposed the intervention and more crucially, pressured the Security Council to retroactively authorize the intervention. ECOWAS' internationalist argument (being one's brother's keeper) was perhaps the strongest position that they had. This argument was boosted by the changed international political environment following the end of the Cold War, when it became fashionable to talk of an emerging

[12] See ECOWAS Decision A/DEC. 1/8/90.

[13] The seven members of the SMC were: Ghana, Nigeria, The Gambia, Sierra Leone, Guinea, Togo, and Mali.

global community and humanitarian intervention. Such intervention did not respect established territorial borders or protocols, such as obtaining the permission of a host state before deployment, especially 'when a state has virtually ceased to exist, [when] there is no effective civil authority, and when subjects are in a quasi state of nature'.[14]

Responding to critics of ECOMOG, then OAU Secretary-General, Salim Ahmed Salim dismissed allegations that the deployment of ECOMOG violated the non-interference clauses of the OAU and UN Charter. He described the criticism as rhetorical, stating that:

> Before ECOWAS undertook its initiative many, including the African media, were condemning the indifference demonstrated by Africa ... (therefore) to argue that there is no legal basis is surprising. Should the countries in West Africa just leave Liberians to fight each other? Will that be more legitimate? Will that be more understandable?[15]

The OAU and ECOWAS placed crucial emphasis on the humanitarian argument. The OAU Secretary-General argued that even if the intervention was construed as of questionable legality, it remained proper. The ECOWAS Chairman was even more categorical when he noted that: 'the wanton killings going on in Liberia has made that country a slaughter-house and the situation could no longer be treated as an internal matter'.[16]

From the outset the international community's response, especially the UN Security Council's, was one of guarded approval. It can be likened to the way it responded to Tanzania's intervention in Uganda in 1979; it validated the result without formally validating the means.[17] But, in its strongest show of support of ECOMOG a senior US administration official observed that,

> in a country where anarchy reigned, ECOMOG provided order and a bastion of security in Monrovia and hundreds of thousands of Liberians flocked to the relative safety of the city ... ECOMOG remains virtually the only force in Liberia unblemished by serious human rights abuses and is the only military force not motivated by personal aggrandizement.[18]

[14] Amadu Sesay, *Humanitarian Intervention in Liberia: Implications for State and Sub-Regional Security and International Society*, paper prepared for the Workshop on Humanitarian Intervention and International Society, London School of Economics, 13 May 1995.

[15] *West Africa Magazine*, August 1990, 1085.

[16] *West Africa Magazine*, August 1990, 1085–7. Scholars of international law at the time questioned the legality of the ECOWAS intervention in Liberia, since it ventured beyond general peacekeeping and attempted to influence the outcome of the civil war in Liberia. For such arguments see Chukwuka Ofodile, 'The Legality of ECOWAS Intervention in Liberia', *Columbia Journal of Transnational Law*, Vol. 32 (1994), 381.

[17] Wippman, 'Enforcing the Peace', 175. David Wippman served as counsel to the interim government of Liberia from November 1990 to May 1992.

[18] For more on this see, 'US Reaffirms Its Policy Toward Liberia', Statement by Leonard H. Robinson, Jr., Deputy Assistant Secretary for African Affairs the Subcommittee on Africa of the House Foreign Affairs Committee, 19 November 1992. Available at http://dosfan.lib.uic.edu/ERC/briefing/dispatch/1992/html/Dispatchv3no48.html.

For its part, the Security Council endorsed the ECOWAS intervention through two presidential statements in 1991 and 1992, and Resolution 788 of November 1992.[19] This is significant because the Security Council, while playing second fiddle to a sub-regional organization, thereby helped to legitimize the intervention, albeit retroactively.

In forcing both the UN and the OAU to legitimize its actions, the ECOWAS intervention in Liberia served as a challenge to the non-interference principles of both organizations. Confronting the sovereignty norm was one of the major consequences of the post-Cold War era. For instance, it was only in the 1990s that the United Nations, the guarantor of sovereignty, began to rethink the notion of sovereignty and the norms of intervention in domestic disputes. Iraq's repression of its Kurdish minority following the Gulf War in 1991 prompted the passage of UN resolution 988 authorizing direct UN intervention into Iraq's internal affairs in order to protect the Kurds. This, according to Stremlau,[20] was an indication of an emerging international consensus on the legitimacy of external collective action to halt domestic oppression as well as external aggression.[21]

Perhaps the most important precedent set by the ECOWAS action was the implied retroactive acceptance of the deployments by both the OAU and UN, which further legitimized them. Both organizations were junior partners in the initial ECOWAS-led peace processes in Liberia and Sierra Leone. The historic significance of the arrangement was not lost on then UN Secretary-General Boutros Boutros-Ghali when he said:

> The peace process in Liberia poses a special opportunity . . . in that UNOMIL . . . will be the first peacekeeping operation undertaken by the UN in cooperation with a peacekeeping mission already set up by another organization, in this case, a sub-regional organization . . . This relationship potentially presents some challenges but . . . with good will . . . this relationship will be successful and may even set a precedent for future peacekeeping missions.[22]

[19] See UN doc. S/22133 of 22 January 1991, UN doc. S/23886 of 7 May 1992, and SC Res. 788 of 19 November, 1992.

[20] See John Stremlau, 'The New Global Order and its Implications for Peace and Security in Africa', U.S. Department of State Dispatch, September, 1991, 159. See also Samantha Power, *A Problem from Hell: America and the Age of Genocide* (New York: Basic Books, 2002). The often controversial subject of sovereignty and non-intervention is discussed by Nicholas G. Onuf, 'Sovereignty: Outline of a Conceptual History', *Alternatives*, Vol. 16/4 (1991), 425–46; Stephen D. Krasner, *Sovereignty: Organized Hypocrisy* (Princeton: Princeton University Press, 1999); Stephen D. Krasner, 'Compromising Westphalia', *International Security*, Vol. 20/3 (1995/1996), 115–51; Saskia Sassen, *Losing Control? Sovereignty in an Age of Globalization* (New York: Columbia University Press, 1996); Hurst Hannum, *Autonomy, Sovereignty, and Self-Determination: The Accommodation of Conflicting Rights* (Philadelphia: University of Pennsylvania Press, 1990); Francis M. Deng, Kimaro Sadikiel, Terrence Lyons, Donald Rothchild, and I. William Zartman, (eds.) *Sovereignty as Responsibility: Conflict Management in Africa* (Washington, DC: Brookings Institution, 1996).

[21] Stremlau, 'The New Global Order', 159.

[22] Quoted in Sesay, *Humanitarian Intervention*.

The Secretary-General's statement and the general response of the international community, though an acceptance of ECOWAS's intervention, fell short of overtly applauding ECOMOG's use of force.[23] Nonetheless, ECOWAS' deployment of troops in Liberia and Sierra Leone was unprecedented in two respects. First, it was the first major intervention by a sub-regional organization in a local conflict; second, the force was deployed without the approval of either the OAU or the UNSC. While this was partly due to international disengagement in less strategic areas of the world, it undoubtedly gave regional and sub-regional entities more room to manoeuvre, especially in the security sphere.[24]

Nigerian Hegemony—A Source of Contested Legitimacy

From the onset, Nigeria's pivotal role in ECOMOG drew fire from opponents of the intervention. For instance, while Côte d'Ivoire was a party to the decision to set up the Standing Mediation Committee (SMC), it did not contribute to the military deployment. Additionally, Togo's withdrawal from ECOMOG and the subsequent denunciation of the decision to intervene by Burkina Faso, a close ally of Côte d'Ivoire, indicated that a rift had developed over the decision to deploy troops into Liberia. In an attempt to build consensus and dampen fears over Nigeria's hegemonic role in the deployment, General Ibrahim Babangida (Nigeria's military ruler and chief architect of ECOMOG), appealed to ECOWAS members when he said:

> Permit me…to remind us all of the basic principle which formed the foundation stone of our organization. The noble ideals of the ECOWAS were anchored on solidarity, unity, mutual trust and good neighbourliness…these attributes impose on us an obligation to adopt a conciliatory situation…we can ill afford at this time to dissipate vital energy on inter-state squabbles…[25]

The focal point of Nigeria's appeal was to invoke common values as a way of fostering consensus and harmonious relationships among member states. In spite of such appeals and reassurances, Côte d'Ivoire and her allies remained suspicious of Nigeria's intentions. Côte d' Ivoire was opposed to the ECOMOG

[23] Wippman, 'Enforcing the Peace', 180.

[24] The four English-speaking states (Ghana, Nigeria, Sierra Leone, Gambia) and, Guinea-Conakry (a lone francophone state), constituted the initial ECOMOG force, leaving nearly all the French speaking states, especially Côte d'Ivoire, and Burkina Faso, vehemently opposed to the intervention. Whilst Burkina Faso and Côte d'Ivoire openly opposed the action (and even supported the Liberian insurgents) other French-speaking states were more muted in their opposition but refused to make any military contribution to ECOMOG; except for Senegal's short deployment in 1992.

[25] See *Journal of ECOWAS*, Vol. 17 (1990), 20.

venture for several reasons, the most important being the perceived threat that came from anglophone West Africa, especially Nigeria. The composition of ECOMOG lent weight to this assumption, and in this context Côte d'Ivoire's attitude in itself spurred the self-fulfilling prophecy. The Ivorian leader was uncomfortable with Nigeria's resort to active military diplomacy, and its long-term impact on the power balance in West Africa. As one astute observer enthused:

> the involvement of the Nigerian armed forces in Liberia changes the military balance of power in West Africa and even further afield. The Nigerian military have demonstrated clearly that it has greater confidence in its ability to influence events outside Nigeria's borders. Given Nigerian aspirations to regional power, this is of some significance (sic).[26]

In the meantime, to incorporate the francophones, Nigeria conceded the leadership of the peacemaking process in Liberia to Côte d'Ivoire. The negotiation process was subsequently adjusted to accommodate this objective. In essence, the substance of the controversy that attended the inception of ECOMOG was not over its legitimacy *per se*. Instead, political disagreements among ECOWAS member states were a function of political differences and the conflicting interests of various leaders.[27] Unsurprisingly, the rifts that emerged over the intervention in Liberia were less pronounced when ECOWAS mounted its second major peace operation in Sierra Leone.

ECOMOG in Sierra Leone

Following the overthrow of the Tejan-Kabbah government in May 1997, the Nigerian-led ECOMOG force was authorized to restore the deposed civilian government. As in Liberia, the intervention did not come without controversy. As the UN pressed for sanctions to be implemented, ECOWAS led mediation for a peaceful settlement and the restoration of the ousted civilian government. The negotiations culminated in the Conakry Accord in which the military junta agreed to step down in April 1998. However, with indications that the junta might not hand over power as agreed, ECOMOG went on the offensive in February 1998, ousting the military junta, cutting short the April deadline reached at Conakry.

[26] See *Journal of ECOWAS*, Vol. 17 (1990), 3.

[27] Ibid, 144–9. See also Amadu Sesay, 'Human Rights and the Maintenance of International Peace and Security in Africa', *Africa Peace Review*, Vol. 3/1 (2001), 19–45; Gani Joses Yoroms, 'Regional Security, Collective Defence and the Problem of Peace Initiatives in West Africa: The case of ECOMOG', *Africa Peace Review*, Vol. 3/1 (2001), 84–112.

Following the Nigerian intervention, *The Economist* commented

> whatever happened to non-interference? Meddling in other countries' affairs, let alone invading them, used to be a taboo, even in the best of causes. But when the Nigerian troops moved against junta officers in Sierra Leone who had overthrown an elected government, their intervention was accepted by the world as if Sierra Leone were Nigerian territory and not an independent state nearly 900 miles away.[28]

Despite such sentiments, then UN Secretary-General, Kofi Annan, appeared to give backing to the use of force when he told the OAU: 'Democracy has been usurped. Let us do whatever is in our power to restore its owners, the people. Verbal condemnation... is not sufficient.'[29]

For its part, the OAU was quick to condemn the coup d'état and called for the restoration of democracy. The UNSC, however, did not act as rapidly. Five months after the coup, the UNSC passed Resolution 1132, requesting the military junta to 'relinquish power' and allow the restoration of the democratically elected government.[30] Although the UNSC found that the situation was a threat to international peace and security in the region, it fell short of authorizing the use of force. It merely authorized ECOWAS to ensure the strict implementation of sanctions.[31]

Following the ousting of the junta, the international community including the UN accepted ECOWAS's actions, apparently willing to turn a blind eye to the legality of the intervention. The OAU welcomed the Nigerian-led intervention almost immediately. For its part, the UNSC issued a statement welcoming the 'fact that the military junta has been brought to an end' and commended 'the important role' that ECOWAS played in the peaceful resolution of the crisis.[32] Despite the international applause, the action raised fundamental questions about the legal norms pertaining to the use of force between sovereign states. This was particularly critical because the UNSC did not authorize the

[28] *The Economist*, June 1997, 49–50. Despite the international acclaim that Nigeria received for its role in restoring the democratically elected government in Sierra Leone, critics of Nigeria's military dictatorship under Gen. Sani Abacha, saw the intervention as a means to divert international attention from the regimes poor human rights record. See Bolaji Akinyemi, 'End the Military Meddling', *The Guardian*, Lagos, 5 June 1997. Following the Nigerian-led restoration of the Kabbah government, a long-time observer of political developments in West Africa commented to this author about the two faces of Nigeria 'in exporting what they didn't have (democracy) and importing what they have (oil)'.

[29] *The Economist*, June 1997, 50.

[30] SC Res. 1132 of 8 October 1997. See also UN doc. S/PV. 2822 of 8 October 1997, Para.1

[31] Karsten Nowrot and Emily Schabacker, 'Military Intervention in Sierra Leone', *International Law Review*, Vol. 4/2 (1998), 328.

[32] Nowrot and Schabacker, 'Military Intervention in Sierra Leone', 338. Commenting on the intervention James Jonah, then Sierra Leone's permanent Representative at the United Nations, invoked Article 51 of the UN Charter as justification for foreign military intervention to restore democracy in Sierra Leone. See Jonah's *Press Conference*, February 18th 1998, UN Headquarters, New York.

ousting of the military junta, though it subsequently supported the action. The intervention not only rekindled the debate on the role of regional organizations with regard to the use of force, but more crucially, it raised questions about the role of the UNSC in authorizing such actions, especially when done retroactively.

ECOWAS' NEW SECURITY ARCHITECTURE

A Broader Mandate

In the Preamble to the 1992 revised treaty, ECOWAS member states agreed that: '...the integration of the Members into a viable regional community may demand the partial and gradual pooling of national sovereignties to the Community within the context of a collective political will...'[33] ECOWAS also adopted a declaration of political principles which committed its members to the recognition and promotion of human and peoples' rights in accordance with the provisions of the African Charter on Human and Peoples Rights; to accountability, economic and social justice and popular participation in development; and promotion and consolidation of a democratic system of governance in each Member State.[34] These instruments preceded the much publicized Human Development Report in 1994. ECOWAS' pioneering role in broadening the conceptualization of security is hardly acknowledged in the policy and academic discourse in western circles.

The adoption of these political principles was a turning point as it was the first time that the fundamental issues of human rights, good governance, accountability, democratic pluralism, and economic development were directly linked to security. The holistic approach to integration presented a unique opportunity for the building of a collective security framework that could address the shortfalls of the *ad hoc* ECOMOG operations in Liberia and Sierra Leone. Additionally, by emphasizing the welfare of the citizens of its member states, ECOWAS reached out to ordinary citizens, thereby increasing its legitimacy among them.

Subsequently, a *Mechanism for Conflict Prevention, Management, Resolution and Security* was adopted in 1999. In its declaration of principles, Article 2 (a) states that 'economic and social development and the security of peoples and States are inextricably linked' adding that 'the consolidation

[33] See Revised Treaty of the Economic Community of West African States, Cotonou, Benin, 24 July 1992.

[34] See Revised Treaty of the Economic Community of West African States, Cotonou, Benin, 24 July 1992, 6–7.

of democratic governments as well as institutions and the protection of fundamental human rights and freedoms and the rules of international humanitarian laws'[35] are fundamental for the effective operationalization of the mechanism.

In a break from previous arrangements, the new mechanism is not limited to inter-state conflicts; it has the mandate to intervene in internal conflicts that pose a threat to human rights and the general peace and security of the sub-region. It is applicable in any of the following cases:

- In case of internal conflict: (i) that threatens to trigger a humanitarian disaster; or (ii) that poses a serious threat to peace and security in the sub-region;
- In the event of serious and massive violations of human rights and the rule of law;
- In the event of an overthrow or attempted overthrow of a democratically elected government.[36]

To reinforce its stance against unconstitutional change or attempted change of government,[37] ECOWAS adopted a supplementary *Protocol on Democracy and Good Governance* in 2001.[38] In the Protocol, it established that in ECOWAS member states, every accession to power must be made through free, fair, and transparent elections; that the organization has no tolerance for power obtained or maintained by unconstitutional means; and that the armed forces must be apolitical and under the command of a legally constituted political authority.[39]

To ensure adherence to these principles enforcement mechanisms ranging from sanctions to military intervention were established. Article 45 (1) of the Supplementary Protocol states that: 'In the event that democracy is abruptly brought to an end by any unconstitutional means or where there is massive violation of human rights in a Member State, ECOWAS may impose sanctions on the state concerned.'[40] The sanctions can take various forms such as suspensions from all ECOWAS decision-making bodies and refusal to support candidates from the state in question for any international posts. ECOWAS has made good on this threat by suspending several members; most notably, Togo,

[35] See ECOWAS, *Protocol Relating to the Mechanism for Conflict Prevention, Management, Resolution, Peacekeeping and Security*, Lome, 10 December 1999.

[36] See ECOWAS, *Protocol on Conflict Resolution*, 17.

[37] See ECOWAS, *Protocol on Conflict Resolution*, Art. 25 (e).

[38] For details see ECOWAS, Protocol A/SP1/12/01 on Democracy and Good Governance—Supplementary to the Protocol relating to the Mechanism for Conflict Prevention, Management, Resolution, Peacekeeping and Security', Dakar, 21 December 2001.

[39] ECOWAS, Protocol A/SP1/12/01, 5–6.

[40] ECOWAS, Protocol A/SP1/12/01, 22.

Guinea, and Niger, all of which are discussed in detail later on in the chapter. Although some might dismiss such moves as symbolic, the suspensions contributed to putting pressure on the military juntas in three cases to return their countries to constitutional civilian rule.

These changes are significant because they entailed an implicit acknowledgement of the perennial problem of coups d'états and the poor human rights record in the sub-region. It was a bold attempt at dealing with the systemic challenge of bad governance by confronting threats to peace and security emanating from poor human rights records, disrespect for the rule of law and corrupt practices. By confronting the issue of good governance in its member states, ECOWAS directly challenged the principles of non-intervention, a principle that had held sway throughout the Cold War.[41]

Decision-making Structures

Meanwhile, to increase the legitimacy of its actions and bolster the emerging norms, ECOWAS had to establish credible decision-making mechanisms. ECOWAS realized that the absence of credible decision-making instruments and the resort to ad hoc mechanisms such as the Standing Mediation Council (SMC) established to deal with the conflict in Liberia undermined its initial peacemaking efforts. Consequently, ECOWAS established several mechanisms as its standing decision-making organs: the Authority (or Summit) of Heads of State and Government; the Mediation and Security Council, and the Executive Secretariat, now transformed to a Commission. The Authority of Heads of State and Government is the supreme institution with responsibility for the general direction and control of the community, while the Mediation and Security Council (MSC) acts as the equivalent of the United Nations Security Council (UNSC). The MSC is one of the most innovative organs of the Protocol, but unlike the UNSC, it has no permanent members.[42] These organs were mandated to take decisions relating to peace and security and perhaps most importantly, to 'authorize all forms of intervention and decide particularly on the deployment of political and military missions'.[43] The decisions of organs are binding on all Member states.

To a large extent, the structure and mandate of these organs was informed by the legitimacy crisis triggered by the intervention in Liberia. The MSC, for example, was a direct response to the challenges posed by what was criticized as the narrow and unrepresentative nature of the SMC which authorized the

[41] For more on ECOWAS' invocation of the Protocol on good governance, see, 'Stepping up to the plate', *Africa Today*, Vol. 9, no. 10, October 2003, 20–2.

[42] ECOWAS *Revised Treaty*, 8.

[43] See ECOWAS, *Protocol on Conflict Resolution*, 9–10.

intervention. ECOWAS moved from ad hoc decision-making bodies to institutionalized structures with the aim of minimizing the controversy and rancour that characterized its first generation interventions in the early 1990s. The creation of these organs is expected to serve as a check against Nigeria's hegemonic dominance of the organization. Dealing with the fears of smaller members through this process of institutionalization is likely to contribute to legitimizing ECOWAS's decisions in the future. As will be seen in the discussion of the Guinea, Togo, and Niger cases later on, the decisions relating to these organs have enjoyed greater support among its members. However, despite this impressive norm development and institutionalization, ECOWAS continues to face a big challenge in ensuring that members comply with its policies, to which attention is now turned.

SECOND GENERATION INTERVENTIONS: THE COMPLIANCE CHALLENGE

Following the intervention in Sierra Leone in 1998, and adoption of its Protocol on Conflict Prevention and Resolution in 1999, ECOWAS has overturned military coups in Guinea-Bissau in 2003 and in Togo 2005, and negotiated the departure of Charles Taylor from Liberia in August 2003. Operationally, ECOWAS deployed two peace operations since 1999: the ECOWAS Mission in Côte d'Ivoire (ECOMICI, 2003) and the ECOWAS Mission in Liberia (ECOMIL, 2003). ECOWAS collaborated with the United Nations, France, and the United States in the two deployments, with troops from both missions subsequently re-hatted to the follow-on UN-led missions. But ECOWAS's key role in resolving the political crisis in Togo (2005) and Guinea (2007) was the most prominent display of its ability to invoke its new instruments to deal with intra-state conflicts before they erupt. Unlike Liberia and Côte d'Ivoire, where ECOWAS intervened to deal with the aftermath of violence, its engagement in Togo and Guinea was credited with averting the eruption of further violence in both countries.

ECOWAS in Togo

In Togo, the death of President Gnassingbé Eyadéma in 2005 threatened to plunge that country into chaos. After his father's death, Faure Gnassingbé's assumption of power was rejected by members of the opposition and ECOWAS as unconstitutional and unacceptable. However, having changed the constitution and with the country's military on his side, Faure initially appeared determined to succeed his father, a move that threatened the stability of the country.

This prompted ECOWAS to intervene by calling for an immediate end to the unconstitutional 'father-to-son' transition and restoration of the old constitution, or Togo risked sanctions and even military intervention; with Nigeria's National Assembly endorsing the latter.[44] Invoking the Togolese constitution and its zero-tolerance policy against unconstitutional change of government (reflecting also the stance of the African Union), ECOWAS succeeded in brokering a deal that saw Faure step aside, and the deputy speaker of the National Assembly assume the Presidency, contrary to the stipulations of the constitution which calls for the speaker to take charge of the government.

Presidential elections, subsequently won by Faure Gnassingbe, were held within sixty days—in line with the constitution but in the face of complaints by the opposition about the short notice, as the sixty days included time spent negotiating with Faure to relinquish power. ECOWAS's success in resolving the crisis can be attributed to three main factors: first, it invoked the Togolese constitution as an entry point to justify its pressure on Faure to relinquish power; second, it invoked its zero-tolerance norm against unconstitutional change of government to justify and legitimize its intervention and; third, its close collaboration with the AU added legitimacy to its actions.

ECOWAS in Guinea

In late January 2007, Guinea was gripped by strike action as calls by the nation's trade union and civic movements for improved working and broader socio-economic conditions metamorphosed into demands for the country's then ailing president, Lansana Conté, to resign. The government reacted with half-measures by appointing a long-time ally of the President as Prime Minister. The government's move further inflamed the civic opposition leading tens of thousands of protesters to take to the streets to protest the appointment. The President responded by declaring a 'state of siege' and unleashed the country's military on the protesters resulting in over 100 civilian deaths with hundreds more injured across the country.[45] ECOWAS, the UN, and bilateral partners unanimously condemned the government's heavy-handedness and warned the military of the repercussions of their actions. ECOWAS dispatched a high-powered mediation team, led by former Nigerian president General Ibrahim Babangida and ECOWAS Commission president Dr. Mohamed Ibn Chambas, to mediate between the parties. The ECOWAS mediation culminated in the appointment of a new prime minister with extensive powers. However, the new prime minister's reign was short-lived as he fell out with the civil society groups that led the

[44] Letogolis.com, *Nigeria National Assembly Endorses Military Action Against Togo*, Lagos, 10 February 2005. Available at http://www.letogolais.com/article.html?nid=1520.

[45] Ofeibea Quist-Arcton, 'Unrest Leaves Guinea in State of Limbo', *NPR*, 23 February, 2007.

demonstrations that led to his appointment, making it easy for president Conté to get rid of him.

Unlike previous attempts at mediation, the 2007 efforts were believed to have succeeded largely because the Guinean authorities realized that their options were dwindling as even some of its parliamentarians voted against an extension of the 'state of siege'. Although ECOWAS' mediation averted Guinea's descent into chaos, President Lansana Conte remained in power until his death on 22 December 2008, precipitating an anticipated crisis.

President Conté's death and the subsequent coup d'état constituted a challenge to ECOWAS' zero-tolerance policy. However, the situation in Guinea, after years of a failing and inept government, posed three critical dilemmas for ECOWAS: first, whether it should strictly enforce its zero-tolerance policy on coup d'états; second, how flexible it should be, given the fragile situation in Guinea and its immediate neighbours in the Mano River basin; third and perhaps most importantly, the initial popularity of the junta amongst Guinea's population, making it difficult for outsiders, including ECOWAS, to be too rigid. The tensions between respecting the 'wishes' of the Guinean public versus implementing its norms exposed the underlying currents between national and supranational institutions.

Faced with these dilemmas, ECOWAS was forced to tread a fine line as it suspended Guinea from its councils, but promised to assist the junta in organizing elections. ECOWAS' pledge to support the junta in organizing the elections was anchored on the wishes of the population. But to reinforce its desire for compliance with existing norms, it objected to the junta's earlier pronouncement of holding elections in two years. The mood within ECOWAS was summed up by Nigeria's Foreign Minister who called on the junta to '...just conduct elections and get out of town'.[46] The Foreign Minister was unequivocal in his condemnation, 'Nigeria has no business with that government in terms of formal recognition...and we know that ECOWAS officially go [sic] in the same direction.'

Moreover, the Minister condemned Senegal's recognition of the junta, an indication of a split among ECOWAS member states. He described Senegal's move as 'unfortunate' adding that '...the issue of undermining the democratic process is not just when a group of adventurers organized a coup and overthrow a democratically elected government. If democratically elected government is giving succour, providing encouragement and giving a signal that that is acceptable, then such a government is guilty by complicity...'[47]

[46] Cited in Timothy Golu, Raliat Ahmed and Nwakpa O. Nwakpa, 'West Africa: ECOWAS to Suspend Guinea, Holds Emergency Summit Friday', *Leadership*, 6 January, 2009. This article can be found at: http://allafrica.com/stories/200901060179.html.

[47] Golu, Ahmed, and Nwakpa, 'West Africa: ECOWAS to Suspend Guinea, Holds Emergency Summit Friday'.

The Nigerian position is significant since it marks a radical expansion of the zero-tolerance norm to include countries that 'fraternise' with coupists. Nigeria's suggestion that the AU should reprimand such countries adds a new and critical dimension to the evolving governance norms.

For its part, the AU initially responded by suspending Guinea from its Councils but like ECOWAS fell short of imposing sanctions. However, both institutions imposed an arms embargo and a travel ban on members of the junta following the killing of over 150 civilians, plus the wounding and disappearance of many more on 28 September 2009. Perhaps, the AU's initial reluctance to impose sanctions was in recognition of the democratic deficit that characterized Guinea under president Conté. Although both the AU and ECOWAS insisted on enforcing their norms, it was obvious that their response was tempered by pragmatism. Nonetheless, the isolation of the junta was critical as it helped to reinforce and further legitimize the policy positions of these organizations.

Meanwhile, ECOWAS' failure to convince president Conté to step aside, even after it was evident that he was incapable of running the country due to deteriorating health, manifested the limitations of the carrots and sticks at its disposal. The limitations are more pronounced in situations involving recalcitrant civilian heads of state. It was thus not surprising that the initial ECOWAS interventions in both Togo (2005) and Guinea (2007) were reactive, rather than proactive. That ECOWAS wielded a big 'stick' in its engagement in Togo and Guinea (2009); compared to its approach with late president Conte highlighted its limitations in dealing with entrenched civilian dictatorships.

ECOWAS in Niger

This challenge is starkly manifested by the standoff between ECOWAS and President Mamadu Tandja of Niger, who despite pressure from ECOWAS violated his country's constitution by allowing himself a third term through a discredited referendum. President Tandja's move contravened the ECOWAS norm prohibiting leaders from unconstitutionally extending their stay in power. ECOWAS suspended Niger from its councils and continued to demand that the president respects the country's constitution and the sub-regional norms it has acceded to. President Tandja's intransigence led to his subsequent ousting in a military coup on 15 February 2010. Although the military takeover was a violation of ECOWAS's zero-tolerance for unconstitutional change of government, it was widely accepted as a necessary step to pull Niger back from the brink. Adhering to its zero-tolerance norm, Niger remained suspended from the Council of ECOWAS as it called on the military junta to ensure a smooth and swift transition to constitutional rule.

The situation in Niger, like the one in Guinea, presented ECOWAS with two dilemmas. First, the country's civilian leadership was largely discredited due to the questionable means that President Tandja employed to prolong his stay in power beyond the two-term limit provided for by the country's constitution. Fearing the ripple effects of such unconstitutional behaviour by elected civilian leaders, ECOWAS was perhaps relieved that Tandja's rule was brought to an end, though it would have favoured more peaceful and constitutional means of doing so. Unfortunately, its mediation efforts had yielded limited results due to Tandja's intransigence. Second, despite its relief, ECOWAS was wary of doing anything that could be interpreted as support for the coup especially at a time when coup d'etats appeared to be making a comeback in the sub-region. The re-emergence of this trend would have profound negative consequences on the fledgling democratic norms in the sub-region, undermining ECOWAS's effort to develop and consolidate such norms in the sub-region.

President Tandja's attempt to perpetuate himself in power through a widely discredited referendum brought to the fore critical questions relating to unresolved tensions between national policies and sub-regional norms. At the heart of the dilemma is whether or what point sub-regional norms trump national policies. ECOWAS's position in Togo, Guinea, and Niger indicates its determination to enforce its norms especially when they conflict with discredited national processes. While ECOWAS has been successful in ensuring compliance among some of its smaller and weaker member states, the true test of its ability to enforce its norms would come when it involves one of its bigger and more powerful members such as Nigeria. But despite some obvious limitations as evidenced by the Niger and Guinea cases under Presidents Conté and Tandja, the fact that it succeeded in reversing several unconstitutional changes of government elsewhere in the sub-region by invoking its norms, and support for its decisions by its members and beyond underscores ECOWAS' growing legitimacy as a pivotal actor in developing and ensuring compliance with its norms.

SEEKING LEGITIMACY BEYOND ITS MEMBER STATES

In a bid to increase support for its actions and bolster its legitimacy, ECOWAS has increased its partnership with civil society in the sub-region and expanded its partnership with other international organizations, most notably, the African Union, European Union, and United Nations. ECOWAS' growing cooperation with civil society is a demonstration of its overarching aim of moving from an 'ECOWAS of States' to an 'ECOWAS of people' as espoused in its Strategic Vision 2020.[48] This dovetails with the normative shift from state security to a more people-centred security and breaks new ground given that ECOWAS's engagement with civil society was strictly limited during the first decade and a half of its existence. At the same time, its deeper cooperation with the AU and UN is relatively new. This cooperation is critical given the growing profile of the AU's Peace and Security Council (PSC) and the fact that the UN Security Council (UNSC) has the primary responsibility for maintaining international peace and security. But it is important for ECOWAS to tread carefully in its engagements with these organizations especially the UNSC, so that it is not viewed as a tool of the UNSC. ECOWAS should maintain its independence in its interaction with these institutions, and increase its engagement with civil society as that would undoubtedly enhance its legitimacy.

Cooperation with Civil Society

The emergence of an active network of civil society organizations (CSOs) on a range of issues from illicit weapons proliferation and governance is perhaps one of the most important linkages between ECOWAS and the public. These cross-border networks are a significant development because it is the first time since the inception of ECOWAS in 1975 that such networks have been involved in integration efforts. Integration schemes in Africa are often criticized for their state-centric focus often with limited consultation with ordinary citizens. The establishment of the West African Civil Society Forum (WACSOF), an umbrella organization for CSOs in the sub-region is a notable development in the emerging ECOWAS–civil society partnership. The objectives of WACSOF can be grouped into two broad categories: deepening the link between citizens of member states and the Organizations; and promoting and monitoring the implementation of ECOWAS's norms domestically.

WACSOF's activities revolve around six major thematic areas: democracy, good governance and human rights; peace and security; gender; youth; economic development; and food, agriculture and environment. These are closely aligned with ECOWAS's priority to ensure optimal complementarity.[49] ECOWAS has also partnered with the West Africa Network for Peace-building (WANEP) on a range of issues including the secondment of a WANEP official to work with the ECOWAS early warning and observation centre at the commission in Abuja. This

[48] For more information see, ECOWAS, *ECOWAS Vision 2020*, ECOWAS Summit, Abuja, Nigeria, June 2008.

[49] http://wacsof.net/aboutus.php.

was unique as it was the first instance of civil society embedding its staff within the ECOWAS Commission.[50]

The involvement of civil society has at least two key effects: first, the activities of these organizations have the potential of influencing government policy in other areas and could foster integration efforts more generally. It has contributed to raising awareness, sense of ownership, and legitimacy of the integration process. And second, it has the potential of serving as a check on governments by making sure they adhere to their sub-regional commitments. Deeper cooperation with civil society would help ECOWAS achieve its objective of creating an 'ECOWAS of people' by increasing the sense of cohesion among citizens of the sub-region. Such a development would allow for greater cooperation among West African civil society on economic, political and security issues. Cooperation on these issues would in the long-run contribute to rolling back the artificial boundaries that have contributed to impeding economic and political integration, the two long-term objectives of ECOWAS.

Cooperation with Other International Organizations

Internationally, the emerging division of labour between ECOWAS and key bi-lateral and multilateral actors, most notably the United Nations and the African Union (AU) indicates its legitimacy internationally. The UN and AU have been involved in conflict resolution programmes in partnership with ECOWAS over the past decade and a half.

In the early 1990s, the UN entered into various co-deployments, starting with the deployment of the United Nations Observer Mission in Liberia (UNOMIL) in 1993, alongside ECOMOG. The UN's first co-deployment in Liberia encountered serious difficulties such as the division of labour between the two parties, whereby ECOMOG provided security while UNOMIL was mandated to monitor implementation of the peace process, and the activities of ECOMOG. This marriage of convenience proved unworkable.[51] However, UNOMIL's deployment was seen as an opportunity to add transparency and legitimacy to the faltering peace process and bolster ECOMOG, which was viewed as partisan by some of the factions in the Liberian conflict. But UNOMIL's dependence on ECOMOG for security compromised its role.[52] The UN faced

[50] See also http://www.wanep.org/wanep/about-us-our-story/about-us.html.

[51] Shepard Forman and Andrew Grene, 'Collaborating with Regional Organizations', in David M. Malone (ed.), *The UN Security Council: From the Cold War to the 21st Century* (Boulder, Co.: Lynne Rienner, 2004), 294–305.

[52] See Clement Adibe, 'The Liberian conflict and the ECOWAS-UN partnership', *Third World Quarterly*, Vol. 3 (1997), 471–88.

similar challenges in neighbouring Sierra Leone when it deployed the United Nations Observer Mission in Sierra Leone (UNOMSIL) to monitor implementation of the peace process, and the activities of ECOMOG.

However, later partnerships between the two institutions in the area of conflict management have benefited from the lessons of the 1990s. In 2003, ECOWAS, working closely with the UNSC, deployed ECOMIL and ECOMICI to Liberia and Côte d'Ivoire, respectively. Unlike earlier partnerships, the UNSC's authorization of both deployments reinforced their legitimacy, and operationally provided ECOWAS with a clear exit strategy. In both cases, the ECOWAS deployments were short-term with clear timelines on when they would transition to UN-led missions. Here the division of labour was based on the comparative advantage of the two institutions, with ECOWAS providing the rapid reaction capability and the UN providing legitimacy and the logistic support.

Meanwhile, ECOWAS's partnership with the African Union (AU) on issues of peace and security has reinforced its legitimacy. For instance, a tri-lateral partnership involving ECOWAS, the AU, and UN has emerged in efforts to deal with the conflict in Côte d'Ivoire. Although ECOWAS continues to play a pivotal role in that country, it has been very strategic in ensuring that its actions are closely aligned with those of the AU. The partnership on this and other instances such as Guinea, Guinea-Bissau, Niger and more recently, Mali has undoubtedly bolstered its legitimacy, thereby strengthening its peacemaking efforts in the sub-region.

CONCLUSION

In the post-Cold War era, ECOWAS has developed a set of norms based on shared values to deal with the legitimacy questions that were precipitated by its first generation interventions in Liberia and Sierra Leone. Drawing on the lessons from its peace operations and the changing international landscape, ECOWAS has put in place robust mechanism, to deal with both inter and intra-state conflicts. It succeeded in doing so partly by institutionalizing decision-making mechanisms and broadening its understanding of security. The establishment of standing decision-making organs such as the Mediation and Security Council has bolstered ECOWAS' legitimacy since these institutions are seen as credible and representative of all member states. The legitimacy deficit that dogged the first generation interventions was due largely to questions about the mandate and authority of the ad hoc mechanism that authorized the interventions. The norms on the other hand, cover a broad spectrum of issues that are seen as important ingredients for sustainable security and development; issues that resonate across the sub-region.

The new security architecture is aimed at applying a non-military approach to security. The prohibition of the unconstitutional change of government either through military takeovers or fraudulent elections is one of the most innovative moves that have bolstered its standing with the civilian populations in its member states. While dealing with the issue of controversial elections is more problematic than undoing military takeovers, ECOWAS' deployment of election observers is proving to be a portent force since its pronouncements could legitimate or discredit a given electoral process. Through this process, ECOWAS is making a remarkable contribution to the improvement of the governance process in the region; thanks to its development of a robust rules-based system.

However, ECOWAS is still plagued by lack of coherence between policy proclamation and implementation. Lack of commitment by some leaders to the agreed norms undermines efforts to implement them, which in the long-run would erode ECOWAS' legitimacy with the civilian population. Publicly ECOWAS speaks with one voice, however, the actions of some of its member states speak differently. For instance, Senegal's embrace of the military junta in Guinea contradicted ECOWAS' zero-tolerance principle.

The analysis also demonstrates the crucial role that Nigeria continues to play in shaping the emerging security architecture. In spite of the controversy over its preponderant role in the region, its commitment of large human and financial resources demonstrates that, if applied properly, Nigeria's resources can be a force for stability. The establishment of a rules-based security regime could be interpreted as an attempt to address the unequal distribution of power, as Barry Buzan observes 'where this power (*in this case Nigeria*—my emphasis) is dominant, states pursue security primarily via establishment and maintenance of what they consider a suitable or stable distribution of power'.[53] While Nigeria's political and economic muscle is unmatched in the region, it is hoped that its influence will be checked by the emerging norms that it is helping to develop. That ECOWAS's legitimacy is rooted on a rules-based normative framework that is predicated on shared common values is its strongest source of legitimacy. However, the true test of its legitimacy would rest on how firmly and effectively it responds to recalcitrant civilian leaders bent on perpetuating themselves in power through unconstitutional means.

[53] Cited in David Lake and Patrick Morgan (eds.), *Regional Orders: Building Security in a New World* (University Park: Pennsylvania State University Press, 1997), 33.

6

Building the Legitimacy of the African Union:
An Evolving Continent and Evolving Organization

Walter Lotze[1]

The transformation of the Organization of African Unity (OAU) into the African Union (AU) in 2002 was based on the recognition that the OAU, founded to promote and protect the interests of newly independent African states during the Cold War era, could no longer adequately articulate and advance the interests of the rapidly evolving continent in the twenty-first century. In essence therefore, African countries recognized that the OAU could no longer serve as the legitimate voice of African states and their people, and that a new organization was required that could legitimately advance and protect the interests of a rapidly changing continent. Since 2002, the AU has worked to develop its legitimacy in the international system as the primary African organization promoting African interests. While the AU has worked to position itself as an actor in the realm of political unity, economic integration, and social upliftment, it is in the peace and security realm in particular that the organization has sought to assert itself as a relevant actor in African affairs. Indeed, over the course of the past decade significant political capital and financial resources have been invested by African states and international partners in the development of what has commonly been referred to as the African Peace and Security Architecture (APSA), and the AU has increasingly come to play a prominent, if not primary, role in conflict situations the continent over. Yet despite this flurry of activity in recent years, some observers have come to question the legitimacy of the AU, in particular when it comes to addressing conflict situations on the continent. While the role of the AU

[1] The views and opinions expressed in this article are those of the author, and not necessarily those of the African Union.

in response to some conflict situations, such as in Burundi (2004 onwards), Sudan (2004 onwards), and Somalia (2007 onwards) is generally recognized as being positive, in other instances the organization has been widely criticized for failing to act in a meaningful and consistent manner. Indeed, in recent years, the AU's role in addressing some conflict situations, such as in Côte d'Ivoire (2011), Libya (2011), and Mali (2012) has proved controversial, both among the organization's partners, but more importantly, also among its member states.

On the basis of the theoretical framework developed earlier in the book, this chapter will investigate the legitimation practices of the AU as an actor in the realm of international peace and security. In particular, the chapter will investigate the manner in which the organization has since 2002, when it replaced the OAU, sought to develop its legitimacy, both vis-à-vis its member states and other actors in the international community, and the practices in which it has engaged to assert and sustain that legitimacy. In this regard, if focuses on three dimensions of legitimacy: first, the extent to which legitimacy is generated through the character of the AU's decision-making processes and the character of its interventions into the affairs of its member states; second, on the role of shared substantive values in justifying the organization's authority; and third, its expertise and ability to advance common goals of its member states. It will do that through the analysis of three aspects: first, the transition from the OAU to the AU; second the organizational structure of the AU; and third, the issue of financing. Building on this analysis, the chapter will move to assess the manner in which the AU has acted in response to particular threats to peace and security on the African continent since its inception, and the manner in which it has asserted legitimacy claims in relation to other organizations in this regard. On the basis of this analysis, the chapter will develop observations with regards to the ability of the AU to legitimize itself by persuading other actors of the unique contribution that it can make to peace and security in Africa.

FROM THE OAU TO THE AU

The founding of the OAU in Addis Ababa, Ethiopia, in 1963 represented the desire of African states to bind themselves into a multilateral arrangement on the basis of common norms and values, and to provide a common political platform that would provide legitimacy to the articulation of common African interests in international relations. The creation of the OAU during the period of decolonization was of course not an uncontested process, and while the establishment of the organization was crucial to processes of security norm socialization in Africa, the question of which norms would govern the workings of the new organization proved a contentious matter. A delicate balancing-act between the competing interests of its member-states would be required if the OAU should become, in Ethiopian Emperor Haile Selassie's words, 'a single institution to which we will all belong, based on principles to which we all subscribe'.[2] In the end, the dominant understanding underpinning the establishment of the OAU was that the organization should work to preserve and defend the borders being established through the process of decolonization, and to foster a sense of nationalism within each state. This understanding was later enshrined in the 1964 Cairo Declaration, and was reinforced through the membership of African states in the United Nations (UN). Thus, Article 3 of the OAU's charter provided the foundations for a collective African security regime that rested on four main principles; namely (1) that imperialism represented a principle obstacle to African unity and that the continent should work to address its own challenges, (2) that the sovereign equality of states was an inviolable norm and that the OAU and African states should work on the basis of consensus, (3) that, on the basis of sovereign equality, intervention in the affairs of member states was not permissible, and (4) that, on the basis of the principle of *uti possideitis,* state borders were inviolable.[3]

While these principles served the organization relatively well throughout the period of decolonization and the Cold War, by the 1990s the OAU was found to be less relevant, unable as it was to address the changing nature of conflict situations across the continent or to meet the aspirations of its member states, many of which had now become democracies and expected the OAU to advance, at least at face value, notions of democratization, economic liberalism, and human rights. Indeed, in matters of peace and security, the OAU had come to be known for its approach of non-intervention in the domestic affairs of its member states. In the 1970s, as Africa witnessed the rise of several regimes with highly problematic human-rights records (Idi Amin in Uganda, Mengistu Haile Meriam in Ethiopia, and Kwame Nkrumah in Ghana, to name but a few), the organization remained silent. In fact, as the Chairmanship of the OAU rotated amongst member states, most of these leaders also chaired the organization at some point in time during their rule. The prevailing Cold War dynamics further served to ensure that no external pressure was placed either on these regimes or on the OAU. Indeed, neither the West nor the Soviet Union displayed any inclination to criticize their real or potential partners in Africa, and continued to provide the resources necessary for their client regimes to remain in power. It was thus with the direct support of the United States that Mobutu Sese Seko in Zaire and Samuel Doe in Liberia were able to routinely suppress internal dissent, often violently so.[4] The political will to

[2] Paul Williams, 'From Non-Intervention to Non-Indifference: The Origins and Development of the African Union's Security Culture', *African Affairs,* Vol. 106/423 (2007), 263.

[3] Williams, 'From Non-intervention to Non-indifference', 264–5.

[4] John Akokpari, 'Introduction: Human Rights Actors and Institutions in Africa' in John Akokpari, and Daniel Shea Zimbler (eds.), *Africa's Human Rights Architecture* (Auckland Park: Fanele, 2008), 2–3.

criticize such actions did not exist within the OAU at the time, and where states may have felt the inclination to criticize others, silence was maintained through the fear of counter-accusations, as hardly any African country could claim to uphold a positive human-rights record during this time.[5] It became increasingly clear to observers, both within and outside the African continent, that the initial wave of security thinking on the African continent had come to be dominated, at least at the level of the OAU, by what would be labelled as a paradigm of 'indifference'.[6]

Increasingly, African states sought to change the manner in which matters of peace and security in particular were addressed at a continental level. In 1991, the Conference on Security, Stability, Development and Cooperation in Africa (CSSDCA) was launched in Kampala to accelerate progress on security and development in Africa. The Conference set out core values that African governments were expected to uphold, including a wide understanding of security encompassing not only military considerations but all other economic, political, and social aspects affecting individuals, the family, community, and the nation.[7] Importantly, the CSSDCA articulated the first notion of what would later become known as 'human security', preceding even the 1994 United Nations Development Programme (UNDP) Human Development Report which many credit with having concretized the concept. This attempt at articulating a new definition of security in Africa, argues Eboe Hutchful, was an effort at decoupling security and sovereignty from one another, and reflected the changing nature of challenges being faced on the continent. In July 1999, the CSSDCA process was endorsed at the OAU summit in Algeria.[8]

A further development which highlighted the changing approach to continental peace and security was the signing of the Abuja Treaty in 1991, creating the African Economic Community (AEC) which formally came into existence in May 1994, and which provided for the establishment of the Pan-African Parliament. The same year, South Africa held its first democratic elections, and the remainder of the 1990s witnessed what appeared to be a revival of democracy throughout Africa. Indeed, by the end of the 1990s, multi-party elections were taking place in over 30 countries across the continent.[9] Increasingly, it

[5] Jeremy Sarkin, 'Humanitarian Intervention and the Responsibility to Protect in Africa' in John Akokpari and Daniel Shea Zimbler (eds.), *Africa's Human Rights Architecture* (Auckland Park: Fanele, 2008), 45–6.

[6] Ben Kioko, 'The Right of Intervention under the African Union's Constitutive Act: From Non-Interference to Non-Intervention', *International Review of the Red Cross*, Vol. 852 (2003), 807–24.

[7] Musifiky Mwanasali, 'From Non-Interference to Non-Indifference: The Emerging Doctrine of Conflict Prevention in Africa' in John Akokpari, et al., *The African Union and its Institutions* (Auckland Park: Fanele, 2008), 49.

[8] Eboe Hutchful, 'From Military Security to Human Security' in John Akokpari, et al., *The Africian Union and its Institutions* (Auckland Park: Fanele, 2008), 76.

[9] Kay Mathews, 'Renaissance of Pan-Africanism: the AU and the New Pan-Africanists' in John Akokpari, et al., *The African Union and its Institutions* (Auckland Park: Fanele, 2008), 32–3.

appeared as though the OAU was out of touch with, or even failing, its members. In his address to the 29th Ordinary Session of the Assembly of Heads of State and Government of the OAU held in Cairo in June 1993, Eritrean President Isaias Aferwerki, vexed perhaps by the reluctance of the OAU to intervene in the conflict between his country and Ethiopia (the seat of the OAU), accused the organization of failing the people of Africa and the people of Eritrea, and argued that it was a 'useless' organization.[10]

Fearing being sidelined, the OAU in 1993 established the Mechanism for Conflict Prevention, Management and Resolution, designed to address the increasingly complex conflict situations being faced on the continent. The Mechanism, however, was quickly criticized for failing to live up to its promise.[11] Indeed, many conflicts never reached the central organ of the Mechanism, or were discussed but never engaged with formally, as the member state involved refused to have the matter taken up by the OAU. Furthermore, heads of state tended not to criticize one another publicly, reinforcing the notion even in the 1990s that the OAU was nothing more than a 'Heads of State Club'.[12] During the 1994 summit in Tunis, South African President Nelson Mandela was the first to speak out publicly, criticizing his peers and the OAU as a whole for failing to be relevant or to act decisively during the Rwandan genocide, still ongoing at the time of the summit.[13] Increasingly, states such as Nigeria, Libya, Senegal, and South Africa began to call for reform within the OAU, arguing that the changing nature of conflict in the post-Cold War era necessitated a changed response from the continental body.[14]

As debates around good governance, transparency, human rights, and democratization intensified throughout the 1990s, these were increasingly linked to efforts aimed at conflict prevention on the African continent. During the Harare summit in June 1997 and again the Algiers summit in July 1999, debate came to centre on whether or not the OAU should be vested with a right of intervention in the internal affairs of member states to protect human rights and constitutional order. Gradually a consensus emerged around the notion of 'sovereignty as responsibility'.[15] Then, at an OAU summit convened specifically to make the organization more relevant in September 1999, Libyan President Muammar Ghadaffi presented his vision of a United States of Africa,

[10] Kioko, 'The Right of Intervention', 813.

[11] Evarist Baimu, and Kathryn Sturman, 'Amendment to the African Union's Right to Intervene—A Shift from Human Security to Regime Security?' *African Security Review*, Vol. 12/2 (2003), 40.

[12] Kioko, 'The Right of Intervention', 814.

[13] Sarjoh Bah, *Dilemmas of Regional Peacemaking: The Dynamics of the AU's Response to Darfur* (Centre on International Cooperation: New York, 2010), 7.

[14] Bah, *Dilemmas of Regional Peacemaking: The Dynamics of the AU's Response to Darfur*, 7.

[15] Musifiky Mwanasali, 'Africa's Responsibility to Protect' in A. Adebajo and H. Scanlon (eds.), *A Dialogue of the Deaf—Essay on Africa and the United Nations* (Auckland Park: Fanele, 2006), 90.

an arguably grandiose vision for the continent complete with a unified defence capability, a single currency, and a powerful central leadership. Following heated exchanges, African states agreed to a process of transitioning the OAU into the AU, of negotiating a new Constitutive Act, and of strengthening the scope and mandate of the organization.[16] By July 2000, discussions on the work of the new AU had been completed, and during the Lomé summit that month the Constitutive Act of the African Union was adopted. The AU was inaugurated in Durban, South Africa, in June 2002, replacing the OAU 39 years after its founding.

Through the drafting and adoption of the new Constitutive Act, member states were able to legitimate the AU in two ways. First, the organization based itself on a set of shared values and principles that member states agreed on to guide their interaction with one another under the auspices of the AU. Second, procedurally it vested the organization with decision-making powers over a range of substantive matters. Key to the further legitimation of the organization however, in particular with regards to peace and security, was the subsequent development of what has commonly come to be known as the APSA.

THE DEVELOPMENT OF THE AFRICAN PEACE AND SECURITY ARCHITECTURE

The Constitutive Act of the African Union tasked the organization with a range of objectives related to the political, social, and economic integration of the African continent, the promotion and advancement of human rights, regional integration, good governance, sustainable development, and the promotion and defence of common African positions in the international system. Yet the radical departures from the OAU were to be seen in the strength of the peace and security mandate vested in the new AU. Already as the transition from the OAU to the AU was being prepared, it became evident that the former principles of non-intervention and sovereign inviolability were coming under assault. Through the late 1990s, the OAU began to play a role in mediation efforts in the Democratic Republic of the Congo (DRC) and Côte d'Ivoire, and in 2000 the OAU had adopted the Declaration Framework for an OAU Response to Unconstitutional Changes of Government.[17]

The AU, it seemed, was going to provide a far more interventionist peace and security architecture than its predecessor, something clearly reflected by the new Constitutive Act, and something for which the majority of its member

[16] Baimu, and Sturman, 'Amendment to the African Union's Right to Intervene', 38.

[17] Sarkin, 'Humanitarian Intervention and the Responsibility to Protect in Africa', 46–9.

states were strongly calling. To reinforce this notion, the first ordinary session of the Assembly of the AU, held in Durban on 9 July 2002, adopted the *Protocol Relating to the Establishment of the Peace and Security Council of the African Union* (commonly referred to as the PSC Protocol). The Protocol led to the creation of the African Union Peace and Security Council (PSC) and its supporting structures, and defined its modalities for action. The Council would replace the defunct Central Organ of the Mechanism for Conflict Prevention, Management and Resolution and would be the central decision-making organ for the prevention, management, and resolution of conflicts. It would be complemented by the work of other actors in the fields of peace and security, namely the Assembly of Heads of State and Government, the Executive Council of the AU, the Pan-African Parliament, the Chairperson of the AU Commission and the relevant Departments and Divisions within the Commission, the Panel of the Wise, the African Standby Force (ASF), and the Military Staff Committee (MSC).

The strongly interventionist stance of the AU appeared to have the solid backing of the organization's member states, and already during its first year of existence, the PSC would come to hold more sessions than its predecessor, the Central Organ of the Mechanism for Conflict Prevention, Management and Resolution, had held in its ten years of existence.[18] In 2004, with the Panel of the Wise and the Pan-African Parliament established, the *Common African Defence and Security Policy* adopted, the ASF rapidly being developed, and the PSC commencing regular sessions, it appeared certain that the AU would come to play a far more prominent role in peace and security on the African continent in the years to come.

Following the establishment of the PSC, attention was turned towards developing the mechanisms of intervention which would give both life and meaning to an interventionist African security regime. Thus, while the PSC was left to find and assert its own role in the security politics of the continent and the international system more broadly, tremendous financial and human effort were exerted to give meaning to the intervention mechanisms at the disposal of the Council and the African Union Commission (AUC). In particular, the AU prioritized the development of the Panel of the Wise, of a mediation support capacity in the Peace and Security Department of the Commission, of the Continental Early Warning System (CEWS), of the PSC Secretariat, of the ASF, and of a Post-Conflict Reconstruction and Development (PCRD) Framework. Indeed, what has come to be known as the APSA consists of a number of key interconnected components that are concerned with political decision-making (the Peace and Security Council), the gathering and analysis of information (the Continental Early Warning System), an advisory capacity (the Panel

[18] Mwanasali, 'From Non-interference to Non-indifference', 44.

of the Wise), peace support operations capacity (the ASF and Military Staff Committee), peacebuilding (the PCRD framework), and financial capacity (the Africa Peace Fund). In essence, with the procedural and shared values dimensions of legitimacy having been established through the adoption of the new Constitutive Act and the creation of the APSA, attention was now turned to addressing the expertise and effectiveness dimensions of legitimacy through the establishment of the operational arms of the APSA, providing the AU with the ability to implement the decisions of its member states.

Despite the significant progress made to date to give operational meaning to the APSA however, numerous challenges persist, and the utility of these mechanisms to the PSC, and to the Commission of the African Union more broadly, remains somewhat limited. Considerable effort has for example gone into the development of the CEWS, and while a level of operational capability has been attained, the utility of the CEWS to the work of the Peace and Security Department, the AU Commission more broadly, and into the decision-making processes of the PSC is not yet clear. In addition, AU member states, especially from North Africa, have proved reluctant to have the system monitor them, impacting on the overall utility of a continental early warning system. Further, the information gathered by the CEWS to date has not systematically fed into the decision-making of the PSC, or into the planning processes of the Commission when responding to emerging crisis situations.

The development of the Panel of the Wise has also received much attention in the past few years. The first members of the Panel were appointed in July 2007, with five members, each holding three-year terms and representing the five security regions, being appointed. In its initial meetings, the Panel adopted criteria to guide its engagements in crisis situations, yet despite the engagement of the Panel in several crises, the work of the Panel has received mixed results to date, and the function of the Panel itself remains unclear.[19] While some observers would argue that the Panel represents a mediation tool for the PSC, others would argue that the Panel can best be used as a mechanism for good offices and behind-the-scenes facilitation, but not in instances where the AU Commission is requested to assist in mediation efforts. In December 2010 the Panel entered its second term, with two members retaining their seats and three new members being appointed. The work of the Panel in its second term will be key to understanding how it fits into the overall APSA framework, and how the operations of the Panel link both to the work of the PSC and the Peace and Security Department overall.

The operationalization of the MSC has also proved problematic to date. Originally the MSC was intended to serve as an advisory body to the PSC on

[19] Tim Murithi, and Charles Mwaura, 'The Panel of the Wise' in Ulf Engel and Jao Gomes Porto (eds.), *Africa's New Peace and Security Architecture—Promoting Norms, Institutionalising Solutions* (Ashgate: Farnham, 2010), 83–4.

peacekeeping matters, composed of the military attaches of the members of the Council. However, the MSC has not yet become operational, and indeed has so far been replaced by the establishment of various ad hoc committees in response to particular conflict situations, and responsibility for its development has been shifted backwards and forwards between the PSC Secretariat and the Peace Support Operations Division (PSOD). The MSC has therefore not yet proved a valuable support mechanism for the decision-making of the PSC or the work of the AU more broadly.

The ASF has perhaps been the APSA mechanism that has witnessed the most progress over the past few years, with the AU becoming incrementally more adept at planning and deploying peace support operations, such as in Burundi, Darfur, Somalia, and Mali and drawing the Regional Economic Communities (RECs) and Regional Mechanisms (RMs) together under the ASF concept. However, progress has repeatedly been stalled, and whereas the ASF was to have attained Full Operating Capability (FOC) by 2010, that timeline has been pushed back to 2015. Thus, while notable progress has been attained to date, the full development of the ASF has consistently been delayed, due primarily to resource constraints, but also in part to political wrangling over whether the ASF should represent a multi-dimensional peace support operations capability, or a reincarnation of the Standing African Army once promoted primarily by the North African states.

The development of the PCRD work of the AU has also been slow to date. While the AU adopted a *Post-Conflict Reconstruction and Development Policy Framework* in 2006, moving beyond the policy framework to implementation has proved challenging. A PCRD Unit has been established in the Peace and Security Department, and post-conflict needs assessment missions have to date been conducted in Liberia, Sierra Leone, the Democratic Republic of the Congo, Burundi, Sudan, and South Sudan. However, by the end of 2012 only some reports of these missions had been presented to the PSC for endorsement and decision-making. In addition, in 2006 the decision was taken to establish a Standing Multidimensional Committee on PCRD, bringing together various departments in the AU Commission, member states, and members of civil society to monitor post-conflict situations in Africa and to generate recommendations for action to the PSC. To date, however, the Committee has not been established, nor has the system of African Union Volunteers (AUV), which is similar to the United Nations Volunteers (UNV) mechanism but specifically aimed at post-conflict reconstruction and development deployments.

Overall, the development of the APSA mechanisms has to date been uneven, and this has impacted on the degree to which the AU has been able to develop legitimacy over the course of the past decade. On the one hand, while the AU has been able to develop legitimacy through establishing shared beliefs about the ends towards which power should be exercised, as witnessed through the adoption of the Constitutive Act and key policy frameworks on peace and security, the uneven development and utilization of the APSA mechanisms has undermined the degree of effectiveness the organization has had in implementing the decisions of its member states on the basis of these policy decisions. In essence, the ability of the AU to achieve the desired outcomes of its member states has at times served to undermine the institutional legitimacy of the organization, witnessed for instance in the organization's responses to conflicts in Côte d'Ivoire and in Libya in 2011.[20] Further, it can also be argued that the weaknesses which exist in the APSA have also impacted negatively on the structural legitimacy of the AU, with both member states and AU partners questioning the degree to which the organization is able to fulfil the functions with which it is vested. Viewed from another perspective, whereas the shared values and procedural dimensions of legitimation appear to have been addressed through the creation of the AU and the adoption of a set of policy frameworks to address peace and security matters on the African continent (in other words, member states have vested the organization with certain responsibilities and powers, and adhere to the decision-making processes of the organization), the uneven development and utilization of the APSA mechanisms to date have highlighted weaknesses in the AU's ability to develop its output legitimacy. Compounding these challenges at developing legitimacy has been the overwhelming financial dependence of the AU not on its member states, but on external partners.

LEGITIMACY AND THE FINANCING OF THE AU

Since its establishment in 2002, the AU has operated on the basis of limited financial contributions on the part of its member states, and has in effect maintained its operations on the basis of financial contributions from external partners. In the negotiation period leading up to the establishment of the AU, a decision was taken that five states (Algeria, Egypt, Libya, Nigeria, and South Africa) would contribute 75% (thus 15% each) of the Commission's annual operating budget, while the remaining 49 Member States would contribute the remaining 25%. In reality however, many member states often do not make any financial contributions to the AU, and where these are made, they are extremely limited. The contributions of some member states, for instance, are insufficient to cover the salary of a single mid-level AU official for a one year period. In previous years, this shortfall was covered by voluntary contributions by some states, such as Libya, yet such arrangements have proved

[20] With regards to Côte d'Ivoire, see Walter Lotze, 'A Tale of Two Councils—The African Union, the United Nations and the Protection of Civilians in Côte d'Ivoire', *Global Responsibility to Protect*, Vol. 3/3 (2011), 365–75.

unreliable. The conflict in Libya in 2011, for instance, placed great financial strain on the AU, as the financial contribution of Libya and by default many other member states was not forthcoming. The operating budget of the AU Commission thus decreased between 2011 and 2012, forcing the organization to make significant budget cuts.

Compounding this situation is that the operational budget of the AU Commission for its programmes and activities has in recent years been funded more by external partners than by member states, with budgetary contributions on average amounting to 40% from member states and 60% from external partners for any given Department in the Commission. In some years this balance is even further skewed. In 2012, for instance, 3% of the programmes of the organization were funded by member states, while 97% of programmes were funded by partners. The ability of the organization to implement its programmes was also extremely limited, with only 40% of the organization's annual programmatic budget having been spent by October 2012.[21]

This situation is even more aggravated with regards to the peace and security work of the organization, which is funded almost exclusively by external partners, either through direct budgetary contributions to the AU, or by means of bilateral arrangements. The operating budget of the Peace and Security Department on average receives only 10% of its resources from member states, and 90% from partners in any given year. The development of the Africa Peace Fund (or Special Fund), designed to provide financial backing for the peace and security work of the AU, has proved extremely challenging. The Fund, which was intended to finance the activities of the APSA, in particular peace support operations, remains largely devoid of the financial resources it was intended to manage. Indeed, most members of the AU, including many members of the PSC, do not contribute the required financial resources to the Fund, leaving the AU largely reliant on support from external partners, in particular the European Union (EU), through its Africa Peace Facility (APF), as well as bilateral partners such as the US, Germany, the UK, and Canada, both for the conduct of its daily work and the implementation of its activities.

The APF has to date been the biggest contributor. It was provided with €250 million by the EU between 2003 and 2007, 80% of which was utilized to fund peace support operations.[22] In June 2008 the EU allocated a further €300 million to the APF from its 10th Economic Development Fund (EDF) for the period 2008 through 2010. In reality these funds were quite limited for African peace support operations, as the annual operating budget of AMISOM in 2011 was estimated at $800 million (in contrast UNAMID's operating budget in 2009 alone was estimated at approximately $1.7 billion,

[21] Presentation made by H.E. Erastus Mwencha, Deputy Chairperson of the AU Commission. October 2012.

[22] The AMIS budget was drawn almost exclusively from the APF.

although this is covered by assessed contributions via the UN). The AU has thus remained financially dependent in its peace support operations on the EU, the US, the UK, and Canada, which funded the bulk of operations in Burundi, Darfur, and Somalia. With regards to Somalia, the African Union Mission in Somalia (AMISOM) was almost entirely reliant on the UN for logistical support, covered by assessed contributions from UN member states, for its operations from 2009 onwards. Even in terms of its physical infrastructure, the AU remains quite dependent on external partners. The German government, for example, has funded the construction of a new building for the PSC and for the Peace and Security Department, while the Chinese government had paid for the construction of an impressive new Secretariat building for the Commission, which was inaugurated in 2012.[23]

As emphasized in the Prodi report,[24] if the AU remains reliant on unpredictable funding sources there is a danger that essential capabilities may not be available when required. This serves, for instance, to dissuade potential contributors to peace support operations, when there is little guarantee that they will be duly reimbursed for their contributions. Indeed, in the past many African countries appeared more willing to contribute to UN missions than to AU missions, as these compensated better financially, though this situation was ameliorated in 2011 when the AU adjusted its compensation terms to those of the UN. Even where member states have been willing to contribute, gaining financial reimbursement can prove challenging. It was only in 2011, for instance, that a Memorandum of Understanding was entered into between the AU Commission and South Africa outlining modalities for the reimbursement of expenses incurred by the South African Government for its deployment in Burundi from the early 2000s onwards.

Thus, while external funding can serve to meet needs in the interim, this does not necessarily lead to a long term development of resources and capacity. While the Africa Peace Fund was established to address this challenge, and to lessen reliance on external partners, most member states do not make the necessary contributions, serving to further jeopardize overall institutional effectiveness, and increasing reliance of the AU on external partner funding.[25] Further, while contributions to the Africa Peace Fund are a pre-requisite for

[23] See Ulf Engel and Jao Gomes Porto, 'Africa's New Peace and Security Architecture: An Introduction' in Ulf Engel and Jao Gomes Porto (eds.), *Africa's New Peace and Security Architecture—Promoting Norms, Institutionalising Solutions* (Farnham: Ashgate, 2010), 4; and Jakkie Cilliers and Johann Pottgieter, 'The African Standby Force' in Ulf Engel and Jao Gomes Porto (eds.), Africa's New Peace and Security Architecture (Farnham: Ashgate, 2010), 130–7.

[24] United Nations General Assembly. *Report of the African Union—United Nations Panel on Modalities for Support to African Union Peacekeeping Operations* UN doc. 2008.A/63/666–S/2008/813, New York, 31 December 2008.

[25] Yvonne Kasumba, and Charles Debrah, 'An Overview of the African Standby Force (ASF)', in Cedric De Coning and Yvonne Kasumba (eds.), *The Civilian Dimension of the African Standby Force* (Addis Ababa: African Union Commission, 2010), 19.

membership in the PSC, in practice this consideration has rarely been followed. Despite these financial constraints, the AU has not made use of Article 21 of the PSC Protocol, which would enable the Commission to defray the cost of peace support operations to member states on the basis of their contributions to the regular budget of the Union.[26] Part of the challenge is of course that only five member states would be requested to contribute 75% of the budget of peace support operations.

This reliance on external financial support has served to significantly constrain the legitimation efforts of the AU, as the organization is required to gain and maintain the legitimacy both of its member states and of external partners simultaneously to function. In certain instances where political agendas align neatly, such as in Burundi or Darfur, this poses few challenges. In others however, such as in Somalia, Côte d'Ivoire, or Libya, this poses significant challenges. The EU, for instance, was unwilling to provide financial resources to the AU to pursue its own agenda in Libya, constraining the ability of the organization to implement the decisions of the PSC. More importantly however, the unwillingness of AU member states to make the required financial contributions to the organization indicates a lack of legitimacy on the part of the AU in the eyes of its member states. West African states, which make generous financial contributions to the Economic Community of West African States (ECOWAS), and Southern African states, which fund the operations of the Southern African Development Community (SADC) to date appear largely unwilling to make the same level of financial commitment to the AU. External actors, on the other hand, appear to view the AU as the legitimate representative of African values and interests, and as the most legitimate regional security mechanism, and therefore continue to provide significant financial assistance, even when the organization's own member states will not. This situation represents a growing legitimacy crisis for the AU, as its efforts to legitimate its role through effectively addressing shared normative concerns are largely reliant on the willingness of external partners to provide the financial resources to do so.

This situation also impacts on the AU's ability to legitimate itself through performance in other ways. The AU Commission in 2011 was staffed by approximately 700 personnel; far fewer than the UN Secretariat or the EU Commission for instance. Funding constraints and the limitations placed on the authorized staffing levels by member states mean that the Commission has remained chronically understaffed. The development of the ASF, for instance, is the task of approximately 30 AU staff, which in 2012 were simultaneously responsible for the management of the AU's ongoing peace support operations in Darfur (the African Union–United Nations Mission in Darfur, UNAMID),

[26] Cilliers, and Pottgieter, 'The African Stand-By Force', 130.

Somalia (the African Union Mission in Somalia, AMISOM), and the Regional Cooperation Initiative against the Lord's Resistance Army (RCI LRA) in the central African region, as well as the planning for potential new operations in Mali and the Eastern DRC.

The same challenge has been encountered, by way of another example, by the PSC Secretariat, which is staffed by just five personnel. The Secretariat is responsible for servicing the regular meetings of the PSC, yet due to resource and personnel constraints is just able to facilitate the bi-weekly meetings of the Council, and the Commission to date has not fully been in a position to facilitate meetings of the Council members at a technical level, or to assist in the preparation of regular policy papers or technical inputs to assist in the decision-making of the Council. Indeed, the Communiqués of the Council are not prepared by the member states in advance, but are prepared by the Commission and circulated during the Council's deliberations for endorsement, as the PSC's Drafting Committee has not yet been established. This means that member states are technically not responsible for the drafting of Communiqués, but more for the endorsement of decisions. Similarly, these resource constraints, and the consensus-style decision-making of the Council, mean that no records of Council deliberations are maintained. Unlike the UN Security Council, where detailed records of meetings and decision-making are kept, only the Communiqués and Press Statements of the PSC are made publicly available, with deliberations and decision-making taking place behind closed doors. This can be viewed as detracting from the accountability and transparency of the Council.

This situation has been compounded in other areas of work as well. The Mediation Unit in the AU in 2012 consisted of 1 staff member, the PCRD Unit consisted of 3 personnel, and the AU had only two staff members dealing with human rights matters. The ability of the organization to implement the decisions of its member states, in other words its ability to support its legitimacy claims with actions, has therefore remained quite limited.

Overall, the AU's reliance on external financial support has elevated the importance of its external audience for legitimacy claims above what could otherwise have been expected, and in certain instances it could even be said that the organization is more reliant on its external audience for legitimation than on its internal audience, its own member states. While this situation has not always proved problematic, in certain instances this does serve to create tensions between the organization's membership and those supporting it through financial assistance. Unfortunately, as the AU at present cannot survive without such external financial assistance, this tension appears set to remain for some time to come, and the AU's legitimation efforts will likely continue to be characterized by these tensions for the foreseeable future.

ASSESSING THE AU'S FIRST DECADE OF ENGAGEMENT

As has been noted above, several challenges have impacted on the ability of the AU to establish its legitimacy in the realm of peace and security on the African continent. These range from resource constraints (both in terms of financial and human resources) to procedural weaknesses, such as a perceived lack of transparency of the PSC. Despite these constraints however, the AU can be credited to a large degree with establishing shared values among its member states, in that African states continue to work through the organization to address threats to peace and security on the continent, and continue to vest decision-making power in the organs of the organization, in particular the PSC. Further, the AU Commission has steadily been developing substantive technical expertise, providing it with increasing legitimacy vis-à-vis its member states. Therefore, despite the serious constraints placed on the organization, it could generally be said that the AU has been relatively successful in developing legitimacy through the procedural and shared values dimensions, and is likely to continue to do so by slowly developing the working methodology of the PSC, by promoting shared values and approaches among its membership, and by investing in the human resource capacity of the Commission. However, the ability of the organization to legitimate itself by persuading both its members and external audiences that it is the 'right' organization to address challenges to peace and security in Africa has not always been automatic. In addition to the organizational challenges highlighted above, it is important to understand how the efforts of the AU to legitimate itself have been impacted on in recent years through an analysis of its responses to a few specific conflict situations, namely Burundi, Darfur, Somalia, the Comoros, Côte d'Ivoire, and Libya. The following section will present a brief assessment of the manner in which the AU has worked to enhance its legitimacy through offering effective responses to conflict situations in Africa over the course of the past decade, and similarly the manner in which it has sought to persuade other actors in the international system of its legitimacy.

The AU had become involved in the conflict in Burundi from 1996 onwards, when regional states, led by Tanzania, commenced with the lengthy negotiations of a peace accord which culminated in the signing of the Arusha peace agreement in 2000. Already in April 2003 the Central Organ of the Mechanism for Conflict Prevention, Management and Resolution of the AU (the Peace and Security Council was only launched in 2004) mandated the deployment of the African Union Mission to Burundi (AMIB) to monitor the partial ceasefire brokered the previous year, the first fully-fledged peace support operation of the AU. AMIB, which commenced operations in May 2003, represented a compromise to support the ailing peace process. As one observer noted, while the 2000 Arusha Agreement originally called for a UN peacekeeping operation to assist with the implementation of the peace agreement, the UN would not authorize a mission in the absence of a comprehensive ceasefire agreement.[27]

Therefore, the AU, regional leaders, and the Burundian parties agreed to the deployment of AMIB for an initial period of one year. At full capacity, AMIB consisted of 3,335 troops from South Africa, Ethiopia, and Mozambique, with additional military observers from Burkina Faso, Gabon, Mali, Togo, and Tunisia. AMIB comprised both a political component and a military contingent, and was designed primarily to verify the implementation of the ceasefire agreement and provide protection for the transitional government.[28] The AU, not even fully operational, was already displaying its eagerness to become actively engaged in the maintenance of peace and security on the continent, and to flex its muscles in the realm of peacekeeping. AMIB operated until 2004, when, after a degree of stability had been established, it was converted into the United Nations Mission in Burundi, known by its French acronym ONUB (*Operation des Nations Unies au Burundi*). While AMIB was generally poorly resourced, and was criticized for not deploying sufficient troops to provide meaningful protection to the civilian population, which bore the brunt of the conflict, the AU intervention did succeed in providing the degree of security required for a UN deployment, and in guaranteeing the level of security required for political leaders to commence with the implementation of the Arusha agreement. The intervention in Burundi also demonstrated the political willingness of the new AU to intervene in conflict situations, and the willingness of its member states to provide the necessary resources, including military muscle, to give operational meaning to the AU's political ambitions.

The next AU intervention came in Darfur when the organization deployed a mission to monitor a ceasefire agreement which had been brokered between the Government of Sudan and armed movements engaged in a conflict in that region. Following the signing of a Humanitarian Ceasefire Agreement for Darfur in April 2004, the AU in August of that year deployed the African Union Mission in Sudan (AMIS), tasked with monitoring and supporting the implementation of the ceasefire agreement. Upon initial deployment, the AU mission consisted of fewer than 100 observers, however, recognizing the gravity of the situation, the AU increased the AMIS presence to include troops, police and, gradually, civilians, and by 2005 the force had been increased to over 7,000. While a transition into a UN operation had been planned for September 2006, this was postponed to January 2008, when AMIS was

[27] Kristiana Powell, *Opportunities and Challenges for Delivering on the Responsibility to Protect: The African Union's Emerging Peace and Security Regime* (Ottawa: The North-South Institute, 2005).

[28] Henri Boshoff, H. and Dara Francis, 'The AU Mission in Burundi: Technical and Operational Dimensions', *African Security Review*, Vol. 12/3 (2003), 41–4.

transitioned from an AU operation into a hybrid AU/UN operation, known as the African Union/United Nations Mission in Darfur (UNAMID).[29] While the AU did succeed in establishing a presence on the ground when the UN could not, and in maintaining political engagement with the Government of Sudan when relations between Sudan and the UN and EU deteriorated to the point of stalemate, AMIS was criticized for being under-resourced to address the security threat posed to humanitarian agencies, and in particular the civilian population, which was being targeted directly both by the Government of Sudan and the armed movements. Despite these shortcomings however, the AU once again displayed a willingness to intervene in a conflict situation when the UN was not able or willing to do so, and to place its troops in the line of fire in an effort to establish a limited degree of stability, paving the way for a joint AU–UN deployment in 2008.

As negotiations for the transition from an AU to a UN operation in Darfur were ongoing, the AU in 2007 launched a further operation in Somalia. In March 2007 the AU deployed the African Union Mission in Somalia (AMISOM), tasked with supporting dialogue and reconciliation by assisting with the free movement, safe passage and protection of all stakeholders involved in a national reconciliation congress. AMISOM was also tasked with providing assistance to the implementation of the National Security and Stabilization Plan, and with contributing to the creation of the necessary security considerations to enable the delivery of humanitarian assistance. While initially mandated with a force of 8,000 peacekeepers, in August 2010 this was increased to a force of 12,000, given the deteriorating security situation in Somalia. Yet by the end of 2011, the AU was struggling to secure pledges from its member states, with only Burundi and Uganda contributing forces to the AMISOM mission, and Djibouti and Sierra Leone pledging to contribute troops by 2012. As in Burundi and Darfur, the AU was once again displaying a willingness to intervene in a conflict situation where the UN was not, and, as was becoming increasingly obvious by 2011, to incur losses to its peacekeeping force which no UN mission would be able to sustain. By 2012 the AU had however managed to turn the situation around, as the force was increased to 17,731 personnel, militant groups were pushed out of the capital, Mogadishu, and a political transition was concluded, leading to the election of Somalia's first functioning government in almost 20 years. Indeed, the AU can be credited with having paved the way for international re-engagement in Somalia, and bringing a large degree of stability to the country.

Shortly after establishing the AMISOM mission, the AU deployed the African Union Electoral and Security Assistance Mission to the Comoros (MAES) in

[29] Fredrik Söderbaum, and Björn Hettne, 'Regional Security in a Global Perspective' in U. Engel and J. G. Porto (eds.) *Africa's New Peace and Security Architecture—Promoting Norms, Institutionalising Solutions* (Farnham: Ashgate, 2010), 23.

May 2007. The mission initially comprised 300 soldiers and police, tasked with providing security assistance during a tense election period. However, tensions soon erupted when one of the islands in the Comoros federation, Anjouan, made a unilateral move towards secession. Failing to secure a political solution to the crisis, the AU in October 2007 imposed sanctions on 168 leaders of the secessionist movement, yet when sanctions too failed to bring a negotiated settlement to the conflict, the AU in March 2008 deployed 1,500 troops from Sudan, Tanzania, and Senegal (with logistical support provided by Libya) to conduct a security operation aimed at restoring the rule of law, and bringing to an end the secessionist attempts of the Anjouan leadership.[30]

Despite building a large degree of legitimacy through its interventions in Burundi, Darfur, and Somalia in particular, notwithstanding the operational challenges that each of these interventions brought with them, in recent years the AU has at times also struggled to persuade its member states and other actors in the international system of its effectiveness, and to persuade in particular other actors in the international system of its legitimacy as an actor in peace and security on the continent. Events in 2011 in Côte d'Ivoire and in Libya in particular served to bring into question the legitimacy claims of the AU.

Following elections in Côte d'Ivoire in November 2010, the country descended into a spiral of violence, leading to attacks against the civilian population, the UN and the international community by early 2011. While the UN and ECOWAS took a firm stance early on, recognizing the election results and calling on the incumbent president to step down, the AU, which also recognized the election results, called for a process of dialogue between the parties in conflict. As the violence escalated, the UN and ECOWAS increased pressure on the regime in Abidjan, while the AU continued to promote a political resolution to the crisis. Finally, frustrated by the lack of results from the AU approach, ECOWAS in April 2011 turned to the UN Security Council, requesting that the use of force be authorized to protect the civilian population, which was being directly targeted by President Laurent Gbagbo's forces in his bid to remain in power. By mid-April Gbagbo had been ousted, and the AU's political approach aimed at generating a negotiated settlement to the conflict had been left in ruins. To make matters worse, ECOWAS, which had initially worked through the AU's Peace and Security Council, decided to bypass the AU and take the matter directly to the UN Security Council instead, following which a swift resolution to the crisis was attained.

While the handling of the Côte d'Ivoire crisis in early 2011 weakened the AU's legitimacy claims, both in terms of the organizations effectiveness at attaining a resolution to the crisis and its ability to persuade other actors

[30] Söderbaum and Hettne, 'Regional Security in a Global Perspective', 23.

that it was indeed the organization best suited to intervening in the conflict, events in Libya throughout 2011 served to bring the legitimacy of the AU into question even further. When civil war first erupted in Libya in February 2011, the AU was quick to condemn the violent repression of the Ghadaffi regime, as were other international organizations. Yet from March 2011 onwards, the AU found itself increasingly isolated from the remainder of the international community, and at odds with the UN, NATO, the EU, the League of Arab States and other members of the Libya Contact Group. From an initial stance of boycotting international meetings on the Libya conflict, the AU by mid-2011 conceded that it did not have the lead on Libya, and started to work together with other organizations. Yet the AU consistently found itself marginalized on Libya, and the decisions of the Peace and Security Council were largely bypassed. The AU's reluctance to recognize the National Transitional Council (NTC) until Ghadaffi's death in October 2011 also weakened the organization's ability to leverage dialogue during the conflict. Although the decision not to recognize the NTC was taken on a principled basis, as the AU recognizes governments and not armed movements, the delay in providing recognition to the NTC long after the UN and several African states had done so did damage the credibility of the AU, which found itself largely sidelined on Libya by late 2011.

Although the AU's responses to the conflicts in Côte d'Ivoire and Libya damaged the reputation of the organization, the AU's legitimacy has also been undermined in other areas in recent years. The legitimacy of the organization has been weakened in particular in terms of both the membership of the PSC and with regards to its ability to ensure member state adherence to its decisions.

Membership in the PSC is based on the principle of equitable regional representation and rotation, with members being in good standing with the AU, having paid their dues, made contributions to the Africa Peace Fund, and respecting constitutional governance and the rule of law. Yet by 2011, of the 35 countries that had served terms on the PSC, at least 14 were suffering from internal conflict, and several had shown little respect for constitutional governance or human rights. To make matters worse, in several instances where the AU has had to intervene in a conflict situation, the country in which the organization intervened sat on the PSC. When the AU deployed AMIS in Darfur in 2004, for instance, Sudan had just been elected to serve a two-year term on the Council. Similarly, both Côte d'Ivoire and Libya were serving terms on the PSC in 2011, when the AU had to intervene in crisis situations in both countries. The impact of the presence of these countries on the Council on the AU's decision-making is difficult to establish, however it certainly did influence the manner in which the organization responded to each conflict situation. In other cases, African states have been able to use their tenure on the Council to advance their own national interests. Ethiopia, for instance, used its term on the Council to ensure that the AU deployed AMISOM to Mogadishu when Ethiopian troops withdrew in 2007, ensuring that Ethiopian regional interests were being advanced. The issue of regional rotation has also come under increasing scrutiny, with Nigeria having served on the Council uninterrupted since 2004.

With regards to ensuring that its member states adhere to the decisions of the PSC, the AU has in recent years witnessed several instances where decisions of the Council are undermined by individual member states, often those serving on the Council itself. In 2003, for instance, the AU condemned a coup in the Central African Republic (CAR), yet the Economic Community of Central African States (ECCAS) accepted the coup leader, François Bozize, as the legitimate president. As highlighted earlier, when the AU in 2011 called for political dialogue in Côte d'Ivoire, ECOWAS, lead by Nigeria, went to the UN Security Council to request more forceful intervention. Friction also arose between Nigeria and South Africa in their response to the crisis, in particular as South Africa was accused of utilizing the Peace and Security Council to undermine the ECOWAS response to the Côte d'Ivoire conflict. The Council was further undermined during the Libya conflict in 2011, when some AU member states, such as Botswana, Ethiopia, Kenya, Nigeria, and Tanzania, moved to recognize the NTC, despite the AU, led in particular by members of the high-level ad hoc committee on Libya (including the Congo, Uganda, Mali, Mauritania, and South Africa), refusing to do so. The AU has therefore increasingly witnessed divisions within the Council, which in turn lead to an inability of the organization to uphold decisions taken in the Council. Though admittedly such occurrences have not been commonplace to date, they do seem to have been on the rise in recent years.

As has been explored above, the AU appears to have been successful in its early years in developing legitimacy, not least by showing its willingness to intervene in conflict situations that the UN was not willing to engage in, such as Burundi, Darfur and Somalia. This appears to have gone a long way in terms of convincing both African states and other actors in the international system that the AU is a serious and credible actor in the peace and security realm in Africa, and can deliver tangible results, despite the numerous constraints the organization still faces. Through this willingness to mount peace operations in extremely dangerous circumstances, the AU therefore appears to have gained a degree of performance legitimation. Despite these initial successes however, in recent years the legitimacy of the AU appears at times to have been weakened, in particular through the inability of the organization, and in particular of the Peace and Security Council, to act decisively in crisis situations where the interests of its more prominent members have been at stake. The consensus-style of decision-making by member states with vastly different interests appears to have the potential to impact on the ability of the AU to take consistently swift and meaningful action when required.

CONCLUSION

The AU has since 2002 worked to establish its legitimacy as a principal actor in peace and security affairs on the African continent, attempting to replace the OAU approach of non-intervention with a new approach based on notions of non-indifference. Accordingly, the AU, in particular through the Peace and Security Council, has become actively involved in the maintenance of peace and security on the African continent, and in articulating and representing Africa's security agenda on the international stage. However, as has been highlighted by this chapter, while the AU does appear to have been relatively successful at legitimating itself procedurally, through reference to shared values, and by building up its reputation as an actor willing to engage in security operations, it has been less consistent at establishing legitimacy by effectively advancing shared norms in its operations. Indeed, in recent years the AU appears at times even to have lost some degree of legitimacy as a peace and security actor in Africa, proving at times in the eyes of its member states and other actors as ineffective in the face of crisis, and unable to persuade its member states and other actors of its primary role in addressing conflict situations on the African continent. Indeed, such was the frustration that in October 2011 Kenyan Prime Minister Raila Odinga argued that the AU had been vague in tackling issues affecting Africa, and remained ineffective. Odinga argued that the AU should 'stand up for Africa's people, and prove that it is not the same old OAU that was well-known for inaction'.[31]

In its initial years, the AU appears to have gained legitimacy by consciously differentiating itself from the OAU, and by displaying not only the political will to address threats to peace and security on the continent, but also by deploying peace support operations under dangerous circumstances. Increasingly however, the AU's legitimacy has come to be viewed not in contrast with the OAU, but on the basis of its own merit. It is in this regard that the organization will need to continue to prove its effectiveness and persuade both its member states and other actors in the international system of its relevance if it is to continue to play a principal role in the maintenance of peace and security on the African continent. Ultimately however, the AU, in its ten years of existence, has evolved dramatically, and today bears little resemblance to its predecessor, the OAU. While the organization will need to continue to work to legitimate itself, especially with regards to its own member states and the continent's people, it is clear that the organization now holds a central and extremely valuable role in the peace and security affairs of the continent, and that this legitimacy is being recognized and increasingly utilized not only by its own member states, but by the international community at large.

[31] Aggrey Mutambo, 'Raila Blames AU for Africa's Woes', *Daily Nation*, 31 October 2011. Accessible at: http://www.nation.co.ke/News/politics/Raila+blames+AU+for+Africa+woes/-/1064/1264324/-/2tp793/-/index.html.

7

The Association of Southeast Asian Nations: *Between Internal and External Legitimacy*

Alice D. Ba

INTRODUCTION

This chapter investigates questions of organizational legitimacy in relation to the Association of Southeast Asian Nations (ASEAN). It seeks to add to ongoing discussions on international organizations and legitimacy in at least two ways. First, its discussion of a regional case study contributes to efforts to expand our sights beyond the Global North and the organizations that are typically the focus of such discussions. This is not to say that regional organizations in the Global South have received no attention but to the extent that they do, the focus is often on how they add to or detract from the legitimacy of existing global organizations rather than the dynamics of regional legitimacy itself.[1] The ASEAN case is used here to illustrate some of the ways that legitimacy challenges may play out differently in non-core regional organizations. Second, discussions have generally focused on legitimacy vis-à-vis an organization's constituent members—that is, how and why members accept the authority and legitimacy of the organizations of which they are a part. In contrast, this chapter highlights how organizations can also face significant external pressures that come from non-member expectations about what

[1] Two particular examples are discussions on regional subsidiarity, especially in relation to the United Nations; and discussions on the unprecedented and growing interest in regional financial cooperation since the 1997–8 Asian financial crisis as a function of the perceived *illegitimacy* of existing 'G7-dominated global financial institutions'. See, for example, Louise Fawcett, 'Exploring Regional Domains: A Comparative History of Regionalism'. *International Affairs*, Vol. 80/3 (2004), 483; Jane Boulden, 'Double Standards, Distance, and Disengagement', *Security Dialogue*, Vol. 37/3 (2006), 409–23; Alice D. Ba, 'Contested Spaces: The Politics of Regional and Global Governance', in Alice D. Ba and Matthew J. Hoffmann (eds.), *Contending Perspectives on Global Governance* (New York: Routledge, 2005), pp. 190–212; Injoo Sohn, 'Asian Financial Cooperation: The Problem of Legitimacy in Global Financial Governance', *Global Governance*, Vol. 11/5 (October 2005), 487–504.

constitutes an organization's legitimacy and how that challenge is often greater for non-European, non-North American organizations like ASEAN for reasons that are structural and material, as well as cultural and historical. In the ASEAN case, the challenge of external legitimacy has moreover become more pronounced since the early 1990s due to three key developments: first, the intensified liberalization of world order since the ending of the Cold War; second, the expanded geographic scope of ASEAN's regionalism(s); and third, the 1997–8 Asian financial crisis. Lastly, in highlighting how such external expectations can interact with internal legitimacy claims in ways that can both add to, and detract from, an organization's overall legitimacy, it draws parallels to developments in state sovereignty where external recognition of a state's legitimacy has been made increasingly contingent on the domestic fulfillment of certain (liberal) standards and norms.[2]

MEASURES AND SOURCES OF LEGITIMACY

This chapter focuses on the sources of organizational legitimacy and what Dominik Zaum in the introduction to this volume describes as the social practice of legitimation—that is, the process by which claims to authority are justified and validated. In particular, the focus here is on the substantive claims and social processes that contribute to the shared acceptance of an organization (in this case, ASEAN) as the most appropriate and best organization to represent a group's particular interests.[3] Such a conceptualization of legitimacy maintains the sense of obligation associated with legitimacy that most scholars emphasize but also explicitly broadens understandings of legitimacy beyond a legal understanding of obligation often emphasized by those who measure legitimacy strictly in terms of contractual compliance.

Discussions on organizational legitimacy have historically focused on conflicts and tensions *within* organizations and between member states. Such a focus makes sense as organizational legitimacy rests most of all on what its member states think of it and whether there exists common agreement about the organization in question. An organization lacking such internal legitimacy will have limited authority to compel state support for its initiatives and processes, which in turn can detract from organizational efficacy and relevance. By the same token, as Ian Hurd argues, legitimacy can also empower an organization, giving an organization authoritative and 'symbolic' power even when

[2] I owe this observation to Dominik Zaum.
[3] Sohn, 'Asian Financial Cooperation', 489.

institutional tools and mechanisms for coordination may be weak.[4] Injoo Sohn similarly describes legitimacy as giving international organizations and institutions an important 'stickiness' that keeps members of a group committed to institutional rules and practices even when benefits fall short or decline.[5]

Thus, discussions typically see the biggest legitimacy challenge facing international organizations as internal. Their biggest challenge has been to convince member states that the organization's normative, material, and social purposes mirror their own. Indeed, the extant international relations literature on international organizations across theoretical perspectives has been defined largely by investigations into domestic–international tensions. Realist and contractual perspectives focus on material concerns and tensions between 'national interest' and the potentially sovereignty-impinging demands that an international institution might make on member-states.[6] Liberal theorists begin with the premise that an individual state's participation (whether it participates, how it participates) will be shaped by states' domestic context and domestic politics. Constructivist, as well as neofunctionalist (and now 'post-functionalist'), perspectives focus on the co-transformation of national and institutional institutions and identities.[7] They, like liberal theorists, have also given attention to the liberal content of key world organizations and institutions as expressions of the liberal identities of their founding states.[8] In short, despite variations in perceived sources of state interest and identity, there is the presumption that the legitimacy of international institutions will be contingent on domestic authoritative structures and expectations projected by member states.

In these discussions, organizational legitimacy is often traced to two general sources—process and performance. Robert Keohane, for example, describes legitimacy in terms of inputs and outputs.[9] 'Input' or 'procedural' legitimacy mostly refers to the process—that is, how accountable, transparent, democratic, and inclusive are an organization's processes and procedures of decision-making

[4] Ian Hurd, 'Legitimacy, Power, and the Symbolic Life of the UN Security Council', *Global Governance*, Vol. 8 (2002), 48. For discussions on the legitimating effects of the 'UN' or 'multilateral' label, see also, Inis L. Claude, 'Collective Legitimization as a Political Function of the United Nations', *International Organization*, Vol. 20/3 (1966), 367–79; Stewart Patrick, 'Beyond Coalitions of the Willing', *Ethics & International Affairs*, Vol. 17/1 (2003), 37–54; Boulden, 'Double Standards'.

[5] Sohn, 'Asian Financial Cooperation'.

[6] For a defining critique, see John Mearsheimer, 'The False Promise of International Institutions', *International Security*, Vol. 19 (1994/95), 5–49.

[7] See, for example, recent discussions and debates in response to Lisbeth Hooghe and Gary Marks, 'A Postfunctionalist Theory of European Integration: From Permissive Consensus to Constraining Dissensus', *British Journal of Political Science*, Vol. 39/1 (2009), 1–23.

[8] See, for example, discussion in Patrick Thaddeus Jackson, 'Bridging the Gap: Toward A Realist-Constructivist Dialogue', *International Studies Quarterly*, Vol. 6 (2004), 337–52. See also, Andrew Moravcsik, 'Taking Preferences Seriously: A Liberal Theory of International Politics', *International Organization*, Vol. 51/4 (Autumn 1997), 540.

[9] Robert Keohane, *Power and Governance in a Partially Globalized World* (London: Routledge 2002), 234.

and implementation? Do members feel appropriately included and consulted? Do members feel that the process is fair? Do members feel that agreed-upon rules and rules of the game have been followed?[10]

'Output legitimacy' is basically 'performance legitimacy'. Much attention, for example has been given to the ways that poor outcomes and poor performance can detract from the legitimacy of an organization or process. For Keohane, performance legitimacy is about the efficiency, efficacy, and sustainability of results.[11] The distinction between efficiency and efficacy, however, deserves particular mention because though often conflated, they are not the same thing. Efficiency is about speed and ease, typically as regards the pursuit of specified, coordinated functional outcomes. Efficacy, in contrast, is about an organization's ability to meet collectively identified and agreed upon goals—goals that may vary depending on the group. Those variations moreover may affect not just the kinds of outcomes and outputs produced but they may also affect how an organization behaves. More to the point, the focus on outcomes has to be qualified by an acknowledgement that international organizations may vary in their functional and social purposes.

Such distinctions point to a third and arguably more important source of internal legitimacy, namely, that of substantive legitimacy.[12] Substantive legitimacy refers to an organization's core values and priorities. In this sense, legitimacy is ultimately a term of appraisal or judgement, not description. The question becomes not just what an organization does, but also whether what it does is consistent with the core values and priorities identified and shared by the group. Put another way, does an organization reflect the 'right' priorities and values? The above distinction between efficiency and efficacy is a case in point. An organization can be fast and decisive in coordinating collective action and outcomes but if it is done at the expense of more valued priorities and aspirations, then efficiency could in fact render an organization less legitimate in the eyes of the community it is supposed to represent. As further discussed below, the ASEAN case in fact compels us to consider how procedural and performance-based criteria for organizational legitimacy are not value free, even if often presented as such. As measures of legitimacy, the two are also not as distinct from each other as sometimes portrayed since procedural questions also reflect substantive legitimacy claims.

[10] See for example Robert Keohane, 'The Contingent Legitimacy of Multilateralism', In Edward Newman, Ramesh Thakur, and John Tirman (eds.), *Multilateralism Under Challenge? Power, International Order, and Structural Change* (Tokyo/New York/Paris: United Nations University Press, 2006), 56–76; Michael Barnett and Martha Finnemore, *Rules for the World: International Organizations in Global Politics* (Ithaca: Cornell University Press, 2004), 166–70; Friederich Kratochwil, 'On Legitimacy', *International Relations*, Vol. 20/3 (2006), 302–8.

[11] Keohane, *Power and Governance.*

[12] Barnett and Finnemore, *Rules for the World*; Kratochwil, 'On Legitimacy'.

In this sense, international organizations are not just sets of rules and procedures, or what some describe as 'forms of hierarchy in which sanctions are employed to make self-interested choices consistent with the social good'.[13] Rather, international organizations, like other social bodies, are expressions of particular socio-cultural and normative frameworks and inter-subjective understandings about what that entity is about. Substantive legitimacy thus goes beyond simply reconciling organizational demands with individual state interest. While different members of an organization may also have distinct and specific ideas and interests vis-à-vis that organization, substantive legitimacy is ultimately about shared and intersubjective agreement about organizational functions, processes, and normative objectives. An organization with substantive legitimacy is one that will be more likely to withstand the disappointments and underperformance that inevitably challenge organizations from time to time. For this reason, substantive legitimacy deserves more weight compared to other criteria such as performance.

External Legitimacy

The questions and challenges highlighted above are ones of *internal* legitimacy—that is, how an organization is collectively understood and assessed by its constituent members, typically states. As noted, there are good reasons to focus on this internal dimension of legitimacy; however, the focus can also obscure the ways that the legitimacy of international organizations can also be informed by expectations *external* to the organization's membership. Moreover, in that internal and external legitimacy can involve distinct sets of expectations, their interaction can have mixed effects on institutional developments. For example, external expectations can substantiate and mobilize internal legitimacy claims, but they can also challenge them. Put another way, what constitutes legitimacy for a particular group need not be the same as that for others. International organizations are also not worlds unto themselves. Instead, they exist amongst and within other communities that provide additional audiences for their actions.

This external dimension of organizational legitimacy has historically drawn less attention. Partly, this is because of the above-noted influence of realist and liberal preoccupations with reconciling national interests and national values with their willingness to participate in international organizations. But partly

[13] Robert H. Bates, 'Contra Contractarianism: Some Reflections on the New Institutionalism', *Politics and Society*, Vol. 16/2–3 (1988), 387. See also Robert Keohane, 'International Institutions: Two Approaches', *International Studies Quarterly*, Vol. 32/4 (1988), 384; Helen Milner, 'Review: *International Theories of Cooperation among Nations: Strengths and Weaknesses*', *World Politics*, Vol. 44/3 (1992), 468.

also, this may be because discussion of organizational legitimacy has focused disproportionately on organizations of global scope, near global membership, and those with universalist claims. As a result, communities external to those organizations were assumed to be small, nonexistent, or inconsequential, thus preempting investigations into questions of external legitimacy. Moreover, globalization and liberalization trends, especially with the ending of old Cold War divisions, are sometimes assumed to have further reduced that external audience and by extension, potential legitimacy challenges from the outside. In short, globalization and liberalization trends seemingly suggest a world 'oneness', making the existence of an external audience even more marginal.

Such assumptions may be premature. World organizations like the United Nations and International Monetary Fund are, in fact, not completely insulated from an external structure of expectations. For example, the same processes of globalization and liberalization mentioned above have also materially and ideologically enabled different actors (non-state actors, transnational networks, substate groups) to question the priorities and processes of global organizations and also to organize more meaningfully against them. Recent discussions have given particular attention to the legitimacy challenge posed to international organizations like the UN, the WTO, and the IMF by societal groups calling for greater accountability, inclusion, and transparency.[14] While many such societal groups may be considered domestic and thus part of the internal audience question discussed above, a growing number are transnational, representing interests and perspectives that transcend states and are thus more appropriately considered outside most international organizations and their constituent states. Indeed, as non-state entities, these societal and transnational actors, if not officially sidelined, are typically given, *at most*, secondary or tertiary status as observers (not full participants) in international organization processes. For these reasons, such societal groups may be better characterized as part of an external, not internal, audience.

At the same time, though such societal challenges come from outside these organizations' memberships and are for the most part materially insignificant against the resources controlled by their state counterparts, such societal pressures can, in fact, pose significant internal legitimacy challenges. This is not just because of the different agendas or priorities these groups may represent; nor is it simply a question of procedural inclusion in global, universalist organizations (as illustrated, most notably, by questions of IMF reform). Rather, it is also because the inclusion question is *made* especially potent by these organization's liberal, substantive claims about the value of universal representation

[14] Keohane, 'Contingent Legitimacy of Multilateralism; Elizabeth Smythe and Peter Smith, 'Legitimacy, Transparency and Informational Technology', *Global Governance*, Vol. 12/1 (2006), 31–53; Michael Zürn, 'Global Governance and Legitimacy Problems', *Government and Opposition*, Vol. 39/2 (2004), 260–87.

and the importance of individuals and societies in relation to state power. The fact that societal groups are speaking directly to these organization's claims to substantive legitimacy is also why the societal challenge, though external in the sense that the challenge comes from outside the referent community of member-states, is also very much an internal one.[15]

Such external audience questions also apply to non-core regional organizations, but the challenge for them is materially and often substantively different. The challenge posed by societal actors, such as those above, offers one example of how external legitimacy questions can play out differently depending on the organization. For example, non-core regional organizations are often comprised of state memberships that are typically less liberal and less democratic than the global powers that originated and still mostly dominate global regimes. Such differences in state identities and an organization's normative-substantive content would make the appeals of societal, non-state groups less compelling and less of a direct legitimacy challenge in and of themselves.

However, in most other respects, non-core regional organizations face more significant external legitimacy challenges. More than global organizations and organizations formed in the Global North, non-core regional organizations have had to confront two worlds of expectations—one within the organization, the other outside the organization. Regional organizations must negotiate not just the normative expectations of their referent community and members, but also a structure of expectations associated with a larger global and mostly liberal post-1945 world system, a system that finds particular expression in key global organizations like the UN, the IMF, and the World Bank. Partly, this is a historical issue. In that the memberships of most non-core regional organizations are comprised of post-colonial entities that mostly emerged in the 1950s, 1960s, and even 1970s, they consequently had little input into shaping the content or structure of the post-World War II order and its institutions. This means that there is considerably more diversity in the value systems represented in the world today than there was in 1945; moreover, if we believe that regional norms and regional authority structures are also products of their specific localities and contexts, then it is reasonable to conclude that there is also greater likelihood of tension, if not conflict, between regional and global expectations and their respective legitimating claims.

The external legitimacy challenge faced by non-core regional organizations is also a power issue. The world of expectations outside non-core organizations is associated with the world's more powerful actors—powers that have dominated much of the post-1945 world system and that are largely responsible for

[15] On the tension between intergovernmentalism and transnationalism, see, for example, Bruce Cronin, 'The Two Faces of the United Nations: The Tension Between Intergovernmentalism and Transnationalism', *Global Governance*, Vol. 8 (2002), 53–71; and the special issue of *Government and Opposition* on legitimacy and accountability in global governance (2004).

imbuing the previously mentioned world organizations with liberal content. Not only can these powers and their organizations grant or deny others important external recognition but those deemed out of conformance with their ideas can also suffer significant material and reputational consequences for it. Put another way, mutually reinforcing normative, institutional, and material forces make up a larger world structure and system in which non-core regional organizations must operate.

In sum, while world organizations like the UN and IMF are not completely insulated from an external structure of expectations, the challenge faced by non-core regional organizations is nevertheless notably different in at least two respects. First, for global organizations, their current external legitimacy challenges stem from expectations mostly of their own making; that is, the challenge tends to be about reconciling institutional practice with internal legitimating claims. This is again not the same for most non-core regional organizations whose members entered the system late and weak and have been 'rule takers' more than 'rule makers'.[16] For them, the potential for normative conflict and tension between internal and external legitimacy claims is thus higher for non-core regional organizations. Second, external legitimacy challenges faced by non-core regional organizations are typically of greater material significance. Unlike global organizations whose external challenges stem mostly from weaker social groups that may lack international recognition and standing, non-core regional organizations find that their external legitimacy challenges stem mostly from organizations and actors that are more materially capable and normatively powerful in their control of economic, security, and legitimacy resources. While the external legitimacy challenges highlighted above may prove in the long run more internally destructive for organizations like the UN if left unaddressed due to their substantive challenge, the external challenges in the non-core cases typically carry penalties that are more direct, immediate, and materially consequential.

In short, for reasons that are both material and normative, non-core regional organizations tend to be much more aware that communities exist outside their memberships and moreover the judgements of these communities affect both their material and normative standing in world politics. That external environment, as a result, conditions in important ways the development and evolution of non-core regional organizations. The ASEAN case below gives particular attention to the tensions between internal and external expectations and how their interactions provide insight into its recent institutional developments and trajectories. In particular, the discussion below shows how recent efforts to reform ASEAN are driven in large part by a need to reconcile

[16] Michael Haas, 'A Functional Approach to International Organization', *Journal of Politics*, Vol. XXVII (1965), 498–517. Jeffrey T. Checkel, 'Norms, Institutions, and National Identity in Contemporary Europe', *International Studies Quarterly*, Vol. 43/1 (1999), 86.

internal and external expectations. It further shows that the external challenge is more than material for ASEAN. In that ASEAN's internal assessments also depend on external recognition, external criticisms and expectations are also destabilizing internal legitimating claims.

ASEAN

Created in 1967, the Association of Southeast Asian Nations (ASEAN)[17] is today among the 'most high profile and successful regional organizations' outside Western Europe and North America.[18] This is because of the organization's association with the region's relative stability (compared to both 1960s Southeast Asia and some other regions), the relative economic success enjoyed by its member states, as well as the interest that larger powers have expressed in associating with ASEAN. That perceived success—in a word, performance—and the external validation that has come with it have helped to bolster ASEAN's internal legitimacy in the eyes of its own members.

This generally favourable assessment, however, has also found itself increasingly challenged, especially since the late 1990s. Against the globalization and liberalization trends highlighted above, ASEAN has been facing growing external criticisms about what the organization does, how it does it, whose voices matter in the decisionmaking process, and what it represents. Put another way, the concerns expressed by external voices are functional, procedural, and substantive-normative. Among the more prominent concerns are that ASEAN is too state centric (not sufficiently inclusive of societal voices and interests), too inefficient and too ineffective (not sufficiently able to coordinate members towards common outcomes in a timely manner), and also undemocratic and illiberal (not sufficiently critical of authoritarian practices and governments within its own ranks).

Underlying each of these concerns has also been a particular judgement made about ASEAN's non-interference norm. While ASEAN has not been

[17] Founding states—Indonesia, Malaysia, Philippines, Singapore, and Thailand—are now joined by Brunei, Vietnam, Laos, Myanmar, and Cambodia.

[18] Richard Stubbs, 'Meeting the Challenge of Regional Building in ASEAN', in Mark Beeson (ed.), Contemporary Southeast Asia, 2nd Edition (New York: Palgrave MacMillan, 2008); Amitav Acharya, *Constructing a Security Community in Southeast Asia* (London: Routledge, 2001). Of course, not everyone agrees that ASEAN has been so successful even during the Cold War. In this chapter, it is argued that what constitutes 'success' will vary depending on the criteria employed and importantly the substantive objectives of an organization. For a representative critical view that focuses on collective coordination as a key measure of efficacy, see David M. Jones and Michael L. R. Smith, 'ASEAN's Imitation Community', *Orbis*, Vol. 46/1 (2001), 93–109. See also, Mark Beeson, 'ASEAN's Ways: Still Fit for Purpose?' *Cambridge Review of International Affairs*, Vol. 22/3 (2009), 333–43.

unique in its attachment to noninterference, the principle (for various reasons to be discussed below) has come to be especially central to and defining for the organization.[19] Not only has it provided a core foundational principle for intra-ASEAN relations, but it has also come to have symbolic, as much as material, value in ASEAN's relations with external actors. Indeed, as discussed below, ASEAN states' attachment to noninterference reflects a principled commitment to basic ideas about peaceful coexistence and mutual respect vis-à-vis both intra-regional and extra-regional actors. The persistent challenges of external interference and intervention and the discursive responses associated with them have moreover given that principle particular salience and even emotional value as an expression of states' fears and aspirations about survival and autonomy.

As with global organizations, some of the external challenge has come from societal and substate groups, as globalization and liberalization processes bear on individual ASEAN states and by extension ASEAN. However, the challenge to ASEAN posed by such societal groups tends to be of a different sort. This is because, again, compared to the European and North American states that dominate most global organizations, ASEAN's member states are generally less democratic, while ASEAN as an organization is nationalist, not liberal, in content.[20] Such differences mean that the legitimacy challenge represented by societal groups is likely to be less substantive for ASEAN compared to an organization like the United Nations.

Instead, the more acutely felt legitimacy challenge for ASEAN has come from states and inter-state groups outside ASEAN. Specifically, ASEAN as an institution has felt compelled to respond to criticisms and authoritative judgements made by various Western liberal states and organizations that include the United States, Australia, Canada, and the European Union, as well as international financial institutions like the IMF and World Bank—actors that are typically more materially and authoritatively powerful in their control of both material and legitimating resources in the world system at large. They also happen to be among collective ASEAN's more important economic, security, and dialogue partners. What this means is that failure to respond to such external assessments can result in immediate, material consequences for individual states and ASEAN as an institution. Indonesia's experience with the IMF and Washington during the 1997–8 Asian financial crisis offers a

[19] Acharya, *Constructing a Security Community.*

[20] See Alice D. Ba, *(Re)Negotiating East and Southeast Asia: Region, Regionalism, and the Association of Southeast Asian Nations* (Stanford: Stanford University Press 2009). Others would describe that content as 'illiberal', though, as highlighted below, this mischaracterizes what I see to be the historical driving preoccupations of ASEAN regionalism, namely, resilience. See, especially, Timo Kivimaki, 'The Long Peace of ASEAN', *Journal of Peace Research*, Vol. *38/1* (2001), 5–25; and Erik Kuhonta, 'Walking a Tightrope: Demoracy versus Sovereignty in ASEAN's Illiberal Peace', *Pacific Review*, Vol. 19/3 (September 2006), 337–58.

particular example of how difficult it can be for states to defy the authoritative judgements of the 'international community' once rendered.[21]

In that these questions and challenges mostly originate outside ASEAN and regard ASEAN's external standing vis-à-vis non-member communities, they constitute external, not internal, legitimacy challenges. As suggested above, the challenge is not just material, but also normative-substantive in the sense that external assessments are also about what external actors think ASEAN *should* be about. In particular, liberal criticisms have come into tension with what has been the nationalist content of ASEAN regionalism. At the same time, though external in origination, such expectations also feed back into intra-ASEAN debates, with possible implications for internal legitimacy claims. This is because ASEAN's internal legitimacy also rests in part on others recognizing the legitimacy and status of ASEAN. Efforts to respond to such external normative expectations have subsequently been accompanied by growing internal, intra-ASEAN debates about what the organization represents and how it should operate.

The discussion below offers a sketch of some of the ways that internal and external legitimacy claims interact in relation to developments concerning ASEAN's noninterference principle, and their institutional consequences for ASEAN.

Sources of Internal Legitimacy

As with most international organizations and political entities, ASEAN did not gain its legitimacy automatically, but rather through reinforcing founding arguments and practices over time, as well as a relatively good track record (in this case, of keeping a relative peace).[22] In particular, that process solidified ASEAN's substantive foundations—foundations that trace their roots to the historical conditions and founding context of recent independence and nationalist conflicts from which it emerged. For all of ASEAN's founding states—including Thailand, the only ASEAN state not to be colonized -independence (and all the sovereign rights associated with it) was also a new and much valued experience; it was also one that remained tenuous in the face of nationalist agendas of neighbouring states and Cold War agendas of extra-regional actors, as well as domestic regime challenges.

The conflicts associated with the 1963 creation of Malaysia were especially emblematic of the multidimensional sovereignty challenges faced by Southeast

[21] Mark Beeson, 'Sovereignty under Siege', *Third World Quarterly*, Vol. 24/2 (2003), 357–74; Mark Beeson, 'Mahathir and the Markets: Globalization and the Pursuit of Economic Autonomy in Malaysia', *Pacific Affairs*, Vol. 73/3 (2000), 335–51.

[22] See Ba, *(Re)Negotiating East and Southeast Asia*.

Asian states: Indonesia, with support from the Philippines, launched a low-level war against Malaysia and its right to exist; Singapore left the newly-created Malaysian state following irreconcilable differences over domestic ethnic political balances—in other words, what properly constituted 'Malaysia'. The need for reconciliation following these conflicts, especially given the associated spectre of extra-regional, Cold War-associated manipulations and interventions, was what provided regional organization with its most immediate and precipitating impetus.[23] However, the immediacy of past conflicts and past interferences into one another's affairs also made the idea of regional organization extremely contentious.

Thus, in this context of recent conflict and recent independence, it was highly unlikely that states would trust their neighbours or any regional organization with the power or authority to make decisions for them. What this meant was that regionalism would have to be of a particular kind if states were to be convinced of its merits. More specifically, in 1960s post-colonial, post-conflict Southeast Asia, a nationalist-bounded regionalism would ultimately be the only kind of regionalism that could be considered legitimate. ASEAN's founding elites, in fact, would commandeer 'nationalist' ideas of self determination (the right to govern and make policies for oneself without interference) towards legitimating an otherwise contentious regionalism.[24]

That nationalism would be given additional local content by Indonesian ideas about national resilience—states' commonly perceived linkage between intra-state political fault-lines and external interventions—a linkage made especially salient by both the US war in Vietnam and China's revolutionary foreign policy goals at the time.[25] National resilience thus came to express states' shared comprehensive security concerns, including the link between internal and external security. Extending ideas of resilience to the region as a whole, *regional* resilience (like national resilience) was premised on the same shared idea that a critical source of Southeast Asian vulnerability was to be found in internal faultlines, only here it was intra-regional and *inter*-state (as opposed to intra-state) faultlines, that provided the opportunities for external manipulations. Security, internally and externally, would thus be found in national and regional unity—in short, resilience.

[23] Michael Leifer, *ASEAN and the Security of South-East Asia* (London: Routledge, 1989).

[24] For an extended discussion on the importance of nationalism and resilience in defining the content of ASEAN regionalism, see Chapters 1 and 2 in Ba, *(re)Negotiating South and Southeast Asia*.

[25] David Dewitt, 'Common, Cooperative, and Comprehensive Security', *Pacific Review*, Vol. 7/1 (1994), 1–15; Donald K. Emmerson, 'Indonesia, Malaysia, and Singapore: A Regional Security Core?' in Richard Ellings and Sheldon Simon (eds.), *Southeast Asia in the New Millennium*, (Armonk, NY: M. E. Sharpe, 1996), 37–9; Amitav Acharya, 'How Ideas Spread: Whose Norms Matter? Norm Localization and Institutional Change in Asian Regionalism', *International Organization* Vol. 58/2 (2004), 239–75.

The heightened insecurity associated with states' pre-ASEAN efforts to meddle and interfere in each others' affairs thus provided the historical context and local conditions of ASEAN's founding that shaped in critical ways the internal, substantive content of regional organization. States' history of conflict and vulnerability to external manipulations—and thus the particular imperative of non-interference principles—ultimately would also provide ASEAN with its internal, legitimating discursive frames and arguments. That substantive content would, in turn, affect ASEAN's resulting institutional form, structure, and culture. A regionalism that was nationalist in content would not, for example, be a sovereignty-abridging or nationalism-negating kind of regionalism. Similarly, a regionalism premised on resilience as its core raison d'être would be a regionalism that demanded respect for states' respective internal struggles—or, in a word, noninterference. The principle of noninterference would then be codified in ASEAN's first and, until 1995, only treaty: The Treaty of Amity and Cooperation (TAC). Thus, *noninterference* came to replace and at least rival what had previously been a destabilizing habit of *interference*.[26] It also helped give rise to an organizational and diplomatic-security culture that values informality over formal treaties, institutional minimalism over binding rules and mechanisms of sanction, and quiet, inclusive diplomacy over confrontational, exclusionary politics.[27] Norms of consensus, not majority rules, would similarly be informed by expectations of noninterference. In this way, noninterference not only provided states with a modus vivendi, but also eventually ASEAN's modus operandi as well.

ASEAN's consensus-based politics deserves special mention as an illustration of the ways that decision-making processes—which are ordinarily associated with an organization's procedural legitimacy—can themselves be products of substantive legitimacy claims. This is in contrast to those discussions that treat procedural legitimacy as value-neutral and where inclusiveness is understood in functional terms, rather than as an expression of underlying values. Keohane is one example. As Keohane explains the importance of inclusion: 'If all voices are heard, more objections will be expressed, deliberation may be enhanced and decisions more widely accepted'.[28] Functionally

[26] To say that non-interference became an important guiding norm and principle is not to say that it was always perfectly upheld. See, for example, Lee Jones 'ASEAN's Unchanged Melody? The Theory and Practice of "Noninterference" in Southeast Asia', *The Pacific Review*, Vol. 23/4 (2010), 479–502; and Alice Ba, 'On Norms, Rule Breaking, and Security Communities', *International Relations of the Asia Pacific*, Vol. 5/2 (2005), 255–66.

[27] On the ASEAN Way as diplomatic and security culture, see especially Jürgen Haacke, *ASEAN's Diplomatic and Security Culture* (London: Routledge, 2003). In Haacke's discussion, he also includes as part of ASEAN's 'diplomatic and security culture', sovereign equality, mutual respect and tolerance, noninterference and nonintervention, non-use of force, ASEAN's non-involvement in unresolved bilateral conflicts.

[28] Keohane, 'The Contingent Legitimacy of Multilateralism'.

understood, inclusion is thus about making sure that everyone has had the opportunity to input their views into the process so as to avoid opposition or defection. For most, it is such input representation that makes outcomes representative of the whole, not just a select few, and that contributes to what Hurd describes as 'the myth of collectivity [that] is essential for the legitimacy of the institution'.[29]

However, what constitutes or defines such understandings of collectivity can vary. Inclusiveness can be pursued in different ways depending on other mitigating values and how inclusion is defined. In majority rules systems, for example, inclusiveness is defined (as in the above discussion) technically in terms of inputting processes and input representation. As long as everyone has input (regardless of whether or not the ultimate outcome reflects their views), the process is considered inclusive. More often than not, such systems are informed by particular notions of liberal democracy, as well as a neoliberal interest and expectation of institutional efficiency. In this way, the 'majority' view becomes the view and expression of the 'collective'.

In contrast, consensual processes, more than majority rules, emphasize the inclusiveness of the outcome. Consensual arrangements are not just about making sure that nobody feels left out of the process; it is also about making sure that the majority does not negate the minority view. Put another way, on the spectrum of decision-making processes, consensual politics, even more than majority rules, is about making sure that everyone 'owns' the organizational and institutional outcome. Similarly, where liberal and neoliberal values inform majority rules systems, community values intervene to shape how states and actors define inclusion and the question of collectivity in consensus politics and processes. In this case, ASEAN's consensus-based processes are also reinforced by additional substantive values—specifically, nationalist and resilience principles that place great value on the importance of mutual respect for states' respective national autonomy. 'Inclusion' is thus about more than input representation; it is also about mutual accommodation and mutual security, where ideas of 'unity' and 'community' also trump, for example, notions of efficiency. As Indonesia's nationalist leader Sukarno put it, the problem with 'Western' majoritarian systems was that they allowed the '50 plus 1' to trample over the other 49, ultimately to the detriment of unity, community, and mutual aid valued in 'Asian' systems.[30]

Others similarly note cultural and local distinctions that make ASEAN's consensus practices more than a question of procedure or mere inclusion. Amitav Acharya, in particular, gives special attention to the ways that

[29] Hurd, 'Legitimacy, Power, and the Symbolic Life of the Security Council', 48.

[30] Michael Vatikiotis, *Indonesian Politics Under Suharto* (London: Routledge 1993). See also Clark Neher, 'Asian Style Democracy', *Asian Survey*, Vol. 34/11 (1994), 949–61; and Laurie Sears, *Colonial Discourse and Javanese Tales* (Durham: Duke University Press, 1996), 123–4, fn. 6.

ASEAN's consensual decision-making processes have been informed by traditional Malay village practices of mutual consultation and consensus (*musjawarah* and *mufakat*), practices that reflect the value given to community, face, and relationships.[31] Along these lines, references to the ASEAN 'family' are also common in the ASEAN discourse. In this way, consensual processes have been about more than the functional imperative of inclusion; rather, they serve ASEAN's larger social purpose and objective of building regional unity, regional relationships, and regional resilience. Viewed in this way, ASEAN's consensus processes are about substantive, as much as procedural, legitimacy.

Precisely because the consensus process is a substantive, not just procedural, question, attempts to change the decision-making process can thus be fraught with difficulty. Indeed, efforts to change the process have the potential to undermine ASEAN's internal legitimacy. This has been the challenge faced by ASEAN and ASEAN states, as the organization's consensus processes have come under increased external criticism. Critics characterize the ASEAN process as too minimalist and also obstructionist to what they see to be larger collective goals—that is, a 'lowest common denominator' approach constrained by the 'negative vetoes' held by individual states. At the same time, such critiques (though technically not incorrect) may also miss the important mutuality and mutual accommodation that supports that process. As Singapore's Tommy Koh, for example, puts it, 'In the true spirit of consensus-making, the majority seeks to accommodate the minority and the minority seeks to align itself with the majority'.[32] Similarly to those who find ASEAN processes inefficient, Muthiah Alagappa notes that consensus-seeking (belaboured though it may be) also reflects an important regard for the collective by ensuring that 'the national interests of all member states are taken into consideration, thereby ensuring ASEAN cohesion, a fundamental if unstated objective of ASEAN'.[33] To underscore the point, as Barley and Tolbert have argued, 'Organizational structures reflect institutional understandings, rather than rational calculations of efficiency'.[34]

[31] Acharya, *Constructing a Security Community*; Neher, 'Asian Style Democracy'.

[32] Tommy Koh, 'Not Perfect but Charter is a Good Start on Road to Regional Progress', *Straits Times* (21 July 2008).

[33] Muthiah Alagappa, 'ASEAN's Institutional Framework and Modus Operandi', in Noordin Sopiee, Chew Lay See, and Lim Siang Jin (eds.), *ASEAN at the Crossroads* (Kuala Lumpur: ISIS-Malaysia, 1987), 187.

[34] Stephen R. Barley and Pamela S. Tolbert, 'Institutionalization and Structuration: Studying the Links between Action and Institution', *Organization Studies*, Vol. 18/1 (1997), 96.

EXTERNAL LEGITIMACY CHALLENGES: 'ASEAN' AND 'THE WORLD'

As suggested above, despite the initial contentiousness of regional organization, ASEAN has gained greater internal legitimacy since its creation in 1967. ASEAN has been able to draw internal legitimacy from a variety of sources—its consistency with national and regional resilience goals, a process that is both inclusive and supportive of individual and collective substantive objectives, and also the actualization of resilience—in a word, performance.[35] Put another way, the stabilization of both ASEAN's intra-regional and extra-regional relations and the generally greater security enjoyed by states over the last 40 years have helped to substantiate the legitimacy of ASEAN as an international organization representative of regional interests and the 'correctness' of ASEAN as a set of institutional practices. Consequently, even though individual states might have frustrations with ASEAN (as when consensus on particular issues is elusive or when collective action is consequently highly constrained, non-existent, and/or inefficient), ASEAN's legitimacy still grew. Here, it is worth underscoring again the difference between efficiency and efficacy. ASEAN was never the most efficient of organizations in terms of speed of decision-making or coordinated action but, during its first decades, that inefficiency was more than offset by ASEAN's relative efficacy in creating the conditions necessary for resilience. The fact that the stabilization of regional relations was also associated with new economic prosperity and growth, which in turn also bolstered ASEAN's external standing, also helped increase ASEAN's internal legitimacy.

ASEAN's general trend of growing legitimacy, however, took a new turn beginning in the mid-1990s when coinciding developments raised questions about ASEAN's approach and practices, especially in relation to non-ASEAN actors. In particular, ASEAN, whose institutional development and processes had been relatively insulated and limited to ASEAN states, found itself as an institution increasingly engaged with (and intruded upon by) the world outside ASEAN. This engagement has driven in important ways intra-ASEAN efforts to reform institutional practices and ASEAN's organizational culture, including the adoption of a new ASEAN Charter. Such efforts, however, today introduce new internal legitimacy challenges that may prove more serious to the organization. Three sets of developments—each illustrative of a different legitimacy challenge—deserve particular mention: the ending of the Cold War

[35] Richard Stubbs, in his discussion of domestic regime legitimacy, gives particular emphasis to the importance of performance legitimacy as more important than procedural legitimacy in sustaining domestic regimes in the global south. See Richard Stubbs, 'Performance Legitimacy and "Soft Authoritarianism,"' in Amitav Acharya, B. Michael Frolic, and Richard Stubbs (eds.), *Democracy, Human Rights, and Civil Society in Southeast Asia* (Toronto: Joint Centre for Asia Pacific Studies, 2001), 37–54.

(substantive), ASEAN's institutional extension into new regionalisms beyond Southeast Asia (procedural), and the Asian financial crisis (performance).

Ending of the Cold War

In Southeast Asia, the ending of the Cold War introduced both new challenges and opportunities for ASEAN as an institution. In particular, the ending of the Cold War enabled a more activist liberal and interventionist agenda, especially as regards human rights and neoliberal economic development, on the parts of global core states and world organizations. Both agendas also meant new external scrutiny of individual ASEAN states, which were mostly authoritarian. All of this might have left ASEAN as an organization relatively unaffected were it not for the fact that ASEAN at this time also began to take the highly symbolic and long awaited process of extending ASEAN membership to Vietnam, Laos, Cambodia, and Myanmar. While that process fulfilled a cherished, founding objective of uniting a divided Southeast Asia, the problem was that among prospective ASEAN members were states whose authoritarian and human rights practices were even more problematic compared to those of the founding members. Myanmar and its military junta drew particular fire from external interstate and transnational coalitions that mobilized against the Myanmar regime, individual ASEAN members, *and* importantly ASEAN for engaging with it.

From 1989 to 1997, external pressures on individual ASEAN states and ASEAN as an institution consequently precipitated a near-decade-long intra-ASEAN debate about Myanmar's ASEAN membership. The internal ASEAN debate is sometimes framed in terms of a liberal–illiberal divide among ASEAN's founding members—but this obscures how influential the external pressure was to this debate. While there were societal and domestic liberalizing trends at play in the cases of Thailand and the Philippines—ASEAN's more democratic members at the time—it is worth noting that they were also Myanmar's initial proponents from 1989–1994, despite the Myanmar military's crackdown on demonstrators in 1988 and Bangkok's first civilian, non-military government (1988–1991) in 12 years. In contrast, Malaysia and Indonesia were most opposed. The mounting external pressure on the Philippines and Thailand, who were also among Washington's historical partners in ASEAN, combined with Indonesia's and Malaysia's objections to major power efforts to interfere with ASEAN's decisionmaking initially led to a shifting of sides (proponents became opponents, while opponents became proponents of Myanmar's scheduled membership[36]). Heightened external pressure on ASEAN, however, would eventually produce an outcome opposite to that

[36] It should be noted that the intra-ASEAN debate was always a question of timing—*when* not *whether* to admit Myanmar, though it theoretically could have been postponed indefinitely.

intended by external liberal critics, with ASEAN defiantly deciding to admit Myanmar in 1997 as planned.

ASEAN's 1997 decision illustrates the tensions that can exist between internal and external legitimacy claims. In this case, external liberal expectations about domestic practices and, by extension, international obligations to comment and bring pressure to bear on those out of conformance came into conflict with ASEAN's internal expectations about states' intra-regional obligations to respect both individual state politics and more importantly a regional peace based on norms of non-interference. While external pressure was not entirely ineffective at first, it was nevertheless always perceived as inappropriate (first, somewhat inappropriate and then, objectionably inappropriate). In addition to directly challenging national and regional autonomy expectations, external pressures also had the effect of fomenting intra-ASEAN tensions, opening the door for greater extra-regional interference and thus illustrating the resilience link between internal instabilities and external pressures. The intensified and even strong-armed external efforts to pressure ASEAN into a different course, eventually reached the limits of appropriateness in ASEAN, convincing collective ASEAN to admit Myanmar in an act of regional self determination, autonomy, and resistance.[37]

As justified as states may have felt in their defence of ASEAN's institutional values, that decision would nevertheless cost ASEAN in terms of its external legitimacy. Indeed, Myanmar became a yearly issue in ASEAN's relations with 'Western' partners, including the United States and European Union, both of which were not above suspending or limiting talks and exchanges with ASEAN on account of Myanmar. Moreover, with Myanmar's membership in ASEAN, the debate became one as much about ASEAN and its institutional practices and values, as it was about Myanmar's military regime.[38]

Extended ASEAN Regionalisms

External scrutiny of ASEAN and its practices was additionally intensified by ASEAN's extension into regionalisms beyond Southeast Asia in the 1990s. Of particular note were the Asia Pacific Economic Cooperation Forum (APEC) and the ASEAN Regional Forum (ARF), both of which included actors whose economic and political development were differently conditioned and for whom internal fragmentation and external intervention were not particular preoccupations. That contrast in historical development and material

[37] Ba, *(Re)Negotiating South and Southeast Asia*, 112–24.

[38] Jürgen Haacke, '"Enhanced Interaction" with Myanmar and the Project of Security Community', *Contemporary Southeast Asia*, Vol. 27/2 (2005), 188–216; See also Robin Ramcharan, 'ASEAN and NonInterference', *Contemporary Southeast Asia*, Vol. 22/1 (2000), 60–88.

condition became a key source of intra-APEC and intra-ARF tensions over both the agendas and processes of ASEAN's extended regionalisms. In particular, ASEAN states tended to extend the emphasis ASEAN placed on long-term relationship-building and relationship-maintaining in their approach to APEC and the ARF, while others like the United States tended to focus more on short-term, discrete functional objectives.

Just as important, those actors also came from different 'Western', legal-rationalist traditions, traditions that sat uneasily with ASEAN's communitarian values and approaches. In one early description of the emerging security dialogue that would become the ARF, Pauline Kerr characterized ASEAN's consensus driven processes as so 'alien' to Western 'results-oriented' (efficiency) preferences and values that Western participants could not get their minds around it and even found the whole process somewhat suspicious.[39] As discussed by Nicole Gallant and Richard Stubbs, similar tensions and culture clashes could also be found in APEC.[40] At minimum, Western, liberal participants in both APEC and the ARF tended to find ASEAN's institutional practices and processes of consensus building frustrating in their time-inefficiency and their unwillingness to compel specific compliance and timeframes through more consequentialist mechanisms.

In short, the issue and disconnect was thus both cultural and functional. For many non-ASEAN participants, despite their participation in the consensus-seeking process, the process nevertheless produced what they saw to be suboptimal outcomes that moreover did not reflect their identities, ideals, or expectations about what international organizations should do. As suggested above, historical and cultural differences also intervened to produce less sympathy for the particular inclusiveness of ASEAN's consensus-driven processes. In other words, in contrast to ASEAN states which tended to value consensus for its communitarian inclusiveness, others tended to see it as unnecessarily extreme in its accommodation of minority voices and as detracting from more 'important' functional objectives. ASEAN's insistence, at and since the APEC's and ARF's founding, that *ASEAN* processes be central to both also likely diminished extra-regional appreciation for the values and priorities that had legitimated those processes within ASEAN. Consequently (and ironically), a consensus whose value lay in its inclusiveness came to be seen by many extra-ASEAN participants of the APEC and ARF processes as insufficiently accommodating of their own institutional

[39] See Pauline Kerr, 'The Security Dialogue in the Asia Pacific', *Pacific Review*, Vol. 7/4 (1994), 397–409. This sense of institutional culture clash remains relevant today. For example, as one US government analyst commented, US participants of ASEAN regional processes still find ASEAN's consensus-driven approach 'foreign'. Informal discussion with author, March 2010, Washington, DC.

[40] Nicole Gallant and Richard Stubbs, 'APEC's Dilemmas: Institution-Building around the Pacific Rim', *Pacific Affairs*, Vol. 70/2 (1997), 203–19.

and practical preferences.[41] The end result for ASEAN has been growing external questions about ASEAN's legitimacy on substantive, procedural, as well as performance grounds.

The Asian Financial Crisis

Lastly, the 1990s brought financial and political crisis to ASEAN. In particular, ASEAN's inability to respond more effectively and quickly to the 1997–8 Asian financial crisis challenged ASEAN's legitimacy and certainly its reputation, in important ways. Perhaps, first and foremost, the crisis became an indictment on ASEAN's performance. There were two aspects to this challenge—one internal, the other external. First, the Asian financial crisis involved questions of performance legitimacy and thus had implications for ASEAN in terms of the commitment of member states. Basically, ASEAN had failed to respond to the crisis in ways that significantly managed or mitigated its effects for member states.[42] Second, the Asian financial crisis dramatically and negatively affected external perceptions of ASEAN as a successful organization—economically, to be sure, but also politically as some states succumbed to competitive posturing.

Moreover, in destabilizing the regimes of key ASEAN member states (Suharto's 30 year rule came to an end; Thailand's prime minister was forced to resign; a deputy prime minister in Malaysia was controversially sacked; separatist movements agitated), the crisis also had the effect of destabilizing the domestic foundations that had underlain individual states' participation in ASEAN. Other challenges—a chronic haze problem caused by land clearing practices in Indonesia, instabilities and political crises in Cambodia, and the shooting of demonstrators in East Timor by Indonesian security forces, to name a few– all similarly seemed to point to the shortcomings of both ASEAN's consensus-based approach and its particular attachment to non-interference, both of which hindered more coordinated, consequential responses to all these various crises.[43] In short, the various crises associated with and intensified by the Asian Financial Crisis diminished ASEAN's legitimacy in the area of performance.

[41] Emmers and Tan, in a similar vein, highlight how the politics of the ARF have, in fact, rigidified states' different positions such that ASEAN processes in the ARF have lost an important flexibility, which had once been its strength. See Ralf Emmers and See Seng Tan, 'The ASEAN Regional Forum and Preventive Diplomacy: Built to Fail?' *Asian Security*, Vol. 7/1 (2010), 44–60.

[42] Douglas Webber, 'Two Funerals and a Wedding? The Ups and Downs of Regionalism in East Asia and Asia-Pacific after the Asian Crisis', *Pacific Review*, Vol. 14/3 (2001), 339–72; Shaun Narine, *Explaining ASEAN: Regionalism in Southeast Asia* (Boulder, CO: Lynne Reinner 2002), 166; Jürgen Ruland, 'ASEAN and the Asian Crisis: Theoretical Implications and Practical Consequences for Southeast Asian Regionalism', *Pacific Review*, Vol. 13/3 (2000), 421–51; Michael Wesley, 'The Asian Crisis and the Adequacy of Regional Institutions', *Contemporary Southeast Asia*, Vol. 21/1 (April 1999).

[43] See, for example, chapter 7 in Narine, *Explaining ASEAN*.

DELEGITIMATION AND RELEGITIMATION?

The above developments have had complex effects on ASEAN as an institution. The difficulties in managing economic, environmental, and political crises, as well as new members, collectively dealt a serious blow to what had previously been considered a successful cooperative enterprise. Most focus on how the above developments have especially affected ASEAN's performance legitimacy. As Joakim Ojendal put it, 'The difficulties in dealing with these (and other) issues have opened up for critical questioning of ASEAN's role and effectiveness in practice, and the real significance of institutionalized regionalization in South-East Asia...'[44] Moreover, while many of the challenges above originated from expectations and forces outside ASEAN, they also began to detract from ASEAN's internal legitimacy and coherence.

Vis-à-vis external actors, one of the more immediate institutional challenges for ASEAN has been how external dissatisfaction with ASEAN has diminished some external interest in ASEAN processes. US participation and interest in the ARF has been of special concern among ASEAN states. While the United States under the Obama administration has stood out for its comprehensive engagement of ASEAN, it is also worth noting that its predecessors (both Clinton and Bush presidencies) came to have important dissatisfactions with ASEAN processes. In particular the constraints imposed by both consensus and non-interference norms, such that they downgraded their presence at ASEAN meetings and/or reverted back to the bilateralism that has historically defined US Asia policy.[45] Nor has the United States been alone in its questions. Australia's most recent Asia Pacific Community (APC) proposal is a particular example of a dissatisfied extra-regional partner pursuing non-ASEAN centric possibilities.[46] While politically challenged in more than one respect and from more than one party, The APC proposal is nevertheless indicative of the growing questions about ASEAN's role, questions that again reflect a lack of external agreement about both ASEAN's institutional practices and its values. For ASEAN, such developments create pressure to change core practices or lose its privileged position in the regional institutional architecture—that is, a centrality that has become itself an additional source of legitimacy in the eyes of ASEAN's member states.

[44] Joakim Ojendal, 'Back to the Future? Regionalism in South-East Asia Under Unilateral Pressure', *International Affairs*, Vol. 80/3 (2004), 519–33.

[45] See, for example, discussion in Alice Ba, 'ASEAN Centrality Imperiled? ASEAN Institutionalism and the Challenges of Major Power Institutionalization', in Ralf Emmers (ed.), *ASEAN and the Institutionalization of East Asia* (Abingdon and New York, Routledge: 2011): 114–29. For a particular discussion on the views held by the George W. Bush presidency, see Ralph Cossa, 'Evolving US Views on Asia's Future Institutional Architecture', in Michael J. Green and Bates Gill (eds.), *Asia's New Multilateralism: Cooperation, Competition, and the Search for Community* (New York: Columbia University Press, 2009), 33–54.

[46] Amy Searight, 'New Challenges, New Vision, Pedestrian Progress', *Comparative Connections* (April 2010), 125–40.

The various developments and conflicts above consequently generated unprecedented discussion and reflection, as well as efforts to reform ASEAN practices, norms, and organizational culture. Shaun Narine summarized well the general consensus among many observers and concerned ASEAN elites: '[U]nless ASEAN the organization can effectively unite its members in times of regional upheaval, it will never regain its international stature'.[47] Such changes include efforts to modify ASEAN's core principle of noninterference since the early 1990s, and states' adoption of an ASEAN Charter in 2007, a document that aims to transform what has been a consensus-based, informal/personal organization into a more 'legalistic' entity and that also includes provisions for human rights and nods to civil society. Though the final document adopted proved less ambitious in its changes than many hoped, the Charter pointed to 'subtle' and notable shifts in intra-ASEAN thinking.[48]

Perhaps most interesting has been the way that above developments reveal how internal legitimacy claims have interacted and dialogued with those outside ASEAN. Most significantly, external *delegitimating* pressures have generated *legitimating* efforts in turn. Those legitimating efforts have taken two general forms. The first is push back where states and elites respond to external claims and pressures with an active defence of ASEAN. The second is adjustment—in essence, efforts to respond to outstanding concerns

Regarding the first, states and elites pushed back against specific criticisms by actively defending ASEAN's practices, its prerogative role, and especially its autonomy to make its own decisions. Moreover, in that external pressures also spoke to historic resilience concerns about opportunistic external manipulations, the ASEAN defence was also able to draw upon longstanding, substantive, internal legitimating arguments in support for the organization. The push back against external pressures also reflected a concern that changing ASEAN practices too much would undermine the very arguments that have legitimated ASEAN's special place and role in both Southeast Asia and extended ASEAN arrangements (see also discussion below).

The case of Myanmar above is one illustration of how external criticisms generated a defence of first, ASEAN's prerogative role in determining what happens in Southeast Asia and second, the value of ASEAN's institutional practices in ameliorating state behavior through dialogue and inclusion. Another example can be found in ASEAN's early responses to external criticisms of its role in the ARF. In that case, criticisms of ASEAN's loose institutionalism and institutional inclusiveness vis-à-vis China, as well as Myanmar and

[47] Shaun Narine, 'ASEAN in the Aftermath: The Consequences of the East Asian Economic Crisis', *Global Governance*, Vol. 8 (2002), 179–94.

[48] Paul Evans, 'Human Security and East Asia: In the Beginning', *Journal of East Asian Studies*, Vol. 4 (2004), 264.

North Korea, precipitated what Johnston characterizes as a 'counter realpolitik' defence of ASEAN's role and practices.[49] As the argument went, ASEAN's institutional informalism (supported by its lesser power status) better served reassurance objectives, was 'a better route to security' than more coercive institutional practices that created a hostile institutional environment, and at minimum, was better able to bring different parties to the regional table and keep them there.[50] In this way states' regular defence of ASEAN vis-à-vis external, extra-regional actors also resulted in sharpened arguments justifying ASEAN's central position and prerogative role in institutional processes.

In contrast, the second form that legitimating efforts have taken is to reform and adjust institutional practices towards *making* ASEAN more legitimate in the eyes of the world outside ASEAN. It was clear, for example, (to quote Robin Ramcharan) that 'the sanctity of the principle of non-interference in ASEAN [was] clearly out-of-step with the emerging practice and rhetoric among the Western states' in the post-Cold War era.[51] Consequently, even at the same time that external criticisms of ASEAN's institutional practices produced sharpened arguments in defence of the legitimacy of ASEAN practices, there were also efforts by states to reframe and retool institutional practices in ways that would appear more legitimate in the eyes of the world outside ASEAN. Examples here would include Bangkok's and Manila's initial policy changes on Myanmar, as well as proposals for 'flexible engagement' and 'enhanced interaction' that, in principle, allowed for legitimate comment and even (limited) action in cases involving especially destabilizing developments to the collective—developments that would otherwise be categorized as 'domestic' and thus beyond ASEAN's reach.[52]

At the same time, such efforts to respond to external criticisms (as also with push back efforts above) are not entirely externally driven. As noted earlier, ASEAN's own internal legitimacy rests at least in part on others affirming the enterprise and recognizing it as a legitimate organization, which means that any loss of external legitimacy will have the potential to destabilize internal assessments. In addition, ASEAN states' efforts to change certain practices,

[49] See Alastair Iain Johnston, 'Socialization in International Institutions', in John Ikenberry and Michael Mastanduno (eds.), *International Relations Theory and the Asia Pacific*, (New York: Columbia University Press, 2003), 107–62.

[50] See, for example, Amitav Acharya, 'Ideas, Identity, and Institution-building: from the "ASEAN Way" to the "Asia-Pacific Way"?' *Pacific Review*, Vol. 10/1 (1997), 319–46; Yuen Foong Khong, 'Making Bricks without Straw in the Asia Pacific?' *Pacific Review*, Vol. 10/2 (1997), 289–300; Evelyn Goh and Amitav Acharya, '*The Asean Regional Forum and US-China Relations: Comparing Chinese and American Positions.*' Draft Paper Prepared for the Fifth China-Asean Research Institutes Roundtable, 'Regionalism and Community Building in East Asia, University of Hong Kong, 17–19 October 2002.

[51] Ramcharan, 'ASEAN and Non-Interference', 84.

[52] For two excellent discussions of this debate, see Haacke, 'Enhanced Interaction'; and Ramcharan, 'ASEAN and NonInterference.'

reflect a concern or realization that ASEAN's external standing affects its ability and efficacy to represent its members vis-à-vis other actors. Thus, even from a purely functional or performance based view, ASEAN's internal legitimacy was sensitive to changing external assessments. The challenge, however, is how to respond to external criticisms but also remain true to established internal expectations and commitments. Internal assessments, after all, are only *partly* informed by what others think of ASEAN. Substantive claims and core institutional values (as the Myanmar case illustrates especially) still apply. Indeed, any effort to respond to extra-regional expectations could backfire if not sufficiently attentive to internal, substantive concerns and foundations. The way that ASEAN states conditioned their new flexibility towards noninterference is a particular example of the fine line often walked.

As noted above, efforts to modify ASEAN's historic position on non-interference responded to external judgements about ASEAN's failure or limited ability to address a range of domestic developments in Myanmar, Cambodia, East Timor, Malaysia, and Indonesia; dissatisfactions with ASEAN processes in the ARF; as well as the damage done to ASEAN's performance legitimacy by ASEAN's weak response to the Asian financial crisis. Intra-ASEAN frustrations about their limitations in controlling or limiting some states' reputation-damaging behavior vis-à-vis ASEAN also played into internal assessments of ASEAN's noninterference norm. Nevertheless, the internal obligations of non-interference remained real parts of ASEAN's 'normative terrain'[53], so it was not a surprise that ASEAN's new flexibility was still characterized as 'interaction' not 'interference'.

States' efforts to balance external and internal expectations were especially evident in the criteria and justifications for 'enhanced interaction'. Most notably, the criteria did *not* focus on the humanitarian or liberal concerns expressed by external critics, but instead on whether a state's practices were *regionally* destabilizing or detrimental to *ASEAN* and regional resilience.[54] As Indonesia's former foreign minister Ali Alatas characterized the new 'enhanced interaction' policy, 'ASEAN should be able to develop an agreed mechanism through which member states could work together to help a member country in addressing internal problems *with clear external implications*' (emphasis added).[55] The criteria and justifications for 'enhanced interaction' clearly frame the internal challenges posed to ASEAN as a functional one of performance, as opposed to a substantive one involving a reassessment of core values. Indeed, in arguing for change, Alatas and others, including Surin Pitsuwan (then Thailand's foreign minister, later ASEAN's 12th Secretary General) who had made the

[53] Haacke, 'Enhanced Interaction'.

[54] Haacke, 'Enhanced Interaction'; Ramcharan, 'ASEAN and NonInterference'.

[55] See 'ASEAN must reinvent itself, loosen non-interference policy: Alatas', *AFP* (7 January 2004).

original argument for 'flexible engagement', were also careful to underscore that respect for the internal affairs of others would remain a guiding principle. Again, the exception was only if a country's domestic practices destabilized the region and a broader regional resilience. In this way, reform efforts were simultaneously constrained by expectations of non-interference and at the same time, legitimated by accepted resilience concerns about regional stability.

The ASEAN Charter similarly illustrates ASEAN states' legitimation efforts vis-à-vis external communities, and at the same time, the strength of internal legitimacy claims and the difficulties that can be associated with efforts to reconcile the two. Adopted in November 2007 and ratified in late 2008 by all ten ASEAN members, the ASEAN Charter aimed to make ASEAN into 'a rules-based, people-oriented and more integrated entity'.[56] Of particular note were explicit references to 'democracy', 'good governance', as well as a provision to create a 'Human Rights Commission'. Towards making ASEAN into a more 'rules based' and even 'legal' institution, the Charter also mandated single chairmanships for 'key high level ASEAN bodies' and took steps to strengthen the ASEAN Secretariat by enhancing its monitoring and diplomatic role.[57] In short, on the external legitimacy questions above, the ASEAN Charter theoretically aimed to address procedural, functional/performance, and substantive concerns.

As many have noted, however, the process of negotiating and ratifying the ASEAN Charter was a protracted affair. In principle and in practice, the ASEAN Charter is also commonly characterized as having fallen short of expectation. Some initiatives—most notably, the creation of an ASEAN Committee of Permanent Representatives—which were originally thought to strengthen the ASEAN Secretariat, have in fact had the opposite effect.[58] The failure of more ambitious proposals during the process of negotiating the Charter, as in the cases above, similarly reflected push back from those inside ASEAN who saw certain proposals as overstepping agreed upon norms. It also may reflect tensions between 'Track II/III' scholars and advisors, who are generally more ambitious in pursuing change than their official 'Track I' counterparts.

Complicating the process in each of the cases above was also the changing content of ASEAN's membership—and not just in terms of newly admitted members. On the question of the ASEAN Human Rights Commission, for example, Jürgen Haacke and others give particular emphasis to a newly democratic Indonesia for pushing 'hard' to liberalize ASEAN's security and

[56] ASEAN Secretariat, 'ASEAN Embarks on New Era: ASEAN Charter Fully Ratified', Media Release (21 October 2008).

[57] ASEAN Website, 'ASEAN Leaders Sign ASEAN Charter', Media Release (20 November 2007)

[58] Surin Pitsuwan, 'ASEAN's Challenge: Some Reflections and Recommendations on Strengthening the ASEAN Secretariat', Report submitted to H. E. Marty Natalegawa, Chair ASEAN Coordinating Council, 2011 (12 December 2011). See also Kavi Chongkittavorn, 'Asean Secretariat Must be Strengthened', *The Irawaddy* (21 May 2012).

diplomatic culture.[59] As early as 2003 and as part of states' discussion on an ASEAN Charter, Indonesia was also a strong proponent of giving ASEAN, as an organization, expanded authority and capacity to talk and act upon destabilizing events in another country.[60] To contrast Indonesia's liberalizing push during the Charter debates with its past positions on, for example, 'flexible engagement' during the Asian financial crisis is to see how democratization has, in an important respect, introduced Indonesia as a different and new member to the ASEAN process.

Nevertheless, the Human Rights Commission is seen by many as significant only in a symbolic sense. States' decision to affirm its inclusion in the Charter was historically unprecedented—but the absence of clear mechanisms to make it operative was also indicative of an uncertain consensus. Especially telling again was what proponents of the mechanism chose to emphasize in their efforts to liberalize ASEAN. As with flexible engagement justifications above, arguments for change focused on functional, not substantive, arguments: Philippine Foreign Affairs Secretary Alberto Romulo argued that the creation of a human rights mechanism was critical and essential if ASEAN were to have any credibility in the international community.[61] ASEAN Secretary General Ong Keng Yong, arguing for the adoption and ratification of the ASEAN Charter, underscored ASEAN's need for a 'legal personality...greater institutional accountability and compliance system' in the interest of 'reinforce[ing] the *perception* of ASEAN as a serious regional player in the future of the Asia Pacific region'.[62] In one effort to explain to Myanmar why ASEAN should be concerned about domestic developments there, one ASEAN leader explained, 'The rest of the world thinks that this is a matter that concerns ASEAN also and have begun to hit at us.'[63] Such arguments surrounding the Charter illustrate well the particular concern and preoccupation states had with external assessments,[64] but also proponents' care to remain consistent with internal expectations and the understood purposes of ASEAN as an organization.

[59] Kavi Chongkittavorn, 'Complex Issues Underlie ASEAN Charter', *Thai Press Reports* (5 November 2007).

[60] See Haacke, 'Enhanced Interaction'.

[61] Al Labita, 'ASEAN Charter: Officials Hope to End Rifts', *Business Times (Singapore)* (27 July 2007).

[62] ASEAN Secretariat, 'ASEAN Leaders Sign ASEAN Charter', Media Release (20 November 2007). Emphasis added.

[63] Alex Au, 'ASEAN Still Toothless After 40 Years', *Asia Times* (27 November 2007).

[64] See especially Hiro Katsumata, 'ASEAN and human rights: resisting Western pressure or emulating the West?' *Pacific Review*, Vol. 22/5 (2009), 619–37; and 'Mimetic Adoption and Norm Diffusion: "Western" Security Cooperation in Southeast Asia?' *Review of International Studies*, Vol.37/2 (2011), 557–76. Katsumata argues that the ASEAN Human Rights Mechanism was created primarily to legitimate ASEAN in the eyes of Western actors.

Lastly, Charter debates also illustrated the new influence of ASEAN's four newest members, all of which joined ASEAN only in the second half of the 1990s. As with the case of a democratizing Indonesia, the addition of new members—because of their different identities and in their case, also different histories—introduce new intra-ASEAN uncertainties that also interact with external pressures. It is generally assumed, for example, that new members are out of step with founding members. Particular attention has focused on Myanmar as the key obstacle to more ambitious changes in ASEAN. As Barry Desker, for example, put it, 'Myanmar's continuing presence in ASEAN's chambers ensures that the traditional emphasis on non-interference and the sovereignty of states will be upheld by ASEAN.'[65] On the other hand, an over-focus on Myanmar and new members in general also risks obscuring what is a real lack of consensus on the issue. As ASEAN's then-Secretary General Ong Keng Yong made sure to emphasize in August 2007,

> When we talk about human rights, don't get the impression that the only guy who objects to whatever provisions we want in the ASEAN Charter is Myanmar... In our discussion on drafting the human rights provision, it was not Burma, as you call it, that caused all the trouble. There were four other countries that had reservations about how this paragraph was drafted and two of them were most vocal and they did not include Burma.[66]

Of those other four, they were reportedly Vietnam, Brunei, Cambodia, and Laos.[67] Singapore would make a fifth.

Still, the predominance of new members in that group is still significant. It is also interesting that these states have proven the most defensive of the principles that have historically defined ASEAN. For ASEAN's newer states, the ASEAN Charter—enhanced authority to comment on developments within another country, a Human Rights Mechanism, as well as a changed consensus principle—represented challenges to the basic conditions and understandings that had informed and substantiated their own decisions to join ASEAN. Moreover, as time went on, concerns heightened. As four out of ASEAN's total ten members, ASEAN's newest members are also able to constrain (and even reverse) efforts to streamline ASEAN's consensus process even under the 'ASEAN minus X' principle (a principle that allows the larger group to

[65] Barry Desker, 'Is the ASEAN Charter Necessary?', *RSIS Commentaries*, Singapore, 17 July 2008.

[66] S. Ramesh, 'ASEAN Charter Being Revised to Include Foreign Ministers' Views', *Channel News Asia* (6 August 2007). See also comments of Tommy Koh, who chaired the High Level Task Force that drafted the Charter following the EPG report. As Koh put it in response to those who blamed Myanmar, 'Myanmar... was not the most difficult colleague I had to deal with.' Koh, 'Not Perfect but Charter is a Good Start on Road to Regional Progress.'

[67] Kavi Chongkittavorn, 'ASEAN Charter: Should We Settle for Second Best?' *Nation* (13 August 2007).

move ahead and individual states to opt out). In addition, new members also defended ASEAN's practice of equal, as opposed to weighted, contributions to the ASEAN Secretariat's operating budget. In each of these cases, the positions taken by new members can also be seen as instances of push back against their perceived second class status in ASEAN where founding states dominate the discourse and dialogue and where newer members in cases like Laos don't even have the capacity to participate in all ASEAN meetings.

CONCLUSION

This chapter on ASEAN has given attention to questions of organizational legitimacy faced by non-core regional organization and how such questions can play out differently compared to the global regimes that are typically the subject of organizational legitimacy discussions. In particular, material and historical forces make questions of external legitimacy much more pressing for non-core organizations, ultimately informing both internal assessments and their institutional development. The specific examples of the Asian financial crisis, post-Cold War Myanmar debates, and ASEAN's relations with non-Southeast Asian actors in expanded ASEAN arrangements illustrate some of the complex effects of that external world of expectations on a non-core regional organization like ASEAN. In particular, these cases illustrate the sensitivity of ASEAN states to external affirmation (and the possible denial of such) and how external expectations and criticisms can challenge, substantiate, and mobilize internal legitimacy claims. On the one hand, they can generate internal changes in an effort to make the organization more legitimate to outside, authoritative actors; on the other hand, they can also result in push back. Thus, as an addendum to Hurd's argument that 'efforts to legitimize an institution naturally generate efforts by others to *de*-legitimize', the cases above illustrate that the converse is also true—that is, efforts to *delegitimize* can also result in refined legitimating arguments and a reaffirmation of internal commitments. The dynamic interactions and exchanges between local/regional expectations and global pressures, especially the ways that the local/regional mediate global norms and expectations, also bear similarities to the 'localisation' processes highlighted by Acharya.[68]

Most of all, the above discussion points to a need to give more attention to the substantive bases of an organization's internal legitimacy. Organizations do not always reflect the same assumptions about efficiency, efficacy, values, or social purpose, and again, non-core regional organizations are likely to reflect

[68] Acharya, 'How Ideas Spread'.

greater variation compared to the global regimes. As the ASEAN case makes clear, a consideration of such differences is important not just because organizations vary in their understood substantive purposes and raison d'etres, but also because substantive bases for legitimacy will also affect assessments of process and performance. In the ASEAN case, the continued validity of substantive claims continues to help sustain the organization despite the organization's clear limitations. For example, as the above discussion makes clear, ASEAN has historically fallen short when it comes to timely coordination and collective responses, but because member-states see ASEAN more in terms of milieu and resilience goals, they have tended to assess ASEAN more favourably than its critics.

The Asian financial crisis offers a specific example of how substantive expectations will affect performance assessments. As highlighted above, there is much agreement about the practical limitations of ASEAN's response to the Asian financial crisis, but while the crisis was highly damaging to ASEAN in terms of its external reputation, internal assessments were generally milder. This is because ASEAN states, unlike their global counterparts, viewed the crisis as having important global sources; and just as important, they tended not to view the management of such external financial forces as something that ASEAN could do.[69] As a result, in the eyes of ASEAN states, the Asian financial crisis did less to delegitimate ASEAN than it did the IMF or APEC, for example.[70]

Indeed, despite the significant external questions raised about ASEAN especially since 1997, the examples above suggest that, internally, ASEAN and its practices continue to enjoy a degree of substantive, procedural, and internal letigimacy. This is also despite the new institutional complexity introduced by processes of domestic liberalization and ASEAN's expanded membership. External critics may see ASEAN's noninterference norm as anachronistic and contrary to liberal standards and norms (in relation to both domestic and international–institutional responsibilities), but internal assessments are more complex. Thus, while the challenges faced by ASEAN during the 1990s have generated interest in reforming and adapting some key ASEAN practices, this does not mean that the old ways have lost relevance—in fact, quite the contrary. As Haacke, for example, has highlighted, one reason that governments have chosen not to be more ambitious in changing ASEAN's noninterference norm is that the practices associated with it have proven successful in other ways. States see them as successfully 'mediating estrangement', minimizing the escalation of conflict, supporting ASEAN's prerogative position in larger forums, engaging major powers in 'norm building'.[71] Such assessments help

[69] See also Narine, 'ASEAN in the Aftermath'.
[70] See discussion in chapter 7 in Ba, *(Re)Negotiating East and Southeast Asia*.
[71] Haacke, *ASEAN's Diplomatic and Security Culture*, 218–23.

explain why change has not been more dramatic in ASEAN. Indeed, the fact that the very institutional practices that have come under external scrutiny are also linked to the successful stabilization of regional relations—in a word, performance—is what makes the tensions between internal and external expectations even more difficult to reconcile for ASEAN.

8

The Shanghai Cooperation Organization: *Legitimacy through (Self-) Legitimation?*

Jochen Prantl

[T]he SCO cannot be exempt from questions about its legitimacy and whether it is ultimately a force for good or ill, as seen from the viewpoint of both its own members' populations and the outside world. In other regions, most multilateral institutions would be judged to be 'effective and (widely accepted as) legitimate' or 'legitimate and ineffective'. In the former case they may be evaluated as doing good and in the latter case at least as doing no harm (unless they create a sense of false security). Prima facie, the SCO may be a rare case of an organization that is relatively effective but not generally regarded—by other institutions, outside powers and some elements in its own member states—as legitimate.[1]

This chapter examines the practices of legitimation in and around the Shanghai Cooperation Organization (SCO). Founded in 2001, the SCO brings together China, Russia, and four Central Asian countries—Kazakhstan, Kyrgyzstan, Tajikistan, and Uzbekistan. It is a striking, though widely understudied, example for the development of regional mechanisms to organize inter-state relations in the post-Cold War order, to address potential tensions, and to manage transnational threats and challenges. As Bailes et al. recently observed, '[t]here is a widespread assumption in the West that, because they involve imperfectly democratic states and often reject externally defined norms of governance, such groups are bound to be illegitimate or ineffective or both'.[2] Examining the SCO from a legitimacy perspective adds to our understanding of how its

[1] Alyson J. K. Bailes and Pál Dunay, 'The Shanghai Cooperation Organization as a regional security institution', in Alyson J. K. Bailes, Pál Dunay, Pan Guang and Mikhail Troitskiy, *The Shanghai Cooperation Organization*, SIPRI Policy Paper No. 17, May 2007, 3.

[2] Bailes and Dunay, '*The Shanghai Cooperation Organization as a regional security institution*', iv.

member states have used the legal framework of an international organization to self-legitimize their policies through mutually recognized practices and beliefs which effectively counter-balance Western claims of SCO illegitimacy.

Departing from this observation, the chapter focuses in particular on the following features of the SCO, each of which elucidates different aspects of legitimation practices:

- the scope of the organization's mandate;
- the organizational structure;
- the homogeneity of membership, including the presence of regional/ global hegemonic powers;
- the underlying norms and principles that guide the workings of the SCO.

Underlying the analysis are three broad questions: first, how the SCO is legitimized from below through its member states; second, how the organization itself claims legitimacy downwards to its membership and sideways towards other international and regional institutions; and third how the SCO is recognized by outsiders who are not (full) members of the organization.

A key theme, running through this chapter, is that the SCO offers a forum for the nurturing of relationships and the building of mutual trust, which is separate from the narrow collective-action problem-solving function generally ascribed to international organizations. Those relationships have strengthened SCO legitimacy and with it the legitimacy of the domestic regimes of SCO member states.

SCOPE: ECONOMIC VERSUS SECURITY COOPERATION

While the SCO itself has a rather short 10-year history, its predecessor, the so-called 'Shanghai Five', originated in the long-term tensions between the Soviet Union and the People's Republic of China over their shared border, which re-emerged on the political agenda in 1991, when the Central Asian states bordering on China—Kazakhstan, Kyrgyzstan, and Tajikistan—declared their independence.[3] The Shanghai Agreement on Confidence Building in the Military Field, and the Agreement on Mutual Reduction of Military Forces, signed in 1996 and 1997 respectively, set out substantial and detailed measures

[3] The Soviet-Chinese border, stretching 4,300 km from the eastern edge of Mongolia to the Tumen River of North Korea and 3,200 km from the western edge of Mongolia to the Tajik-Afghanistan border junction, had been drawn primarily by the Russian Empire and the Qing Dynasty in the late 19th century.

of military restraint and transparency along all five states' mutual borders. The Shanghai Five thus emerged as a confidence-building mechanism, facilitating the conclusion of further bilateral agreements on frontier delineation, trade, and cooperation.[4] In June 2001 the same group of countries, along with Uzbekistan, consolidated their relations by setting up the SCO as a formalized institution with the declared objectives of

> strengthening mutual trust and good-neighborly friendship among the member states; encouraging effective cooperation among the member states in political, economic and trade, scientific and technological, cultural, educational, energy, communications, environment and other fields; devoting themselves jointly to preserving and safeguarding regional peace, security and stability; and establishing a democratic, fair and rational new international political and economic order.[5]

The new organization broadened its scope beyond border and regional economic cooperation to include security cooperation particularly aimed at combating terrorism, separatism, and religious extremism, which SCO members, especially China, usually refer to as the 'three evils'.[6] The SCO's 2001 Convention on Combating Terrorism, Separatism and Extremism adopted a common framework on the meanings of those terms and established a mutual commitment of guaranteed extraditions or forcible return of individuals committing such crimes. In essence, the convention presents an alternative model of counter-terrorism approaches. The underlying rules and principles constitute, according to the NGO Human Rights in China, 'fundamental challenges to the international community's efforts to ensure protection of human rights in counter-terrorism approaches, including within the UN Global Counter-Terrorism Strategy'.[7] At the heart of SCO security cooperation is the Regional Anti-Terrorism Structure (RATS) as further developed in Section 2. It is the permanent body entrusted with the implementation of SCO counter-terrorism strategies. Over the years, the SCO held a number of major multilateral anti-terrorism exercises to strengthen security cooperation and confidence amongst its members.[8] The first exercise was held in 2003 aiming

[4] The first meeting took place in Shanghai, in April 1996.

[5] Declaration on the Establishment of Shanghai Cooperation Organization, signed on 15 June 2001, available at www.sectsco.org.

[6] Preamble to the Shanghai Convention on Combating Terrorism, Separatism and Extremism, signed on 15 June 2001, available at www.sectsco.org.

[7] Human Rights in China, *Counter-Terrorism and Human Rights: The Impact of the Shanghai Cooperation Organization*, A Human Rights in China Whitepaper, New York, March 2011, ii.

[8] For example, The 'Peace Mission-2010' exercise, hosted by Kazakhstan, included over 5,000 personnel from China, Russia, Kazakhstan, Kyrgyzstan, and Tajikistan. Notably, Uzbekistan did not participate in the multilateral exercise. See Julie Boland, 'Learning from the Shanghai Cooperation Organization's "Peace Mission-2010" Exercise', *Brookings Opinion*, 29 October 2010, available at http://www.brookings.edu/research/opinions/2010/10/29-asia-war-games-boland.

at preventing Uighur separatists from crossing the border into Kazakhstan in order to launch attacks against China. Another multilateral exercise, carried out in 2006, involved Kyrgyzstan, Tajikistan, and Uzbekistan, and aimed at preventing terrorists from attacking critical infrastructure with the purpose of undermining the stability of the respective regimes in the countries concerned. SCO security cooperation has strengthened its legitimacy through the close rhetorical association with the US-led 'War on Terror' and subsequently with the UN Global Counter-Terrorism Strategy, adopted in 2006. However, while SCO declaratory policy pays lip-service to the objectives of UN-sanctioned counter-terrorism efforts,[9] SCO (regional) operational policy is driven by the much narrower concern about SCO member states' regime security and territorial integrity. The global counter-terrorism strategy, along with the SCO's much broader definition of terrorism which includes religious extremism and separatism, provides the legitimizing framework for the SCO 'to nullify any threat to the integrity of their nation states or regimes'.[10]

Security cooperation and economic development remain the key priorities for the SCO, as the heads of states and government confirmed in their 10th Anniversary Astana Declaration, adopted in June 2011. But they also further expanded their scope by adopting a new Counter-narcotics Strategy for 2011–16 in order 'to strengthen pragmatic interaction with the aim of jointly preventing a negative impact from the narcotic threat in the SCO region and safeguarding a steady regional development'.[11]

Yet, the general agreement on the broader objectives of the SCO does not come without tensions. China tends to emphasize the economic dimension of the SCO; the Russian Federation is more interested in strengthening the SCO's capacity to address security concerns. While China has been pushing for the creation of a SCO free trade area by 2020, Russia has been keen to delay this process, since the comparative cost advantage of Chinese products may eventually jeopardize Russian exports to Central Asia. Looked at from a Chinese perspective, the SCO provides a convenient platform to develop economic relationships with Central Asian countries without antagonizing Russia. It has become the arena to address and manage differences between China and Russia within an institutionalized framework. Such a framework

[9] For example, the 2008 Dushanbe Declaration of Heads of SCO Member States 'reaffirm[ed] their commitment to strengthening the central coordinating role of the UN in mounting an international response to the threat of terrorism, to consistent implementation of the UN Global Counterterrorism Strategy, [and] earliest possible approval of the Comprehensive Convention on International Terrorism', available at http://www.sectsco.org/news_detail.asp?id=2360&LanguageID=2.

[10] Stephen Aris, 'The Shanghai Cooperation Organisation: 'Tackling the Three Evils'. A Regional Response to Non-Traditional Security Challenges or an Anti-Western Bloc?', *Europe-Asia Studies*, Vol. 61, No. 3, May 2009, 467.

[11] Astana Declaration of the 10th Anniversary of the Shanghai Cooperation Organization, 15 June 2011, Paragraph VII.

provides reassurance to the Central Asian governments, and larger political space to navigate their interests vis-à-vis the great powers. Despite their policy differences, Central Asian states are united by the key objective 'at least formally, to take part in generating regional approaches to cooperation and security on an equal basis with the larger regional powers'.[12] At the same time, they perform the function of balancers between East and West, defying the interpretation of the SCO as an anti-Western bloc. For example, all Central Asian countries participate in NATO's Partnership for Peace programme. Uzbekistan has been—especially after the terrorist attacks of 11 September 2001—an ally of the United States and signed a Declaration on Strategic Partnership and Cooperation Framework in 2002, which sought to establish new bilateral relations in the political, economic, military, and humanitarian fields.[13] Kyrgyzstan still hosts a military installation of the United States, which was opened in 2001 to support Operation Enduring Freedom in Afghanistan. Kazakhstan became the first Central Asian state to assume the status of NATO partner country, after concluding an Individual Partnership Action Plan with the Atlantic Alliance in 2006. In sum, while the SCO has been a convenient policy forum for Central Asian states to institutionalize their interaction with China and Russia within a stable organizational framework, association with NATO has allowed Central Asian countries to balance carefully their policy agendas in a region that has turned into a contested space between East and West.

Since the creation of the SCO, Chinese enterprises have attempted major inroads to Central Asian energy markets in order to challenge Russian control over oil and gas resources in the region. For example, in 2005, China National Petroleum Corporation (CNPC) and Russian Lukoil engaged in an acquisition race for the Turgai Petroleum joint venture in North Kumkol, Kazakhstan. When CNPC acquired PetroKazakhstan in October 2005, President Nazarbayev signed a law which forced the Chinese corporation to sell one third of its shares back to the Kazakh national oil company KazMunaiGaz.[14] While the Russian Federation is aware that it cannot keep China out of the Central Asian region, it has aimed at regulating and controlling this process to the greatest possible extent. Supported by Uzbekistan and Kazakhstan, then-President Vladimir Putin proposed in summer 2006 the establishment of an 'Energy Club' to coordinate energy policies of SCO members under a single umbrella, addressing the interests of both oil and gas producers as well

[12] Ruslan Maksutov, The Shanghai Cooperation Organization: A Central Asian Perspective, SIPRI Project Paper, August 2006, 4.

[13] Bilateral relations with the United States (and other Western countries) temporarily deteriorated after Uzbek troops fired into a crowd of protesters in Andijan on 13 May 2005, which reportedly left hundreds dead.

[14] Artyom Matusov, 'Energy Cooperation in the SCO: Club or Gathering', *China and Eurasia Forum Quarterly*, Vol. 5/3 (2007), 83–99.

as consumers. The Chinese response to the proposed 'Energy Club' has been extremely lukewarm, since it does not want to be tied down by rules and principles that may eventually constrain its advances into the Central Asian energy market. As Matusov has rightly observed:

> When officials and experts talk about an 'energy club' or 'cooperation and coordination' within the SCO what some of them really want are mechanisms to defuse potentially damaging competition among producers, consumers and transit states. What could this damaging competition entail other than a more open market where China is able to have greater choice as to who it gets its energy from and how much it pays for it? It doesn't seem very likely that China would buy into such a scheme.[15]

And indeed, China has been extremely selective in choosing cooperative frameworks, institutional and non-institutional, for pursuing its energy security interests in Central Asia. The multilateral SCO framework has been primarily used for a triple purpose: first, to gain access to a region that is of vital strategic importance to Russia without antagonizing the regional hegemon; second, to develop economic relationships (and dependencies) through the SCO framework, for example, by channeling loans to SCO member states;[16] and third, to provide a regional conduit beyond the more narrow concerns of Sino-Russian relations in order to occupy political space in and around which regional relationships could be organized—at the expense of the European Union, NATO, and the United States.

Although the proposal to form an 'Energy Club' is still on the table, it has now been overtaken by events. The Astana Declaration of the SCO 10th Anniversary does not specifically mention the club but only refers to the potential advancement of major projects in the area of energy-saving technologies for which the '[c]reation of the relevant funding mechanisms will be expedited'.[17] Energy security relations have evolved through a matrix of relationships—bilateral, trilateral, plurilateral—in and around the SCO, involving members and non-members of the organization.[18] For example, Uzbekistan sells gas to both China and Russia on the basis of bilateral agreements; at the

[15] Matusov, *'Energy Cooperation in the SCO: Club or Gathering'*, 97.

[16] For example, at the SCO Yekaterinburg Summit in June 2009, China announced plans of a US$10 billion loan to SCO member states to support their struggling economies after the 2008 global financial crisis. See Xinhua News, 16 June 2009, available at http://news.xinhuanet.com/english/2009-06/16/content_11552439.htm. At the SCO Beijing Summit in June 2012, China offered another loan of US$10 billion to boost regional economic development and support economic cooperation amongst SCO members. See Xinhua News, 7 June 2012, available at http://news.xinhuanet.com/english/china/2012-06/07/c_131637089.htm.

[17] Astana Declaration of the 10th Anniversary of the Shanghai Cooperation Organization, 15 June 2011, Paragraph VIII.

[18] Examples of those energy security relationships include: China—Kazakhstan, Uzbekistan, and Turkmenistan; Russia—China; China—Iran; Russia—Iran; Iran—Pakistan. See M. K. Bhadrakumar, 'Sino-Russian baby comes of age', *Asia Times*, 13 June 2009.

same time, it has accepted bilateral Russian foreign direct investments over the next five years, thereby circumventing any potential multilateral agreement within the SCO structures.

Energy security cooperation between Russia, the world's largest oil producer, and China, the top global energy consumer, is also noteworthy in this context. Since 2008, the relationship has been organized through the Sino-Russian energy negotiation mechanism. While the Chinese perception of energy security is primarily driven from a demand-side that is concerned about access to resources, the Russian perception of energy security is driven from a supply-side that is concerned about the control of energy supplies and prices. Those diverging perceptions are not necessarily mutually exclusive and can be made mutually beneficial, as the deepening of Sino-Russian energy cooperation suggests. Cooperation has been facilitated by a confluence of five factors: (1) the creation of the SCO that provided the institutional framework to build trust and confidence between the great powers, settling border disputes and dampening Russian concerns over China's advances into the Central Asian region; (2) the falling energy demand in European markets; (3) the strained European Union—Russia energy relationship; (4) the Russian desire for diversification of its Asian markets; (5) the rising Chinese energy demand and its desire for diversification of its energy supplies. The Sino-Russian cooperation culminated in January 2011, when the first crude oil pipeline opened, running between East Siberia and the northeastern Chinese city of Daqing.

When the SCO marked its 10th anniversary at the summit meeting in Astana, there were many indicators that this regional organization could turn into the premier forum to build intergovernmental relationships in the Eurasian landmass.This relationship-building function is qualitatively different from, let's say, European style 'integration', that is, the pooling of sovereignty to generate collective goods that could not be achieved otherwise. The primary function of relationship-building is to occupy political space rather than collective-action problem-solving proper. Institutional platforms allow for the nurturing of relationships and the building of mutual trust. They create a political environment that is conducive to cooperation. Implicitly, it makes it harder for 'regional outsiders'—individual or collective—such as the United States and NATO to pursue political and military objectives in the region.

STRUCTURE: STRONG INTERGOVERNMENTALISM—WEAK INSTITUTIONS

Analyzed from a comparative institutional perspective, 'the SCO stands near the opposite end of the scale from the EU in being extremely intergovernmental with only minimal central institutions and centrally managed resources'.[19] According to Gregory Chin, 'members are not bound by the clear set of legal obligations of a multilateral security alliance, but have pledged to work together to gradually forge a collective mission and identity through consensus-building'.[20] In essence, the SCO appears as an intergovernmental network, which is led by annual summits and by regular meetings of the heads of government and foreign ministers or other high-level representatives of the member states.[21] As Anne-Marie Slaughter has observed:

> [I]t seems that what the members have really done is pledge to continue working with one another—to keep meeting at multiple levels, exchanging information, identifying synergies and opportunities for cooperation, and developing trust and personal relationships. The organisation's charter states the SCO's purposes so broadly—and, thus, vaguely—that no international lawyer could find a concrete obligation in the aspirational text.[22]

SCO decision-making procedures are based on consensus, which may easily lead to institutional stalemate. Such deadlock has been most visible in efforts to create an SCO free trade zone by 2020 as well as the expansion of SCO membership where Beijing and Moscow have effectively blocked each other's policy proposals. This may appear, at first sight, as an institutional liability. However, in fact, those procedures establish institutional checks and balances that constitute an important source of legitimation, as the SCO provides a forum to manage Sino-Russian differences of interest within an institutionalized framework, which facilitates their peaceful coexistence in Central Asia.

The main governing body of the SCO is the Council of the Heads of State, which meets once a year (see Figure 1). Summits of the Council rotate from one member to another (according to the Russian alphabetical order).[23] The country holding the annual rotating presidency usually convenes the summit. There are also mechanisms for regular meetings at the level of Speakers of Parliament, Secretaries of Security Councils, Foreign Ministers, Ministers of Defence, Emergency Relief, Economy, Transportation, Culture, Education, Healthcare, Heads of Law Enforcement Agencies, Supreme Courts and Courts of Arbitration, Prosecutors General. The Council of National Coordinators of SCO Member States (CNC) is in charge of coordinating interaction within the

[19] Alyson J K Bailes, 'The Shanghai Cooperation Organization and Europe', *China and Eurasia Forum Quarterly*, Vol. 5/3 (2007), 13.

[20] Gregory Chin, 'China's Rising Institutional Influence', in Alan S. Alexandroff and Andrew Cooper (eds.), *Rising States, Rising Institutions: Challenges for Global Governance* (Washington, DC: Brookings Institutions Press, 2010), 89.

[21] Bailes and Dunay, 'The Shanghai Cooperation Organization as a regional security institution', 5.

[22] Anne-Marie Slaughter, 'Networking Government to Government: The Asian Way,' *International Review* (Shanghai), Autumn 2008.

[23] See Oksana Antonenko, *The EU should not ignore the Shanghai Co-operation Organisation*, Centre for European Reform, Policy Brief, May 2007.

SCO framework. The SCO's work is supported by a small secretariat, located in Beijing, comprising 30 permanent staff members.[24] The under-institutionalization of the SCO strongly suggests a purely administrative function of the Secretariat, with very limited capacity to play an autonomous role. Such an institutional structure is in line with the intergovernmental network character of the organization, which is primarily driven by SCO member states. The very thin organizational shell provides just *enough* structure to provide a legitimizing frame for the recognition and validation of member states' policies.

The SCO's second most important institution, after the Secretariat, is the Regional Anti-Terrorist Structure (RATS).[25] Based in Tashkent, Uzbekistan, RATS coordinates the collection and sharing of information amongst member states, and maintains a (classified) database on terrorist, separatist and extremist organizations, including their members and associated individuals. It also assists in special operations to conduct international searches for individuals listed on the database. The identification (and elimination) of terrorists is carried out by member governments, not by RATS. RATS subsequently widened the scope of its activities, including now the harmonization of anti-terrorist legislation in the member-states and tracking the financing of terrorist bodies. In international fora such as the United Nations, the SCO tries to present common positions, for example on definitions of terrorism or lists of banned organizations. However, the effectiveness of RATS in delivering on these policy goals is extremely difficult to evaluate. According to some, RATS 'has succeeded in foiling over 500 terrorist plots'.[26] The institution focuses on the individual priorities of the SCO member states, for example, on suppressing terrorist activities by groups in the Uighur province or in Chechnya, which accommodates the national interests of China and Russia respectively.

The establishment of the SCO Secretariat and RATS allowed for the implementation of the declared policy goals, which has been best epitomized in the holding of regular joint anti-terrorism military exercises since 2003.[27] The largest exercise thus far, 'Peace Mission 2005', was held in August 2005 in Vladivostok and involved about 10,000 troops, including air, sea, and ground units. In essence, the missions aim at achieving four objectives:[28] (1) the projection of power; (2) joint operations; (3) joint command; and (4) strategic consultation among SCO members.

[24] The Secretariat opened in 2004. The initial budget was US$ 2.6 million.

[25] RATS became operational in 2004. It is based in Tashkent, Uzbekistan, comprising 30 staff members. Financial contributions are shared among SCO member states with Russia and China each providing 25%, Kazakhstan 21% and the other members proportionately less.

[26] M K Bhadrakumar, 'SCO steps out of Central Asia', *Asia Times*, 18 June 2011; Erica Marat, 'SCO's Tipping Point in Central Asia', *Eurasia Daily Monitor*, Vol. 8/117 (2011), 17 June 2011.

[27] See Jing-dong Yuan, 'China's Role in Establishing and Building the Shanghai Cooperation Organization (SCO)', *Journal of Contemporary China*, Vol. 19/67 (2010), 855–69.

[28] See Roger N. McDermott, *The Rising Dragon: SCO Peace Mission 2007*, Occasional Paper (Washington, DC: The Jamestown Foundation, October 2007).

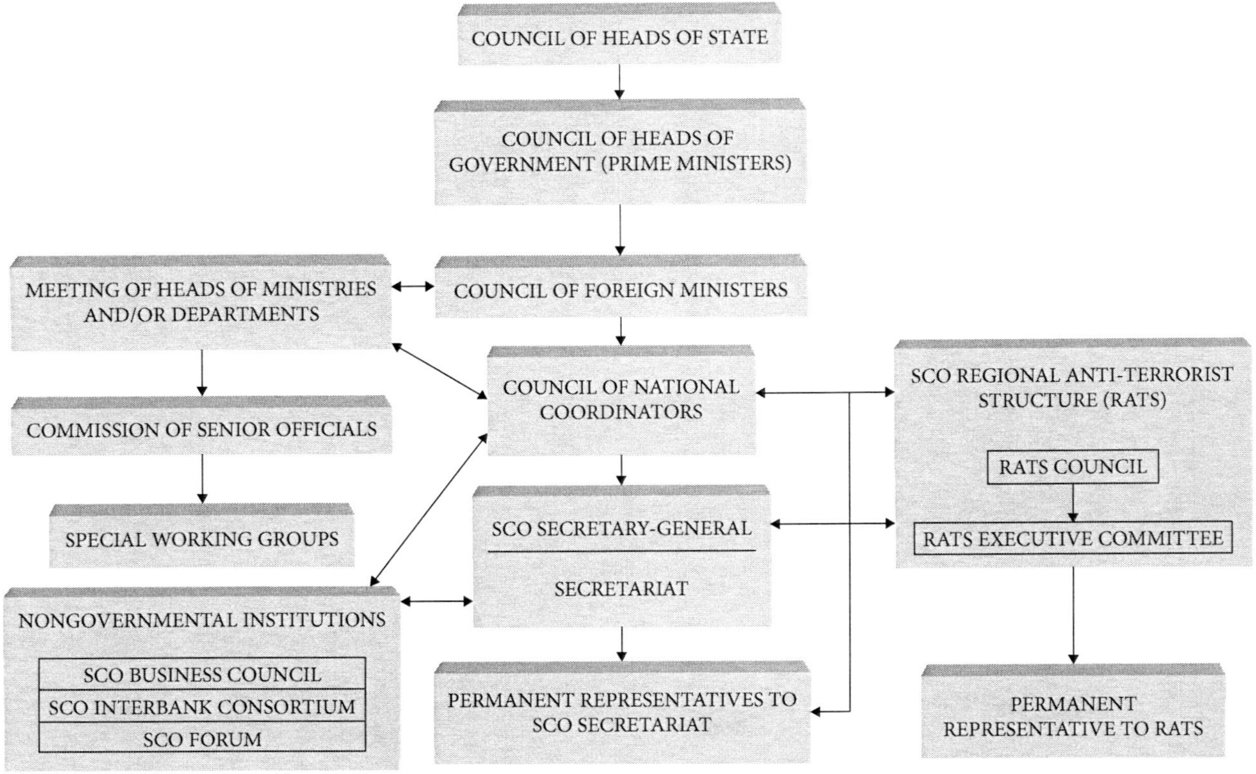

Fig. 1. Shanghai Cooperation Organization—Structure

Source: SCO

In conclusion, the institutional set-up of the SCO reveals a heavy reliance on both a network structure and network modes of operation, which has considerable implications for compliance. Without compliance mechanisms in place, it is very tempting to dismiss the effectiveness of the SCO in accomplishing its mandate. However, the network character of the organization allows for the development and cultivation of diplomatic relations, as well as informal contacts, facilitating confidence-building among SCO member states. The purpose of the SCO is first and foremost cooperation in itself on a bilateral rather than on a multilateral basis (before collective-action problem solving). Institution building appears therefore more like a strategy on its own rather than a means to achieve a particular common good. In a nutshell, SCO legitimacy is therefore not primarily derived from its institutional effectiveness in solving problems but from the wider recognition by third parties—e.g. other international or regional organizations and states.

MEMBERS, OBSERVERS, PARTNERS, GUESTS: BUILDING REGIONAL RELATIONSHIPS

The SCO covers one of the largest geographical areas of any regional organization, from Kaliningrad to Vladivostok and from the White Sea to the South China Sea. Together with its observer states, it stretches to the Indian Ocean and the Middle East as well. SCO member and observer states control 17.5% of the world's oil reserves, 47–50% of the natural gas reserves and contain roughly 45% of the world's population.[29]

SCO membership is highly diverse with sharp differences in strategic position and influence by China and Russia, on the one hand, and by the four Central Asian members on the other. While the strategic outlook of the former is far more global in nature, the latter are landlocked with only limited relative power and only little aspirations of acting beyond the region. Even within the group of four Central Asian countries, significant differences exist in terms of size and the extent to which countries possess oil and gas reserves. China and Russia, for their part, are linked by their permanent membership on the UN Security Council, as well as by their status as nuclear powers. The Rules of Procedure and the Statute on the Order of Admission of New members to the SCO, adopted at the Tashkent summit in June 2010, have been kept deliberately vague and simply state that the minimum eligibility criteria for full membership are: a) to be geographically located in Eurasia, b) to have pre-existing

[29] See Bailes and Dunay, 'The Shanghai Cooperation Organization as a regional security institution', 3–4.

observer or partnership status within the SCO, c) to entertain diplomatic relations and active economic and humanitarian ties with all SCO members, d) not to be subject to UN sanctions, and e) not to be in a state of armed conflict with another country.

The observer status was originally not foreseen in the SCO statutes, which provide only that 'membership shall be open for other States in the region that undertake to respect the objectives and principles of this Charter and to comply with the provisions of other international treaties and instruments adopted in the framework of SCO'.[30] Thus far, Afghanistan, India, Iran, Mongolia, and Pakistan have been accepted as observers, providing those countries with access to all high-level meetings.[31] Belarus, Sri Lanka, and Turkey are so-called dialogue partners, and the Commonwealth of Independent States, the Association of Southeast Asian Nations, and Turkmenistan are guest attendees. The overriding motivation for association with the SCO that is shared by perhaps all these countries is a strong interest in developing deeper economic relations across Central Asia, including common initiatives to facilitate access to trans-Asian energy infrastructure and networks.[32]

In addition to the material incentives, for India and Pakistan the SCO paves a way right into (Central) Asian geopolitics, which allows both countries to act beyond their relatively narrow sub-regional confines. Besides, the SCO provides a platform to address a wide range of issues that are of paramount importance for their bilateral relations, including border management and terrorism and insurgency, which the South Asian Association for Regional Cooperation (SAARC) is unable to resolve. For India, a regulated and peaceful multilateral framework for addressing the regional and global rise of China is also of interest for reasons partly analogous to those of Russia. However, some observers have expressed rather serious doubts about the prospects of SCO enlargement, because the full accession of the two SAARC heavy-hitters (and rivals), Pakistan and India, may simply transfer SAARC's institutional weakness right into the SCO and undermine the Sino-Russian condominium.[33] This obviously would be neither in China's nor in Russia's interest.

At the same time, Beijing and Moscow use the prospect of full SCO membership as a quid-pro-quo to induce change in the foreign policies of interested candidates such as Iran. For example, at the 10th Anniversary Summit in

[30] www.sectsco.org. Please note that the charter does not further define the boundaries of the region. Granting observer status is therefore essentially a political decision.

[31] Mongolia became an observer in 2004; India, Iran, and Pakistan joined as observers in 2005.

[32] Iran has shown a particular interest in energy cooperation, which is also illustrated by its growing bilateral engagement with China. In 2006, President Mahmoud Ahmadinejad invited the six SCO member states to Tehran to discuss ways and means of energy exploitation and development.

[33] Anonymous interview.

Astana, Presidents Hu and Medvedev engaged in bilateral talks with Iranian President Mahmoud Ahmadinejad pressing him to resume talks about Iran's nuclear programme and to develop a more cooperative strategy with 'the international community'.[34] Looked at from this perspective, the SCO offers a conduit that provides an alternative to Western-led engagement—i.e. the EU3+3—and allows for the pursuance of different strategies in addressing Iran's controversial nuclear programme.

In sum, relationship-building through full membership, associate membership, observer status, or guest status ultimately propels the SCO into a source of legitimation that provides a seal of approval for domestic abuses of international law. Those abuses are established and mutually accepted practice among the SCO membership. While the SCO observers, guests, and other partners do not necessarily subscribe to the same practices, the broad engagement of countries and other international organizations—such as the United Nations, the Collective Security Treaty Organization, the Eurasian Economic Community, and the UN Economic and Social Commission for the Asia-Pacific—significantly enlarges the policy space of the SCO. For example, the UN General Assembly adopted on 13 December 2010 a resolution on cooperation between the United Nations and the SCO, which stated that the SCO 'has become an essential regional organization for addressing security in the region in all its dimensions'.[35] In effect, the enlargement of policy space ultimately strengthens the legitimacy of the organization by way of recognition through third parties.

NORMS AND PRINCIPLES: MAINTAINING THE STATUS QUO

The SCO is the only international organization where China has been a stakeholder from its creation. Institutional design and evolution of the SCO, including its underlying rules and principles, have been strongly shaped by the Chinese government.[36]

The SCO Charter lists several underlying basic principles of international law as its normative framework, including territorial integrity, the sovereign equality of states, non-interference in internal affairs, the rejection of hegemony and coercion, and the settlement of disputes through consultation. The

[34] See Richard Weitz, 'Balancer-in-Chief: China Assumes SCO Chair', *China Brief*, Vol. XI/12 (2011), 9–12.

[35] Draft resolution on cooperation between the United Nations and the Shanghai Cooperation Organization (SCO), UN-Doc. A/65/L.29, preambular paragraph.

[36] See Yuan, 'China's Role in Establishing and Building the Shanghai Cooperation Organization (SCO)'.

charter also includes a statement that the SCO is 'not directed against other States and international organisations'.[37]

Unsurprisingly absent from this list are principles such as respect for human rights and self-determination of peoples. This absence serves first and foremost as mutual reassurance among SCO members. Looked at from this perspective, the underlying norms and principles are essentially a means for regime survival and therefore heavily focused on maintaining the status quo. China and Russia accept the formal equality of the smaller Central Asian countries and commit themselves to refrain from intervention in their internal affairs without invitation.[38] Working through the SCO lends greater weight and legitimacy to the diplomacy of its members, especially its most powerful ones, who can claim to speak on behalf of Central Asia.[39]

The circumstance that all of the SCO member states have more or less autocratic forms of government clearly impacts on the scope, structure, and process of the organization, hence the focus on the so-called three evils of terrorism, separatism, and religious extremism, including the strong aversion against intervention, which have featured highly on the SCO's policy agenda. Consequently, SCO proceedings exclusively take place at an intergovernmental level. Transparency, accountability, and democratic control do not constitute major concerns. Mutual recognition is the core underlying principle of SCO policies, as stipulated in the 2005 Concept of Cooperation. Any individual or group identified by one member state as a terrorist, separatist, or religious extremist must be recognized as such by the SCO membership as a whole. Furthermore, SCO agreements stipulate that member states are required to target separatists and extremists, as defined by the organization, 'whether or not they use violence'.[40] The principle of mutual recognition, in combination with the excessively broad interpretation of terrorism by SCO member states, renders the application of counter-terrorist policies extremely arbitrary, leading to unconditional expulsion and extradition of suspects. In fact, the principle of mutual recognition deprives individuals from their right to seek asylum in SCO countries, because their suspected involvement in terrorist, separatist, or religious-extremist activities will automatically trigger extradition to their state of origin without consideration of whether they may face torture there. While those practices violate international norms against *refoulement*, the SCO provides a framework of self-legitimation, from above,

[37] See Declaration on the Establishment of Shanghai Cooperation Organization, available at www.sectsco.org.

[38] The charter does not include any reference to potential rights of non-state actors or more direct representation of citizens.

[39] For example, in March 2008, the SCO issued a statement that supported China's suppression of demonstrations in Tibet; available at www.sectsco.org.

[40] Andrew J. Nathan and Sarah McKune, 'The Dubious Agenda of the SCO', *The National Interest*, 16 June 2011.

below, and side-ways, defining the rules and principles of counter-terrorism strategies within the Central Asian regional context.[41]

The SCO process is driven by what is often referred to as the so-called Shanghai spirit (*Shanghai jingshen*), which includes, according to Chinese Foreign Minister Yang Jiechi, 'mutual trust, mutual benefit, equality, consultation, respect for diversified civilisations and pursuit of common development' as well as 'the democratisation of international relations', and 'a multipolar world'.[42] The major aspiration of a multipolar world is a call for an alternative model to the underlying norms and principles of a hegemonic US-led international order. Consequently, the SCO serves an inward and an outward function: on the one hand, it regulates relations between a highly diverse group of autocratic or semi-autocratic member states, providing a platform for cooperation; on the other hand, it provides a bulwark against and an alternative model to the perceived threat of the Western liberal order. For both China and Russia, the SCO is a multilateral forum to articulate and legitimize those claims, as the organization constitutes a source of alternative values for an international system that is still heavily dominated by the United States.[43] The Astana Declaration of the SCO's 10th Anniversary effectively adopted the Russian language on missile defence by highlighting that the 'unilateral and unlimited build-up of anti-missile defence by a particular country or a narrow group of countries could damage strategic stability and international security'.[44]

Similar observations can be made with regard to Iran. Facing the danger of isolation over its nuclear programme, Iran has been eager to instrumentalize the SCO as a multilateral alternative, which stands in stark contrast to the policies of the Western powers. While the bulwark function of the SCO may be one of its great attractions, this naturally comes with a price tag, as Bailes and Dunay observed in 2007:

> The most clearly negative aspect of the SCO's relations with the world lies in its inability to establish a cooperative dialogue with any institution outside its own region (or individual Western states), in spite of having won official observer status at the UN General Assembly in December 2004. This in turn is a reminder that reputation can limit an organisation's options as much as its capacities or actual behaviour.[45]

[41] Non-refoulement is a key property of refugee law that protects refugees from being extradited to countries where their lives could be endangered. See Human Rights in China, *Counter Terrorism and Human Rights*.

[42] Xinhua News Agency, 11 June 2011.

[43] Both countries have used the SCO at times to criticize perceived Western double standards.

[44] Astana Declaration of the 10th Anniversary of the Shanghai Cooperation Organization, 15 June 2011, Paragraph V.

[45] Bailes and Dunay, 'The Shanghai Cooperation Organization as a regional security institution', 29.

Although such statements seemed to be an accurate observation then, the SCO has recently established a whole range of partnerships with ASEAN, the United Nations, the Commonwealth of Independent States, the Collective Security Treaty Organization, the Eurasian Economic Community, and others, which in fact enhances the SCO's options to engage in dialogue outside its own region. In sum, relationship-building has had the following two effects. First, it has strengthened SCO legitimacy horizontally vis-à-vis third parties by gaining recognition from other international organizations and established partnerships. Second, it has strengthened the legitimacy of the domestic regimes of SCO member states. By extension, the SCO has also gained recognition of their larger vision of international order, which is closely linked especially to China's and Russia's belief in a multipolar world.

CONCLUSIONS: LEGITIMACY THROUGH (SELF-) LEGITIMATION?

This chapter has posed three broad questions at its outset: first, how the SCO is legitimized from below through its member states; second, how the organization itself claims legitimacy downwards to its membership and other international institutions; and third how the SCO is recognized by outsiders who are not (full) members of the organization.

In addressing the first question, the chapter illustrated that the legitimation of the SCO from below occurs at two levels: (1) through the existence of a Sino-Russian condominium which creates a political environment conducive to regional cooperation; (2) through the followership of the Central Asian governments which use the SCO as a platform to manage China's growing presence in the region and to balance Russia's predominance. At the same time, China legitimizes its presence in the region by channelling loans through the organization, which helps to reduce suspicions of Chinese hegemonial ambitions. By working through the SCO, Moscow demonstrates its willingness to recognize and legitimize Beijing's ascendancy in the Central Asian region.

In addressing the second question, the chapter showed that the SCO has succeeded remarkably well in (self-)legitimizing itself, especially its counterterrorism strategies to address the 'three evil forces' of terrorism, separatism, and religious extremism, which violate international norms against *refoulement*. Those policies become further legitimized through the acceptance by and engagement of third parties—e.g. United Nations, the Collective Security Treaty Organization, the Eurasian Economic Community, and the UN Economic and Social Commission for the Asia-Pacific—which recognize the SCO as an important regional organization.

In addressing the third question, the chapter highlighted the growing attractiveness of the SCO as an alternative model to Western-type international organizations. Countries like Iran may use the organization as a means to escape from the scrutiny of Western liberal ordering. However, this does not come without a price-tag. Both China and Russia have used Iran's interest as a lever to influence (and change) Iranian nuclear policies.

Finally, despite much anti-Western rhetoric, the SCO does not directly challenge Western liberal ordering. Yet, by building relationships with governments and international organizations in Central Asia and beyond, the SCO occupies policy space and provides an alternative model to Western-type international organizations. In doing so, it ultimately may prevent liberal institutions such as the European Union, NATO, and the OSCE from making further inroads into the Central Asian region.

9

A European Re-invention of Indirect Legitimacy?

Christopher Lord

The legitimacy of the European Union is of special interest to scholars of international organizations. Of all bodies that exercise political power from beyond the state, its legitimacy has probably been most studied, and, helpfully, it has been examined by both political philosophers and empirical political scientists. Above all, the Union is usually considered an interesting case on the grounds that it seemingly does most to challenge the assumption that international bodies need to be indirectly legitimated by their component member states. It has its own representative institutions, including a directly elected Parliament. It has a Court which claims inherent authority for Union law. It even has member states which have (albeit unsuccessfully) proposed that the Union should be given its own constitutional authority; which have not done much to challenge the European Court of Justice (ECJ)'s claims to the autonomy and superiority of Union law; and which have implicitly renounced their own claims to a monopoly on the representation of their own citizens in the European arena.

Whether by fashioning its own democratic politics, its own legal order or its own constitutional authority, the assumption, then, is that the Union need not depend exclusively on its member states for legitimation. Rather it can develop at least some of its own legitimacy in direct interaction with the governed. Some commentators even suggest that the Union should 'come out' as a state; or, to put the point less frivolously, that the underlying structure of its authority, and justifications for it, will only be adequately aligned once it is understood that the EU can and should be legitimated by means and standards similar to those which apply to the democratic state.[1] In the view

[1] Daniel Gaus, *Der Sinn Von Demokratie. Die Dikurstheorie der Demokratie und die Debatte über die Legitimät der EU* (Frankfurt: Campus Verlag, 2009); Glynn Morgan, *The Idea of a European Superstate, Public Justification and European Integration* (Princeton: Princeton University Press, 2005).

of others, though, the Union offers its own 'third way' between stateness and an international organization of states. It challenges any assumption that polities must be classified in binary fashion as either having the 'inherent' legitimacy of a state or the 'delegated' legitimacy of an international organization. Thus assorted neologisms—including a Federation of States,[2] a Region State,[3] a non-state political system,[4] a *Condominio*[5]—have been proposed as means of portraying the Union as a composite form, part dependent on its member states for its legitimacy, part capable of generating that legitimacy independently from within its own system. Amongst philosophers who have written on European integration, Jean-Marc Ferry argues that the Union reflects its own dual, direct and indirect, legitimation by treating both individuals and its component political communities as the 'double normative reference points' of its actions (2000).[6]

Rather than add any further conjectures to this debate, this chapter questions an assumption that seems to lie behind it: namely, that the Union should be considered novel in proportion to how far it shows any signs of directly legitimating itself autonomously of its member states. Such a focus, it seems to me, runs the risk of overlooking just how far the study and practice of European integration have also 're-invented' indirect legitimacy. I develop this argument in the following stages. First, I set legitimacy and indirect legitimacy in their European Union context (Section 2). Second, I identify ways in which the study of European integration has contributed to conceptual innovation in the study of indirect legitimacy (Section 3). Third, I develop a case study of some of the legitimation claims real actors make in their attempts to justify the institutions and policies of the Union. By comparing attempts by the British and French governments to justify the Constitutional Treaty to their publics, my case study shows how governments appeal to considerations of both direct and indirect legitimacy, and how that, in turn, means that the European re-invention of indirect legitimacy extends to its deployment in composite forms, and not just to new understanding of how it might work on its own (Section 4).

[2] Jacques Delors, *L'Europe en tant quantité politique. Combats pour l'Europe* (Paris, Economica, 1996); C. Leben, *Fédération d'Etats Nations ou Etat Fédéral?*, Harvard Law School Symposium, Jean Monnet Working Papers no. 7, 2000.

[3] Vivien Schmidt, 'The European Union: Democratic Legitimacy in a Regional State?', *Journal of Common Market Studies*, Vol. 42/5 (2004), 975–97.

[4] Simon Hix, *The Political System of the European Union* (Basingstoke: Palgrave Macmillan, 2005).

[5] Philippe Schmitter, 'Examining the Present Euro-Polity with the Help of Past Theories', in Gary Marks, Fritz Scharpf, Philippe Schmitter, and Wolfgang Streeck (eds.), *Governance in the European Union* (London: Sage, 1996), 121–50.

[6] Jean-Marc Ferry, *La Question de l'État Européen* (Paris: Gallimard, 2000).

INDIRECT LEGITIMACY IN THE EU CONTEXT

A polity is legitimate in so far as the governed are under a moral obligation to obey its rule. It is worth labouring the point that mere support or approval is not enough. Political legitimacy is more demanding than that. It consists of a series of institutional rights—to decide some matters collectively and in certain ways—which the addressees of those institutions must acknowledge on account of their own moral obligations. As Habermas puts it, legitimacy consists in those 'political obligations' actors 'put themselves under' through the propositional logic of their own 'moral claims'.[7] This sets the hurdle high, conceptually and practically. Yet, a definition which grounds legitimacy in those obligations which the governed put themselves under of their own free will, avoids the circularity of assuming the justifiability of those very distributions of power or interest that are in need of justification. It also grasps the point that a liberal political order—which assumes individuals should judge what is morally right and good for themselves—can only rightfully coerce individuals in ways they can themselves accept as right and good.[8]

What, though, of indirect legitimacy? At a minimum it consists in the claim that a body whose 'authority is recognized and confirmed by the acts of other legitimate authorities' is itself legitimate.[9] Yet it would be a mistake to see indirect legitimacy as a simple matter of the legal authorization of international bodies by their member states. On the one hand, not all legal authorizations of 'beyond-state' bodies need be understood as issuing in indirect legitimacy. They can even be interpreted as alienations rather than delegations of power. That, indeed, is precisely the interpretation which the ECJ has put on the European Communities Treaties: 'By contrast with ordinary international treaties...the member states have limited their sovereign rights [in favour of]...an independent source of law.'[10] On the other hand, legality cannot be a sufficient justification for the non-arbitrary exercise of political power where the law itself conflicts with deeply-held normative convictions.[11]

A second mistake is to believe that indirect legitimacy implies that an international body need only be legitimate with its Member Governments. Consider the following quotation from Fritz Scharpf:

> If the function of legitimacy is to motivate compliance with *undesirable obligations*, what matters for the EU is the compliance of governments, parliaments,

[7] Jürgen Habermas, *Between Facts and Norms* (Cambridge: Polity 1996), 67.

[8] Rainer Forst, *Das Recht auf Rechtfertigung. Elemente einer Konstruktivistischen Theorie der Gerechtigkeit* (Frankfurt am Main: Suhrkamp, 2007), John Rawls, *Political Liberalism* (New York: Columbia University Press, 1993), 138.

[9] David Beetham, and Christopher Lord, *Legitimacy and the European Union* (Harlow, Essex: Addison, Wesley, Longman, 1998), 11.

[10] Case 6/64 Flaminio Costa v ENEL [1964] ECR 585.

[11] David Beetham, *The Legitimation of Power* (London: Macmillan, 1991).

> administrative agencies and courts within member states...Empirically, therefore, the EU is best understood as a government of governments, rather than a government of citizens.[12]

Thus, Scharpf argues, enquiry into the legitimacy of the Union should focus 'primarily' on 'normative arguments that could oblige governments to comply with undesired rules'.[13] Rodney Barker likewise questions how far it is meaningful to ask whether the Union is legitimate in relation to individuals as opposed to its member states: 'legitimacy is a concept which can usefully be applied to rule or challenges to rule. It cannot usefully be applied where rule is absent, hypothetical or so indirect as to be invisible to the ruled.'[14] He then puts his finger on what, in his opinion, it is about the EU which only requires it to have indirect legitimacy. As he puts it, 'the EU may govern' but 'it does not follow that it has subjects in the same way a state has'.[15] In other words, the Union does not, for the most part, require the obedience of individuals, since its laws are only enforced on the latter through the medium of national law. Thus understood, indirect legitimacy allows the Union to seek solutions to collective action problems which elude single states whilst relying on those same member states for the most state-like of their characteristics: namely their pre-acknowledged monopoly of legitimate coercive power.

Yet it is hard to make sense of the notion that indirect legitimacy removes the need for EU law to be legitimate with the individuals to whom it is eventually applied. If it really is the case that the only source of legitimacy available to post-traditional, non-authoritarian, and non-superstitious political orders is that individuals should be able to see themselves as controlling those who make the laws by which they are bound, then that presumably applies to all polities which exercise power and make laws, the EU included. All, then, that indirect legitimacy can do is hold out the possibility that laws made at the Union level can be legitimate *via* the moral obligations individuals owe to their own member states. Given, moreover, a free and critical media, and temptations on governments to pose as the reluctant enforcers of law made elsewhere, it cannot be assumed that the origins of Union laws in Union institutions are undiscoverable and invisible to individual citizens in the member states.

Instead it seems more plausible that attempts to secure the EU's legitimacy indirectly have to be justifiable for what they really are: namely, a lending out of national enforcement structures to laws made according to the procedures

[12] Fritz Scharpf, 'Reflections on Multilevel Legitimacy', *EUSA Review*, Vol. 20/3 (2007), 5.

[13] Scharpf, *'Reflections on Multilevel Legitimacy'*, 5.

[14] Rodney Barker, 'Legitimacy, Legitimation and the European Union: What Crisis?', in Paul Craig and Richard Rawlings (eds.), *Law and Administration in Europe. Essays in Honour of Carol Harlow* (Oxford: Oxford University Press, 2003), 159–60.

[15] Barker, *'Legitimacy, Legitimation and the European Union: What Crisis?'*, 159–60.

of the Union. Whilst, then, indirect legitimation is self-evidently an attempt to derive the legitimacy of the Union from that of its member states, it has also to be capable of justifying a form of authority exercised by those states that is itself profoundly changed by their membership of the Union.[16] The object of legitimation is, as it were, 'the state within the Union': the member state, rather than the nation state; the state that obliges itself through its commitments to the Union to act as the enforcer for Union law in exchange for decision rights in the making of that law.

In this regard the challenge of indirect legitimation is, arguably, greater in the case of the European Union than that of other international bodies for the simple reason that the 'lending out' of national enforcement structures to laws made elsewhere is of greater consequence. Whilst other international bodies produce legal obligations that then have to be enforced domestically, none is quite like the Union in the scope of its legal outputs, in its claims to legal supremacy, in its sheer functional dependence for its core goals (notably the single market programme) on a body of law that can be systematized and enforced in a manner that ensures legal unity, and in its provision for making some of those laws without the consent of all member states. Indeed, many legal obligations are the result of judicial interpretation, with no requirement for the consent of any member states, rather than legislative procedures in which member states can be out-voted. In sum, then, there are good reasons to anticipate that even where Union rule is indirect—or, in other words, mediated through national enforcement structures—it may require significant reserves of legitimation. Moreover, those concerns cannot be brushed aside by observing that the proportion of laws made by the Union has been exaggerated;[17] or by claiming that in all things which really matter—tax and spend, social security, and physical security—citizens continue to be ruled by their member states, rather than the Union. It is not just on account of its quantum that Union law needs legitimation, but on account of its ultimately coercive nature too.

Indeed, a final mistake is to regard indirect legitimacy as a 'soft option'. First, to labour the argument made earlier, any kind of law ultimately requires democratic legitimacy in societies governed by liberal democratic values, and democratic legitimacy, in turn, requires that citizens should be able to control the representatives who make the laws by which they are bound. This may be quite a challenge where arrangements intended to deliver indirect legitimacy presuppose systems of representation at the European level that not only operate

[16] Reik Oddvar Eriksen, And John Erik Fossum, *Reconstituting European Democracy*, ARENA Working Paper 01/2007, Oslo, 2007, 14.

[17] For a balanced assessment, see Annette E. Töller, 'Measuring and Comparing the Europeanisation of National Legislation', *Journal of Common Market Studies*, Vol. 48/2 (2010), 417–44.

at the end of a longer chain of delegation to any found in the domestic arena, but also entrust the exercise of legislative powers to the executive branches of national governments.[18] The latter concern is not to deny that elected national executives may even be very good at representing the views of national publics. It is merely to point out that they assemble together at the European level for the purposes of bargaining or of pooling technical expertise, and not for those of realizing the procedural requirements of legitimate legislation, such as providing justifications in a very public place of alternatives which have been tested in adverse controversy against one another.[19]

A further reason why indirect legitimacy is not a 'soft option' is that it presupposes what is at first sight a precarious enforcement structure. Although, in the case of the EU, member states can be fined for non-compliance, held liable by private actors for the consequences of not meeting obligations established under Union law,[20] or just reminded of any shortcomings in their own implementation when they request new obligations of others, any indirect account of the Union's legitimacy has to find some way of accommodating the difficulty that indirect legitimacy necessarily implies limits to the powers of EU institutions to sanction those very states it understands as the Union's own principals.

Assuming, indeed, that notions of indirect legitimacy understand the monopoly of legitimate violence as remaining with member states, they would seem to rule out the escalation beyond a certain point in Union sanctions against non-compliant states. Likewise, in so far as indirect legitimacy assumes a continued monopoly of the national arena on the ingredients of democracy and political community,[21] its supporters cannot answer the question 'what is the basis of political obligation to the Union?' in any way that presupposes that Union institutions can enjoy inherent, rather than delegated, democratic authority. These sources of fragility—the difficulty of justifying from within the assumptions of indirect legitimacy why the Union should have ultimate sanctioning powers or democratic trumps over those entities whose compliance it needs—in turn rule out the means by which modern polities typically deal with the problem that legitimacy partly depends on individual actors having confidence in the compliance of others.[22]

[18] Joseph Weiler, 'The Reform of European Constitutionalism', *Journal of Common Market Studies*, Vol. 35/1 (1997), 97–131.

[19] John Stuart Mill, *Utilitarianism, On Liberty and Considerations on Representative Government* (London: Dent, 1972 [1861]).

[20] Jonas Tallberg, *European Governance and Supranational Institutions: Making States Comply* (London: Routledge, 2003).

[21] Fritz Scharpf, *Governing in Europe: Effective and Democratic?* (Oxford: Oxford University Press, 1999).

[22] Føllesdal, *Legitimacy Theories*, 15–17.

INDIRECT LEGITIMACY REDUX?

The last section argued that the European Union amounts to a hard case for those who hold that indirect legitimacy is sufficient to justify any exercise of political power from beyond the state. Notwithstanding that difficulty, I now show how key contributions to the European integration literature may be assembled into a theory of how indirect legitimacy might be sufficient even for a polity that is as ambitious as the European Union in its policy scope, its institutional structures and its legal order. Thus my first example of what I term a European re-invention of indirect legitimacy comes from the study, rather than the practice of integration.

Consider the following answer Giandomenico Majone gives to the question 'which policies could be legitimately included in the agenda of a European federal state?'

> Aside from foreign and security, the public agenda would mostly include efficiency-enhancing, market preserving policies... Unlike redistribution—zero-sum game—efficiency issues may be thought of as positive sum games where everyone can gain. Hence, efficiency-enhancing policies do not need a strong normative foundation: output legitimacy (accountability by results) is generally sufficient.[23]

If, then, the European Union can be made to work as a pareto-improving relationship—or, in other words, one that leaves all relevant parties feeling better off in terms of their own felt preferences—it would in Majone's view need little further justification. Now, in the assessment of one of the most influential theories of European integration—liberal intergovernmentalism—most Union policies can, indeed, be explained by the mutual gains member states can secure by clubbing together to sort out 'collective action' problems they cannot solve individually. Thus, in their view, most Union policies are means of providing international public goods or of removing 'negative externalities'—or, in other words, harms—such as market distortions, competitive devaluations, or environmental pollution, which member states could otherwise impose on one another.[24]

At first sight, however, it is by no means obvious that all the legal obligations that the Union calls upon its member states to observe can be legitimated as a 'pareto-improving' bargain to which they all consent from which they all benefit. To the contrary, some of those obligations derive from policies which re-allocate values between members; others from decision-rules which

[23] Giandomenico Majone, *Dilemmas of European Integration. The Ambiguities and Pitfalls of Integration by Stealth* (Oxford: Oxford University Press, 2005), 19.

[24] Andrew Moravcsik, 'Preferences and Power in the European Community: A Liberal Intergovernmentalist Approach', *Journal of Common Market Studies*, Vol. 31/4 (1993), 473–524.

impose outcomes upon them. Yet, those who defend the view that the Union can be justified as a mutually advantageous bargain between its member states might reply that truly efficient 'efficiency-seekers' do not seek anything as crude as pareto-improvement in relation to single policies. Rather, they trade their vetoes, even if that means losing out here and there. As for majority voting, that can be seen as little more than a closure device for the efficient and timely pursuit of objectives that are themselves supported by a consensus of member states.[25] Not only, as Rousseau might have put it, does majority voting 'presuppose unanimity, on one occasion at least',[26] but it is in practice only used sparsely and, it would seem, with regret in so far as the search for consensus often continues after member states have been out-voted.[27] Comitology committees—which play the key executive function in the Union of agreeing implementing instructions—are often used to achieve real-time adjustments between common obligations and the preferences of individual governments.[28]

Indeed, member state preferences are, in the view of some scholars, sufficient to explain much of the Union's institutional design and its legal order.[29] Union institutions are, in their assessment, 'passive'[30] in the sense they are delegated just those powers, and no more, that allow member states to realize mutual gains. On this account member states delegate agenda-setting and monitoring powers to the Commission, and tacitly acknowledge the Court's claims to legal supremacy, in order to make more credible commitments to one another,[31] to save bargaining costs, to raise decision-making speeds, to pool expertise,[32] and to deal with problems of incomplete contracting[33]: all in the expectation of increasing the number and scope of mutually advantageous bargains they can reach with one another. In sum, then, the binding nature of Union institutions is really little more than a series of *self*-binding commitments by its own

[25] Moravscik, 'Preferences and Power', 510.

[26] Jean Jacques Rousseau, *The Social Contract or Principles of Political Right* (London: Everyman, 1973 [1762]), 173.

[27] Dorothee Heisenberg, 'The Institution of "Consensus" in the European Union: Formal versus informal Decision-making in the Council', *European Journal of Political Research*, Vol. 44/1 (2005), 65–90; Mikko Mattila and Jan Erik Lane, 'Why Unanimity in the Council? A Roll-Call Analysis of Council Voting', *European Union Politics*, Vol. 2/1 (2001), 31–53.

[28] Charles Sabel, and Jontahan Zeitlin, *Learning from Difference: the New Architecture of Experimentalist Governance in the European Union*, European Governance Papers (EuroGov), 2007.

[29] Moravscik, 'Preferences and Power', 508; Mark Pollack, *The Engines of European Integration. Delegation, Agency and Agenda-Setting in the EU* (Oxford: Oxford University Press, 2003), 377.

[30] Moravscik, 'Preferences and Power', 508.

[31] Andrew Moravcsik, *The Choice for Europe: Social Purpose and State Power from Messina to Maastricht* (Ithaca, NY: Cornell University Press, 1998), 73; Giandomenico Majone, 'Two Logics of Delegation: Agency and Fiduciary Relations in EU Governance', *European Union Politics*, Vol. 2/1 (2001), 103–21.

[32] Majone, 'Two Logics of Delegation'.

[33] Geoff Garrett, 'The Politics of Legal Integration in Europe', *International Organization*, Vol. 49/1 (1995), 172.

member states. Like Ulysses they only tie their hands to the mast, so that they can realize their own objectives.[34]

The notion, though, that the Union can be justified as a 'pareto-improving polity' is open to the further objection that a theory of mutual benefit cannot amount to one of political obligation. We cannot, in other words, infer the legitimacy of the European Union from any claim that member states use it to bargain to their mutual advantage. However, defenders of bargaining theory might counter that they make no such claim. To the contrary, by identifying where the collective choices of the Union can also be the individual choices of each member states, they do no more than identify those conditions where the legitimacy of Union laws can be inferred, not from any bargain between states, but from any standards of political and moral obligation that are internal to each member state: conditions where each member state can make its own judgement—according to its own internal arrangements for the legitimation of decisions—about any questions of right and value that may be involved in co-operation. Moreover, mutually advantageous bargains between member states do not just allow the Union to draw its legitimacy from domestic sources. They also stabilize conditions for indirect legitimacy. The risk that enforcement structures may be precarious under assumptions of indirect legitimacy will be reduced in so far as member states will have no obvious incentives to defect from obligations they have bargained to their mutual advantage, except, perhaps, through fears others may do so: fears that can, in turn, be overcome with the right 'commitment technologies'.

Hybrid Legitimation

The last section showed how some leading authors in the European integration literature continue to regard the Union as indirectly legitimated by its member states. If correct, this view would imply that indirect legitimacy need not be limited to international organizations with limited remits and unambiguously intergovernmental methods. It can also work for a body that is as ambitious as the European Union in its policy scope, decision rules and its claims to legal superiority.

However, the stretching of indirect legitimacy to cover the Union may depend on assumptions that are more heroic than plausible. Thus Fritz Scharpf has argued that it takes only small departures from ideal conditions to turn consensus decision-rules from a kind of pareto-improving paradise in which all member states gain and all consent into 'joint-decision traps' which lock member states into obligations which are anything but to their

[34] Jon Elster, *Ulysses and the Sirens, Studies in Rationality and Irrationality* (Cambridge: Cambridge University Press, 1984).

mutual benefit (2006).[35] Elsewhere I enlarge on Scharpf's critique,[36] by showing that it also implies that the Union's attempt to combine legal obligation with consensus decision rules is unlikely to satisfy two conditions political philosophers have proposed for the non-arbitrary exercise of political power: namely a 'scheme of co-operation' which is 'fair' between conflicting yet equally reasonable values;[37] and, closely related to that, a condition of 'democratic self-legislation' in which citizens can control the making of laws by which they are bound without arbitrary procedural biases in how they can exercise that control.[38]

Rather, though, than reproducing these theoretical objections in full, I want to consider a very different objection in the remainder of this chapter: the objection that even the actors who might be most expected to rely on indirect legitimacy in their attempts to justify the Union to their own publics—the member state governments and especially those considered to be most uncomfortable with constraints on their own sovereignty and control—prefer, instead, to mix and match elements of direct and indirect legitimacy in the justifications they offer their publics for their own participation in the Union.

Why this emphasis on the legitimation claims that political actors' themselves make? At first it might seem to get things the wrong way round: surely, it might be objected, the legitimation claims of power-holders need to be judged against standards which are independent of the self-serving claims of those who exercise the powers of institutions? To understand, though, where it can be helpful to analyse the legitimation claims of power holders themselves, it helps to consider some observations Rodney Barker has made about the academic literature on legitimacy. Using, as it happens the example of contributions to the debate on the legitimacy of the EU, he criticizes as excessively 'deductive' and 'ahistorical' those studies which appraise institutions against assumed academic criteria for the rightful use of political power without bothering to consider whether anyone even remotely expects those standards to be met. As an antidote, he proposes that we should indeed give a role in our investigations to what real people think and say about legitimacy in context. As he puts it, 'legitimation (is) an action or series of actions –speech, writing, ritual, display—whereby people justify to themselves or others the actions they are taking and the identities they are expressing'.[39]

[35] Fritz Scharpf, 'The Joint-Decision Trap Revisited', *Journal of Common Market Studies*, Vol. 44/4 (2006), 845–64.

[36] Christopher Lord, *Polecats, Foxes and Lions. Social Choice, Moral Philosophy and the Justification of the EU as a Restrained yet Capable form of Political Power*, ARENA Working Paper 15/2009, Oslo, ARENA.

[37] Rawls, *Political Liberalism*.

[38] Richard Bellamy, *Political Constitutionalism, A Republican Defence of the Constitutionality of Democracy* (Cambridge: Cambridge University Press, 2007).

[39] Barker, 'Legitimacy, Legitimation and the European Union', 159–64.

Barker's discussion clearly implies that the actors whose statements we should study are, indeed, power-holders themselves. Whilst, of course, we could study the responses of publics to the legitimation claims of power holders—rather than the claims themselves—it is not always obvious that publics respond at all. As Barker puts it elsewhere, it is often easier to identify 'failures than successes';[40] or, perhaps to put the point more exactly, 'failures' can too easily be mistaken for 'successes' to the extent that legitimation problems can remain latent with public opinion for a long time. Needless to say, empirical political scientists have attempted to devise all kinds of methods to fill this gap. Prominent amongst them are attempts to infer legitimacy from evidence of public support expressed in public opinion poll data.[41] A difficulty, though with this measure is that it fails to capture what is most interesting about legitimacy, for legitimacy, as Jean-Jacques Rousseau pointed out long ago, consists in an obligation to comply even with those policies we do *not* support.[42]

While public opinion might therefore not always provide conclusive evidence of legitimacy, the apparently self-serving claims of power-holders may be worth studying where those power holders come under pressure to justify themselves in normative environments they cannot entirely control. As implied by Jon Elster's observation that even 'hypocrisy' can have 'civilising effects',[43] we may not need to judge how sincere or how strategic are the appeals which power-holders make to standards in their legitimating claims. That they seem to believe those standards are expected of them may in itself be significant.

As it happens there is a clear and consistent pattern in the legitimation claims member state governments employ in their attempts to justify the Union to their own publics. Since at least the end of the 1990s, they have adopted the mantra that the Union is subject to a dual form of democratic legitimation. Typical of the genre is Tony Blair's contribution to the future of Europe debate in 2000. After claiming that 'the directly elected and representative institutions of the nation states—the national governments and parliaments—are the primary sources' of democratic control at Union level, Blair went on to argue that 'the European Parliament is' none the less 'a vital part of the checks and balances of the EU'.[44] By the time of the Lisbon Treaty, the governments of the

[40] Rodney Barker, 'Democratic legitimation: what is it, who wants and why?' in Achim Hurrelman, Steffen Schneider, and Jens Steffek (eds.), *Legitimacy in an Age of Global Politics* (Basingstoke: Palgrave Macmillan, 2007), 30.

[41] For a discussion of various attributes of system support and performance which might be measured by public opinion surveys, see M.Stephen Weatherford, 'Measuring Political Legitimacy', *American Political Science Review*, Vol. 86/1 (1992), 149–66.

[42] Rousseau, *Social Contract*, 250.

[43] Jon Elster, 'Deliberation and Constitution Making' in Jon Elster (ed.), *Deliberative Democracy* (Cambridge: Cambridge University Press, 1998), 111.

[44] Tony Blair, *The Prime Minister's Speech to the Polish Stock Exchange*, Warsaw, 6 October 2000.

member states agreed that the 'European Union shall be founded on representative democracy' before going on to assert that a) citizens are directly represented at Union level in the European Parliament and b) that member states are represented in the European Council by their Heads of Government and in the Council by their governments, themselves democratically accountable either to their national parliaments or to their citizens.[45]

Member states have, however, not just agreed to a mixture of greater national and European parliamentary control over their own decisions in the Union arena, they have also flirted with the constitutionalization of the Union. Perhaps even more significant than their endorsement in 2004 of a 'Constitutional' Treaty has been the absence of any serious and sustained challenge by Member states to the development since the 1960s of what Joseph Weiler calls a material constitution—in which the European Court of Justice has set out a hierarchy of laws which accords Union law primacy over national law, and developed a rights jurisprudence.[46]

In sum, then, two matters that can hardly be more central to the legitimacy of Union laws—the Union's ordinary law-making procedures and member states' own understanding of their constitutional relationship with the Union—would seem to mix and match elements of direct and indirect legitimacy. Co-decision, which is now needed to pass most Union laws and to agree annual budgets too, is the most obvious way in which powers are divided between member state governments in the Council and representatives directly elected to the European Parliament. On the other hand, the role of the member states in 'neither confirming nor denying' the superiority of Union law in its field of competence means that for all practical purposes the Union is, as John-Erik Fossum and Agustin Menendez put it, 'at one and the same time a derivative order (from all national constitutions) and the supreme law of the land'.[47] Ordinary procedures—such as co-decision—that are themselves hybrid between direct and indirect forms of legitimation are thus embedded in a constitutional relationship between the Union and its member states that is itself hybrid.

But how agreed are member state governments between themselves in how they mix direct and indirect legitimation claims in their justifications of the contemporary Union; and, indeed, in the weights they give to the two elements? Whilst space does not permit that question to be answered in full here, it is possible to demonstrate some of the most salient elements of agreement and disagreement through a brief summary of a case study I have published

[45] Treaty of Lisbon, Art. 8(a)

[46] Joseph Weiler, 'A Constitution for Europe? Some Hard Choices', *Journal of Common Market Studies*, Vol. 40/2 (2002), 563–80.

[47] John Erik Fossum, and Agustin Menendez, *The Constitutional Path of the European Political Project. Lessons from Laeken and Lisbon*, Unpublished Manuscript. Oslo, ARENA, 2010, 7.

elsewhere on the basis of a content analysis of documents and speeches in which the British and French Governments sought to justify the Constitutional Treaty to their own publics.[48]

Hybrid Legitimation: British and French Legitimation of the Constitutional Treaty

Differences in how far the British and French governments appealed to considerations of direct and indirect legitimacy are reflected in how they represented the origins and character of the Constitutional Treaty (CT), as well as the obligations and entitlements created by it. The CT lent itself to being variously described as a constitution, a constitutional treaty or a treaty. It could also be variously presented as conferring entitlements on citizens or member states; and its authorship could also be variously attributed to the Convention or to the Intergovernmental Conference (IGC). The British government was, indeed, the more likely to describe it in 'indirect legitimacy language' as a treaty approved by an IGC; and the French the more likely to characterize it as a constitution authored by a convention, whose legitimacy derived only partly from member states.[49] Whilst the French government saw advantage in claiming that 'in practice, nine-tenths of the text is that of the Convention',[50] the British Government was more eager to claim that the acceptability of the final text rested on its prior sieving by an IGC. An annex to the British White Paper went to the lengths of setting out all 80 amendments the IGC made to the Convention draft, before claiming 39 of these had been sponsored by the British government alone; that it had no objection to a further 38; and that it had secured changes that allowed it to accept the remaining three in spite of its initial opposition.[51]

Given its eagerness to present the CT as a delegation of powers from the member states, it is unsurprising that the British government used the principle of conferral set out in Article I-9 to claim that 'the Treaty makes clear that the EU derives its powers from its member states, not the other way round'.[52] In other words, the British government presented constitutionalization as an exercise

[48] Christopher Lord, 'Polity Empowering or Polity Constraining? A Comparison of British and French attempts to legitimise the Constitutional Treaty', *Journal of European Public Policy*, Vol. 15/7 (2008), 1001–18.

[49] Lord, 'Polity Empowering or Polity Constraining? A Comparison of British and French attempts to legitimise the Constitutional Treaty', 1007.

[50] République Française, *Constitution Pour L'Europe, Mode D'Emploi*, Paris, 2004, 8.

[51] Foreign and Commonwealth Office. *White Paper on the Treaty Establishing a Constitution for Europe, Command 6309* (London: HMSO, 2004), 15 and Annex 2.

[52] Foreign and Commonwealth Office. *White Paper on the Treaty Establishing a Constitution for Europe*, 19.

in the constraint and delimitation of institutions, rather than as a step towards their empowerment: as confirming that the Union was defined by its *origins* in an agreement between member states, rather than teleologically defined by any presumed *ends* of ever closer union. In contrast, the French government was much more likely to treat the origins of the CT, and the relationship to which it would give rise, as two distinct questions. By emphasizing that the whole point of a 'Constitutional Treaty' was to use a treaty to create a constitution, the French government was eager to emphasize its transformative potential. Indeed, in so far as the French government presented the Constitutional Treaty as constraining, it was often with a view to constraints it would put on member states. Thus, for example, the decision to base the first part of the Constitutional Treaty on the Charter of Fundamental Rights of the Union (drawn up by an earlier convention in response to concerns that European Union law could theoretically over-ride national rights protections without codifying rights at the European level)[53] was justified by the French Government as a move that would be constraining of member states to the extent that it would 'make clear the ethical engagements of the European Union'.[54]

Indeed, on the assumption that a Treaty is best understood as a 'contract' between states for the pursuit of specific interests, whilst a Constitution involves a mutual according of rights within a general purpose governance structure, it is important to distinguish how often the justifications offered by the two governments referred to 'rights' and 'values', as opposed to functional considerations of interest and performance (economic growth, security, capacity to solve cross-border problems). The finding in my content analysis, that only the French government made much attempt to argue that a constitutional relationship could be justified by shared rights and values,[55] can be illustrated from key passages in its documents. The *Exposé* was sub-titled 'A Union founded on common values and objectives',[56] whilst the *Mode d'Emploi* claimed the CT aimed to 'build a common house resting on shared values and rules'.[57] In contrast, British references to the Charter were largely defensive. More space was given to limits to its application than to the document itself.[58] The British government was also eager to claim that the rights in question were derived and not original: 'in each area the rights are expressly limited to those available under existing national and Union law'.[59]

[53] J. Schönlau, *Drafting the Charter: Rights, Legitimacy and Process* (Basingstoke: Palgrave Macmillan, 2005).

[54] République Française, *Apports de la Constitution Européenne*. Paris, 2004.

[55] Lord, 'Polity Empowering or Polity Constraining', 1010.

[56] République Française, *Référendum du 29 Mai 2005. Projet de loi autorisant la ratification du traité établissant une Constitution pour l'Europe. Exposé des motifs*, Paris, 2005.

[57] République Française, *Mode D'Emploi.*

[58] FCO, *White Paper*, 36.

[59] FCO, *White Paper*, 36.

Continuing its claim that the Union would operate as a delegation of powers even under a Constitution, the British government repeatedly claimed that the CT would even tighten control by member states. By giving slightly more prominence than the French to the role of the new Article 11 in classifying competences, and by giving much more attention to new arrangements for enforcing subsidiarity,[60] it suggested that the boundaries between Union and member states would in future be better defined and policed. Even the *passarelle*—which allowed the European Council—to transfer some matters to qualified majority voting (QMV) without going through the full procedures for treaty change, was portrayed by the British Government as a procedure that could even be used to return power to member states.[61]

Above all, the seemingly paradoxical finding that the British Government was the more likely to mention the EU Foreign Minister and the new Presidency of the European Council[62] is easily explained by the British Government's determination to present those new leadership structures as a means of moving the Union closer to a well-supervised delegation of powers from the member states. Blair told the House of Commons that the creation of a new European Council Presidency—elected for up to 5 years by the heads of government—would be 'crucial in placing the power to set Europe's agenda in the hands of Europe's intergovernmental body'.[63] Likewise, the British government presented the new post of European Union Minister for Foreign Affairs as very much the agent of the Council. Whereas the French government simply repeated the calculated ambiguity of the CT which presented the Foreign Minister as mandated by the Council but a member of the Commission,[64] the British emphasized that the Minister would only be bound by Commission rules in so far as they were consistent with the mandate from the Council.[65]

Whilst arguing that the member states would exercise greater control over the Union, the British government also suggested that the CT would make Union membership more flexible, and more voluntaristic from the point of view of member states themselves. That, at least, was their interpretation of new arrangements for enhanced co-operation between selected members, as well as the point of the many mentions of opt-outs old and new. In contrast the French government, as seen, presented the CT as clarifying the obligations of member states. Indeed, at one point constitutionalization was presented as a deductive exercise in which the text began by agreeing shared

[60] Lord, 'Polity Empowering or Polity Constraining', 1008.

[61] FCO, *White Paper*, 20; FCO, *A Constitution for our kind of Europe. Speech by the Foreign Secretary*, 7 December 2004.

[62] Lord, 'Polity Empowering or Polity Constraining'.

[63] House of Commons debate on the European Council, 21 June 2004.

[64] République Française, 'Apports de la Constitution Européenne', 29.

[65] FCO, *White Paper*, 22.

values and then went on to set out the rules and obligations on member states which would follow.[66]

Attempts to justify the CT also tested the relative weight the two governments gave to direct and indirect forms of democratic control: to control of the Union through its own democratic institutions and politics or through those of its member states. The French government was, indeed, the more likely to claim that the CT would further empower the European Parliament, notably by extending co-decision to the whole of the budget and 95% of first legislation.[67] Whilst, however, the French government portrayed the CT as moving the Union closer to a system of mutually constraining majorities *within* the EU polity, the British government made more of provisions which would strengthen national parliamentary constraint *of* the EU polity. Indeed, its interpretation of the new Article I-11 was significant. It argued that 'if a third of national parliaments were against a proposal, so would their governments be'. Since it would then be 'hard to put together the qualified majority needed to pass the proposal' it would be 'unlikely to prosper further'. The British government then went on to hope that national parliaments would 'work together' to use the new procedure.[68] Putting these points together, it presented the CT as allowing a third of national parliaments and governments to operate as a blocking minority at the agenda-setting stage, and as encouraging cross-national parliamentary alignments into the different veto groups that would be possible under the new rules.

Whilst, though, the British and French Governments put different emphases on direct and indirect legitimation claims in their attempts to justify the CT, both kinds of claim featured to some degree in the case made by each government. It would be a caricature to present the British and French cases for the Constitutional Treaty as resting on a black and white contrast between one government that claimed it would strengthen national parliaments and clarify member states' rights and another that claimed it would strengthen the European Parliament and define individual rights. To give just one example, even if the warmer comments the British government made about the Charter presented it as an opportunity for individuals to deploy rights *against* Union institutions, it conceded the point that it was desirable for individuals, and not just member states, to have the 'right to have rights' at the European level. Whilst, moreover, the British Government at one point poured cold water on a list of rights it claimed was more 'derived than original', that did not stop it from also claiming that the Charter had some value in articulating 'new generation

[66] République Française *Mode D'Emploi*, 12.

[67] Assemblée Nationale, *Déclaration du Gouvernement sur le référendum portant sur le projet de loi autorisant la ratification du traité établissant une Constitution pour l'Europe par Jean-Pierre Raffarin Premier Ministre*, Paris, Assemblée Nationale, 5 April 2005 (http://www.assemblée-nationale.fr/12/cri/2004-2005).

[68] FCO, *White Paper*, 19.

rights' such as 'solidarity between generations' and the 'rights to the child'.[69] In sum, then, *single* governments mix and match claims that are commonly associated with direct and indirect legitimacy. It is simply not the case that legitimation claims are only composite when aggregated at the Union level.

CONCLUSION

In recent years the history of European integration has come to be told as one of legitimacy. According to a standard account the history of European integration can be divided into two periods: one of permissive consensus before the early 1990s; and one of legitimation crisis from then onwards.[70] Whilst before the 1992 Treaty on European Union decision-making by intergovernmental bargaining, judges, and experts seemingly provided sufficient legitimation, it has since become more common to question whether that combination really is enough to satisfy conditions for the rightful exercise of political power. As seen here, member states have often responded by claiming that the Union enjoys dual legitimation: indirectly through the role of elected national governments in sanctioning and controlling Union decisions and, directly, through the exercise of the powers of the European Parliament by elected representatives. A possible counter view, however, is that attempts to introduce elements of direct legitimation only risk exacerbating any legitimation crisis in so far as they assume something that is by no means obvious: namely, that the peoples of the member states want to associate together at the European level as a single people.[71] That might, in turn, suggest that the Union would be better advised to explore means of linking collective problem solving at the European level with mechanisms of democratic control at the domestic level.[72] Note, though, that even that would amount to a re-invention of indirect legitimacy in so far as changes needed to secure the democratic control of the Union through the domestic politics of its member states cannot be accommodated within their established arrangements for the public control of external policy. Whether, then, as an experiment in composite forms of direct and indirect legitimacy, or just as a source of change in the latter, the European Union remains central to any enquiry into what indirect legitimacy is and can be.

69 FCO, *White Paper*, 19.

70 William Wallace, and Julie Smith, 'Democracy or Technocracy? European Integration and the Problem of Popular Consent', *West European Politics*, Vol. 18/3 (1995), 137–57.

71 Majone, *Dilemmas of European Integration*, 40.

72 Scharpf, *Governing Europe*.

10

Legitimacy and International Organizations—the Case of the OSCE

*Ingo Peters**

INTRODUCTION

Is the Organization for Security and Cooperation in Europe (OSCE) in a crisis of legitimacy? If so, what are the implications of such a crisis for the OSCE's contribution to regional governance in Europe? Anecdotal evidence certainly supports the notion of an OSCE in crisis. First, numerous public statements, books or journal articles by political actors or by OSCE experts refer to the organization standing 'at the crossroad' between political significance and irrelevance. Others explicitly speak of the organization's 'crisis', some ending more pessimistically with an exclamation mark and some more optimistically with a question mark.[1]

Second, there are clear doubts about the effectiveness of the OSCE. After all, war has come back to Europe since the 1990s, first in the Balkans and later in the post-Soviet space, twice in Chechnya (1994–6, 1999–2009), and then in Georgia (2008). Moreover, OSCE missions have been deprived by host governments of their ability to do their job, or have even been expelled by some participating states, apparently rendering the organization helpless in the face of traditional power games and 'ethnic conflicts'. Third, since the end of the cold war, the OSCE has not emerged as the overall 'clearing house' for European security as it had been foreseen in the OSCE Security Charter of 1999. Instead the OSCE has been

* The author is very grateful for the constructive comments on earlier versions of this paper by Dominik Zaum as well as for the valuable comments and research assistance by Max A. von Bargen (Stanford University) and Koen van der Schoor (Zuyd University of Applied Sciences Maastricht) during their internship in Berlin.

[1] See, for example Anvar Azimov, 'OSCE at the Crossroads', *International Affairs (Moscow), 2* (2005), 57–66; Robert Barry, *The OSCE at a Turning Point?* (London: British American Security Information Council, 2004); Pál Dunay, *OSCE in crisis* (Paris: EU Institute for Security Studies, 2006); Victor-Yves Ghebali, *OSCE between Crisis and Reform* (Geneva: Centre for the Democratic Control of Armed Forces (DCAF), 2005).

confined to a 'niche of common and cooperative security'.[2] While in absolute terms the OSCE might still perform vital work in this niche, it has been largely marginalized compared to other major European security organizations, first and foremost the European Union and NATO.

Fourth, and most important, from the mid-1990s onwards Russia in particular has harshly criticized the OSCE for its ineffectiveness in terms of guaranteeing security for all, and in preventing war. Moscow has complained about double standards and unfair practices related to what it considers interferences in the domestic affairs of participating states, and about some OSCE agencies claiming unwarranted political autonomy at the expense of political control by the participating states and governments. As a possible remedy, Russia has suggested fundamental reforms by submitting proposals for reforming specific aspects of concern, and a 'legally binding European Security Treaty' (EST) as a comprehensive framework for reform. Western states, though open to some adjustments around procedural issues, have rejected this drive for structural reform. They have generally favoured the status quo since they see the OSCE as continuing to serve the promotion of liberal values; first and foremost human rights, democracy, and the rule of law. The reforms advocated by Russia and the CIS states, especially the EST proposal, in their eyes could easily devalue the OSCE's role.[3]

The ongoing debate about the OSCE's proposed role between Russia and most CIS states on the one hand, and Western states on the other highlights the erosion of the formal consensus of the early 1990s amongst participating states on the core values and norms governing European security affairs, and the institutional functions and form of the OSCE. As Marc Perrin de Brichambaut, the Organization's Secretary General since 2005 aptly put it:[4]

> Tensions have increased as some states have proved less willing to accept the intrusiveness inherent to some of the mechanisms adopted in previous eras, while others have been unwilling to invest in the organization beyond areas that directly interest them. All sides have been tempted to hold the organization hostage, leaving it in a state of permanent crisis, struggling from one ministerial council to the next[5]

[2] See Ingo Peters, 'The OSCE, NATO and the EU within the "Network of Interlocking European Security Institutions": Hierarchization, Flexibilization, Marginalization', *OSCE Yearbook 2003* (Baden-Baden: Nomos, 2004), 381–402.

[3] Sergej Lavrov, *Speech by Russia Minister of Foreign Affairs at the 16th Meeting of the OSCE Ministerial Council in Helsinki* (5 December 2008), available at http://www.mid.ru/bdomp/brp_4.nsf/e78a48070f128a7b43256999005bcbb3/ab6b61362ca33952c3257523003f9f6c!OpenDocument.

[4] Marc Perrin de Brichambaut, 'The OSCE and the 21st Century', *Helsinki Monitor: Security and Human Rights*, Vol. 3 (2007), 183.

[5] Marc Perrin de Brichambaut, 'Mid-Life Crisis?' *The National Interest*, Vol. 75/2 (2007), 37–41.

All this suggests that the OSCE is not recognized by all participating states as a highly significant security organization, and that it suffers from a 'crisis of legitimacy'.[6] Moreover, as it lacks coercive power of its own, and remains confined to the realm of cooperative security and soft power, legitimacy is the key requirement for the OSCE to become or remain a relevant element of international governance beyond the nation state, in terms of facilitating international cooperation, making states and governments comply with its normative standards, and significantly contributing to European security governance.

The OSCE's legitimacy is not so much an objective category as it is a social practice grounded in inter-subjective meanings and values, and needs to be claimed, justified, and recognized. It is these competing efforts to justify the OSCE's legitimacy, and the competing frameworks within which these claims are evaluated and recognized, that are at the heart of this analysis. Given the lack of legal personality of the OSCE, the analysis focuses on the efforts of member states to legitimize the organization and its practices. Through the lens of official statements by three key member states—Russia, the US, and Germany—the chapter explores two distinct legitimation narratives, sketched out briefly above, and identifies how participating states either support (justify, endorse) or challenge (question, criticize, or complain about) the OSCE's legitimacy. The analysis highlights the role of the OSCE as a forum within which member states try to legitimate competing visions of international order, rather than an autonomous actor aiming to legitimate its own authority.

Evaluating the status of the OSCE's legitimacy and investigating its causal underpinnings, however, is not an end in itself. It becomes meaningful only if related to the second question stated at the outset: what are the implications for regional governance? Therefore, the discussion will also address the specific functions of the OSCE, and assess the implications of its legitimacy crisis for its effectiveness in terms of a) fostering cooperation among participating states; b) states'/governments' compliance with principles and norms, and c) its declared assignments and mandate?

The remainder of this chapter is structured as follows. Section two will provide some background to the on-going debates about the OSCE's appropriate roles and mandate, to contextualize the contending claims of Russia and CIS states, and Western states. Sections three to five will investigate both camps'

[6] According to Christian Reus-Smit, a crisis of legitimacy of an institution exists 'when the level of social recognition that its identity, interest, practices, norms, or procedures are rightful declines to the point where the actor or institution must either adapt (by reconstituting the social bases of its legitimacy, or by investing more heavily in material practices of coercion or bribery) or face disempowerment'. Christian Reus-Smit, 'International Crises of Legitimacy', *International Politics*, Vol. 44/2–3 (2007), 158.

legitimation strategies by scrutinizing political actors' practices of legitimation with regard to the contested institutional framework, the regimes and norms embedded in the OSCE, and the contested practices and activities of the OSCE. In the final section, the implications of the previous findings for the prospects of the OSCE's contribution to European governance will be evaluated.

HISTORICAL BACKGROUND

The Conference on Security and Cooperation in Europe (CSCE), which emerged in the early 1970s as part of East–West détente policy, had originally been a brainchild of the Soviet Union, not least intended to reach Western political recognition of Moscow's sphere of influence and borders in Europe. The negotiation process of the early 1970s resulted in the Helsinki Final Act of 1975. It established the CSCE (and later the OSCE) as the European security organization with the widest coverage in terms of both participants—the number of states participating in the CSCE/OSCE rose in stages during the first half of the 1990s from 35 to 56—and geographical reach: 'from Vancouver to Vladivostok'. Embedded in a comprehensive concept of security, the CSCE/OSCE's traditional policy areas—politics and security ('Basket I' containing the fundamental principles of relations between states as well as a set of military confidence- and security-building measures), economic relations ('Basket II') and humanitarian matters and human rights issues ('Basket III')—remained the Organization's domain following the end of the Cold War.

With the end of the cold war, participating states including the Soviet Union—and after the breakdown of the Soviet Union in December 1991, Russia—negotiated and accepted the Charter for Europe and its related documents, defining—along the lines of liberal cultural traditions and political values and norms—a common political denominator in terms of democracy, human rights, and rule of law as the fundamental values supposedly governing the future practice of international relations in Europe in 1990.[7] New institutions and structures, and the instruments the OSCE has used to perform its new specific functions were largely in place by 1995.[8] Since then, participating states have mostly been content to consolidate the institutions and their

[7] See for example Gregory Flynn and Henry Farrell, 'The CSCE and the "Construction" of Security in Post-Cold War Europe' *International Organization*, Vol. 53/3 (1999), 505–35. See also OSCE, *Charter of Paris for a New Europe*, Paris, 1990.

[8] For a systematic earlier comparison of the institution pre-and post 1989/90, see Ingo Peters, 'From the CSCE to the OSCE—Institutional Quality and Political Meaning', in Ingo Peters (ed.), *New Security Challenges: The Adaptation of International Institutions. Reforming the UN, NATO, EU and CSCE since 1989* (Münster/New York: Lit Verlag/ St. Martin's Press, 1999), 85–122.

operational activities. This has generally been a matter of making organizational changes in the light of practical experience.[9]

At the operational level, the frequently arduous everyday work of the OSCE in conflict prevention and the promotion of democracy, the rule of law, and human rights remain largely unreported. However, the OSCE Office for Democratic Institutions and Human Rights (ODIHR), frequently in co-operation with the Council of Europe, has been involved in training members of the executive, judicial, and legislative branches of government in the new democracies of Central and Eastern Europe. Fact-finding and monitoring missions have served to examine standards in political life, and have formed the basis for institutional recommendations. The OSCE High Commissioner on National Minorities (HCNM) has played a key role in pursuing these goals and has received considerable recognition. Long-term OSCE missions have attempted to head off potential crisis situations and to eliminate deficits in the application of OSCE principles and norms. Despite the political controversies over the deployment and authority of field operations discussed in more detail below, the number of operations has remained relatively high: while in 2001, OSCE field operations were present in 17 countries and employed some 4,000 personnel, in 2012, 20 operations were deployed. The mandates of OSCE field missions have ranged across concrete conflict-management efforts, the promotion of human and minority rights, democratization and election monitoring and the monitoring of ceasefires and peacekeeping forces.[10]

Since the mid-1990s, Russia has tried to promote the conference as the prime European security organization and to formalize it into an organization under international law. The West, first and foremost NATO and its member states, however, have frustrated these political elements of Russian reform plans, since these were seen to infringe upon other European security organizations, especially NATO and the EU. While the conference became nominally an *organization* and the CSCE the OSCE, it has continued to lack international legal personality, and did not become the top-dog in a hierarchy of European security organizations. Russian frustration was compounded by the OSCE's missions and its normative ambitions, especially by the CSBM (Confidence and Security-building Measures) documents and the CFE treaty, the regulations of which have been viewed by Moscow as unacceptable infringement on Russia's freedom to act during the wars in Chechnya in the mid- and late 1990s.[11]

[9] For details of the institutional development see Peters, 'OSCE, NATO, and the EU'.

[10] See OSCE, *Annual Report 2001 on Interaction between Organizations and Institutions in the OSCE Area (1. Nov. 2000–31. Oct. 2001)*, Vienna, 26.11.2001, 27–88. OSCE. Survey of OSCE Field Operations (SEC.GAL/207/12; 25 October 2012).

[11] See Peters 'From the CSCE to the OSCE' for the context and debates of the early 1990s.

This brief historical sketch is important for understanding contemporary debates on OSCE reforms in general and the basic ambiguity of Russia's stance on the OSCE in particular.[12] Today, Russia perceives the OSCE challenged by, as Foreign Minister Sergey Lavrov stated, 'negative tendencies in the evolution of the OSCE' leading towards a 'fragmentation of the pan-European space' and possibly towards a collapse of the European security architecture.[13] In this interpretation 'the OSCE in recent years got stuck at a crossroads' of choosing a direction of further relevance or irrelevance. It is perceived to lack effectiveness concerning its 'main vocation', which is 'to provide equal and indivisible security for all', and to prevent wars such as the 1999 '78-day bombing of Yugoslavia, or the military attack on South Ossetia'.[14] Hence, according to Moscow's analysis, the authority of the OSCE is questionable: 'Unfortunately, the OSCE both as a real instrument for ensuring security and as a forum for dialogue and a search for mutually acceptable solutions continues to remain out of the mainstream of events.'[15] Overall, the European security architecture 'still bears the stamp of an ideology from the past':

> An organization such as the OSCE could, it would seem, embody European civilization's newfound unity, but it is prevented from doing so, prevented from becoming a full-fledged general regional organization. The problem is not just in the organization's own incomplete institutional development but also in the obstruction created by other groups intent on continuing the old line of bloc politics.[16]

In contrast, the United States—a CSCE sceptic at the outset, which was merely won over to the conference project due to a strong urge coming from its West European partners[17]—today praises the OSCE for its contribution to uniting Europe and ending the East-West conflict.[18] US President Gerald Ford's assertion at the signing ceremony of the Helsinki Final Act in

[12] See Victor-Yves Ghebali, 'Growing Pains at the OSCE: The Rise and Fall of Russia's Pan-European Expectations', *Cambridge Review of International Affairs, 18/3* (2005), 375–88; Wolfgang Zellner, *Managing Change in Europe. Evaluating the OSCE and Its Future Role: Competencies, Capabilities, and Mission*, Hamburg, CORE Working Paper 13, 2005.

[13] Lavrov, *Speech at the 15th OSCE Ministerial Council.*

[14] Sergey Lavrov, *Speech by Russian Minister of Foreign Affairs at the 16th Meeting of the OSCE Ministerial Council in Helsinki (5. Dec. 2008)*, http://www.mid.ru/bdomp/brp_4.nsf/e78a48070f128a7b43256999005bcbb3/ab6b61362ca33952c3257523003f9f6c!OpenDocument

[15] Lavrov, *Speech at the 15th OSCE Ministerial Council.*

[16] Dmitry Medvedev, *Speech at Meeting with German Political, Parliamentary, and Civic Leaders in Berlin (5 June 2008)*, http://archive.kremlin.ru/eng/speeches/2008/06/05/2203_type82912type82914type84779_202153.shtml

[17] See John Maresca, *To Helsinki. The Conference on Security and Cooperation in Europe, 1973-1975* (Durham and London: Duke University Press, 1987).

[18] Julie Finley, 'Ambassador Finley on Looking Ahead to OSCE Ministerial' 14 Nov. 2008, U.S. Department of State, http://iipdigital.usembassy.gov/st/english/texttrans/2008/11/20081114114439eaifas0.3973963.html#axzz2PIQF4AzR; Condoleezza Rice, 'Rice Urges European Parliamentarians To Think Boldly, Globally', U.S. Department of State, 2005. http://www.america.gov/st/washfile-english/2005/July/20050701183551 1CJsamohT0.4665338.html.

1975: 'History will judge this Conference, not by what we say here today but by what we do tomorrow, not by the promises we make, but by the promises we keep', has served as a premise of US policy ever since.[19] Very much in this vein, the US has underscored the OSCE's broad mandate, and its comprehensive concept of security,[20] and has defined its 'paramount objectives' as 'preserving the integrity of OSCE principles and ensuring that the OSCE continues to be an agent of peaceful, democratic transformation'.[21] In response to Russia's critique of the OSCE, the US has underlined the organization's significance for promoting the principles and values enshrined in the Helsinki Final Act, and has generally regarded the OSCE as a success story:

> Its record over the past 15 years in fostering post-conflict stabilization and reconciliation; in striving to resolve peacefully the region's still frozen conflicts; in assisting the development of domestic democratic institutions and procedures; in promoting democratic elections; and in the development of a vibrant civil society, is unmatched.[22]

In the same spirit, the German government holds the OSCE in high esteem, not least since it contributed to the re-unification of Europe and of Germany. The Helsinki principles 'and adherence to these principles have brought Europe the longest period of peace in its history. The long-term confidence building which we practise is certainly regarded as a model in other regions of the world.'[23] Accordingly, these attributes render the OSCE 'an indispensable contribution to security, stability and strengthening the rule of law in Europe'.[24] Referring to the war in Georgia in August 2008, German Foreign Minister Frank-Walter Steinmeier, stressed that 'in times when new mistrust and occasional old, confrontational ways of thinking are becoming noticeable—in Europe as well', the OSCE is 'absolutely essential' for defining a new order: 'by strengthening

[19] Cited in Rice, 'Rice Urges European Parliamentarians'.

[20] David Kramer, *Speech on the Future of the OSCE. OSCE transforms a continent divided by force into one united in peace*, 17 October 2008, Washington DC. http://www.america.gov/st/text-trans-english/2008/October/20081020103033xjsnommis9.714907e-02.html; Kurt Volker, 'State's Volker Outlines Vision of Reformed but Flexible OSCE' Washington, DC, 2005. http://www.america.gov/st/washfile-english/2005/September/200509121158051CJsamohT0.3265802.html

[21] Rice, 'Rice Urges European Parliamentarians'; see also William Burns, *United States Intervention to the 2008 OSCE Ministerial Council* Vienna, United States Mission to the OSCE, 2008, http://osce.usmission.gov/media/pdfs/mc/mc_120408_burns_intervention.pdf; Kramer, *Speech on the Future of the OSCE*.

[22] Burns, *US Intervention to the 2008 Ministerial Council*; Volker, 'Reformed but Flexible OSCE'.

[23] 'German Foreign Minister Steinmeier urges for EU-OSCE Cooperation in Vienna Speech', *The Seoul Times*, 18 January 2007; Frank-Walter Steinmeier, *Speech by Federal Minister for Foreign Affairs, at the OSCE Ministerial Council in Madrid*, 29 Nov. 2007. http://www.osce.org/mc/29301

[24] Frank-Walter Steinmeier, *Rede des Bundesministers des Auswärtigen beim Ministerrat der OSZE*, 5. Dez. 2005 in Laibach, http://www.bundesregierung.de/nn_774/Content/DE/Bulletin/2001__2005/2005/12/2005-12-05-rede-des-bundesministers-des-auswaertigen-dr-frank-walter-steinmeier-beim-ministerrat-.html; Frank-Walter Steinmeier, 'Partnerschaft wagen—für eine Erneuerung der Sicherheitspolitik im 21. Jahrhundert', Frankfurter Allgemeine Zeitung, 4 December 2008.

democracy and the rule of law, and through its commitment to human rights and basic freedoms the OSCE is bringing about greater security in Europe, more trust, and also deeper mutual understanding'.[25]

In sum, with regard to the organization's legitimacy, Western states praise the organization for facilitating security and cooperation in Europe. Russia's stance, however, is more ambiguous: though Moscow has continued to emphasize the importance of the OSCE, its praise has been diluted by its concerns about the scope of the OSCE's operations and its involvement in the domestic affairs of member states. The ongoing debate on the organization's reforms is fundamentally framed by the fact that 'the consensus between participating states of the early post-Cold War years has eroded'.[26] What the OSCE is facing today are contesting views on its legitimacy: While western states take the position that preserving the organization's norms and functions relating to human rights, democratization and the rule of law are essential to its legitimacy, Russia—at least since Vladimir Putin became president and Moscow's policy became more assertive in 1999—has been taking the position of a revisionist power arguing that these interventions undermine the organization's legitimacy, and has tried to push institutional reforms that would advance more traditional understandings of sovereignty and non-interference with domestic affairs. These different and sometimes incompatible views of the OSCE's legitimacy will structure the following investigation into competing perceptions of the legitimacy of institutional structures, norms, and regimes, as well as operational activities of the organization.

A CONTESTED INSTITUTIONAL FRAMEWORK

The Issues of a Treaty Foundation and Legal Personality

Even after the change from the *Conference* to the *Organization* for Security and Cooperation in Europe in 1995, the OSCE has remained a cooperative body based on political agreement, and has not been established as a formal organization under international law, based on an international treaty deposited at the United Nations. Its principles, norms, and rules therefore remained *soft law* and the organization lacks legal personality with the privileges and immunities for its actions and personnel that such status would involve. Whether

[25] Frank-Walter Steinmeier, *Rede des Bundesaußenministers beim OSZE-Ministerrat in Helsinki*, 4 December 2008. http://www.bundesregierung.de/nn_774/Content/DE/Bulletin/2008/12/136-3-bmaa-osze.html.

[26] De Brichambaut, 'The OSCE and the 21st Century', 183.

and how this should be changed has been an issue since Russia and its CIS partners in 1994 started to push for reforms rendering the OSCE *de jure* an international organization like NATO or the UN. However, what at first glance looks like a mere judicial issue becomes a severe challenge to the main features of the OSCE, and a bone of political contention concerning the form and the functions (and thus the legitimacy) of the organization.

While Moscow accepted in the 1990s that the formal foundations of the organization would remain unchanged, the issue re-emerged in the renewed reform debate in 2004/2005, not least because of the recommendation of the *Panel of Eminent Persons Report* that participating States 'devise a concise statute or charter of the OSCE containing its basic goals, principles and commitments, as well as the structure of its main decision-making bodies'. The panel also suggested that participating States 'agree on a convention recognizing the OSCE's legal capacity and granting privileges and immunities to the OSCE and its officials'.[27]

Russia and its CIS partners remained the *demandeur* on this issue: The lack of authority and effectiveness of the OSCE, according to the Russian view, have been 'strongly affected by its incomplete institutionalization'. Consequently, Russia has pushed for the transformation of its institutional form into a 'full-fledged regional organization' to be founded on an OSCE charter or a statute.[28] According to President Dmitry Medvedev's initiative of May 2008, as well as the draft statute Russia proposed together with the CIS states, a Pan-European summit should decide on a kind of 'Helsinki 2',[29] advancing a legally binding European Security Treaty (EST) establishing an all-European collective security system, 'a truly indivisible space of equal security of all states in the Euro-Atlantic area'. Upgrading the formal status of the OSCE would make Russia a key member in a European security institution formally on an equal footing with NATO and the EU. Intrinsically linked to the formal treaty was the question of legal personality. Russia and CIS states have always taken the position that the latter should be an integral part of the new treaty foundation and should not be treated separately. As discussed further below, this has

[27] OSCE. *Common Purpose: Towards a More Effective OSCE*, Final Report and Recommendations of the Panel of Eminent Persons On Strengthening the Effectiveness of the OSCE, Vienna, 27 June 2005.

[28] Lavrov, *Speech at the 15th Ministerial Council Meeting*.

[29] Lavrov, *Speech at the 15th Ministerial Council Meeting*; Lavrov, *Speech at the 16th Ministerial Council Meeting*; Medvedev, *Speech at Meeting with German Leaders*; Dmitry Medvedev, European Security Treaty, Moscow, 29 November 2009, http://eng.kremlin.ru/text/docs/2009/11/223072.shtml; OSCE. *Draft Decision On The Charter Of The OSCE submitted by Armenia, Belarus, Kazakhstan, Kygyzstan, Uzbekistan, Russian Federation, Tajikistan*, PC.DEL/897/07, Vienna, 18 September 2007. See also Margarete Klein, 'Russia's Plan for a New Pan-European Security Regime: A Serious Proposal or an Attempt at Division?' *Russian Analytical Digest*, Vol. 55 (2009), 6–9.

put western states on the defensive, since while they have disapproved of any treaty, they have generally favoured a legal status for the OSCE.[30]

The US and Germany have continuously taken a cautious stance on Russian proposals for institutional reforms. Washington has always stressed that the OSCE 'as it is now structured, does excellent work. Reform can strengthen what OSCE does best, but the organization does not need major surgery.'[31] The baseline for Washington has been that 'new procedures must not come at the expense of principles', and 'any institutional reforms should be geared to strengthening OSCE's ability to produce results on the ground, particularly through its field missions'.[32] Consequently, the US government has remained opposed to 'any effort that—either in its intent or its effect—would diminish OSCE's credibility, dilute the commitments of signatory states, divert OSCE's attention from tough Human Dimension issues or undermine OSCE's effectiveness on the ground'.[33] The US therefore originally resisted any treaty or charter establishing the OSCE as an international organization with legal personality, since it asserted that such a formal treaty would 'misdirect our energies and political capital away from the OSCE's substantive work'.[34] Rather it suggested that 'the Helsinki Document and the OSCE's *acquis* of agreements and decisions speak for themselves'. However, over time, the US government increasingly considered the proposals as distinct issues, which did not necessarily have to go together, and ultimately 'firmly supported' the adoption of the legal convention granting the OSCE legal personality but no formal treaty foundation.[35] Germany has also considered an OSCE charter and a convention on its legal personality distinct issues, and has been in favour of the latter.[36] Its baseline concerning institutional reforms has been that 'a dynamic organization needs change and renewal'. In support of the US position, Berlin

[30] On the evolution of the debate on the OSCE's legal status, see Sonya Brander, 'Making a credible case for a legal personality for the OSCE', *OSCE Magazin*, March/ April 2009, 18–22.

[31] Volker, 'State's Volker Outlines Vision'.

[32] Rice, 'Rice Urges European Parliamentarians'; Burns, *United States Intervention to the 2008 OSCE Ministerial Council*; Kramer, *Speech on the Future of the OSCE*.

[33] Kramer, *Speech on the Future of the OSCE*.; See Elizabeth Pryor, *Criticism of OSCE by Nine CIS Countries Draws the Response*, U.S. Helsinki Commission, 2004, http://www.brama.com/news/press/2004/07/040729csce.html, for a pointed treatment of Lavrov's main points (i. e. non-interference with internal affairs principle; imbalance of baskets, unfair standards in the human dimension and election monitoring).

[34] Volker, 'State's Volker Outlines Vision'.

[35] See Julie Finley, *Response to Russian Foreign Minister Lavrov*, Vienna, 23 May 2007. http://osce.usmission.gov/media/pdfs/2007-statements/lavrov_5-23-07.pdf: 'Recalling the 2006 Ministerial Decision, we do not believe that a "Charter" should be negotiated, nor is it necessary, to give the OSCE the same legal status as other international organizations.' See also Julie Finley, 'Ambassador Finley on Looking Ahead to OSCE Ministerial', 14 November 2008, http://georgia.usembassy.gov/tr-11142008.html

[36] Frank-Walter Steinmeier, *Speech by Federal Minister for Foreign Affairs, at the OSCE Ministerial Council in Madrid*, 29 November 2007, http://www.osce.org/documents/mcs/2007/11/28493_en.pdf.

also emphasized that 'it is therefore very important... that there is no move to encroach upon the OSCE's basic values, values which we all share and which make up the organization's strength.'[37] Efficiency and transparency of OSCE's work should be improved on the premises of reform and consensus, partnership, common responsibility, and enhanced geographic balance.[38]

Concerning Medvedev's proposal for negotiations of a new all-European security treaty, German and American officials repeatedly emphasized the OSCE as indispensable for establishing a new political order in Europe and adjured the need for open dialogue in order to 'restore the consensus and the comprehensive operability of the OSCE', a consensus the lack of which had become apparent by the fact that since 2002 no Declaration of Ministers had been adopted at its annual Council meetings.[39] However, as Steinmeier stressed, a new order 'will not come out of the blue: neither the Charter nor the European security architecture. Too much confidence has been lost, and alienation has become too immense. Therefore, now we need prudent—and concrete—steps, which facilitate the re-establishment of confidence.'[40]

At least since 2007, across the changing US administrations, Washington has argued for avoiding 'harsh rhetoric, which sometimes makes it sound as if the relationship itself is in question', and in favour of finding 'ways to manage our differences with Russia where they persist, and stand firm where our principles or our vital interests are at stake.'[41] Likewise, German OSCE policy in the wake of the 2008 war in Georgia emphasized the role of the organization as a vehicle for dialogue, referring explicitly to the dangers of a revival of 'old confrontational thinking in Europe.'[42] From a German perspective, using the OSCE as an overall instrument for political dialogue across all dividing lines explicitly paralleled the CSCE process in the 1970s, and both Berlin and Washington pushed for involving an OSCE presence in Georgia based on 'sovereignty, independence and territorial integrity of Georgia'. While Western states have acknowledged Russian and CIS concerns, and wider discussions on the role of the OSCE within the wider European security architecture continued under the umbrella of the 'Corfu process' since 2009, the underlying divisions have remained largely unresolved.

[37] Gernot Erler Speech by the Minister of State in the Federal Foreign Office at the OSCE Ministerial Council in Brussels, 4. December 2006. Gernot Erler was Minister of State of the German Foreign Office 1998/2002–5.

[38] Steinmeier, *Rede beim Ministerrat der OSZE*.

[39] Steinmeier, *Rede beim Ministerrat der OSZE*. In fact the first substantial Ministerial Document since 2002 was adopted in December 2009.

[40] Steinmeier, 'Partnerschaft Wagen'. Translation by the author.

[41] Finley, *Respnse to Lavrov*; Hillary Rodham Clinton, *Secretary Clinton's Remarks After NATO Meeting*, New York, Council on Foreign Relations, March 2009.

[42] Steinmeier, *Rede beim OSZE Ministerrat in Helsinki*.

Diverging Views on OSCE Principles

In addition to its fundamental critique of the OSCE's lack of political significance and its vigorous demand for reforming its formal foundations, Moscow has criticized 'double standards' with regard to the principle of equality of OSCE participating states—one of the ten principles laid down in the Helsinki Final Act of 1975 and reiterated in many of the OSCE documents adopted after 1990. A case in point was Kazakhstan's offer (supported by all CIS states) to take on the OSCE chairmanship in 2009, an offer which was opposed by some participating states doubting this country's 'suitability'.[43] Based on the premise 'that any Chair of the OSCE must be in substantial compliance with all OSCE commitments', the US State Department left no doubt that this bid was unacceptable unless Kazakhstan substantially would implement its OSCE commitments, especially those on human rights and democratization.[44] Germany expressed similar concerns but was more conciliatory, in principle supporting application for OSCE chairmanship, which Kazakhstan actually took on in January 2010.[45]

More significantly, Moscow's proposal for the reform of the overall structure of the OSCE, and especially for a legally binding treaty was directly linked to the demand that all participants

> reaffirm their commitment to fundamental principles of the international law, such as the non-use of force and peaceful settlement of disputes, sovereignty, territorial integrity and non-interference in internal affairs as well as the inadmissibility of strengthening one's own security by infringing upon the security of others.[46]

Russian arguments have rested on both its perceived interests and shared norms. It has identified the challenges posed to the OSCE's legitimacy as rooted in 'profound differences in perceptions about the role, the vocation and the future of OSCE', stemming directly from 'group interests being placed above pan-European' ones:[47] In the words of Sergej Lavrov,

> There are those who want everything to be kept as it was in the 1990s. In other words, a group of countries positioning themselves as being civilizationally the most advanced determine and monitor the movement parameters for the rest.

[43] Lavrov, *Speech at the 15th OSCE Ministerial Council Meeting.*

[44] Robert Herman, 'Testimony: Dr. Robert Herman before the U.S. Helsinki Commission', Washington DC, 21 September 2007. http://csce.gov/index.cfm?FuseAction=ContentRecords.ViewWitness&ParentType=H&ContentRecord_id=861&ContentType=D&CFID=14870214&CFTOKEN=68024409; Christopher H. Smith, 'Kazakhstan's Candidacy for OSCE Chairmanship', U.S. House of Representatives: Proceedings of the 109th Congress, 2nd Session, 29. June 2006, Congressional Record 152 (2006), 87.

[45] Erler, *Speech at the Ministerial Council.*

[46] Lavrov, *Speech at the 15th OSCE Ministerial Meeting.*

[47] Lavrov, *Speech at the 15th OSCE Ministerial Meeting.*

> Therefore they demand that all institutions and mechanisms of the Organization be kept intact, like a kind of gold standard. Yet history shows that if these standards do not meet the tasks of contemporaneity, then the teacher of life, as the ancient Greeks called history, consigns them to a museum or archive at best. And this is not a question of somebody's wishes or will—it's an objective process.[48]

Arguably, the Russian Federation's prompting for a return to the traditional principle of non-interference has posed the most significant challenge to the organization's credibility, diluting the signatory states' commitments. Western states have generally rejected such moves with references to the OSCE's 'comprehensive concept of security',[49] supposedly legitimizing concerns of OSCE states about domestic affairs of fellow-participating states' implementation of OSCE principles, norms, and rules. Holding up the mirror to those participating states trying to undo what they had signed up to in core OSCE documents, not least the Moscow Document of 1991, Washington has argued that:

> Not surprisingly, it is from those participating states where fundamental freedoms are most challenged by government actions, and where democratic safeguards are the weakest, that we tend to hear the most criticism by state officials of the way the OSCE and its institutions and field missions conduct their work. It is precisely where the distance between commitment and conduct is greatest that the OSCE must continue to concentrate its efforts.[50]

The German government likewise spoke out for a necessary dialogue on what traditionally were considered states' domestic affairs.[51] However, Western states feared that Russian reform proposals and specifically an OSCE Statute 'may undermine the commitments of member states that have been built up within the OSCE', a critique rejected by Russia as 'groundless'.[52]

Restoring National Control or Maintaining Autonomy of the ODIHR?

Another core target of Russian criticism on the level of the overall setup of OSCE institutions has been the Office for Democratic Institutions and Human Rights (ODIHR), located in Warsaw. This major operational agency of the Organization, was accused of ascribing to

> Groundless claims...to autonomy from the member states and attempts to put themselves above the member states while ignoring the directives from the

[48] Lavrov, *Speech at the 16th OSCE Ministerial Meeting.*
[49] Kramer, *Speech on the Future of the OSCE.*
[50] Kramer, *Speech on the Future of the OSCE.*
[51] Frank-Walter Steinmeier, *Rede des Bundesministers des Auswärtigen vor dem Ständigen Rat der OSZE in Wien,* 18 January 2007, http://www.bundesregierung.de/nn_774/Content/DE/Bulletin/2007/01/04-4-aa-osze.html.
[52] Lavrov, *Speech at the 15th OSCE Ministerial Meeting.*

> intergovernmental bodies of the OSCE and the division of member states into 'first and second rate' countries, particularly in organizing the observation of elections. It seems to us that a 'point of no return' has been reached: either we will all together agree on the rules for electoral monitoring or differences in this area will put in jeopardy the prospect of ODIHR as an institution of the Organization.[53]

Moscow's proposal for reforming the ODIHR's procedures included a requirement for the OSCE Permanent Council to approve all ODIHR election monitoring reports. Given the requirement for consensual decision-making in the Council, the proposal would have given each state a veto over ODIHR's assessments.[54]

The US and the German government rejected such attacks on the ODIHR as cutting to the bone of the organization's operational activities. Instead, both governments favoured institutional reforms as those 'valuable and necessary' proposals elaborated by the Eminent Persons Panel.[55] Washington especially welcomed those buttressing the operational level by increasing 'capacities and maintaining independence of ODIHR and OSCE Representatives', as well as strengthening human rights and the effectiveness of field missions.[56] As a marked feature of the OSCE's strength, the German government also emphasized 'the independence of its institutions, field missions and election observation missions'.[57] These policy preferences undoubtedly were meant to maintain the delegated operational autonomy of the ODIHR and thus rebuffed Russia's plans to put the Office on a shorter political leash. However, as will be discussed further below, Washington and Berlin also indicated their readiness to address Russia's concerns.

Summing up, Russia considered OSCE standards and practices as no longer reflecting norms shared by all OSCE participant states, but as one-sidedly reflected western values. To redress this imbalance, Moscow has questioned the institutional status quo of the OSCE and demanded profound institutional reforms, to be crowned by a new European Security Treaty. In contrast, the US and Germany have argued in favour of reforms strengthening its performance first and foremost 'on the ground', rather than major structural changes, arguing against a new 'European Security Treaty' or an OSCE Charter, not least because they have considered the OSCE's 'flexible and un-bureaucratic' structures and procedures to facilitate its transformative power. From their perspective, an inherent tension exists between Russia's call for, on the one hand, a new legally binding treaty allegedly strengthening the OSCE's effectiveness

[53] Lavrov, *Speech at the 15th OSCE Ministerial Meeting*.

[54] See Herman, *Testimony*; OSCE, *Draft Decision on OSCE/ODIHR Observation of National Elections*.

[55] OSCE, *Common Purpose;* Steinmeier, *Rede beim Ministerrat der OSZE*.

[56] Pryor, *Criticism of OSCE.*; Burns, *United States Intervention*.

[57] Erler, *Speech at OSCE Ministerial Council*; see also Steinmeier, *Speech at the OSCE Ministerial Council in Madrid*.

and, on the other hand, the aim to redefine the constitutive as well as the regulative norms governing OSCE work, i.e. the rules of procedure as well as the substantive norms as laid down in various OSCE documents concerning state performance in human rights, rule of law, and democratization policies, to which Russia has not always adhered. They consider Russian efforts as not aiming at a 'progressive' process of institutionalized cooperation and regional integration, but rather as an effort to roll-back the scope of its activities. Evidence for this may be Moscow's strive for undoing normative CSCE standards which diluted the traditional principle of non-interference with domestic affairs if OSCE participating states are concerned about the others' conduct with regard to OSCE norms and values, or when Russia is trying to cut back autonomy of OSCE agencies and restoring national control. In response to growing Russian assertiveness, however, western states have made efforts to accommodate Russia and discuss problems of election monitoring as well as actively promoting election monitoring on their territories.

REGIMES AND NORMS

The Treaty on Conventional Forces in Europe (CFE)

Arms control and disarmament had been part of the original proposals of the Soviet Union for a European security conference as early as the 1950s. However, since this was considered an unbearable attack on NATO as the key Western security institution, not least on the insistence of the US the CSCE became concerned with soft arms control only, i.e. Confidence and Security-building measures. Hard arms control was instead assigned to the Mutually Balanced Forces Reduction talks (MBFR) among the Eastern and the Western alliances, i.e. the Warsaw Treaty Organization and the North Atlantic Treaty Organization (NATO). In the wake of the breakdown of the East–West conflict these talks resulted in the CFE Treaty (1990), generating significant reductions in conventional arms of the member states of the Eastern and Western alliance. Negotiated separately, arms control became 're-integrated' to the CSCE since it was assigned with overseeing the implementation of the CFE Treaty. This arms control regime together with the Basket 3 agreements thus became the prime regimes in the CSCE/OSCE framework.[58]

[58] SeeIvo Daalder, 'The Role of Arms Control in the New Europe', *Contemporary Security Policy*, Vol. 12/1 (1991), 20–34; Jonathan Dean and Randell Forsberg, 'CFE and Beyond: The Future of Conventional Arms Control', *International Security*, Vol. 17/1 (1992), 76–121.

However, with the breakdown of the Soviet Union and the Warsaw Pact, some Eastern European states joining NATO, and the military conflicts in the Balkans as well as parts of Russia, adjustments and reforms of the original treaty as well as of the complementing CSBM regime became inevitable.[59] Thus, the CFE Treaty was updated so as to meet the new situation in Europe by the Adaptation Agreement signed in November 1999. However, in 2001 NATO states deferred the ratification of the adapted treaty until Russia had adjusted its forces to the new limits and also had fulfilled its commitments to withdraw its military forces from Moldova and Georgia.[60] While NATO confirmed that the first condition was fulfilled in 2002, the second precondition remains unfulfilled, not least because Russia never accepted that it had made such a commitment. Russia regretted the continuing situation of 'legal uncertainty', complained about the CFE regime's loss of 'contact with reality', and finally suspended the Treaty in December 2007.

At the same time, however, Moscow continuously stressed its openness for 'dialogue and a joint search for solutions to ensure entry into force of the adapted CFE Treaty as soon as possible and the restoration of the viability of European control over conventional arms as a whole' and urged for a response to the draft Russian–American 'package deal'.[61] While emphasizing that the Treaty 'should be restored', Moscow simultaneously accused NATO countries of pursuing 'unilateral advantages and solving questions having no relationship to arms control, then a further erosion of the existing regimes will become inevitable'. Russia moreover demanded in general 'an unbiased overview of the existing norms and documents for their conformity with present day realities', and in particular proposed a revision of the Vienna Document, i. e. the regime of Confidence and Security-building Measures (CSBM) in line with its own proposal.[62]

The United States has also favoured preserving the benefits of the CFE Treaty, which 'transformed European security and contributed to the dramatic decline of conventional forces in Europe'.[63] Likewise Germany has emphasized

[59] See Richard Falkenrath, 'The CFE Flank Dispute: Waiting in the Wings', *International Security, Vol. 19/4* (1995), 118–44; Zellner, *Managing Chaos in Europe.*

[60] See Arms Control Association, *The Adapted Conventional Armed Forces in Europe Treaty at a Glance*, Washington DC, 2009, http://www.armscontrol.org/factsheets/adaptcfe; OSCE, *Istanbul Summit Document*, 18–19 November 1999, 46–58. http://www.osce.org/documents/mcs/1999/11/4050_en.pdf.

[61] Lavrov, *Speech at the 15th OSCE Ministerial Council;* Sergey Lavrov, *Speech by Russian Minister of Foreign Affairs Sergey Lavrov at the 17th OSCE Ministerial Council Meeting, Athens,* 1 December 2009. http://www.norway.mid.ru/news_fp/news_fp_146_eng.html.

[62] Lavrov, *Speech at the 16th OSCE Ministerial Meeting*; Lavrov, *Speech at the 17th OSCE Ministerial Meeting.*

[63] Burns, *United States Intervention*; see also Finley, *Response to Lavrov*; Finley, *Looking ahead to OSCE Ministerial.*

the essential role of the adapted CFE Treaty for buffering the transformation in Europe after the end of the Cold War and praised the treaty's contribution to security and stability in Europe as a 'cornerstone of European security'. Both have argued that the politico-military dimension of the OSCE, i.e. the Adapted CFE Treaty and the CSBM, should be 'preserved, fully implemented and further strengthened'.[64] While accusing Russia of putting the treaty at risk by its suspension of implementation and its continuing military presence in Moldova and Georgia, the US and the other NATO countries have also stressed their readiness for negotiations to overcome the impasse and facilitate the Treaty's ratification.[65] The arms control regime has thus remained, despite disagreements, one of the areas where agreement on OSCE rules and norms has remained strong.

The Human Dimension of the OSCE

Concerning the human rights dimension of the OSCE, Russia—while criticizing the Organization's operational policy and emphasizing the need 'for an overview of the existing norms and documents for their conformity with present day reality'—has explicitly referenced the OSCE's human rights principles in its military engagement in Georgia (August 2008). Foreign minister Lavrov asserted that human rights and the protection of national minorities are of 'everlasting significance',[66] and Georgia's treatment of South Ossetia an 'urgent humanitarian matter'.[67] Moscow admitted that the human rights dimension remained an 'integral part of the concept of security' but has opposed what it perceived as OSCE efforts to substitute its own human rights instruments for 'anything and everything', even if the UN's Human Rights Council and the Council of Europe operate with 'efficient mechanisms and agreed rules for monitoring and reporting'.[68] Moreover, it criticized 'a selective approach' concerning the freedoms laid down in the Paris Charter for a New Europe (1990), with the promises of freedom of movement and eased visa regimes

[64] Steinmeier, *Rede vor dem Ständigen Rat der OSZE*; Frank-Walter Steinmeier, *EU Statement in response to H.E. the Minister of Foreign Affairs of the Russian Federation, Mr. Sergei Lavrov*, 23 May 2007. http://www.eu2007.de/en/News/Statements_in_International_Organisations/May/0523OSCERussia.html.

[65] Burns, *United States Intervention*; see also Finley, *Response to Lavrov*; Finley, *Looking ahead to OSCE Ministerial*.

[66] Lavrov, *Speech at the 16th OSCE Ministerial Meeting*.

[67] Lavrov, *Speech at the 16th OSCE Ministerial Meeting*. For Russia's narrative on aggression of Georgia on South Ossetia and Abkhasia and Russia's recognition of their independence, see Sergey Lavrov, *Address of the Foreign Minister of the Russian Federation, at the 63rd Session of the UN General Assembly*, New York, 27 September 2008. http://www.norway.mid.ru/pr08-12_nor.html.

[68] Lavrov, *Speech at the 17th OSCE Ministerial Council*.

being neglected, and requested a mandate for ODIHR to monitor the visa situation in OSCE countries.[69]

In accordance with its vigorous support for the OSCE's human rights principles, Washington has strongly emphasized the organization's important role in promoting democracy, human rights, and rule of law, and especially for combating anti-Semitism and other forms of discrimination.[70] Germany has based its assessment of the OSCE's Basket 3 principles very much on the same premise when asserting that '(s)ecurity and stability in the OSCE area are inconceivable without democracy, human rights and the rule of law'.[71] For western states, the human rights dimension is considered to be at the 'heart of the work of the OSCE'.[72] Accordingly, following the war in August 2008 the US and Germany argued strongly in favour of re-establishing an OSCE mission in Georgia in view of human rights abuses in South Ossetia. Based on the principles of sovereignty, independence, and territorial integrity the mandate had to cover the whole of Georgia explicitly.[73]

Both the human rights and the politico-military regimes have been closely linked by Russia as well as by the United States and Germany to the 'frozen conflicts' in Europe—though for contrary reasons. While Washington and Germany accused Russia of violations of OSCE principles and norms in the cases of Moldova and Georgia, Moscow tried to steal the others' thunder by pointing towards Western policy on Kosovo. Complaining about 'disrespect for the documents adopted in the OSCE', Russia asserted the bypassing of the UN Security Council in the Kosovo case as undermining 'the very foundation of the Organization, primarily its mainstay—the Helsinki Final Act'. The US and Germany considered Kosovo as a *sui generis* case, which could not be a precedent for other conflicts in Europe.[74] The above discussion of the issues and lines of argument of Russia (and its CIS partners) and the Western states again point to the manifest conflict of established norms and what are considered to be vital state interests implying a severe controversy about the legitimacy of these regimes as well as of the OSCE. It also highlights how the OSCE has become a forum within which key member states try to advance and legitimize their broader understandings of international order, and with that legitimize or de-legitimize the OSCE and its practices.

[69] Lavrov, *Speech at the 17th OSCE Ministerial Council.*

[70] Kramer, *Speech on the Future of the OSCE*; Rice, 'Rice urges Parliamentarians to Think Boldly'.

[71] Steinmeier, *Speech at the Madrid Ministerial Council.* For the new government's position, see Werner Hoyer, *Rede des Staatsministers im auswärtigen Amt beim OSZE Ministerrat in Athen,* 1 December 2009, http://www.auswaertiges-amt.de/diplo/de/Infoservice/Presse/Reden/2009/091201-HoyerOSZE.html.

[72] Steinmeier, *EU Response to Sergej Lavrov.*

[73] Finley, *Final Statement at the Helsinki Council*; Steinmeier, *Rede beim OSZE Ministerrat in Helsinki.*

[74] Lavrov, *Speech at the 15th Ministerial Council*; Steinmeier, *Rede beim Ständigen Rat.*

OSCE OPERATIONAL ACTIVITIES

With the institutional structures established by the Charter of Europe in 1990 and their respective adjustment and consolidation until 1995, the OSCE has acquired agencies assigned to monitoring the compliance of participating states with OSCE norms and regimes as well as promoting values and norms by providing assistance and advice to governments. Moreover, its agencies have been holding seminars for educating civil servants of the participating state on improving standards of performance in the realm of democratic elections, rule of law, as well as human and minority rights, and peaceful conflict resolution. The prime instrument for monitoring of and assistance to participating states are various kinds of missions working in the respective countries with a specified mandate agreed to within the overall OSCE framework, and with the consent of the respective country. The most prominent agencies for these purposes are the High Commissioner for National Minorities (HCNM) located in The Hague, the Office for Democratic Institutions and Human Rights (ODIHR) located in Warsaw, and the Conflict Prevention Center (CPC) in Vienna.[75]

Election Monitoring and Observation Missions

Aside from qualms about the normative foundations of the OSCE, Russia has increasingly complained about the implementation of norms and regimes, i.e. the practices on the level of operational activities. Joined by its CIS partners, Russia criticized a general shift towards 'humanitarian problems' and field missions because of the latter's alleged exclusive focus 'on the functions of monitoring the situation in the sphere of human rights and democratic institutions'.[76] The prime target of Moscow's criticism has been the ODIHR due to the Office's conduct of and reporting on election monitoring missions. With the vast majority of its election monitoring missions in Eastern European and CIS countries, Moscow has alleged that the majority of states hosting such missions on their territory wish to get rid of them, and branded the presence of these missions as a manifestation of inequality in the OSCE. In addition, it considered the missions as insufficiently accountable, especially in relation to the states hosting them, and to whom they are expected to hand over their functions. Additionally, Lavrov claimed an 'increased frequency of cases of non-observance of the procedures for

[75] OSCE, *Survey of OSCE Field Operations,* SEC.GAL165/09, Vienna, 9 October 2009.

[76] Commonwealth of Independent States (CIS). *Statement by CIS Member Countries on the State of Affairs in the OSCE,* Moscow, 3 July 2004. http://www.kremlin.ru/eng/text/docs/2004/07/74223.shtml.

appointment of heads of field presences of the Organization' becoming manifest in a total neglect of the host country's view or these posts going to but one country.[77] The growing criticism of the ODIHR by Russia and other CIS countries culminated in accusations of 'groundless claims...to autonomy from the member states',[78] and the proposal to subordinate the Office to the political control of the Permanent Council.[79]

In contrast to Russia, the US government has continuously supported OSCE's work 'on the ground' through ODIHR, 'the world's premier election monitoring organization',[80] and its field missions.[81] Though Washington has conceded some problems concerning the variance of standards in practices applied by ODIHR and the OSCE Parliamentary Assembly,[82] it has stood firmly behind what has been considered these institutions' valuable work:

> Due to the imposition of serious constraints on the exercise of fundamental freedoms, key elections in some participating States have fallen short—in a number of cases—egregiously short—of OSCE commitments. The United States rejects all efforts to undermine the effectiveness, objectivity and independence of OSCE election observation....[83]

In operational terms and concerning the balance of the OSCE elections monitoring practice, the US sought to address part of Russia's concern and conceded room for compromise[84] by expending the geographic scope of election monitoring through inviting observers to US elections, supposedly contributing towards a more balanced practice.[85]

Berlin also stressed the interconnectedness of the normative and the operational level of the organization: 'Common values; institutions, field and election monitoring missions have acquired model character enabling a crucial

[77] Lavrov, *Speech at the 15th Ministerial Council*; Lavrov, *Speech at the 16th Ministerial Council*. The CIS countries had already complained in 2004 about the practice of human rights and democratic institutions as not corresponding to main principles of the OSCE: 'Selectively paying more attention to some countries while ignoring the problems in other member countries is a violation of the OSCE mandate, and shows that the Organisation has a practice of double standards and selective approaches, and does not wish to pay attention to the peculiarities and specifics of individual nations.' CIS, *Statement by CIS Members*.

[78] Lavrov, *Speech at the 15th Ministerial Council*.

[79] Lavrov, *Speech at the 15th Ministerial Council*. See also OSCE, *Draft Decision On The Charter Of The OSCE submitted by Armenia, Belarus, Kazakhstan, Kygyzstan, Uzbekistan, Russian Federation, Tajikistan*, PC.DEL/897/07, Vienna, 18 September 2007.

[80] Burns, *United States Intervention*.

[81] Volker, 'State's Volker Outlines Vision of Reformed but Flexible OSCE'.

[82] R. Spencer, Oliver, *Remarks on Election Observation by Secretary General of the OSCE Parliamentary Assembly, to the U.S. Helsinki Commission*, Washington DC, 15 September 2008. http://www.freedomhouse.org/uploads/TESTIMONYOLIVER.pdf

[83] Kramer, *Speech on the Future of the OSCE*.

[84] Finley, *Response to Lavrov*; see also Hrair Balian, 'Older and wiser: Election observation benefits from lessons learned', *OSCE Newsletter*, Vol. 10/3 (2003), 11–13.

[85] Burns, *United States Intervention*; see also: Kramer, *Speech on the Future of the OSCE*.

role concerning conflict prevention, crisis management and arms control.'[86] In contrast to Russian allegations, foreign minister Steinmeier emphasized the significant and successful contributions of OSCE field missions as well as the professional and impartial activities of more than 150 election observation missions.[87] Representing EU presidency, Steinmeier called for an active role of all states concerned about OSCE missions, stressing that such dialogue should not be misinterpreted as 'lecturing, showing up, or even denouncing'.[88] On behalf of the EU and its member states, he explicitly endorsed the High Commissioner on National Minorities, the Representative on Freedom of the Media, as well as the ODIHR and the field and election observation missions as 'key institutions and instruments whose viability and efficiency we have to preserve and strengthen'.[89]

Though Germany conceded that the criticism of states which fear that missions are directed against them should be taken seriously, it rejected some states' scepticism and allegations that monitoring missions 'are used to bring about changes of regime', since 'democratic changes of government take place due to election results and not due to the monitoring of the elections'. Steinmeier however, added that 'it is important that the election observers do not just come from a few states but rather that the composition is as balanced as possible in geographical terms',[90] And added that 'the receiving states [should] regard these missions not as foreign interference but rather as partners—as an offer of support at a difficult time and in a challenging process of transition'.[91] Berlin did not refrain from speaking out on Moscow's decision—contrary to 2012—not to allow OSCE election monitoring during the 2007 state elections in Russia, not least since Russia had already failed to meet OSCE and Council of Europe commitments on the occasion of the Duma elections in 2003.[92] However, in order to reassure Russia and other critics and thus to respond constructively to Lavrov's and others' concerns, Steinmeier emphasized Germany's own experience with OSCE monitoring missions and the domestic learning process spurred by these activities:

> Germany too faces up to the mechanisms of the OSCE and the sometimes uncomfortable criticism of the community and tries to use it proactively to

[86] Steinmeier, *Rede beim OSZE Ministerrat*; Steinmeier, *Rede beim OSZE Ministerrat in Helsinki.*

[87] Steinmeier, *Rede bei OSZE Ministerrat*; see also Steinmeier, *Speech at the Madrid Ministerial Council.*

[88] Steinmeier, *Rede vor dem Ständigen Rat der OSZE.*

[89] Steinmeier, *Rede vor dem Ständigen Rat der OSZE.*

[90] The Seoul Times, 'Steinmeier urges for OSE-EU Cooperation'; Steinmeier, *Speech at the Madrid Ministerial Council*; Erler, *Speech at the Ministerial Council.*

[91] Erler, *Speech at the Ministerial Council.*

[92] Mikhail Evstafiev, 'Observing Russia's Duma elections is a hard day's night', *OSCE Magazine* Vol.1/1 (2004), 19–21.

bring about improvements. As recently as this spring, the report by the Personal Representative of the Chairman-in-Office, Ambassador Orhun, criticizing the naturalization laws of German Länder for Muslim minorities, sparked off a fruitful domestic-policy debate in our country. Moreover, my country emphatically supports the OSCE Declarations against anti-Semitism, racism and all forms of discrimination.[93]

Civil Society Involvement in OSCE Activities

Another issue questioning the OSCE's underlying normative foundations as well as its purpose to promote security and cooperation in Europe has been the place of civil society in OSCE activities. As became clear from some statements of Foreign Minister Lavrov, Russia has been increasingly critical of the involvement of civil society actors in OSCE activities, suggesting that the invitation of 'marginal and indeed utterly "phantom" NGOs with extremist views' to OSCE events was detrimental to constructive cooperation among member states.[94] In 2007, Russia (together with Tajikistan and Uzbekistan) submitted a proposal for more restrictive NGO regulations, along the lines of those of the UN.[95] In contrast, the US and Germany have always viewed a 'vibrant civil society' as one of the pillars of good governance and thus one of the desired political effects of the OSCE process. They have accordingly considered close cooperation of the OSCE with civil society actors an integral part of the organization's human rights dimension and efforts in conflict prevention and post-conflict rehabilitation.[96]

In sum, OSCE operational activities and the involvement of civil society actors obviously resemble the basic tensions characterizing the CSCE from its very beginning, that is, the intrinsic tension between the aims of stability and change. After some time of sullen toleration due to the break-down of the communist systems, Russia and with different degrees also the CIS states have become resurgent and try to re-reform the OSCE on the level of operational practices towards a *status qua ante* and dismiss formerly agreed standards of democratic rule, human rights, and rule of law. In contrast, the US and Germany supported by other NATO and EU member states not surprisingly favour the established rules, procedures, and operational activities of the OSCE which were so successfully built on Western values of democracy and human rights. Hence, they do favour the status quo and favour further reforms

[93] Erler, *Speech at the Ministerial Council.*

[94] Lavrov, *Speech at the 15th Ministerial Council.*

[95] OSCE. *Proposal for Clarifying the Rolle of NGOs in OSCE Activities*, PC.DEL/1029/07, Vienna, 30 October 2007.

[96] See Steinmeier, *EU Response to Lavrov*; Volker, 'Volker Outlines Vision for Reformed OSCE'; Burns, *United States Intervention.*

only in terms of adjustments strengthening the OSCE when it comes to these political norms.

CONCLUSIONS: IMPLICATIONS FOR THE PROSPECTS AND LIMITS OF REGIONAL GOVERNANCE

In the words of OSCE Secretary-General de Brichambaut, 'It is difficult for a value-based organization to do better than its constituent parts; the OSCE is no exception to the rule.'[97] This discussion of the assessments of the Organization's principles, structures, and practices and their legitimacy highlights two competing views of and narratives about the OSCE. On the one hand, Russia and CIS states question the legitimacy and the effectiveness of the OSCE across all dimensions, no matter whether concerning the organization's general functions or its special functions. For them, the organization fails when it comes to the heart of its mandate, preventing conflicts and war, and in turn providing peace and security. Its institutional structures and procedures are considered to inappropriately discriminate against Russia and its CIS partners. Its regimes and norms are said to be implemented in an unequal manner at the expense of the Eastern participating states and OSCE's missions are criticized for undermining the stability of governments and countries.

On the other hand, western states (analysed here through the lens of the US and Germany) have generally a more positive view of the OSCE's legitimacy and effectiveness. They focus on the desirability of the Organization's transformative power, and argue that its principles, norms, and values have 'brought Europe the longest period of peace in history'.[98] The deficient commitment of some states and governments to OSCE regimes and norms, i.e. the difference between the promises made and the promises kept, are said to undermine stability and security in Europe. In contrast to Moscow, Washington and Berlin do criticize participating states but not the organization as such. The OSCE's institutional structures are praised for their contribution to translating abstract principles and norms in operational activities, and for having succeeded in promoting the norms of democracy, the rule of law, human rights, and a strengthened civil society. OSCE activities 'on the ground', and specifically OSCE missions are strongly supported in their successful work.

The organization's legitimacy has thus been hotly contested, but more importantly has been judged according to distinct and incompatible normative

97 de Brichambaut, 'The OSCE and the 21st Century', 180.

98 Burns, *United States Intervention*; Steinmeier, *Speech at the Madrid Ministerial Council.*

frameworks: a traditional 'pluralist' framework emphasizing state sovereignty and non-intervention on the one hand; and a more 'solidarist' framework emphasizing human rights norms and the conditionality of sovereignty on the other. These disputes have been rumbling since the mid-1990s, and are cutting to the bone of what is the major resource for its authority and operational activities. In that regard, the OSCE is suffering a crisis of legitimacy, and the depth of the normative disagreement makes it difficult to see how competing legitimacy claims could be reconciled. What Russia criticizes about the OSCE, the US and Germany praise; what Russia urgently wants to change, the US and Germany want to preserve. The diverging understandings of what should be the OSCE's function and form undermine the Organization's output legitimacy in terms of the routine implementation of principles (such as good governance, and stability and security in Europe), norms and rules; and also procedural legitimacy (in terms of perceived procedural fairness). The limited common ground in terms of normative and functional interests facilitated another reform process in 2005, resulting in the Report of the Panel of Eminent Persons, however, it was insufficient to sustain negotiations and reach agreement on contested issues, and resolve the organization's legitimacy crisis. The formal consensus of the early 1990s, eased at that time by Russia's weakness, concerning participating states' definitions of interests and the institutional functions and form of the OSCE has eroded not least due to Russian resurgence.

What are the implications of the previous analysis for the political significance of the OSCE in terms of fostering cooperation among participating states; their compliance with OSCE principles and norms; and its declared functions and goals? The analysis has shown that, based on conflicting normative frameworks and interests, there are fundamental differences of states' evaluation of the OSCE's legitimacy and fundamental differences in the ways in which they argue its legitimacy could be strengthened. These differences not only undermine its effectiveness in terms of substantive outcomes that the organization can achieve, but also in terms of its role as facilitator for cooperation among participating states. Moreover, the fundamental tension between simultaneously stabilizing the status quo and facilitating change, which was already part and parcel of the Helsinki Basic Principles of 1975, has re-emerged. In contrast to the Cold War years, the status quo is now contested by the Russians longing for a resurrection of sovereignty and non-interference, and its maintenance is seen as essential to the OSCE's legitimacy by the West. This basic tension, linked with the comprehensive concept of security on which the OSCE is built, has resulted in conflicts on multiple issues and levels: 'frozen' (sometimes 'boiling') conflicts in Georgia, Kosovo, Moldova, and Chechnya, the issue of a US/NATO Ballistic Missile Defence system in Europe, or concerns about NATO enlargement are not *external* to the OSCE but are an *integral part* of the organization's business. All these issues are related to OSCE norms and regimes; dealing with Europe's frozen conflicts, for example, and the use of military force directly touch upon the CFE Treaty, the CSBM agreements, and also relate to the Basket 3 dimension of the OSCE.

However, especially in times of political tensions running high, like the Georgia war in 2008, all sides seem to remember the times of the Cold War before 1990, when the OSCE—than still the CSCE—very much functioned as a vehicle for sustaining some basic channel of communication and dialogue despite fundamental ideological differences. All seem to be eagerly trying to resurrect this function, though the issues on the agenda today are different. But whether the OSCE will be able to continue its socialization function very much depends on changing calculations and normative orientation of the governments and states involved, and today remains an open question. Thus, the underlying challenge to the OSCE's legitimacy is likely to remain, and as OSCE Secretary General de Brichambaut cautiously remarked, 'participating states must act with care to ensure that the call for further "reform" does not become a poisoned chalice of recrimination and disappointment'.[99]

[99] de Brichambaut, 'The OSCE and the 21st Century', 184; see also de Brichambaut, 'A Mid-Life Crisis?'

11

Conclusion

Dominik Zaum

The central focus of the preceding chapters has been the legitimation practices of international and regional organizations—that is conscious efforts to enhance their legitimacy in the eyes of diverse audiences, both internal and external. While legitimation efforts are characterized by diversity, and each organization displays unique experiences, a range of common themes emerge from the chapters. This suggests that examining the practices of international and regional organizations from the perspective of legitimation adds to our understanding of these organizations and of international order more generally.[1]

This brief conclusion aims to summarize and evaluate the book's findings about international organizations' legitimation practices. To that end, it will first briefly summarize the key findings and identify similarities across the cases. Second, it will evaluate how different legitimation practices contribute to the three purposes of legitimation by international organizations identified in the first chapter: confirming the status quo against rival authority claims, recategorizing and extending authority relationships, and addressing the legitimacy gaps that have arisen from social and political change. The chapter will conclude with a brief discussion of two wider contributions that this analysis suggests a legitimation perspective can make to the understanding of international organizations and international order.

AN OVERVIEW OF THE FINDINGS

Legitimacy Challenges

All international organizations examined here have faced challenges to their legitimacy claims. The underlying sources of these challenges tend to be quite

[1] This concluding chapter draws on the analysis and insights of the preceding chapters. The views expressed here, however, are of the author and not necessarily of the other contributors.

similar. In most of the cases, legitimacy challenges are rooted in either changes in the distribution of power in international society and the (re)emergence of powers like China, Russia, India, Brazil, and South Africa, or in normative changes. Even challenges to organizations' output legitimacy—their apparent inability to advance common desirable goals—are often rooted in social and normative change and a perceived need to advance additional—or different—shared norms. However, the specific character that legitimacy challenges have taken varies widely between organizations. Across the cases, one can identify four different legitimacy challenges.

The first are challenges to decision-making structures and practices. With regard to structures, challenges have focused in particular on the lack of representativeness (in the case of the UN Security Council), or on the dominance of hegemomic powers in an organization's decision-making, as with regard to the US role in the UN Security Council after the cold war, or Nigeria's hegemonic role in ECOWAS. Concerning decision-making practices, challenges often focus on a lack of transparency and openness across a wide range of the cases. Generally, challenges to the legitimacy of decision-making structures and practices are internal, coming from member states who feel excluded or marginalized. One important exception to this is the challenge to ASEAN's decision-making structures and practices, which have been criticized for effectively being too inclusive and consensual, and seen as hindering effective decision-making and offering too many veto opportunities for obstructionist states.[2] Importantly, though, such challenges have come from external actors—especially Western states and organizations—and the existing structures continue to enjoy strong legitimacy amongst ASEAN members. As Alice Ba notes in Chapter 7, changing them would threaten to undermine ASEAN's internal legitimacy (see page 146).

The second challenge arises from non-compliance of member states with an international organization's decisions, or unwillingness to enforce its decisions. The problem of non-compliance has been highlighted in particular in the discussions of the AU and the UN Security Council, and includes uses of force (as in Iraq or Kosovo) where the Council was divided and unable to authorize such action; or the pursuit by states of policies in contravention of those decided upon by the African Union's Peace and Security Council—as

[2] A similar criticism has been made by some commentators of the UN Security Council, where concerns about obstructionism through the use of the veto by non-liberal permanent members led to proposals for a League of Democracies. Interestingly, the proponents of such a league sought to address the problem posed by the veto not by abolishing it (the proposed decision-making mechanism was consensual), but by restricting membership to democratic states. The proposal gained very little traction. See John G. Ikenberry and Anne-Marie Slaughter, *Final Report of the Princeton Project on National Security, Forging a World of Liberty Under Law: US National Security in the 21st Century* (Princeton, NJ: Woodrow Wilson School of Public and International Affairs, 2006).

Nigeria and ECOWAS states did over Cote d'Ivoire in 2011. Non-compliance challenges can also be external, for example non-compliance of non-state actors such as rebel forces with the demands made in UN Security Council resolutions.[3] With regard to legitimacy, however, non-compliance by member states, especially powerful member states with a strong voice in the organization, poses a much greater challenge to an organization's legitimacy.

The third legitimacy challenge comes from member states who want to limit the existing authority and autonomy of international organizations. The cases examined here include two examples of this: debates about the balance between European supranational institutions and member states in the debates about the EU constitutional treaty, and the Russian efforts to reduce the autonomy of OSCE institutions such as the Office for Democratic Institutions and Human Rights (ODIHR), and its electoral observer missions who have been critical of practices by Russia and its allies. The changed Russian position very much reflects the (re)emergence of Russian power, and an attempt to roll back the liberal norms and institutions advanced by the OSCE in the wake of the end of the Cold War.

The final set of legitimacy challenges arises from institutions and practices conflicting with or failing to reflect, international norms. Most dramatically, this led to the replacement of the OAU with the AU when it was seen as increasingly irrelevant and unable to address the post-cold war realities on the African continent. Importantly, this challenge came from within the OAU's membership. Another example is the SCO, whose legitimacy amongst some external (especially Western) audiences is compromised by its challenge to liberal norms, but where this challenge and the political and normative alternatives it opens up make it attractive and more legitimate to states who feel their interests threatened or marginalized by international organizations dominated by liberal Western states.

Legitimation Practices

The legitimation practices of international organizations identified in the earlier chapters, just like legitimation challenges, are quite varied. Given that organizations differ in their mandates, the degree of institutionalization, and the character of their membership, this is not surprising. Still, despite this variation, one can identify three broad categories of legitimation practices employed across the cases identified here.

[3] The International Peace Institute has compiled an extensive dataset on compliance with UN Security Council Resolutions, and has found that compliance with the Council's demands by civil war parties is generally low. See www.ipacademy.org/coping-with-crisis/compliance-with-security-council-resolutions/programlist.html (accessed 29 January 2013).

One of the most common forms of legitimation—practiced by almost all organizations discussed in this book—is the creation of new institutions and structures. The wholesale transformation of the OAU into the AU, with a whole new institutional architecture, is arguably the most dramatic instance of this practice. Other organizations, however have also reformed or expanded their institutions—ASEAN's new charter and the creation of the Human Rights Commission, the expansion of the UN Security Council's committee system, or the EU's institutional changes under the Lisbon treaty are all cases in point. Even the most weakly institutionalized international organization examined here, the SCO, has sought to increase its internal legitimacy through strengthened issue-specific coordination mechanisms like the RATS.

Importantly, not all of these institutional changes are targeted at strengthening the internal legitimacy of international organizations, by strengthening the relevance of the organization to key members and their concerns. Especially in non-Western organizations that rely on the support or recognition of external actors and do not count great powers amongst their members—such as the AU, ECOWAS, or ASEAN—institutional change is targeted also at external audiences to sustain their recognition and support.

Second, almost all international organizations examined here seek external validation for their authority claims. This can take several forms. One is through links and partnerships with other organizations which bestow a stamp of approval and recognition of authority: the SCO's desire to forge links with other international organizations like the UN and the Collective Security Treaty Organization is an example of this, as are the links between the AU and ECOWAS, and between both AU and ECOWAS and the UN. Another one is to seek the authorization of the UN for uses of force by organizations like ECOWAS, the EU, or NATO. A third form of seeking such external validation is through efforts to involve external actors, especially great powers or important organizations, in dialogue and in an institution's processes, as ASEAN has tried with regard to the US in particular.

Third, international organizations and their member states have engaged in rhetorical affirmation of the importance and legitimacy of existing institutional arrangements and practices in light of specific challenges to these arrangements, or broader social and political change. The efforts by the US and Germany to defend the autonomy of the OSCE's institutions against efforts to bring them under tighter member-state control, and their affirmation of the continued importance of their autonomy, is a key example of this practice.

THE OBJECTIVES OF LEGITIMATION

Even when eschewing judgements on the legitimacy of different organizations, it is worth evaluating their legitimation practices and examining how they contribute to the three key purposes of legitimation identified in the book's introduction: confirming the status quo against rival authority claims, re-categorizing and extending authority relationships, and addressing the legitimacy gaps that have arisen from social and political change. It is worth noting that these different purposes are not mutually exclusive, but often inter-related: the desire to extend authority relationships into issue areas such as regional security, for example, can be informed by a need to address legitimacy gaps that have arisen from normative change. As a consequence, individual legitimation efforts might address several of these purposes, not just one.

Confirming the Status Quo

Asserting existing authority relationships against rival claims and challenges is an important purpose of the legitimation practices of almost all the organizations examined in this book. Such legitimation efforts have come in response to challenges from inside an organization—for example the American and German efforts in the OSCE to legitimate the existing scope of the mandates of the ODIHR and electoral monitoring missions, or UN Security Council members asserting the need for Council authorizations in the light of unilateral and unauthorized uses of force by key member states. More often, though, such legitimation occurs in response to claims from external actors and organizations, for example the AU and ECOWAS asserting their role as speaking for and coordinating their regional and sub-regional communities respectively, regional organization's challenging the Security Council's monopoly on the authorization of the use of force, or ASEAN's admission of Myanmar despite Western pressure to not grant it membership.

The main practice associated with confirmations of the status quo is rhetorical affirmation. States or the bureaucracies of international organizations emphasize the continued utility for member states of the existing institutional arrangements and practices, and the potential negative consequences of any change. These efforts are also often conducted with reference to well-established normative frameworks. In addition to rhetorical affirmation, to defend the status quo international organizations and their member states often also seek external validation of their legitimacy claims. ECOWAS seeking an ex-post endorsement of its intervention in Liberia is an obvious example of this. Some organizations, such as the Security Council, have also used institutional change in pursuit of legitimating the status quo, for example through its efforts to strengthen its epistemic capacities, so that it could justify and defend its primacy with regards to addressing threats to international peace and security.

Re-categorizing and Extending Authority Relationships

Legitimation efforts with the purpose of re-categorizing and extending authority relationships have been much more contested and have arguably been less successful than legitimation to counter authority challenges from other actors. Efforts have been aimed, on the one hand, at procedurally changing the relationship between an international organization and its member states, often focussing on greater accountability and transparency, re-balancing the relationship between the authority of an organization versus its member states, and on changing decision-making structures and practices to make them more inclusive or effective. Such issues were central to the legitimation efforts of France and the UK over the Lisbon treaty, and to Security Council reform efforts. On the other hand, such efforts have aimed at extending an organization's authority into new issue areas (or in some cases seeking a retrenchment of an organization's authority). Sometimes, such efforts are not particularly controversial—for example the UN Security Council's pronouncements on the applicability of the laws of war to non-state actors.[4] In other cases, such as the Council's greater engagement in peacebuilding or the promotion of the responsibility to protect by some of its member states, or ECOWAS' engagement in security issues and the use of force, such efforts have met with greater resistance.

The legitimation of re-categorizations and extensions of authority relationships has most frequently occurred through institutional changes to underpin such legitimacy claims. Examples include the establishment of the UN peacebuilding commission, the establishment of the RATS, and most dramatically the transformation of the OAU into the AU, and the later establishment of the APSA. It is worth noting that institutional changes that are poorly resourced, or insufficiently backed by great powers, have done little to support organizations' legitimacy claims. The AU's experience, with the persistent weakness of the APSA, and the lack of compliance by key member states during the crises in Libya and Cote d'Ivoire, is a reflection of this.

Addressing Legitimacy Gaps in Light of Social and Political Change

All international organizations examined here have been challenged by social and political change, and they and their members have sought to sustain their

[4] Georg Nolte, 'The Different Functions of the Security Council With Respect to Humanitarian Law', in Vaughan Lowe, Adam Roberts, Jennifer Welsh, and Dominik Zaum (eds.), *The United Nations Security Council and War: The Evolution of Thought and Practice since 1945* (Oxford: Oxford University Press, 2008), 519–34.

legitimacy vis-à-vis key audiences by responding to it either through institutional adaption, or through resistance. One reason for the emergence of legitimacy gaps has been changes in the balance of power and the composition of international society. Another reason for the emergence of legitimacy gaps has been normative change, with international and regional norms no longer reflected in the structures and practices of international organizations. Such changes affect different states in different ways, depending on their internal characteristics, their economic or military capacity, or their geopolitical position. They do not simply deprive an organization's legitimacy of its normative underpinnings, rather, changes within international society open up spaces for contestation, either because of diverging expectations or because previously existing differences come into the open—as reflected in the vociferous debates in the UN over the use of force and the responsibility to protect, in the EU over the balance of power between member states and supranational institutions, or in the OSCE over human rights and democracy promotion. Such changes can create opportunities for states and international organizations to challenge existing contested normative frameworks, as highlighted by the SCO's challenge to liberal norms.

Unsurprisingly, legitimation to address legitimacy gaps has occurred almost exclusively through institutional change. As legitimacy gaps have arisen because of changes in the political and normative underpinnings of previous legitimacy claims, rhetorical affirmations and external validations of unchanged claims are unlikely to resonate with relevant audiences. Most of the institutional changes sought or pursued in the cases examined in the previous chapters are responses to legitimacy gaps—from ASEAN's new charter and the Lisbon treaty, to the transformation of the OAU into the AU and UN Security Council reforms. The record of such changes has generally been mixed, either because substantive change has remained largely elusive (as over UN Security Council reform), or because social change has undermined the emergence of a substantive normative consensus around which institutions could be reformed and an organization could be legitimized. As a result, institutional change has left the legitimacy of international organizations either internally contested—as with the UN Security Council, the African Union, or the EU—or has had divergent effect on the internal and external legitimacy of international organizations, as with ASEAN and the SCO.

THE CONTRIBUTION OF A LEGITIMATION PERSPECTIVE

What can an analysis of international organizations from the perspective of legitimation add to our understanding of international order and the politics and practices of international organizations? From the preceding chapters, two wider themes emerge.

First, examining international organizations from a legitimation perspective sheds light on the normative fault lines of international and regional orders, as legitimacy claims and counter-claims are regularly structured around these divisions. The analysis in the preceding chapters suggests that the key normative divisions that international and regional organizations face are very similar across the cases—though they sometimes occur within an organization's membership, and sometimes between an organization's members and key external audiences.

While particular contestations over legitimacy are organizationally specific, and reflect the character of the organization's membership, institutional structures, and unique political challenges, at the heart of many of the legitimation efforts examined is the tension between key aspects of the two global practices into which, as Mervyn Frost suggests in Chapter 2, all international organizations are embedded: global civil society, and the society of sovereign states. Across the cases examined here, divisions over human rights and responsibilities to uphold them on the one hand, and the rights to non-intervention associated with state sovereignty on the other, are at the heart of legitimacy debates. These divisions have shaped debates over the scope of UN Security Council authority and its authorizations of the use of force, are at the heart of the OSCE's debates over the authority of electoral observer missions and democracy promotion institutions, and have defined the debates over the 'non-indifference' norm and its institutional and policy implications in the AU and ECOWAS. In the context of ASEAN, it has shaped the debate about membership of Myanmar, then governed by a highly illiberal military regime; and, finally, the SCO has to some extent styled itself as an institutional alternative to the 'coercive solidarist'[5] order associated especially by many developing countries with the practice of global civil society and Western-dominated international organizations.

That this particular normative fault line is central to contestations over legitimacy across the different organizations, and across different regions, is not necessarily surprising. It reflects an international order characterized on the one hand only by a shallow normative consensus, and on the other hand by substantial power inequalities, with power still—despite the less liberal character of emerging powers—disproportionately concentrated in liberal states. It is these liberal states and organizations dominated by them that have frequently been an important external audience for the legitimacy claims of non-Western organizations. For example, should ASEAN increasingly look towards China or India rather than the US, or were China and Russia, rather than

[5] Andrew Hurrell, *On Global Order: Power, Values, and the Constitution of International Society* (Oxford: Oxford University Press, 2007), 63.

the European Union, a major financial contributor to AU peace and security operations, the character of their legitimation efforts would almost certainly be very different. While the mostly liberal norms associated with the practice of global civil society and promoted by Western powers have remained contested, the continued political and economic reach of these states nonetheless requires other states, and international and regional organizations they participate in, to engage with these norms—be it through adaption or resistance.

Second, a focus on legitimation as a practice, rather than on legitimacy as an institutional attribute, brings out the role of international organizations as institutional frameworks within which other actors—especially the organizations' bureaucracies and individual member states—engage in legitimation, not only of the organization itself vis-à-vis different audiences, but importantly also of their particular understandings of regional or international order. There are three reasons for this. First, the structured character of interaction in the context of international organizations can constrain the exercise of coercion and power politics,[6] creating a more permissive environment for norm-based discourses. This offers a platform to actors (especially states) who would otherwise find it more difficult to have their voices heard, and to advance their visions of order. Second, as Thomas Risse has argued, international organizations are characterized by a 'repertoire of collective understandings'[7] that structure their debates. Legitimation efforts that reflect these shared normative frameworks are more likely to resonate with an organization's wider membership than those that do not reflect them, and are more persuasive than others.[8] Consequently, international organizations offer a particularly conducive environment for norms-based discourses, and a structured yet permissive framework to contest competing norms. A third reason why international organizations act as frameworks for legitimation is their role in facilitating cooperation amongst member states vis-à-vis external audiences. As the chapters on the AU, ASEAN, and the SCO suggest, this function is particularly important for regional organizations advancing normative positions at odds with wider international norms, or norms advanced by powerful external actors. Advancing particular conceptions of order multilaterally through an international or regional organization weakens counter-claims that they merely reflect narrow national political interests, but allows them to be framed as principled normative commitments that have wider regional support.

[6] Martha Finnemore, 'Fights about rules: the role of efficacy and power in changing multilateralism', *Review of International Studies*, Vol. 31/S1 (2005), 187–206.

[7] Thomas Risse, 'Let's Argue! Communicative Action in World Politics', *International Organization*, Vol. 54/1 (2000), 11.

[8] Ian Johnstone, 'Security Council Deliberations: The Power of the Better Argument', *European Journal of International Law*, Vol. 14/3 (2003), 437–80.

These brief conclusions provide only some selective reflections and perspectives on the legitimation practices of international and regional organizations. They highlight how their legitimacy relates both to the interactions between states and other actors within the organizations, and to the dynamics of the wider social and material dimensions of international order. Examining international organizations through the lens of legitimation practices highlights that while international organizations structure and constrain the behaviour and interactions of states, ultimately it is predominantly through the actions of states that their legitimacy is reproduced and recognized. It also points to an international order characterized by relatively shallow normative agreement, and by deep divisions between the key international practices of global civil society and the society of sovereign states. These divisions not only structure international organizations' legitimation efforts, but importantly also tightly delineate the political and normative space within which they can successfully legitimate themselves. If nothing else, therefore, the analysis in this book underlines David Beetham's observation that the maintenance and reproduction of legitimacy is not independent of the wider social and material structures of power,[9] and that international organizations cannot transcend the wider order in which they are embedded.

[9] David Beetham, *The Legitimation of Power* (Basingstoke: Palgrave Macmillan, 1991), 104.

Bibliography

Acharya Amitav (1997), 'Ideas, Identity, and Institution-building: from the 'ASEAN Way' to the 'Asia-Pacific Way'?' *Pacific Review* Vol. 10/1, 319–46.

Acharya Amitav (2001), *Constructing a Security Community in Southeast Asia* (London: Routledge).

Acharya Amitav (2004), 'How Ideas Spread: Whose Norms Matter? Norm Localization and Institutional Change in Asian Regionalism', *International Organization*, Vol. 58/2, 239–75.

Acharya, Amitav and Alastair Iain Johnston (eds.) (2007), *Crafting Cooperation* (Cambridge: Cambridge University Press).

Adebajo, Adekeye (2002), *Building Peace in West Africa* (Boulder, CO: Lynne Rienner,).

Aderinwale, Ayodele (2000), 'The Conference on Security, Stability, Development and Cooperation in Africa—Framework and the Role of Regional Institutions', in Moufids Goucha and Jakkie Cilliers (eds.) *Peace, Human Security and Conflict Prevention in Africa* (Paris/Pretoria: ISS/UNESCO), 59–66.

Adibe, Clement (1997), 'The Liberian conflict and the ECOWAS-UN partnership', *Third World Quarterly*, Vol. 18/3, 471–88.

Adisa, Jimmi (1994), 'Nigeria in ECOMOG: Political Undercurrents and the Burden of Community Spirit', *Small Wars and Insurgencies*, Vol. 5/1, 83–110.

Adler, Emmanuel and Michael N. Barnett (eds.) (1998), *Security Communities* (Cambridge: Cambridge University Press).

African Union (2005), *The Common African Position on the Proposed Reform of the United Nations: 'The Ezulwini Consensus'*, AU doc. Ext/EX.CL/2(vii), March 7–8.

African Union (2005), *Roadmap for the Operationalization of the African Standby Force*, AU doc. EXP/AU-RECs/ASF/4(I), 22–23 March.

African Union and United Nations (2008), *Report of the African Union-United Nations panel on modalities for support to African Union peacekeeping operations*, UN doc. A/63/666-S/2008/813, 31 December.

Akinyemi, Bolaji (1997), 'End the Military Meddling', *The Guardian*, Lagos, 5 June.

Akokpari John (2008), 'Introduction: Human Rights Actors and Institutions in Africa' in John Akokpari, and Daniel Shea Zimbler (eds.) (2008), *Africa's Human Rights Architecture* (Fanele: Auckland Park), 1–23.

Alagappa, Muthiah (1987), 'ASEAN Institutional Framework and Modus Operandi', in Noordin Sopiee, Chew Lay See, and Lim Siang Jin (eds.), *ASEAN at the Crossroads* (Kuala Lumpur: ISIS-Malaysia).

Almqvist, Jessica (2008), 'A Human Rights Critique of European Judicial Review: Counter Terrorism Sanctions', *Comparative Law Quarterly*, Vol. 57/2, 303–31.

Alter, Karen (2001), *Establishing the Supremacy of European Law: The Making of an International Rule of Law in Europe* (Oxford: Oxford University Press).

Alvarez, José E. (2005), *International Organizations as Law-Makers* (Oxford: Oxford University Press).

Andreopoulos, George (2008), 'The challenges and perils of normative overstretch', in Bruce Cronin and Ian Hurd, *The UN Security Council and the Politics of International Authority* (London: Routledge), 105–28.

Annan, Kofi (2005), *In Larger Freedom: Towards Security, Development and Human Rights for All—Report of the Secretary General*, UN Doc. A/59/2005 of 21 March.

Antonenko, Oksana (2007), *The EU should not ignore the Shanghai Co-operation Organisation*, Centre for European Reform, Policy Brief, London.

Arendt, Hannah (1954), 'What is Authority', in Hanna Arendt, *Between Past and Future: Eight Exercises in Political Thought* (New York: Viking Press), 91–141.

Aris, Stephen (2009), 'The Shanghai Cooperation Organisation: '"Tackling the Three Evils". A Regional Response to Non-Traditional Security Challenges or an Anti-Western Bloc?', *Europe-Asia Studies*, Vol. 61/3, 457–82.

Asante, S.K.B. (1991), *African Development: Adebayo Adedeji's Alternative Strategies* (Ibadan, Nigeria: Spectrum).

ASEAN Secretariat (2007), 'ASEAN Leaders Sign ASEAN Charter', Media Release, 20 November.

ASEAN Secretariat (2008), 'ASEAN Embarks on New Era: ASEAN Charter Fully Ratified', Media Release, 21 October.

Assemblée Nationale (2005), *Déclaration du Gouvernement sur le référendum portant sur le projet de loi autorisant la ratification du traité établissant une Constitution pour l'Europe par Jean-Pierre Raffarrin Premier Ministre*, Paris, Assemblée Nationale, 5 April (http://www. assemblée-nationale.fr/12/cri/2004-2005).

Au, Alex (2007), 'ASEAN Still Toothless After 40 Years', *Asia Times*, 27 November.

Ba, Alice D. (2005) 'On Norms, Rule Breaking, and Security Communities', *International Relations of the Asia Pacific*, Vol. 5/2, 255–66.

Ba, Alice D. (2005), 'Contested Spaces: The Politics of Regional and Global Governance', in Alice D. Ba and Matthew J. Hoffmann (eds.), *Contending Perspectives on Global Governance*, (New York: Routledge), 190–212.

Ba, Alice D. (2009), *(Re)Negotiating East and Southeast Asia: Region, Regionalism, and the Association of Southeast Asian Nations* (Stanford: Stanford University Press).

Ba, Alice D. (2011), 'ASEAN Centrality Imperiled? ASEAN Institutionalism and the Challenges of Major Power Institutionalization', in Ralf Emmers (ed.), *ASEAN and the Institutionalization of East Asia*, (Abingdon and New York, Routledge), 114–129.

Bah, Sarjoh (2010), *Dilemmas of Regional Peacemaking: The Dynamics of the AU's Response to Darfur*, Centre on International Cooperation, New York.

Bailes, Alyson J. K. (2007), 'The Shanghai Cooperation Organization and Europe', *China and Eurasia Forum Quarterly*, Vol. 5/3, 13–18.

Bailes, Alyson J. K., and Pál Dunay (2007), 'The Shanghai Cooperation Organization as a regional security institution', in Alyson J. K. Bailes, Pál Dunay, Pan Guang and Mikhail Troitskiy, *The Shanghai Cooperation Organization*, SIPRI Policy Paper No. 17, Stockholm, 1–29.

Bailey, Sydney and Sam Daws (1998), *The Procedure of the UN Security Council*, 3rd Edition (Oxford: Oxford University Press).

Baimu, Evarist and Kathryn Sturman (2003), 'Amendment to the African Union's Right to Intervene—A Shift from Human Security to Regime Security?', *African Security Review*, Vol. 12/2, 37–45.

Barker, Rodney (1990), *Political Legitimacy and the State* (Oxford: Clarendon Press).

Barker, Rodney (2001), *Legitimating Identities: The Self-Representation of Rulers and Subjects* (Cambridge: Cambridge University Press).

Barker, Rodney (2003), 'Legitimacy, Legitimation, and the European Union: What Crisis?', in P. Craig and R. Rawlings (eds.), *Law and Administration in Europe: Essays in Honour of Carol Harlow* (Oxford: Oxford University Press), 163–4.

Barker, Rodney (2007), 'Democratic legitimation: what is it, who wants and why?' in Achim Hurrelman, Steffen Schneider, and Jens Steffek (eds.), *Legitimacy in an Age of Global Politics* (Basingstoke: Palgrave Macmillan), 19–34.

Barley, Stephen R. and Pamela S. Tolbert (1997), 'Institutionalization and Structuration: Studying the Links between Action and Institution', *Organization Studies*, Vol. 18/1, 93–117.

Barnett, Michael N. (2002), *Eyewitness to Genocide: The United Nations and Rwanda* (Ithaca: Cornell University Press).

Barnett, Michael N. (2006), 'Building a Republican Peace: Stabilizing States after War', *International Security*, Vol. 30/4, 87–112.

Barnett, Michael N. and Raymond Duvall (eds.) (2005), *Power in Global Governance* (Cambridge: Cambridge University Press).

Barnett, Michael N. and Martha Finnemore (1999), 'The Politics, Power, and Pathologies of International Organizations', *International Organization*, Vol. 53/4, 699–732.

Barnett, Michael N. and Martha Finnemore (2004), *Rules for the World: International Organizations in Global Politics* (Ithaca, NY: Cornell University Press).

Bassey, Celestine (1993), 'Nigeria in ECOMOG: Dilemma of Preventive Diplomacy?' in J. Owoeye (ed.) *Nigeria in International Institutions* (Ibadan: College Press Ltd), 159–70.

Bates, Robert H. (1988), 'Contra Contractarianism: Some Reflections on the New Institutionalism', *Politics and Society*, Vol. 16/2-3, 387–401.

BBC Africa News (2010), 'West Africa volunteers scheme launched', 26 March.

Beeson, Mark (2000), 'Mahathir and the Markets: Globalisation and the Pursuit of Economic Autonomy in Malaysia', *Pacific Affairs*, Vol. 73/3, 335–51.

Beeson, Mark (2003), 'Sovereignty Under Siege', *Third World Quarterly*, Vol. 24/2, 357–74.

Beeson, Mark (2009), 'ASEAN's Ways: Still Fit for Purpose?' *Cambridge Review of International Affairs* Vol. 22/3, 333–43.

Beetham, David (1991), *The Legitimation of Power* (Basingstoke: Palgrave Macmillan).

Beetham, David and Christopher Lord (1998), *Legitimacy and the European Union* (Harlow, Essex: Addison, Wesley, Longman).

Bellamy, Alex J. (2002) *Kosovo and International Society* (Basingstoke: Palgrave-Macmillan).

Bellamy, Alex J. (2006) *Just Wars* (Cambridge: Polity).

Bellamy, Alex (2010), 'The Responsibility to Protect—Five Years On', *Ethics and International Affairs*, Vol. 24/2, 143–69.

Bellamy, Alex J. and Paul Williams (2005), 'Who's Keeping the Peace? Regionalization and Contemporary Peace Operations', *International Security*, Vol. 29/4, 157–95.

Bellamy, Alex J. and Paul D. Williams (2009), 'The West and Contemporary Peace Operations', *Journal of Peace Research*, Vol. 46/1, 39–57.

Bellamy, Alex J. and Paul D. Williams (2010), *Understanding Peacekeeping*, 2nd edition (Cambridge: Polity).

Bellamy Alex J. and Paul D. Williams (2011), 'The new politics of protection? Cote d'Ivoire, Libya, and the Responsibility to Protect', *International Affairs*, Vol. 87/4, 825–50.

Bellamy, Richard (2007), *Political Constitutionalism, A Republican Defence of the Constitutionality of Democracy* (Cambridge: Cambridge University Press).

Berdal, Mats (2003), 'The UN Security Council: Ineffective but Indispensable', *Survival*, Vol. 45/2, 7–30.

Berdal, Mats and Spyros Economides (eds.) (2007), *United Nations Interventionism: 1991-2004* (Cambridge: Cambridge University Press).

Bergholm, Linnea (2009), *The African Union-United Nations Relationship and Civilian Protection in Darfur, 2004-2007* (Unpublished Ph thesis, Aberystwyth University, Department of International Politics).

Bhadrakumar, M.K. (2009), 'Sino-Russian baby comes of age', *Asia Times*, 13 June.

Bhadrakumar, M.K. (2011), 'SCO steps out of Central Asia', *Asia Times*, 18 June.

Bjola, Corneliu (2005), 'Legitimating the Use of Force in International Politics: A Communicative Action Perspective', *European Journal of International Relations*, Vol. 11/2, 266–303.

Blair, Tony (2000), *The Prime Minister's Speech to the Polish Stock Exchange*, Warsaw, 6 October.

Blondel, Jean (1990) *Comparative Government: An Introduction* (New York: Philip Allan).

Boland, Julie, 'Learning from the Shanghai Cooperation Organization's 'Peace Mission-2010' Exercise', *Brookings Opinion*, 29 October 2010.

Boshoff, Henri and Dara Francis (2003), 'The AU Mission in Burundi: Technical and Operational Dimensions', *African Security Review*, Vol. 12/3, 41–4.

Boucher, David (2003), 'Oakeshott', in David Boucher and Paul Kelly (eds.), *Political Thinkers: From Socrates to the Present* (Oxford: Oxford University Press), 459–79.

Boulden Jane (2006), 'Double Standards, Distance, and Disengagement: Collective Legitimization in the Post-Cold War Security Council', *Security Dialogue*, Vol. 37/3, 409–23.

Boulden, Jane (2008), 'The Security Council and Terrorism', in Vaughan Lowe, Adam Roberts, Jenifer Welsh, and Dominik Zaum (eds.), *The United Nations Security Council and War* (Oxford: Oxford University Press), 608–23.

Brysk, Alison and Gershon Shafir (eds.) (2007), *National Insecurity and Human Rights: Democracies Debate Counterterrorism* (Berkeley: University of California Press).

Buchanan Allen (2002), 'Political Legitimacy and Democracy', *Ethics*, Vol. 122, 689–719.

Buchanan, Allen and Robert Keohane (2006), 'The Legitimacy of Global Governance Institutions', *Ethics and International Affairs*, Vol. 20/4, 405–37.

Bull, Hedley (1995), *The Anarchical Society: A Study of Order in World Politics*, 2nd edition (Basingstoke: Macmillan).

Bull, Hedley (1966), 'The Grotian Conception of International Society', in Herbert Butterfield and Martin Wight (eds.), *Diplomatic Investigations: Essays in the Theory of International Politics*, (London: Allen and Unwin, 1966), 51–73.

Buzan, Barry (1991), *People, States and Fear: An Agenda for International Security Studies in the Post-Cold War Era*, 2nd ed. (Boulder: Lynne Rienner).

Call, Charles T. (2008), 'Knowing peace when you see it: Setting standards for peace-building success', *Civil Wars*, Vol. 10/2, 173–94.

Caney, Simon (2005), *Justice Beyond Borders* (Oxford: Oxford University Press).

Centre for International Cooperation (2009), *Robust Peacekeeping: The Politics of Force* (New York University: Center on International Cooperation, 2009).

Checkel, Jeffrey T. (1999), 'Norms, Institutions, and National Identity in Contemporary Europe', *International Studies Quarterly*, Vol. 43/1, 84–114.

Chesterman, Simon (2006), 'Does the UN have Intelligence?' *Survival*, Vol. 48/3, 149–64.

Childress, Sarah (2010), 'Civilian casualties dog troops in Somalia', *Wall Street Journal*, 29 July.

Chin, Gregory (2010), 'China's Rising Institutional Influence', in Alan S. Alexandroff and Andrew Cooper (eds.), *Rising States, Rising Institutions: Challenges for Global Governance* (Washington, DC: Brookings Institutions Press), 83–104.

Chongkittavorn, Kavi (2007), 'ASEAN Charter: Should We Settle for Second Best?' *Nation*, 13 August.

Chongkittavorn, Kavi (2007), 'Complex Issues Underlie ASEAN Charter', *Thai Press Reports*, 5 November.

Chongkittavorn, Kavi (2012), 'Asean Secretariat Must be Strengthened', *The Irawaddy*, 21 May.

Cilliers, Jakkie and Johann Pottgieter (2010), 'The African Standby Force' in Ulf Engel and Jao Gomes Porto (eds.), *Africa's New Peace and Security Architecture—Promoting Norms, Institutionalising Solutions* (Farnham: Ashgate), 111–42.

Clark, Ian (1998), *The hierarchy of states: Reform and resistance in the international order* (Cambridge: Cambridge University Press).

Clark, Ian (2005), *Legitimacy in International Society* (Oxford: Oxford University Press).

Claude, Inis L. (1996), 'Peace and Security: Prospective Roles for the Two United Nations', *Global Governance*, Vol. 2/3, 289–98.

Claude, Inis L. (1966), 'Collective Legitimization as a Political Function of the United Nations', *International Organization*, Vol. 20/3, 367–79.

Coicaud, Jean-Marc and Veijo Heiskanen (eds.) (2001), *The Legitimacy of International Organizations* (Tokyo: United Nations University Press).

Coleman, Katharina (2007), *International Organisations and Peace Enforcement: The Politics of International Legitimacy* (Cambridge: Cambridge University Press).

Connolly, William E. (1983), *The Terms of Political Discourse*, 2nd ed. (Oxford: Martin Robertson).

Cossa, Ralph (2009), 'Evolving US Views on Asia's Future Institutional Architecture', in Michael J. Green and Bates Gill (eds.), *Asia's New Multilateralism: Cooperation, Competition, and the Search for Community* (New York: Columbia University Press), 33–54.

Crawford James (2006), *The Creation of States in International Law*, 2nd ed. (Oxford: Oxford University Press).

Crocker, Chester et al. (eds.) (2011), *Rewiring Regional Security in a Fragmented World* (Washington DC: US Institute of Peace Press).

Cronin, Bruce (2002), 'The Two Faces of the United Nations: The Tension Between Intergovernmentalism and Transnationalism', *Global Governance*, Vol. 8/1, 53–71.

Cronin, Bruce and Ian Hurd (2008), *The UN Security Council and the Politics of International Authority* (Abingdon: Routledge).

Delors, Jacques (1996), *L'Europe en tantquantité politique. Combats pour l'Europe* (Paris, Economica).

Deng, Francis M., Kimaro Sadikiel, Terrence Lyons, Donald Rothchild and I. William Zartman, (eds.) (1996), *Sovereignty as Responsibility: Conflict Management in Africa* (Washington, DC: Brookings Institution).

Desker, Barry (2008), 'Is the ASEAN Charter Necessary?' *RSIS Commentaries*, Singapore, 17 July.

Dewitt, David (1994), 'Common, Cooperative, and Comprehensive Security', *Pacific Review*, Vol. 7/1, 1–15.

Diehl, Paul F. and Daniel Druckman (2010), *Evaluating Peace Operations* (Boulder, CO: Lynne Rienner).

Duffield, John S. (2006), 'International Security Institutions' in R.A.W. Rhodes et al. (eds.), *The Oxford Handbook of Political Institutions* (Oxford: Oxford University Press), 633–54.

Durch, William J. (ed.) (2006), *Twenty-first Century Peace Operations* (Washington DC: US Institute of Peace Press).

ECOWAS (1999), *Protocol Relating to the Mechanism for Conflict Prevention, Management, Resolution, Peacekeeping and Security*, Lome, 10 December.

ECOWAS (2008), *ECOWAS Vision 2020*, ECOWAS Summit, Abuja, Nigeria, June.

Eldon, Stewart (2004), 'East Timor', in David Malone (ed.), *The UN Security Council: From the Cold War to the 21st Century* (Boulder: Lynne Rienner), 551–66.

Elster, Jon (1984) *Ulysses and the Sirens, Studies in Rationality and Irrationality* (Cambridge: Cambridge University Press).

Elster, Jon (1998) 'Deliberation and Constitution Making' in Jon Elster (ed.), *Deliberative Democracy* (Cambridge: Cambridge University Press), 97–122.

Emmers, Ralf and See Seng Tan (2010), 'The ASEAN Regional Forum and Preventive Diplomacy: Built to Fail?' *Asian Security*, Vol. 7/1, 44–60.

Emmerson, Donald K. (1996), 'Indonesia, Malaysia, and Singapore: A Regional Security Core?' in Richard Ellings and Sheldon Simon (eds.), *Southeast Asia in the New Millennium* (Armonk, NY: M. E. Sharpe), 1963–6.

Engel, Ulf and Jao Gomes Porto (2010), 'Africa's New Peace and Security Architecture: An Introduction', in Ulf Engel and Jao Gomes Porto (eds.), *Africa's New Peace and Security Architecture—Promoting Norms, Institutionalising Solutions* (Farnham: Ashgate), 1–12.

Eriksen, Reik Oddvar, and John Erik Fossum (2007), *Reconstituting European Democracy*, ARENA Working Paper 01/2007, Oslo.

Erskine Toni (ed.) (2003), *Can Institutions Have Responsibilities?* (Basingstoke: Palgrave MacMillan).

Erskine, Toni (2004), '"Blood on the UN's Hands?" Assigning Duties and Apportioning Blame to an Intergovernmental Organisation', *Global Society*, Vol. 18/1, 21–42.

Evangelista, Matthew (2008), *Law, Ethics and the War on Terror* (Cambridge: Polity Press).

Evans, Paul (2004), 'Human Security and East Asia: In the Beginning', *Journal of East Asian Studies*, Vol. 4/2, 263–84.

Fawcett, Louise (2004), 'Exploring Regional Domains: A Comparative History of Regionalism', *International Affairs*, Vol. 80/3, 429–46.

Feinstein, L. and Anne-Marie Slaughter (2004), 'The Duty to Prevent', *Foreign Affairs* Vol. 83/1, 136–50.

Feldman, Noah (2004), *What We Owe Iraq: War and the Ethcis of Nationbuilding* (Princeton: Princeton University Press).

Ferry, Jean-Marc (2000), *La Question de l'État Européen* (Paris: Gallimard).

Finnemore Martha (2005), 'Fights about rules: the role of efficacy and power in changing multilateralism', *Review of International Studies*, Vol. 31/S1, 187–206.

Foong Khong, Yuen (1997), 'Making Bricks without Straw in the Asia Pacific?' *Pacific Review*, Vol. 10/2, 289–300.

Foot, Rosemary (2005), 'Collateral damage: human rights consequences of counterterrorist action in the Asia-Pacific', *International Affairs*, Vol. 81/2, 411–25.

Foreign and Commonwealth Office (FCO) (2004), *White Paper on the Treaty Establishing a Constitution for Europe, Command 6309* (London: HMSO).

Foreign and Commonwealth Office (FCO) (2004), *A Constitution for our kind of Europe. Speech by the Foreign Secretary*, 7 December.

Forman, Shepard and Andrew Green (2004), 'Collaborating with Regional Organizations', in David M. Malone (ed.), *The UN Security Council: From the Cold War to the 21st Century* (Boulder: Lynne Rienner), 294–305.

Forst, Rainer (2007), *Das Recht auf Rechtfertigung. Elemente einer Konstruktivistischen Theorie der Gerechtigkeit* (Frankfurt am Main: Suhrkamp).

Fortna, Virginia Page (2003), 'Inside and Out: Peacekeeping and the Duration of Peace after Civil and Interstate Wars', *International Studies Review*, Vol. 5/4, 97–114.

Fortna, Virginia Page (2004) 'Does Peacekeeping Keep Peace? International Intervention and the Duration of Peace after Civil War', *International Studies Quarterly*, Vol. 48/2, 269–92.

Fortna, Virginia Page (2008), *Does Peacekeeping Work? Shaping Belligerents' Choices after Civil War* (Princeton, NJ: Princeton University Press).

Fossum, John Erik and Agustin Menendez (2010), *The Constitutional Path of the European Political Project. Lessons from Laeken and Lisbon*, Unpublished Manuscript. Oslo, ARENA.

Franck, Thomas M. (1990), *The Power of Legitimacy Among Nations* (Oxford: Oxford University Press).

Franck, Thomas M. (1995), *Fairness in International Law and Institutions*, (Oxford: Clarendon Press).

Frost, Mervyn (1996), *Ethics in International Relations: A Constitutive Theory* (Cambridge: Cambridge University Press).

Frost, Mervyn (2009), *Global Ethics: Anarchy, Freedom and International Relations* (London: Routledge).

Gallant, Nicole and Richard Stubbs (1997), 'APEC's Dilemmas: Institution-Building around the Pacific Rim', *Pacific Affairs*, Vol. 70/2, 203–19.

Gallis, Paul (2003), *NATO Decision-making Procedures*, Washington, DC: Congressional Research Service Report RS-21510.

Gambetta, Diego (1996), *The Sicilian Mafia: The Business of Private Protection* (Cambridge MA: Harvard University Press).

Garrett, Geoff (1995), 'The Politics of Legal Integration in Europe', *International Organization*, Vol. 49/1, 171–81.
Gaus, Daniel (2009), *Der Sinn Von Demokratie. Die Dikurstheorie der Demokratie und die Debatte über die Legitimät der EU* (Frankfurt: Campus Verlag).
Gharekan, Chinmaya (2006), *The Horseshoe Table: An Inside View of the UN Security Council* (Delhi: Dorling Kindersley).
Gilligan, Michael and Stephen John Stedman (2003), 'Where do the peacekeepers go?', *International Studies Review*, Vol. 5/4, 37–54.
Goh, Evelyn and Amitav Acharya (2002), 'The Asean Regional Forum and US-China Relations: Comparing Chinese and American Positions.' Draft Paper Prepared for the Fifth China-Asean Research Institutes Roundtable, 'Regionalism and Community Building in East Asia', University of Hong Kong, 17–19 October.
Golu, Timothy, Raliat Ahmed, and Nwakpa O. Nwakpa (2009), 'West Africa: ECOWAS to Suspend Guinea, Holds Emergency Summit Friday', *Leadership*, 6 January.
Greenstock, Jeremy (2008) 'The Security Council in the Post-Cold War World', in in Vaughan Lowe, Adam Roberts, Jenifer Welsh, and Dominik Zaum (eds.) *The United Nations Security Council and War* (Oxford: Oxford University Press), 248–64.
Greig, J. Michael and Paul F. Diehl (2005), 'The Peacekeeping–Peacemaking Dilemma', *International Studies Quarterly*, Vol. 49/4, 621–45.
Haacke, Jürgen (2003), *ASEAN's Diplomatic and Security Culture* (London: Routledge).
Haacke, Jürgen (2005), '"Enhanced Interaction" with Myanmar and the Project of Security Community', *Contemporary Southeast Asia*, Vol. 27/2, 188–216.
Haas, Michael (1965), 'A Functional Approach to International Organization', *Journal of Politics* Vol. XXVII, 498–517.
Haas, Peter M. (1992), 'Introduction: Epistemic Communities and International Policy Coordination', *International Organization*, Vol. 46/1, 1–35.
Habermas, Jürgen (1996), *Between Facts and Norms* (Cambridge: Polity).
Hafner-Burton, Emilie (2005), 'Trading Human Rights: How Preferential Trade Agreements Influence Government Repression', *International Organization*, Vol. 59/3, 593–629.
Hannum, Hurst (1990), *Autonomy, Sovereignty, and Self-Determination: The Accommodation of Conflicting Rights* (Philadelphia: University of Pennsylvania Press).
Heisenberg, Dorothee (2005), 'The Institution of "Consensus" in the European Union: Formal versus informal Decision-making in the Council', *European Journal of Political Research*, Vol. 44/1, 65–90.
Heiskanen, Veijo (2001), 'Introduction', in Jean-Marc Coicaud and Veijo Heiskanen (eds.), *The Legitimacy of International Organizations* (Tokyo: United Nations University Press,), 1–47.
Heldt, Birger (2008), 'Trends from 1948 to 2005: How to view the relation between the United Nations and non-UN entities' in Donald Daniel, Patricia Taft, and Sharon Wiharta (eds.), *Peace Operations: Trend, Progress and Prospects* (Washington DC: Georgetown University Press), 9–26.
Hix, Simon (2005) *The Political System of the European Union* (Basingstoke: Palgrave Macmillan).

Holt, Victoria and Glyn Taylor, with Max Kelly (2009), *Protecting Civilians in the Context of UN Peacekeeping Operations* (New York: UN DPKO/OCHA).

Hooghe, Lisbeth and Gary Marks (2009), 'A Postfunctionalist Theory of European Integration: From Permissive Consensus to Constraining Dissensus', *British Journal of Political Science*, Vol. 39/1, 1–23.

Howe, Herbert M. (2001) *Ambiguous Order: Military Forces in African States* (Boulder, CO: Lynne Rienner).

Human Rights in China (2011), *Counter-Terrorism and Human Rights: The Impact of the Shanghai Cooperation Organization*, A Human Rights in China Whitepaper, New York.

Hurd, Ian (1999), 'Legitimacy and Authority in International Politics', *International Organization*, Vol. 53/2, 379–408.

Hurd, Ian (2002), 'Legitimacy, Power, and the Symbolic Life of the UN Security Council', *Global Governance*, Vol. 8/1, 35–51.

Hurd, Ian (2007), *After Anarchy: Legitimacy and Power at the UN Security Council* (Princeton: Princeton University Press).

Hurd, Ian (2008), 'Theories and tests of international authority', in Bruce Cronin and Ian Hurd (eds.), *The UN Security Council and the Politics of International Authority* (Abingdon: Routledge), 23–40.

Hurrell, Andrew (2005), 'Power, Institutions, and the Production of Inequality', in Michael Barnett and Raymond Duval (eds.), *Power in Global Governance* (Cambridge: Cambridge University Press, 2005), 33–58.

Hurrell, Andrew (2005), 'Legitimacy and the Use of Force: Can the Circle be Squared?', *Review of International Studies*, Vol. 31, special issue on Force and Legitimacy in World Politics, 15–32.

Hurrell, Andrew (2007), *On Global Order: Power, Values, and the Constitution of International Society* (Oxford: Oxford University Press).

Hutchful, Eboe (2008), 'From Military Security to Human Security' in in John Akokpari, Angela Ndinga Muvumba, and Timothy Murithi (eds.), *The African Union and its Institutions* (Fanele: Auckland Park), 63–84.

Ikenberry, G. John (2001) *After Victory: Institutions, Strategic Restraint, and the Rebuilding of Order after Major Wars* (Princeton: Princeton University Press).

Ikenberry, G. John and Anne-Marie Slaughter (2006), Final Report of the Princeton Project on National Security, *Forging a World of Liberty Under Law: US National Security in the 21st Century* (Princeton, NJ: Woodrow Wilson School of Public and International Affairs).

Independent International Commission on Kosovo (2000), *The Kosovo Report: Conflict, International Response, Lessons Learned* (Oxford: Oxford University Press).

International Commission on Intervention and State Sovereignty (2001), *The Responsibility to Protect* (Ottawa: International Development Research Centre).

Jackson, Patrick Thaddeus (2004), 'Bridging the Gap: Toward A Realist-Constructivist Dialogue', *International Studies Quarterly*, Vol. 6/2, 337–52.

Johnson, Shaun (1993), *Strange Days Indeed* (London: Bantam Press).

Johnston, Alastair Iain (2001), 'Treating International Institutions as Social Environments', *International Studies Quarterly*, Vol. 45/3, 487–515.

Johnston, Alastair Iain (2003), 'Socialization in International Institutions', in John Ikenberry and Michael Mastanduno (eds.), *International Relations Theory and the Asia Pacific* (New York: Columbia University Press), 107–62.

Johnstone, Ian (2003), 'Security Council Deliberations: The Power of the Better Argument', *European Journal of International Law*, Vol. 14/3, 437–80.

Johnstone, Ian (2008), 'The Security Council as Legislature', in Bruce Cronin and Ian Hurd (eds.), *The UN Security Council and the Politics of International Authority* (Abingdon: Routledge), 80–104.

Jones, Bruce with F. Cherif (2004), *Evolving Models of Peacekeeping* (UN: Peacekeeping Best Practices Unit).

Jones, David M. and Michael L. R. Smith (2001), 'ASEAN's Imitation Community', *Orbis*, Vol. 46/1, 93–109.

Jones, Lee (2010), 'ASEAN's Unchanged Melody? The Theory and Practice of "Noninterference" in Southeast Asia', *The Pacific Review*, Vol. 23/4, 479–502.

Kagan, Robert (2007), 'The world divides... and democracy is at bay', London, *Sunday Times*, 2 September.

Karns, Margaret and Karen Mingst (2010), *International Organizations: The Politics and Process of Global Governance* (Boulder, Co.: Lynne Rienner).

Kasumba, Yvonne and Charles Debrah (2010), 'An Overview of the African Standby Force (ASF)', in Cedric De Coning and Yvonne Kasumba (eds.), *The Civilian Dimension of the African Standby Force* (Addis Ababa: African Union Commission), 10–19.

Katsumata, Hiro (2009), 'ASEAN and human rights: resisting Western pressure or emulating the West?' *Pacific Review*, Vol. 22/5, 619–37.

Katsumata, Hiro (2011), 'Mimetic Adoption and Norm Diffusion: 'Western' Security Cooperation in Southeast Asia?' *Review of International Studies*, Vol. 37/2, 557–76.

Keating, Colin (2004), 'Rwanda: An Insider's Account', in David Malone (ed.), *The UN Security Council: From the Cold War to the 21st Century* (Boulder: Lynne Rienner), 500–11.

Keck, Margaret and Kathryn Sikkink (1998), *Activists beyond Borders: Advocacy Networks in International Politics* (Ithaca: Cornell University Press).

Keene, Edward (2007), 'A Case Study of Construction of International Hierarchy: British Treaty-Making Against the Slave Trade in the Early Nineteenth Century', *International Organization*, Vol. 61/2, 311–39.

Kelly, Paul (2003), 'Hume', in David Boucher and Paul Kelly (eds.) *Political Thinkers*, (Oxford: Oxford University Press), 198–216.

Kelman, Herbert (2001), 'Reflections on Social and Psychological Processes of Legitimization and Delegitimization', in John T. Jost and Brenda Major (eds.), *The Psychology of Legitimacy: Emerging Perspectives on Ideology, Justice, and Intergroup Relations* (Cambridge: Cambridge University Press), 54–73.

Kennedy, Paul (2006), *The Parliament of Man: The Past, Present, and Future of the United Nations* (New York: Random House).

Keohane, Robert O. (1984), *After Hegemony: Cooperation and Discord in the World Political Economy* (Princeton: Princeton University Press).

Keohane, Robert O. (1988), 'International Institutions: Two Approaches', *International Studies Quarterly*, Vol. 32/4, 379–96.

Keohane, Robert O. (2002), *Power and Governance in a Partially Globalized World* (London: Routledge).

Keohane, Robert O. (2003), 'Political authority after Intervention: gradations in sovereignty' in J.L. Holzgrefe and Robert O. Keohane (eds.), *Humanitarian Intervention: Ethical, Legal, and Political Dilemmas* (Cambridge: Cambridge University Press), 275–98.

Keohane, Robert O. (2006), 'The Contingent Legitimacy of Multilateralism', In Edward Newman, Ramesh Thakur, and John Tirman (eds.), *Multilateralism Under Challenge? Power, International Order, and Structural Change* (Tokyo/New York/Paris: United Nations University Press), 56–76.

Kerr, Pauline (1994), 'The Security Dialogue in the Asia Pacific', *Pacific Review*, Vol. 7/4, 397–409.

Kioko, Ben (2003), 'The Right of Intervention under the African Union's Constitutive Act: From Non-Interference to Non-Intervention', *International Review of the Red Cross*, Vol. 852, 807–24.

Kivimaki, Timo (2001), 'The Long Peace of ASEAN', *Journal of Peace Research*, Vol. 38/1, 5–25.

Koh, Tommy (2008), 'Not Perfect but Charter is a Good Start on Road to Regional Progress', *Straits Times*, 21 July.

Krasner, Stephen D. (1995/6), 'Compromising Westphalia', *International Security*, Vol. 20/3, 115–51.

Krasner, Stephen D. (1999), *Sovereignty: Organized Hypocrisy* (Princeton: Princeton University Press).

Krasner, Stephen D. (2004), 'Sharing Sovereignty: New Institutions for Collapsed and Failing States', *International Security*, Vol. 29/2, 85–120.

Kratochwil, Friederich (2006), 'On Legitimacy', *International Relations*, Vol. 20/3, 302–8.

Krisch, Nico (2008), 'The Security Council and the Great Powers'. In Vaughan Lowe et al. (eds.), *The United Nations Security Council and War: The Evolution of Thought and Practice since 1945* (Oxford: Oxford University Press), 133–53.

Kuhonta, Erik (2006), 'Walking a Tightrope: Democracy versus Sovereignty in ASEAN's Illiberal Peace', *Pacific Review*, Vol. 19/3, 337–58.

Kupchan, Charles A. (2008), 'Minor League, Major Problems', *Foreign Affairs*, Vol. 87/6, 96–109.

Labita, Al (2007), 'ASEAN Charter: Officials Hope to End Rifts', *Business Times (Singapore)*, 27 July.

Lake, David A. (2007), 'Escape from the State of Nature: Authority and Hierarchy in World Politics', *International Security*, Vol. 32/1, 47–79.

Lake, David A. and Patrick Morgan (eds.) (1997), *Regional Orders: Building Security in a New World* (University Park: Pennsylvania Staten University Press).

Leben, C. (2000), *Fédération d'Etats Nations ou Etat Fédéral?*, Harvard Law School Symposium, Jean Monnet Working Papers no. 7.

Leifer, Michael (1989), *ASEAN and the Security of South-East Asia* (London: Routledge).

Letogolis.com (2005), *Nigeria National Assembly Endorses Military Action Against Togo*, Lagos, 10 February. Available at http://www.letogolais.com/article.html?nid=1520.

Levitt, Jeremy L. (2003), 'The Peace and Security Council of the African Union: The Known Unknowns', *Transnational Law and Contemporary Problems*, Vol. 13/1, 110–38.

Lord, Christopher (2008), 'Polity Empowering or Polity Constraining? A Comparison of British and French attempts to legitimise the Constitutional Treaty', *Journal of European Public Policy*, Vol. 15/7, 1001–18.

Lord, Christopher (2009) *Polecats, Foxes and Lions. Social Choice, Moral Philosophy and the Justification of the EU as a Restrained yet Capable form of Political Power*, ARENA Working Paper 15/2009, Oslo, ARENA.

Lotze, Walter (2011), 'A Tale of Two Councils—The African Union, the United Nations and the Protection of Civilians in Côte d'Ivoire', *Global Responsibility to Protect*, Vol. 3/3, 365–75.

Lowe, Vaughan, Adam Roberts, Jennifer Welsh, and Dominik Zaum (eds.) (2008), *The United Nations Security Council and War: The Evolution of Thought and Practice since 1945* (Oxford: Oxford University Press).

Luck, Edward C. (2005), 'The UN Security Council: Reform or Enlarge?', in Paul Heinbecker and Patricia Goff (eds.), *Irrelevant or Indispensable? The United Nations in the 21st Century* (Waterloo, On: Wilfred Laurier University Press), 143–52.

Lundestad, Geir (1986), 'Empire by Invitation? The United States and Western Europe, 1945-1952', *Journal of Peace Research*, Vol. 23/2, 263–77.

MacQueen, Norrie (2006), *Peacekeeping and the International System* (Abingdon: Routledge).

Majone, Giandomenico (2001), 'Two Logics of Delegation: Agency and Fiduciary Relations in EU Governance', *European Union Politics*, Vol. 2/1, 103–21.

Majone, Giandomenico (2005), *Dilemmas of European Integration. The Ambiguities and Pitfalls of Integration by Stealth* (Oxford: Oxford University Press).

Maksutov, Ruslan (2006), 'The Shanghai Cooperation Organization: A Central Asian Perspective', *SIPRI Project Paper*, Stockholm.

Malan, Mark (2008), 'Africa: Building Institutions on the Run', in Donald Daniel, Patricia Taft, and Sharon Wiharta (eds.), *Peace Operations: Trend, Progress and Prospects* (Washington DC: Georgetown University Press), 89–118.

Malone, David M. (2000), 'Eyes on the Price: The Quest for Nonpermanent Seats in the UN Security Council', *Global Governance*, Vol. 6/1, 3–23.

Marat, Erica (2011), 'SCO's Tipping Point in Central Asia', *Eurasia Daily Monitor*, Vol. 8/117 (2011), 17 June.

Matheson, Michael (2006), *Council Unbound: The Growth of UN Decision Making on Conflict and Post-Conflict Issues after the Cold War* (Washington D.C.: USIP Press).

Mathews, Kay (2008), 'Renaissance of Pan-Africanism: the AU and the New Pan-Africanists' in in John Akokpari, Angela Ndinga Muvumba, and Timothy Murithi (eds.), *The African Union and its Institutions* (Fanele: Auckland Park), 25–40.

Mattila, Mikko and Jan Erik Lane (2001), 'Why Unanimity in the Council? A Roll-Call Analysis of Council Voting', *European Union Politics*, Vol. 2/1, 31–53.

Matusov, Artyom (2007), 'Energy Cooperation in the SCO: Club or Gathering', *China and Eurasia Forum Quarterly*, Vol. 5/3, 83–99.

Mbeki, Thabo (2011), 'What the world got wrong in Cote D'Ivoire', *Foreign Policy*. 29 April.

McDermott, Roger N. (2007), *The Rising Dragon: SCO Peace Mission 2007*, Occasional Paper (Washington, DC: The Jamestown Foundation).

Mearsheimer John (1994/5) 'The False Promise of International Institutions', *International Security*, Vol. 19/3, 5–49.

Menon, Anand (2009), 'Empowering Paradise? The ESDP at Ten', *International Affairs*, Vol. 85/2, 227–46.

Mill, John Stuart (1972) *Utilitarianism, On Liberty and Considerations on Representative Government* (London: Dent [1861]).

Milner, Helen (1992), 'Review: International Theories of Cooperation among Nations: Strengths and Weaknesses', *World Politics*, Vol. 44/3, 466–96.

Moravcsik, Andrew (1993), 'Preferences and Power in the European Community: A Liberal Intergovernmentalist Approach', *Journal of Common Market Studies*, Vol. 31/4, 473–524.

Moravcsik, Andrew (1997), 'Taking Preferences Seriously: A Liberal Theory of International Politics', *International Organization*, Vol. 51/4, 513–53.

Moravcsik, Andrew (1998), *The Choice for Europe: Social Purpose and State Power from Messina to Maastricht* (Ithaca, NY: Cornell University Press).

Morgan, Glynn (2005), *The Idea of a European Superstate, Public Justification and European Integration* (Princeton: Princeton University Press).

Morris, Justin and Nicholas J. Wheeler (2007), 'The Security Council's Crisis of Legitimacy and the Use of Force', *International Politics*, Vol. 44, nos. 2/3, 214–31.

Murithi, Timothy and Charles Mwaura (2010), 'The Panel of the Wise' in Ulf Engel and Jao Gomes Porto (eds.), *Africa's New Peace and Security Architecture—Promoting Norms, Institutionalising Solutions* (Ashgate: Farnham, 2010), 77–90.

Mutambo, Aggrey (2011), 'Raila Blames AU for Africa's Woes', *Daily Nation*, 31 October.

Mwanasali, Musifiky (2006), 'Africa's Responsibility to Protect', in Adekeye Adebajo and Helen Scanlon (eds.), *A Dialogue of the Deaf—Essay on Africa and the United Nations* (Auckland Park: Fanele, 2006), 89–110.

Mwanasali, Musifiky (2008) 'From Non-Interference to Non-Indifference: The Emerging Doctrine of Conflict Prevention in Africa', in John Akokpari, Angela Ndinga Muvumba, and Timothy Murithi (eds.), *The African Union and its Institutions* (Fanele: Auckland Park), 41–62.

Nardin, Terry (1983), *Law Morality and Relations of States* (Princeton, N.J.: Princeton University Press).

Nardin, Terry (1998), 'Legal Positivism as a Theory of International Society', in David Maple and Terry Nardin (eds.), *International Society: Diverse Ethical Perspectives* (Princeton, NJ: Princeton University Press), 17–35.

Narine, Shaun (2002), *Explaining ASEAN: Regionalism in Southeast Asia* (Boulder, CO: Lynne Reinner 2002)

Narine, Shaun (2002), 'ASEAN in the Aftermath: The Consequences of the East Asian Economic Crisis', *Global Governance*, Vol. 8/2, 179–94.

Nathan, Andrew J. and Sarah McKune (2011), 'The Dubious Agenda of the SCO', *The National Interest*, 16 June.

Neher, Clark (1994), 'Asian Style Democracy', *Asian Survey*, Vol. 34/11, 949–61.

Newman, Edward, Roland Paris and Oliver Richmond (eds.) (2010), *New Perspectives on Liberal Peacebuilding* (Tokyo: UN University Press).

Nolte, Georg (2008), 'The Different Functions of the Security Council With Respect to Humanitarian Law', in Vaughan Lowe, Adam Roberts, Jennifer Welsh, and Dominik Zaum (eds.), *The United Nations Security Council and War: The Evolution of Thought and Practice since 1945* (Oxford: Oxford University Press), 519–34.

Novosseloff, Alexandra (2003), 'Les "missions spéciales" du Conseil de Sécurité des Nations Unies', *Annuaire français de droit international*, Vol. 49, 165–75.

Nowrot, Karsten and Emily W Schabacker (1998), 'The Use of Force to Restore Democracy: International Legal Implications of the ECOWAS Military Intervention in Sierra Leone', *International Law Review*, Vol. 14 (1998), 321–412.

Nye, Joseph (2004), *Soft Power: The Means to Success in World Politics* (Jackson: PublicAffairs).

Ofodile, Chukwuka (1994), 'The Legality of ECOWAS Intervention in Liberia', *Columbia Journal of Transnational Law*, Vol. 32, 381–418.

Ojendal, Joakim (2004), 'Back to the Future? Regionalism in South-East Asia Under Unilateral Pressure', *International Affairs*, Vol. 80/3, 519–33.

Onuf, Nicholas G. (1991), 'Sovereignty: Outline of a Conceptual History', *Alternatives*, Vol. 16/4, 425–46.

Paris, Roland (2003), 'Peacekeeping and the Constraints of Global Culture', *European Journal of International Relations*, Vol. 9/3, 441–73.

Paris, Roland (2004), *At War's End* (Cambridge: Cambridge University Press).

Paris, Roland (2010), 'Saving Liberal Peacebuilding', *Review of International Studies*, Vol. 36, 337–65.

Parsons, Talcott (1958), 'Authority, Legitimation, and Political Action' in Carl Friedrich (ed.), *Authority* (Cambridge, MA: Harvard University Press), 197–221.

Patrick, Stewart (2003), 'Beyond Coalitions of the Willing', *Ethics & International Affairs*, Vol. 17/1, 37–54.

Paul, James (2004), 'Working with Non-Governmental Organizations', in David Malone (ed.), *The UN Security Council: From the Cold War to the 21st Century* (Boulder: Lynne Rienner), 373–90.

Pirozzi, Nicoletta (2009), *EU Support to African Security Architecture: funding and training components*, Occasional Paper 76 (Paris: European Union Institute for Security Studies).

Pitsuwan, Surin (2011), 'ASEAN's Challenge: Some Reflections and Recommendations on Strengthening the ASEAN Secretariat', Report submitted to H. E. Marty Natalegawa, Chair ASEAN Coordinating Council, 12 December.

Pogge, Thomas (1997), 'Creating Supra-National Institutions Democratically: Reflections on the European Union's "Democratic Deficit"', *Journal of Political Philosophy*, Vol. 5/2, 163–82.

Pollack, Mark (2003) *The Engines of European Integration. Delegation, Agency and Agenda-Setting in the EU* (Oxford: Oxford University Press).

Pouligny, Béatrice (2006), *Peace Operations Seen from Below: UN Missions and Local People* (London: Hurst).

Powell, Kristiana (2005), *Opportunities and Challenges for Delivering on the Responsibility to Protect: The African Union's Emerging Peace and Security Regime* (Ottawa, The North-South Institute).

Power, Samantha (2002), *A Problem from Hell: America and the Age of Genocide* (New York: Basic Books).

Prantl, Jochen (2005), 'Informal Groups of States and the Security Council', *International Organization*, Vol. 59/3, 559–92.

Quist-Arcton, Ofeibea (2007), 'Unrest Leaves Guinea in State of Limbo', *NPR*, 23 February.

Ramcharan, Robin (2000), 'ASEAN and NonInterference', *Contemporary Southeast Asia*, Vol. 22/1, 60–88.

Ramesh, S. (2007), 'ASEAN Charter Being Revised to Include Foreign Ministers' Views', *Channel News Asia*, 6 August.

Rawls, John (1993), *Political Liberalism* (New York: Columbia University Press).

Raz, Joseph (1990), 'Introduction', in Joseph Raz (ed.), *Authority* (New York: New York University Press), 1–19.

République Française (2004), *Constitution Pour L'Europe, Mode D'Emploi*, Paris.

République Française (2004), *Apports de la Constitution Européenne.* Paris.

République Française (2005), *Référendum du 29 Mai 2005. Projet de loi autorisant la ratification du traité établissant une Constitution pour l'Europe. Exposé des motifs*, Paris.

Reus-Smit, Christian (2004), *American Power and World Order* (Cambridge: Polity).

Reus-Smit, Christian (2007), 'International Crises of Legitimacy', *International Politics*, Vol. 44, 157–174.

Righter, Rosemary (2008), 'Let's join the new democracy gang', *The Times*, London, 29 May.

Risse, Thomas (2000), 'Let's Argue! Communicative Action in World Politics', *International Organization*, Vol. 54/1, 1–39.

Risse, Thomas and Mareike Kleine (2007), 'Assessing the Legitimacy of the EU's Treaty Revision Methods', *Journal of Common Market Studies*, Vol. 45/1, 69–80.

Roberts, Adam (2001), 'The so-called "right" of humanitarian intervention', *Yearbook of International Humanitarian Law*, Vol. 3, 3–51.

Roberts, Adam (2003), 'Law and the Use of Force after Iraq', *Survival*, Vol. 45/2, 31–56.

Rousseau, Jean Jacques (1973), *The Social Contract or Principles of Political Right*, (London: Everyman [1762]).

Ruland, Jürgen (2000), 'ASEAN and the Asian Crisis: Theoretical Implications and Practical Consequences for Southeast Asian Regionalism', *Pacific Review*, Vol. 13/3, 421–51.

Sabel, Charles and Jontahan Zeitlin (2007), *Learning from Difference: the New Architecture of Experimentalist Governance in the European Union*, European Governance Papers (EuroGov).

Sarkin Jeremy (2008), 'Humanitarian Intervention and the Responsibility to Protect in Africa' in John Akokpari, and Danielo Shea Zimbler (eds.), *Africa's Human Rights Architecture* (Fanele: Auckland Park), 45–67.

Sassen, Saskia (1996), *Losing Control? Sovereignty in an Age of Globalization* (New York: Columbia University Press).

Schlesinger, Stephen (2009), 'Why a League of Democracies Will Not Work', *Ethics and International Affairs*, Vol. 23/1, 13–18.

Scharpf, Fritz (1999), *Governing in Europe: Democratic and Effective?* (Oxford: Oxford University Press).

Scharpf, Fritz (2006), 'The Joint-Decision Trap Revisited', *Journal of Common Market Studies*, Vol. 44/4, 845–64.

Scharpf, Fritz (2007), 'Reflections on Multilevel Legitimacy', *EUSA Review*, Vol. 20/3, 2–11.

Schmidt, Vivien (2004) 'The European Union: Democratic Legitimacy in a Regional State?' *Journal of Common Market Studies*, Vol. 42/5, 975–97.

Schmitter, Philippe (1996), 'Examining the Present Euro-Polity with the Help of Past Theories', in Gary Marks, Fritz Scharpf, Philippe Schmitter, and Wolfgang Streeck (eds.), *Governance in the European Union* (London: Sage), 121–50.

Schnabel, Albrecht and Ramesh Thakur (eds.) (2000), *Kosovo and the Challenge of Humanitarian Intervention* (Tokyo: UN University Press).

Schönlau, J. (2005), *Drafting the Charter: Rights, Legitimacy and Process* (Basingstoke: Palgrave Macmillan).

Schroeder, Paul (1989), 'The nineteenth century system: balance of power or political equilibrium?' *Review of International Studies*, Vol. 15, 135–53.

Searight, Amy (2010), 'New Challenges, New Vision, Pedestrian Progress', *Comparative Connections*, April.

Sears, Laurie (1996), *Colonial Discourse and Javanese Tales* (Durham: Duke University Press).

Security Council Report (2010), *Security Council Working Methods—A Work in Progress?* New York, 30 March.

Sesay, Amadu (1995), *Humanitarian Intervention in Liberia: Implications for State and Sub-Regional Security and International Society*, paper prepared for the Workshop on Humanitarian Intervention and International Society, London School of Economics, 13 May.

Sesay, Amadu (2001), 'Human Rights and the Maintenance of International Peace and Security in Africa', *Africa Peace Review*, Vol. 3/1, 19–45.

Simma, Bruno (1994), 'From Bilateralism to Community Interest in International Law: Bilateralism and Community Interest Confronted', *Recueil des Cours*, 250, 229–55.

Simpson, Gerry (2004), *Great Powers and Outlaw States: Unequal Sovereigns in the International Legal Order* (Cambridge: Cambridge University Press).

Slater, Jerome (1964), 'The Limits of Legitimization in International Organizations: The Organization of American States and the Dominican Crisis', *International Organization*, Vol. 23/1, 48–72.

Slaughter, Anne-Marie (2008), 'Networking Government to Government: The Asian Way', *International Review* (Shanghai), 56–72.

Smythe, Elizabeth and Peter Smith (2006), 'Legitimacy, Transparency and Informational Technology', *Global Governance*, Vol. 12/1 (2006), 31–53.

Söderbaum, Fredrik and Björn Hettne (2010), 'Regional Security in a Global Perspective', in Ulf Engel and Jao Gomes Porto (eds.), *Africa's New Peace and Security*

Architecture—Promoting Norms, Institutionalising Solutions (Farnham: Ashgate), 13–30.

Sohn, Injoo (2005), 'Asian Financial Cooperation: The Problem of Legitimacy in Global Financial Governance', *Global Governance*, Vol. 11/5, 487–504.

Steffek, Jens (2003), 'The Legitimation of International Governance: A Discourse Approach', *European Journal of International Relations*, Vol. 9/2, 249–75.

Stremlau, John (1991), 'The New Global Order and its Implications for Peace and Security in Africa', *U.S. Department of State Dispatch*, September.

Stubbs, Richard (2001), 'Performance Legitimacy and "Soft Authoritarianism"', in Amitav Acharya, B. Michael Frolic, and Richard Stubbs (eds.), *Democracy, Human Rights, and Civil Society in Southeast Asia* (Toronto: Joint Centre for Asia Pacific Studies), 37–54.

Stubbs, Richard (2008), 'Meeting the Challenge of Region-Building in ASEAN', in Mark Beeson (ed.), *Contemporary Southeast Asia*, 2nd Edition (New York: Palgrave MacMillan, 2008), 234–47.

Mark Sutchman (1995), 'Managing Legitimacy: Strategic and Institutional Approaches', *Academy of Management Review*, Vol. 20/3, 571–610.

Tallberg, Jonas (2003) *European Governance and Supranational Institutions: Making States Comply* (London: Routledge).

Tavares, Rodrigo (2009), *Regional Security: The capacity of international organizations* (Abingdon: Routledge).

Thomas, Daniel Charles (2001), *The Helsinki Effect: International Norms, Human Rights, and the Demise of Communism* (Princeton, NJ: Princeton University Press).

Thompson, Alexander (2009), *Channels of Power: The UN Security Council and U.S. Statecraft in Iraq* (Ithaca: Cornell University Press).

Töller, Annette E. (2010), 'Measuring and Comparing the Europeanisation of National Legislation', *Journal of Common Market Studies*, Vol. 48/2, 417–44.

Tyler, Tom R. (2001), 'A Psychological Perspective on the Legitimacy of Institutions and Authorities', in John T. Jost and Brenda Major (eds.), *The Psychology of Legitimacy: Emerging Perspectives on Ideology, Justice, and Intergroup Relations* (Cambridge: Cambridge University Press), 416–36.

United Nations (1988), *Human Rights: A Compilation of International Instruments* (New York: United Nations).

United Nations (2004), *A More Secure World—Our Shared Responsibility: Report of the Secretary General's High Level Panel on Threats, Challenges and Changes*, UN doc. A/59/565 of 2 December.

United Nations (2005), *In Larger Freedom: Towards Security, Development and Human Rights for All*, Report of the UN Secretary-General, UN doc. A/59/2005, 21 March.

United Nations (2005), *World Summit Outcome Document*, UN doc. A/Res/60/1 of 24 October.

United Nations (2008), *UN Peacekeeping Operations: Principles and Guidelines*, New York: DPKO.

United Nations Development Program (UNDP) (1994), *Human Development Report 1994: New Dimensions of Human Security* (New York: Oxford University Press).

United Nations General Assembly (2008), *Report of the African Union—United Nations Panel on Modalities for Support to African Union Peacekeeping Operations* UN doc. 2008.A/63/666 – S/2008/813, New York, 31 December.

United Nations Human Rights Council (2012), Report of the Independent International Commission of Inquiry on the Syrian Arab Republic, UN doc. A/HRC/21/50, 15 August 2012.

United Nations Human Rights Council (2012), *Oral Update of the Independent International Commission of Inquiry on the Syrian Arab Republic,* UN doc. A/HRC/20/CRP.1 of 26 June.

United Nations Security Council (2010), *Note by the President of the Security Council,* UN doc. S/2010/507 of 26 July.

Vatikiotis, Michael (1993), *Indonesian Politics under Suharto* (London: Routledge).

Voeten, Erik (2005), 'The Political Origins of the UN Security Council's Ability to Legitimize the Use of Force', *International Organization*, Vol. 59/3, 527–57.

Wallace, William and Julie Smith (1995), 'Democracy or Technocracy? European Integration and the Problem of Popular Consent', *West European Politics*, Vol. 18/3, 137–57.

Waltz, Kenneth (1979), *Theory of International Politics* (New York: Addison-Welsey).

Weatherford, M. Stephen (1992), 'Measuring Political Legitimacy', *American Political Science Review*, Vol. 86/1, 149–66.

Webber, Douglas (2001), 'Two Funerals and a Wedding? The Ups and Downs of Regionalism in East Asia and Asia-Pacific after the Asian Crisis', *Pacific Review*, Vol. 14/3, 339–72.

Weber, Max (1968) *Economy and Society* (New York: Bedminster Press).

Weiler, Joseph (1997), 'The Reform of European Constitutionalism', *Journal of Common Market Studies*, Vol. 35/1, 97–131.

Weiler, Joseph (2002), 'A Constitution for Europe? Some Hard Choices', *Journal of Common Market Studies*, Vol. 40/2, 563–580.

Weiss, Thomas G., Tatiana Carayannis, and Richard Jolly (2009), 'The "Third" United Nations', *Global Governance*, Vol. 15/1, 123–42.

Weitz, Richard (2011), 'Balancer-in-Chief: China Assumes SCO Chair', *China Brief*, Vol. XI/12, 9–12.

Weller, Marc (2008), 'Kosovo's Final Status', *International Affairs*, Vol. 84/6, 1223–43.

Welsh, Jennifer (2007), 'The Responsibility to Protect: Securing the Individual in International Society', in Benjamin Goold and Liora Lazarus (eds.), *Security and Human Rights* (Oxford: Hart), 363–83.

Welsh, Jennifer (2008), 'The Security Council and Humanitarian Intervention', in Vaughan Lowe, Adam Roberts, Jennifer Welsh, and Dominik Zaum (eds.), *The United Nations Security Council and War* (Oxford: Oxford University Press), 535–62.

Wendt, Alexander (1992), 'Anarchy Is What States Make of It: The Social Construction of Power Politics', *International Organization*, Vol. 46/2, 391–425.

Wendt, Alexander and Daniel Friedheim (1996), 'Hierarchy under anarchy: informal empire and the East German state', in Thomas Biersteker and Cynthia Weber (eds.), *State sovereignty as social construct* (Cambridge: Cambridge University Press), 240–77.

Wesley, Michael (1999), 'The Asian Crisis and the Adequacy of Regional Institutions', *Contemporary Southeast Asia*, Vol. 21/1, 54–73.

Whalan, Jeni (2010) 'The power of friends: The Regional Assistance Mission to Solomon Islands' *Journal of Peace Research*, Vol. 47/5, 627–37.

Wheeler, Nicholas J. (2000) *Saving Strangers: Humanitarian Intervention in International Society* (Oxford: Oxford University Press).

Wiharta, Sharon (2009), 'The legitimacy of peace operations' *SIPRI Yearbook 2009* (Oxford: Oxford University Press), 95–116.

Williams, Paul D. (2007), 'From Non-Intervention to Non-Indifference: The Origins and Development of the African Union's Security Culture', *African Affairs*, Vol. 106/423, 253–79.

Williams, Paul D. (2008), 'Keeping the peace in Africa: Why "African solutions" are not enough', *Ethics and International Affairs*, Vol. 22/3, 309–29.

Williams, Paul D. (2009), 'The African Union's Peace Operations: A Comparative Analysis', *African Security*, Vol. 2/2–3, 97–118.

Williams, Paul D. (2010), 'Peace Operations' in Robert A. Denemark (ed.), *The International Studies Encyclopedia: Volume IX* (Malden, MA: Wiley-Blackwell), 5551–78.

Wills, Siobhán (2009), *Protecting Civilians: The Obligations of Peacekeepers* (Oxford: Oxford University Press).

Wippman, David (1993), '"Enforcing the Peace: ECOWAS and the Liberian War', in L.F. Damrosch, (ed), *Enforcing Restraint: Collective Intervention in Internal Conflicts* (New York: Council on Foreign Relations Press), 157–204.

Woods, Ngaire (2003), 'The United States and the International Financial Institutions: Power and Influence within the World Bank and the IMF' in Rosemary Foot, Neil MacFarlane, and Michael Mastanduno (eds.), *US Hegemony and International Organizations* (Oxford: Oxford University Press), 92–114.

Yoroms, Gani Joses (2001), 'Regional Security, Collective Defence and the Problem of Peace Initiatives in West Africa: The case of ECOMOG', *Africa Peace Review*, Vol. 3/1, 84–112.

Yuan, Jing-Dong (2010) 'China's Role in Establishing and Building the Shanghai Cooperation Organization (SCO)', *Journal of Contemporary China*, Vol. 19/67, 855–69.

Zaum, Dominik (2006), 'The Authority of International Administrations in International Society', *Review of International Studies*, Vol. 32/3, 458–61.

Zaum, Dominik (2007), *The Sovereignty Paradox: The Norms and Politics of International Statebuilding* (Oxford: Oxford University Press).

Zelditch, Morris (2001), 'Theories of Legitimacy', in John T. Jost and Brenda Major (eds.), *The Psychology of Legitimacy: Emerging Perspectives on Ideology, Justice, and Intergroup Relations* (Cambridge: Cambridge University Press), 33–53.

Zürn, Michael (2004), 'Global Governance and Legitimacy Problems', *Government and Opposition*, Vol. 39/2, 260–87.

Index